D1347446

Technology-Based Assessments for 21st Century Skills

Theoretical and Practical Implications from Modern Research

A volume in
Current Perspectives on Cognition, Learning, and Instruction
Daniel H. Robinson and Gregory Schraw, *Series Editors*

Technology-Based Assessments for 21st Century Skills

Theoretical and Practical Implications from Modern Research

edited by

Michael C. Mayrath
Harvard University

Jody Clarke-Midura
Harvard University

Daniel H. Robinson
University of Texas at Austin

Gregory Schraw
University of Nevada–Las Vegas

INFORMATION AGE PUBLISHING, INC.
Charlotte, NC • www.infoagepub.com

Library of Congress Cataloging-in-Publication Data

Technology-based assessments for 21st century skills : theoretical and practical implications from modern research / edited by Michael C. Mayrath ... [et al.].
       p. cm. – (Current perspectives on cognition, learning, and instruction)
 Includes bibliographical references.
 ISBN 978-1-61735-632-2 (pbk.) – ISBN 978-1-61735-633-9 (hardcover) – ISBN 978-1-61735-634-6 (ebook)
1. Educational tests and measurements–Data processing. 2. Educational tests and measurements–Computer programs. 3. Education–Effect of technological innovations on. I. Mayrath, Michael C.
 LB3060.55.T43 2011
 371.26–dc23

                                                          2011038817

CONTENTS

FOREWORD

The new skills of the 21st century are not destined to closely match educational standards of the 20th century. We live in a new world now after computer technologies have evolved for a half a century. Educational practices are shifting from the industrial revolution to the knowledge revolution, so assessments also need to be different. Meanwhile, everyone worries whether our tests, teachers, and policies are moving quickly enough to keep pace.

When I went to school, I did not receive any training or experiences with 21st century skills. I never played multiparty games that required timely opportunistic communication and negotiation strategies with invisible players. Collaborative problem solving to achieve group goals was not part of our curriculum. I never learned how to manage limited resources and understand tradeoffs between factors with an interactive simulation. I lived primarily in a world of print in books rather than a rich colorful world of visualizations and multimedia. I never was encouraged or taught how to ask deep questions (why, how, what-if, so what) and to explore novel hypotheses because all of our curriculum in history, social studies, and science was preplanned by the teacher. There was no Google, blogs, and quick electronic access to millions of information sources that vary from clandestine to free association to rigorously validated wisdom. All of our educational materials were edited by experts, so I rarely worried about the truth of what I read. I had no concept of the value of cross-checking multiple information sources to converge closer on the truth. I never designed or modified a game to make it interesting, challenging, or educational. I had to live without Facebook, so my social network was limited to two dozen friends rather than 1000 acquaintances. All of these 21st century activities—and many more—were absent when I went to school.

Technology-Based Assessments for 21st Century Skills, pages vii–xi

Interestingly, these 21st century skills also are conspicuously absent from most of our current curricula, standards, and high stakes assessments in K16. Our society continues to perseverate on assessing 20th century reading, writing, mathematics, science, and academic knowledge, typically with multiple choice and other psychometrically validated tests that can be efficiently administered in one or a few hours. The landscape of skills and knowledge being tested does not stretch to the 21st century. The testing format does not sufficiently tap the functional cognitive procedures and social practices of today. Many groups are trying desperately to correct this misalignment, both inside and outside of the assessment industries. But the process is slow and laborious, with politics complicating everything.

Technologies are currently available to perform fine-grained formative assessments of knowledge and skills over long stretches of time that can be measured in months or years. Formative evaluation uses assessments at one point in time to guide training at subsequent points in time. These assessments are used to select learning activities rather than merely measuring the result of learning activities. The measures can diagnose problems or deficits at varying levels of detail. Imagine 100,000 data points being collected from each student over a period of a year and the computer tracking the learning rate of 200 different skills. Imagine the computer tracking everything the student reads from digital media in both formal and informal learning environments over the course of a year. Educational data mining techniques can be applied to these rich data sets in order to discover productive versus unproductive learning trajectories. This is a very different methodology than the standard psychometric practice of crafting 67 multiple choice questions to assess reading comprehension ability in a one-hour, anxiety-ridden, high stakes test.

There needs to be a more rapid but rigorous methodology for assessing the 21st century skills. Evidence centered design is a highly regarded approach to meet the demands. Researchers first identify what key knowledge and skills need to be mastered and then devise tasks with measures that are aligned with the knowledge and skills. Thus, the functional or theoretical constructs guide the details of the test construction. This methodology can be readily applied, but first there needs to be some agreement on the skills to be measured. And this indeed is a moving target. The important skills today may be passé 10 years from now. I have no confidence that the futurists have enlightened intuitions on what these skills will be. However, we should at least be able to modify our assessments quickly in the face of our dynamic, multifaceted world.

Games are currently at the crossroads between formal and informal learning environments. They are also at the crossroads between learning and motivation. Younger students like to play games because they are engaging and fun. They are skeptical of any academic content that interferes with a game's hedonic quality. Meanwhile, those in education try to find ways to smuggle in serious academic content. Which drum does the student follow? There is also an interesting tradeoff between learning efficiency and time-on-task persistence in comparisons of games with traditional no-nonsense learning environments. Learning is less efficient because of the non-germane cognitive load from the game features, but the game features motivate the student to spend more time learning in a self-regulated fashion. Both efficiency and persistence need to be considered in a satisfactory assessment of learning from games. Any assessment that targets only one of these criteria is missing the big picture.

The chapters in this book provide a glimpse of technology-based assessment at this point in history. The book has a stellar cast of contributors who collectively have made major advances in education, technology, assessment, and the social sciences. Just as important, they have a deep understanding of the current ecology of 21st century skills and of the poverty of business as usual in the assessment world.

—**Arthur C. Graesser**
University of Memphis

CHAPTER 1

INTRODUCTION TO *TECHNOLOGY-BASED ASSESSMENTS FOR 21ST CENTURY SKILLS*

Michael C. Mayrath and Jody Clarke-Midura
Harvard University

Daniel H. Robinson
University of Texas at Austin

ABSTRACT

Creative problem solving, collaboration, and technology fluency are core skills requisite of any nation's workforce that strives to be competitive in the 21st century. Teaching these types of skills is an economic imperative, and assessment is a fundamental component of any pedagogical program. Yet, measurement of these skills is complex due to the interacting factors associated with higher order thinking and multifaceted communication. Advances in assessment theory, educational psychology, and technology create an opportunity to innovate new methods of measuring students' 21st century skills with validity, reliability, and scalability. In this book, leading scholars from multiple disciplines present their latest research on how to best measure com-

1

plex knowledge, skills, and abilities using technology-based assessments. All authors discuss theoretical and practical implications from their research and outline their visions for the future of technology-based assessments.

We are not using the full flexibility and power of technology to design, develop, and validate new assessment materials and processes for both formative and summative uses.
—U.S. National Educational Technology Plan, March, 2010

INTRODUCTION

Educational organizations around the world are calling for 21st Century Skills (21CS) and looking to technology as a means to improve learning, motivation, and collaboration. Research supports the use of technology for content delivery (Atkinson & Wilson, 1968; Mayer, 2001; Mayrath, Nihalani, & Robinson, 2011), tutoring (Aleven & Koedinger, 2002; Anderson, Corbett, Koedinger, & Pelletier, 1995; Graesser, Person, Lu, Jeon, & McDaniel, 2005), simulations (de Jong & van Joolingen, 1998; Gredler, 2004; Behrens, Mislevy, Bauer, Williamson, & Levy 2004), virtual worlds (Clarke, Dede, Ketelhut, & Nelson, 2006; Clarke-Midura, Mayrath, & Dede, 2010; Dede, 2009a; Kafai, 2006; Mayrath, Traphagan, Jarmon, Trivedi, & Resta, 2010), games (Barab & Dede, 2007; Gee, 2003; Shaffer, 2006; Squire, 2006), and assessment (Wainer, 1990; Quellmalz & Pellegrino, 2009; Clarke-Midura & Dede, 2010). However, only over the last ten to twelve years has a research base been established that systematically explores the use of technology-based assessments to measure complex Knowledge, Skills, and Abilities (KSAs) (Bennett, 1999; Sandene et al., 2005; Quellmalz & Zalles, 2002).

Modern research on cognition and human learning, combined with emerging technologies, offers new possibilities for teaching and assessing higher-order thinking skills (Bransford, Brown, & Cocking, 2000; Collins, 1991; Jonassen & Rohrer-Murphy, 1999; White & Frederiksen, 1990). However, systematic research is needed to determine how to best measure these complex KSAs using technology-based assessments. The field of technology-based assessments is in its infancy, and as the field explores how to create valid, reliable, and scalable assessments of 21CS, it is important to build upon the past twenty years of research on complex, performance-based assessments (Cronbach, Linn, Brennan, & Haertel, 1997; Darling-Hammond, 1994; Linn, Baker, & Dunbar, 1991; Messick, 1989, 1995; Mislevy, Steinberg, & Almond, 2002; Shavelson, Baxter, & Pine, 1992; Wilson & Sloane, 2000).

This book represents an effort to aggregate leading researchers' latest findings and ideas about the direction of the field. All authors were requested to discuss theoretical and practical implications from their research and push their own boundaries by envisioning the future of technology-based assessments. This chapter provides background on 21st Century Skills, Technology-Based Assessments, and the chapters in this book.

21ST CENTURY SKILLS

It is frequently argued in the U.S. that the public education system's focus on measuring a student's declarative knowledge of discrete facts has taken critical focus away from teaching the skills truly necessary for success in the modern workplace (Darling-Hammond, 2007). Twenty-first Century Skills (21CS) is a term commonly used to represent a set of KSAs associated with success in today's workplace, such as high levels of cognitive processing and complex communication. Conceptual frameworks for 21CS have been published by numerous organizations and scholars: American Association of Colleges and Universities (2007), Dede (2005, 2009b), Educational Testing Service (2007), International Society for Technology in Education (2007), Jenkins, Clinton, Purushotma, Robinson, & Weigel (2006), the Metiri Group and NCREL (2003), National Science Foundation Cyberinfrastructure Council (2006), Partnership for 21st Century Skills (2006), and the Organization for Economic Cooperation and Development (2005). The *Assessment and Teaching of 21st Century Skills Project* (www.atc21s.org) is an international collaboration sponsored by Cisco, Microsoft, and Intel that is pulling together top researchers to explore 21CS. The Partnership for 21st Century Skills Framework is fairly encompassing of the other organization's lists and includes the following 21CS:

- Core subjects (as defined by No Child Left Behind)
- 21st century content: global awareness, financial, economic, business and entrepreneurial literacy, civic literacy and health and wellness awareness
- Learning and thinking skills: critical thinking and problem solving skills, communications skills, creativity and innovation skills, collaboration skills, contextual learning skills and information and media literacy skills
- Information and communications technology literacy
- Life skills: leadership, ethics, accountability, adaptability, personal productivity, personal responsibility, people skills, self-direction and social responsibility

At the heart of 21CS is creative problem solving through evaluation, reasoning, and decision making. Humans have used these skills for thousands of years to survive; however, implied in 21CS is the ability to use digital technologies because these are the tools of the modern workplace, and being properly prepared requires knowledge of how to use these tools to create, communicate, collaborate, and problem solve.

Assessment is fundamental for any instructional objective, and assessing 21CS is challenging due to the interacting factors inherent to expert thinking, complex communication, and creative problem solving. Yet, advances in assessment theory, understanding of human learning, and technology have opened the door to a new range of possibilities for technology-based assessment for 21CS.

TECHNOLOGY-BASED ASSESSMENTS

Research on Technology-Based Assessments (TBAs) goes back three decades and was originally focused on computer adaptive testing (Almond & Mislevy, 1999; Wainer & Mislevy, 2000; Weiss & Kingsbury, 1984). However, in the late 1990s researchers began investigating how technology could be used to measure complex performances and higher order thinking skills (Baker & Mayer, 1999; Bennett, 1999; Quellmalz & Haertel, 2000; Quellmalz & Zalles, 2002).

In the early 2000s, research was conducted by numerous organizations to explore the potential of TBAs. The U.S. National Assessment of Educational Progress's 2001–2003 Technology-Based Assessment Project investigated issues related to measurement, equity, efficiency, and logistical operation in online math and writing assessments (Bennett, Persky, Weiss, & Jenkins, 2007). Findings suggested that although the majority of students reported being familiar with technology, differences in computer proficiency may introduce "irrelevant variance into performance on NAEP mathematics test items presented on computer, particularly on tests containing constructed-response items" (Sandene et al., 2005, p. ix). As computers become more ubiquitous, familiarity with technology should not be an issue; however, poor instructional design, specifically usability and accessibility, can overload a user's cognitive resources and impede performance (Sweller, 2005). Universal Design for Learning principles (Rose & Meyer, 2000), multimedia learning principles (Ginns, 2005; Mayer, 2001; Mayer & Johnson, 2008), and instructional technology design research (Kalyuga, Ayres, Chandler, & Sweller, 2003; van Merriënboer, Kirschner, & Kester, 2003) should guide the design and development of TBAs.

An issue that limited the potential of TBAs until recently was operationalizing how an activity in a digital environment would elicit a student performance rich enough to make valid and reliable inferences about levels of proficiency (Baker, Chung, & Delacruz, 2008). This issue was at least partially solved by the use of logdata and a new theory of assessment. One of the most promising functionalities of TBAs is known by many names including logdata, tracedata, and/or clickstream data. Logdata is the history of everything a student does while using the system. This large amount of data must be organized and processed appropriately to extrapolate patterns or inferences that best represent the students' KSAs. Logdata is complex and rich; thus, numerous researchers have emphasized the importance in designing observations that are fine-grained, interrelated, and process-oriented (Baker & Mayer, 1999; Pellegrino, Chudowsky, & Glaser, 2001).

Logdata provides a robust data source; however, the issue of how to interpret the logdata remains. For example, in a flight simulation assessment there is an interaction of complex variables, including the student, task, evidence in the form of logdata and decisions made, the usability of the simulation, and the systemic assembly of all of these variables interacting with each other. Such interrelatedness requires a comprehensive framework for making valid inferences about learning.

One such framework is Evidence Centered Design (ECD), which provides a formal, multi-layered approach to designing assessments (Mislevy, 2006; Mislevy, & Haertel, 2006; Mislevy & Riconscente, 2006; Mislevy, Steinberg, & Almond, 2003). ECD formalizes the procedures generally done by expert assessment developers (Shute, Hansen, & Almond, 2008). Using the ECD approach, an evidentiary assessment argument is formed that connects claims, evidence, and supporting rationales. "It provides a framework for developing assessment tasks that elicit evidence (scores) that bears directly on the claims that one wants to make about what a student knows and can do" (Shute, Hansen, & Almond, 2008, p. 6).

The ECD framework underlies some of the most innovative and rigorous current research studies on TBAs for 21CS (Clarke-Midura & Dede, 2010; Clarke-Midura, Mayrath, & Dede, 2010; Frezzo, Behrens, & Mislevy, 2010; Mislevy et al., 2010; Quellmalz & Pellegrino, 2009; Rupp, Gushta, Mislevy, & Shaffer, 2010; Shute, Ventura, Bauer, & Zapata-Rivera, 2009). ECD is a core component of the research discussed in numerous chapters within this book.

BOOK CHAPTERS

In this book, Chapters Two through Seven discuss game-based or simulation-based assessments developed using the ECD framework. In Chapter 2, Behrens, Mislevy, DiCerbo, and Levy lay the foundation for how Evidence Centered Design can be used to drive the assessment process and the changing landscape of technology-based assessments. They describe *PacketTracer*, a simulation tool used by Cisco to train students in computer networking skills, as an illustration of ECD. In Chapter 3, Quellmalz, Timms, Buckley, Davenport, Loveland, and Silberglitt discuss 21st Century dynamic assessments and describe *SimScientists*, a simulation game that teaches scientific thinking. In Chapter 4, Shute and Torres introduce a new public school called *Quest to Learn* where the curriculum is based on principles of game design, immersion, and active learning. In Chapter 5, Clarke-Midura, Code, Dede, Mayrath, and Zap discuss the *Virtual Performance Assessment Project* and their feasibility studies of immersive virtual performance assessments used to measure scientific inquiry. In Chapter 6, Zapata-Rivera and Bauer present examples of their game-based assessments including *English ABLE*, the *English and Math ABLE*, and the *Student Interactive Score Report*. In Chapter 7, Goldman, Lawless, Pellegrino, Braasch, Manning, and Gomez examine ways to assess multiple source comprehension using digital technologies.

In Chapters 8 and 9, the authors continue to explore the use of simulation- and games-based approaches to assessment. In Chapter 8, Shaffer and Gee present *Good Assessment for Twentyfirstcentury Education* (GATE) and outline a framework for using games as assessments. In Chapter 9, Baker, Chung, and Delacruz present an architecture for game-based assessment and describe relationships of learning goals, cognitive demands, and domain and task features.

In Chapters 10 and 11, the authors focus specifically on using technology to assess inquiry learning. In Chapter 10, de Jong, Wilhelm, and Anjewierden discuss technology-enhanced inquiry learning environments—in particular simulations—and describe how the rich data from these environments can be used for instructional interventions. In Chapter 11, Songer discusses how technology can be utilized to teach and assess essential science to nascent inquirers.

In Chapters 12, 13, and 14, the authors use cognitive load theory as a framework for designing technology-based assessments. In Chapter 12, Low, Jin, and Sweller explore the congruence of assessments with cognitive principles of human information processing, and they offer suggestions for optimizing cognitive load. In Chapter 13, Kalyuga discusses diagnostic assessments in digital learning environments such as adaptive online tutors. In Chapter 14, Nihalani and Robinson explore task selection procedures for individual versus collaborative assessments.

We conclude the volume with Chapters 15 and 16, which explore technology-based assessments at a meta-level. In Chapter 15, van Merriënboer and van der Vleuten present a four-component instructional design model (4C/ID-model) to be used as guidelines for technology-based assessment within a competence-based curriculum. In Chapter 16, Russell speculates on the potential of new, empirically-untested approaches to assessment. We hope the reader finds all chapters to be helpful summaries of the most current, cutting edge technologies and approaches to assessment.

CONCLUSION

Teaching today's students how to use digital technologies for higher order cognitive processes is an economic imperative for any nation (Dede, Korte, Nelson, Valdez, & Ward, 2005). Economists Levy & Murnane (2004) have suggested:

> Declining portions of the labor force are engaged in jobs that consist primarily of routine cognitive work and routine manual labor—the types of tasks that are easiest to program computers to do. Growing proportions of the nation's labor force are engaged in jobs that emphasize expert thinking or complex communication—tasks that computers cannot do. (pp. 53–54)

The chapters in this book reflect the current state of the art for using technology-based assessment to measure 21st Century Skills. The authors of these chapters are top experts in education research, and their chapters collectively push forward an ambitious research agenda for a new field at a time in history when these tools are needed most.

REFERENCES

Aleven, V.,1 & Koedinger, K. (2002). An effective metacognitive strategy: Learning by doing and explaining with a computer-based Cognitive Tutor. *Cognitive Science, 26,* 147–179.

Almond, R. G., & Mislevy, R. J. (1999). Graphical models and computerized adaptive testing. *Applied Psychological Measurement, 23,* 223–237.

American Association of Colleges and Universities. (2007). *College learning for the new global century.* Washington, DC: AACU.

Anderson, J. R., Corbett, A., Koedinger, K., & Pelletier, R. (1995). Cognitive tutors: Lessons learned. *Journal of the Learning Sciences, 4,* 167–207.

Atkinson, R., & Wilson, H. (1968). Computer-assisted instruction. *Science, 162*(3849), 73–77.

Baker, E. L., Chung, G. K. W. K., & Delacruz, G. C. (2008). Design and validation of technology-based performance assessments. In J. M. Spector, M. D. Merrill, J. J. G. van Merriënboer, & M. P. Driscoll (Eds.), *Handbook of research on educational communications and technology* (3rd ed., pp. 595–604). Mahwah, NJ: Erlbaum.

Baker, E. L., & Mayer, R. E. (1999). Computer-based assessment of problem solving. *Computers in Human Behavior, 15,* 269–282.

Barab, S, A., & Dede, C. (2007). Games and immersive participatory simulations for science education: An emerging type of curricula. *Journal of Science Education and Technology, 16,* 1–3.

Behrens, J. T., Mislevy, R. J., Bauer, M., Williamson, D. M., & Levy, R. (2004). Introduction to evidence centered design and lessons learned from its application in a global e-learning program. *The International Journal of Testing, 4,* 295–301.

Bennett, R.E. (1999). Using new technology to improve assessment. *Educational Measurement: Issues and Practice, 18,* 5–12.

Bennett, R. E., Persky, H., Weiss, A. R., & Jenkins, F. (2007). *Problem solving in technology- rich environments.* A Report from the NAEP Technology-Based Assessment Project, Research and Development Series. NCES 2007-466.

Bransford, J. D., Brown, A. L., & Cocking, R. R. (2000). *How people learn: Brain, mind, experience, and school: Expanded edition.* Washington, DC: National Academy Press.

Clarke, J., Dede, C., Ketelhut, D. J., & Nelson, B. (2006). A design-based research strategy to promote scalability for educational innovations. *Educational Technology, 46(3),* 27–36.

Clarke-Midura, J., Mayrath, M., & Dede, C. (2010, April). *Designing immersive virtual environments for assessing inquiry.* Paper presented at the annual meeting of the American Education Research Association. Denver, Colorado.

Clarke-Midura, J., & Dede, C. (2010). Assessment, technology, and change. *Journal of Research in Technology and Education, 42,* 309–328.

Collins, A. (1991). Cognitive apprenticeship and instructional technology. In L. Idol & B. F. Jones (Eds.), *Educational values and cognitive instruction: Implications for reform.* (pp. 119–136). Hillsdale, NJ: Lawrence Erlbaum Associates.

Cronbach, L. J., Linn, R. L., Brennan, R. L, & Haertel, E. H. (1997). Generalizability analysis for performance assessments of student achievement or school effectiveness. *Educational and Psychological Measurement, 57,* 373–399.

Darling-Hammond, L. (1994). Performance-based assessment and educational equity. *Harvard Educational Review, 64*(1), 5–29.

Darling-Hammond, L. (2007). Evaluating "No Child Left Behind." *The Nation.* Retrieved March, 12, 2011 from http://www.leland.stanford.edu/~hakuta/ Courses/Ed205X%20Website/Resources/LDH_%20Evaluating%20 %27No%20Child...pdf

de Jong, T., & van Joolingen, W. R. (1998). Scientific discovery learning with computer simulations of conceptual domains. *Review of Educational Research, 68,* 179–201.

Dede, C. (2005). Planning for "neomillennial" learning styles: Implications for investments in technology and faculty. In J. Oblinger and D. Oblinger (Eds.), *Educating the net generation* (pp. 226–247). Boulder, CO: EDUCAUSE Publishers.

Dede, C. (2009a). Immersive interfaces for engagement and learning. *Science 323*(5910) (Jan 2nd), 66–69.

Dede, C. (2009b). *Comparing frameworks for "21st Century skills."* Harvard Graduate School of Education. Retrieved March 12, 2011 from http://www.watertown. k12.ma.us/dept/ed_tech/research/pdf/ChrisDede.pdf

Dede, C., Korte S., Nelson, R., Valdez, G., & Ward, D. J. (2005). *Transforming learning for the 21st century: An economic imperative.* Naperville, IL: Learning Point Associates. Retrieved March 12, 2011, from http://www.learningpt.org/tech/transforming.pdf

Educational Testing Service. (2007) *Digital transformation: A framework for ICT literacy.* Princeton, NJ: ETS.

Frezzo, D. C., Behrens, J. T., & Mislevy, R. J. (2010). Design patterns for learning and assessment: Facilitating the introduction of a complex simulation-based learning environment into a community of instructors. *Journal of Science Education and Technology, 19,* 105–114. doi:10.1007/s10956-009-9192-0

Gee, J. (2003). *What video games have to teach us about learning.* New York: Palgrave.

Ginns, P. (2005). Meta-analysis of the modality effect. *Learning And Instruction, 15,* 313–331.

Graesser, A. C., Person, N., Lu, Z., Jeon, M. G., & McDaniel, B. (2005). Learning while holding a conversation with a computer. In L. PytlikZillig, M. Bodvarsson, & R. Bruning (Eds.), *Technology-based education: Bringing researchers and practitioners together* (pp. 143–167). Charlotte, NC: Information Age Publishing.

Gredler, M. (2004). Games and simulations and their relationships to learning. *Handbook of research on educational communications and technology,* 571–581.

International Society for Technology in Education. (2007). *The national educational technology standards and performance indicators for students.* Eugene, OR: ISTE.

Jonassen, D., & Rohrer-Murphy, L. (1999). Activity theory as a framework for designing constructivist learning environments. *Educational Technology Research and Development, 47,* 61–79.

Jenkins, H., Clinton, K., Purushotma, R., Robinson, A. J., & Weigel, M. (2006). *Confronting the challenges of participatory culture: Media education for the 21st century.* Chicago, IL: The MacArthur Foundation.

Kafai, Y. B. (2006). Playing and making games for learning: Instructionist and constructionist perspectives for game studies. *Games and Culture, 1,* 36–40.

Kalyuga, S., Ayres, P., Chandler, P., & Sweller, J. (2003). The expertise reversal effect. *Educational Psychologist, 38,* 23–31.

Levy, F., & Murnane, R. J. (2004). *The new division of labor: How computers are creating the next job market.* Princeton, NJ: Princeton University Press.

Linn, R. L., Baker, E. L., & Dunbar, S. B. (1991). Complex, performance-based assessment: Expectations and validation criteria. *Educational Researcher, 20,* 15–21.

Mayer, R. E. (2001). *Multimedia learning.* New York: Cambridge University Press.

Mayer, R. E., & Johnson, C. (2008). Revising the redundancy principle in multimedia learning. *Journal of Educational Psychology, 100,* 380–386.

Mayrath, M. C., Nihalani, P. K., & Robinson, D. H. (2011). Varying tutorial modality and interface restriction to maximize transfer in a complex simulation environment. *Journal of Educational Psychology,* doi:10.1037/a0022369.

Mayrath, M.C., Traphagan, T.T., Jarmon, L., Trivedi, A., & Resta, P. (2010). Teaching with virtual worlds: Factors to consider for instructional use of Second Life. *Journal of Educational Computer Research, 43,* 403–444.

Messick, S. (1989).Validity. In R. L. Linn (Ed.), *Educational Measurement* (3rd ed., pp. 13-104). New York: Macmillan.

Messick, S. (1995). Validity of psychological assessment: Validation of inferences from person's responses and performances as scientific inquiry into score meaning. *American Psychologist, 50*, 741–749.

Metiri Group & NCREL. (2003). *EnGauge 21st century skills: Literacy in the digital age.* Chicago, IL: NCREL.

Mislevy, R. J. (2006). Cognitive psychology and educational assessment. In R. L. Brennan (Ed.), *Educational measurement* (4th ed., pp. 257–305). Westport, CT: American Council on Education/Praeger Publishers.

Mislevy, R.J., Behrens, J.T., Bennett, R.E., Demark, S.F., Frezzo, D.C., Levy, R., Robinson, D.H., Rutstein, D.W., Shute, V.J., Stanley, K., & Winters, F.I. (2010). On the roles of external knowledge representations in assessment design. *Journal of Technology, Learning, and Assessment, 8*(2). Retrieved from http://escholarship.bc.edu/jtla/vol8/2.

Mislevy, R. J., & Haertel, G. D. (2006). Implications of evidence-centered design for educational testing. *Educational Measurement: Issues and Practice, 25*(4), 6–20.

Mislevy, R. J., & Riconscente, M. M. (2006). Evidence-centered assessment design: Layers, structures, and terminology. In S. Downing & T. Haladyna (Eds.), *Handbook of test development* (pp. 61–90). Mahwah, NJ: Lawrence Erlbaum Associates.

Mislevy, R. J., Steinberg, L. S., & Almond, R. G. (2002). On the roles of task model variables in assessment design. In S. Irvine & P. Kyllonen (Eds.), *Item generation for test development* (pp. 97–128). Mahwah, NJ: Lawrence Erlbaum Associates.

Mislevy, R. J., Steinberg, L. S., & Almond, R. G. (2003). On the structure of educational assessments. *Measurement: Interdisciplinary Research and Perspectives, 1,* 3–67.

National Science Foundation Cyberinfrastructure Council. (2006). *NSF's cyberinfrastructure vision for 21st century discovery (draft 7.1).* Washington, DC: National Science Foundation.

Organization for Economic Cooperation and Development. (2005). *The definition and selection of key competencies: Executive summary.* Paris, France: OECD.

Partnership for 21st Century Skills. (2006). *A state leader's action guide to 21st century skills: A new vision for education.* Tucson, AZ: Partnership for 21st Century Skills.

Pellegrino, J., Chudowsky, N., & Glaser, R. (Eds.). (2001). *Knowing what students know: The science and design of educational assessment.* Washington, DC: National Academy Press.

Quellmalz, E. S., & Pellegrino, J. W. (2009). Technology and testing. *Science Magazine, 323,* 75–79.

Quellmalz, E. S., & Zalles, D. (2002). *Integrative performance assessments in technology.* SRI International: US Department of Education.

Quellmalz, E. S., & Haertel, G. (2000). *Breaking the mold: Technology-based science assessment in the 21st Century* [Online]. Retrieved from http://pals.sri.com

Rose, D., & Meyer, A. (2000). Universal design for learning. *Journal of Special Education Technology, 15*(1), 67–70.

Rupp, A. A., Gushta, M., Mislevy, R. J., & Shaffer, D. W. (2010). Evidence-centered design of epistemic games: Measurement principles for complex learning environments. *Journal of Technology, Learning, and Assessment, 8*(4). Retrieved from http://escholarship.bc.edu/jtla/vol8/

Sandene, B., Horkay, N., Bennett, R., Allen, N., Braswell, J., Kaplan, B., & Oranje, A. (2005). *Online assessment in mathematics and writing: Reports from the NAEP Technology- Based Assessment Project, Research and Development Series (NCES 2005–457).* U.S. Department of Education, National Center for Education Statistics. Washington, DC: U.S. Government Printing Office. Retrieved March 12, 2010 from http://nces.ed.gov/nationsreportcard/pdf/studies/2005457_1.pdf

Shaffer, D. W. (2006). *How computer games help children learn.* Palgrave: Macmillan.

Shavelson, R. J., Baxter, G. P., & Pine, J. (1992). Performance assessments: Political rhetoric and measurement reality. *Educational Researcher, 21*(4), 22–27.

Shute, V. J., Hansen, E. G., & Almond, R. G. (2008). *An assessment for learning system called ACED: Designing for learning effectiveness and accessibility.* ETS Research Report, RR-07-26 (pp. 1–54), Princeton, NJ.

Shute, V. J., Ventura, M., Bauer, M., & Zapata-Rivera, D. (2009). Melding the power of serious games and embedded assessment to monitor and foster learning: Flow and grow. In U. Ritterfeld, M. J. Cody, & P. Vorderer (Eds.), *The social science of serious games: Theories and applications* (pp. 295–321). Philadelphia, PA: Routledge/LEA.

Squire, K. (2006). From content to context: Videogames as designed experiences. *Educational Researcher, 35*(8), 19–29.

Sweller, J. (2005). The redundancy principle in multimedia learning. In R. E. Mayer (Ed.), *The Cambridge handbook of multimedia learning* (pp. 147–158). New York: Cambridge Press.

U.S. Department of Education. (2010). *National educational technology plan 2010 draft.* Office of Educational Technology. Retrieved from http://www.ed.gov/technology/netp-2010

Wainer, H. (1990). *Computerized adaptive testing: A primer.* Hillsdale, NJ: Lawrence Erlbaum Associates.

Wainer, H., & Mislevy, R.J. (2000). Item response theory, calibration, and estimation. In H. Wainer (Ed.), *Computerized adaptive testing: A primer.* Mahwah, NJ: Lawrence Erlbaum Associates.

Weiss, D. J., & Kingsbury, G. G. (1984). Application of computerized adaptive testing to educational problems. *Journal of Educational Measurement, 21,* 361–375.

White, B. Y., & Frederiksen, J. (1990). Causal model progressions as a foundation for intelligent learning environments. *Artificial Intelligence, 24,* 99–157.

Wilson, M., & Sloane, K. (2000). From principles to practice: An embedded assessment system. *Applied Measurement in Education, 12*(2), 181–208.

van Merriënboer, J. J. G., Kirschner, P. A., & Kester, L. (2003). Taking the load off a learner's mind: Instructional design for complex learning. *Educational Psychologist, 38,* 5–13.

CHAPTER 2

EVIDENCE CENTERED DESIGN FOR LEARNING AND ASSESSMENT IN THE DIGITAL WORLD

John T. Behrens
Cisco

Robert J. Mislevy
University of Maryland

Kristen E. DiCerbo
Independent Researcher

Roy Levy
Arizona State University

INTRODUCTION

If the 21st century unfolds as previous centuries have, all we can be sure about is that time will be uniformly distributed, technological and social change will increase exponentially, and almost any attempt at further pre-

Technology-Based Assessments for 21st Century Skills, pages 13–53

diction will under-estimate the amount of change that will occur in the next 90 years. What is most salient to us about the 21st century, in its current nascent state, are the social and personal changes brought about by the Information and Communication Technologies (ICT) of digitization, computation, and information transmission via communications networks such as the World Wide Web (WWW). Consider, for instance, how you would have completed undertaking each of the following activities in 1990:

1. Purchase a shirt from a company 1,000 kilometers away for whom you do not know the address or phone number.
2. Determine the height of the St. Joseph river in Elkhart, Indiana today.
3. Show someone living on another continent, in real time, what your child looks like when dancing.

These are relatively simple tasks now because of the ubiquity of digitization devices (cameras, remote sensors), computation on the digital information, the transmission of information via computer and other information networks, and display via the world wide web. Each task was difficult 20 years ago, often requiring expensive and time-intensive physical movement or access to information previously held by proprietary groups (e.g., the local phone company) but now in the public domain. But for the examples above, search engines (e.g., Google.com; Ask.com) now provide global contact information, NOAA.gov provides data sensors to thousands of rivers and creeks in the United States, and numerous free internet-based video chatting services are available. Technologies interacting through the web allow us to see into homes and schools around the world, visualize data from space, and talk "face to face" with a colleague in another country. We will refer to this breadth of technological advances as the "digital revolution" (DR). Technologies are advancing so rapidly and with such ubiquity that we hardly notice. These advances change what is relevant to assess, how we are able to assess knowledge, skills, and attributes (KSAs), and how we think about the very nature of assessment. In this chapter we will discuss how we might understand the impacts of these technological and social shifts in terms of the Evidence Centered Design (Mislevy, Steinberg, & Almond, 2003) conceptual framework for assessment. We have been using this approach in our work for over 10 years to undergird the delivery of 100 million exams in over 160 countries, along with development of innovative simulation-based curricular and assessment tools (e.g., Frezzo, Behrens & Mislevy, 2010). The scope and scale of such work would hardly have been imagined 20 years ago. For each of the major sections of the ECD framework, we offer thoughts about how emerging technologies will influence the future of assessment and provide examples from our own emerging work.

HISTORY AND CONTEXT

The context of our assessment research and experience is the Cisco Networking Academies (CNA; see http://cisco.com/go/netacad/), a public-private partnership between Cisco and over 9,000 educational institutions in over 160 countries. Cisco, previously called Cisco Systems, is the world's largest maker of computer and data networking hardware and related equipment. Cisco provides partnering schools with free on-line curriculum and on-line assessments to support local school instructors in teaching ICT skills in areas related to personal computer (PC) repair and maintenance, as well as computer and data network design, configuration, and maintenance in alignment with entry-level industry certifications. The value of the program from the perspective of corporate social responsibility was discussed by Porter and Kramer (2002), while the logical origins of the e-learning approach have been described by Levy and Murnane (2004). Behrens, Collison, and DeMark (2005) provide a conceptual framework for the many and varied aspects of the assessment ecosystem in the program.

The instructional cycle in the Networking Academies typically consists of the students working through the interactive on-line curriculum in advance of class, followed by face-to-face interaction in class to provide group activities, additional clarification by the instructor, and hands-on interaction with networking equipment. The e-learning environment includes facilities for simulations of networks that are too complex or varied to operate with hardware in the classroom (Frezzo et al., 2010). To be successful in this domain, students must learn a broad range of planning, design, implementation, operating, and troubleshooting skills that combine a conceptual understanding of how networking systems work with the physical aspects of network connectivity (such as management of cables and alignment of hardware in physical spaces), and facility with the programming language of computer and data networks called the Cisco Internetwork Operating System (IOS) (Frezzo, Behrens, & Mislevy, 2009). Student-initiated formative assessment and curriculum-embedded feedback occur throughout the learning progression with built-in interactive curricular objects, in-line fixed-response quizzes, simulation-based "challenge labs" that simulate complex tasks and provide performance feedback, and numerous simulation-based practice activities. In addition, a separate on-line assessment system provides instructor initiated assessments for end-of chapter, and end-of course fixed-response exams and simulation-based performance exams.

WHY ECD?

In 2000, the Networking Academies undertook a two-pronged effort to advance its nascent assessment program. On one hand, efforts were begun to redesign the large-scale fixed-response assessment system used for chapter and final exams for students as they progressed through the learning experience. On the other hand, a new strand of work was initiated to investigate the possibility of automated performance-based assessment, which eventually produced the NetPass system (Behrens, Mislevy, Bauer, Williamson, & Levy, 2004; Williamson et al., 2004). In the first effort, the primary concern was balancing the need for a framework that could be implemented in a more or less standard way (i.e., a large-scale multiple-choice testing program) but was sufficiently abstract that it could be extended as needed in the very unclear future. In the second effort, the primary concern was that the traditional assessment language was inadequate for the job. Assessment designers and teachers involved in the program could easily create real-world tasks and corresponding scoring systems with ostensibly high ecological validity. However, the open-ended structure of the work was a poor fit for the fixed-response oriented language and technologies that ground familiar large-scale testing. Presenting a learner with a computer network and asking her to fix it is a relevant and straightforward task. However, we were at a loss to match these tasks that occur naturally in the professional world with the need for automated scoring in the global on-line educational system. Where does the language of "question" and "answer," "correct" and "incorrect" response fit in to the fluid, seamless, and interactive experience of working on computer networking equipment? There is no "question," only a task. There is no "answer," only a working (or not working) network, and myriad ways to get there. "Options" and "distractors" were likewise difficult to map to in this environment. We required a language that subsumed fixed-response tasks, but did not constrain us to them.

Relevant experience and research was available, of course, in the form of studies of performance assessment in education (e.g., Kane & Mitchell, 1996), simulation testing in professional settings (e.g., Tekian, McGuire, & McGahie, 1999), and intelligent tutoring systems with implicit assessments of students' capabilities (e.g., Shute & Psotka, 1996). Further, theoretical pieces such as those by Messick (1994) and Wiley and Haertel (1996) had begun to lay out a way of thinking about assessment that could unify the principles that underlie assessment of all forms, from multiple-choice and performance tasks, to extended projects and informal interactions with students. A quotation from Messick (1994) neatly summarizes the core idea of an assessment argument:

> A construct-centered approach would begin by asking what complex of knowledge, skills, or other attributes should be assessed, presumably because they are tied to explicit or implicit objectives of instruction or are otherwise valued by society. Next, what behaviors or performances should reveal those constructs, and what tasks or situations should elicit those behaviors? Thus, the nature of the construct guides the selection or construction of relevant tasks as well as the rational development of construct-based scoring criteria and rubrics. (p. 17)

The ECD framework provides terminology and representations for layers at which fundamental entities, relationships, and activities continually appear in assessments of all kinds, to the end of instantiating such an argument. We submit that the essential structure will remain useful for thinking about assessments even as technology and psychology advance. We will see, however, that these advances can provoke radically different answers to Messick's (1994) questions about the nature of what to assess, what situations hold evidence, and what performances to observe and how to evaluate them. ECD nevertheless provides a common conceptual framework for designing and making sense of assessments across a range of surface forms.

In the case of Cisco Networking Academies, ECD has served us by providing a sufficiently high degree of abstraction in the language to encompass standard practice while providing a set of constructs that are equally well applied to describe teacher-student interactions and a wide array of interactions with complex automated assessment systems. A key feature to the usefulness of ECD in our work has been that the model is fundamentally descriptive, not prescriptive. Where the ECD model states that an evidence model bridges the statistical model and the task model, it is not asserting that you should construct an evidence model of any particular kind, but that the way you have always moved from a task to an inference is by using an evidence model to reason from observation to conclusion, no matter how informal or implicit the activity is. This step may be explicit and technical in one assessment and implicit and intuitive in another, but recognizing it as an essential link in web of reasoning of all assessments helps us both understand existing assessments and design new ones; we recognize what we are doing when it is implicit and know what kinds of structures and relationships will need to be in place when we need to make it explicit. Such conceptualizations give us a comprehensive language for some of the unarticulated steps in common assessment development work. Where people might have said "it just works," or "just make some items and see what sticks," ECD provides a more detailed and explicit language to help us understand the ways our activities are working for which purposes. As technologies and the social changes around them accelerate at an increasing pace, we have found that the value of ECD to make sense of technologies and their possible uses also increases.

AN OVERVIEW OF THE ECD FRAMEWORK AND ITS RELATIONSHIP TO TECHNOLOGY

Educational assessment involves characterizing aspects of student knowledge, skill, or other attributes (KSAs), based on inferences from the observation of what students say, do, or make in certain kinds of situations. The

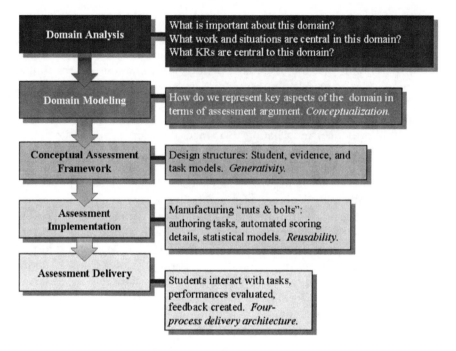

Figure 2.1 Layers in Evidence-Centered Design. KR = Knowledge Representations (adapted from Mislevy & Riconscente, 2006).

following sections describe key parts of the ECD framework as end-to-end processes in several conceptual layers (Mislevy, 1994; Mislevy, Steinberg, & Almond, 2002, 2003). The first step in starting the assessment process is considering those aspects of the world that are relevant to the assessment one wishes to construct. This is represented by the top layers of the ECD model, as illustrated in Figure 2.1 (adapted from Mislevy & Riconscente, 2006). The first layer is marshalling facts and theory about the domain, and the second is organizing the information in the form of assessment arguments. The middle layer, the Conceptual Assessment Framework (CAF), specifies more technical models for task creation, evaluation procedures, measurement models, and the like—in essence, blueprints for the pieces and activities that instantiate the argument in the real world. The next layer concerns the manufacturing of the assessment artifacts and the specifics for their usage. The lower layer describes a four-process architecture for understanding assessment delivery.

Below we discuss the major elements of the ECD framework and note how technological advances affect the conceptualization of the element and/or its implementation in an assessment system. In some areas the technological directions are clear; in other areas, they are more speculative.

DOMAIN ANALYSIS

Domain analysis and domain modeling define the high-level content or experiential domains to be assessed and document relationships among them. This is the content knowledge or subject matter related to the educational enterprise, the ways people use it, and the kinds of situations they use it in. What constitutes mathematics or troubleshooting or teamwork for the context at hand? What do we know about progressions of thought or skill, patterns of errors or common representations? For the current context, what knowledge, skill, goals, tools, enablers, representations and possible distractions are relevant? How do people interact with the physical environment, conceptual representations, and other people to accomplish things? By what standards are these efforts judged? To answer such questions, designers conduct a domain analysis. They consider the domain from a number of perspectives, such as cognitive research, available curricula, professional practice, ethnographic studies, expert input, standards and current testing practices, test purposes, and the various requirements, resources and constraints to which the proposed assessment might be subject.

Developments in psychology have had profound effects on domain analysis in recent decades (Mislevy, 2006). Domain analysis under behaviorist psychology, for example, focused on identifying concrete and precisely-defined actions in a domain, to be expressed as behavioral objectives (Mager, 1962). The information-processing perspective of the cognitive revolution (exemplified by Newell & Simon, 1972) called attention to the internal and external knowledge representations people work with, the procedures and strategies they use, and the features of problems that make them hard—all holding clear implications for assessment design. A sociocognitive perspective further widens domain analysis to the range of cognitive, cultural, and physical tools people use and the ways they interact with situations and each other to accomplish goals in some sphere of activity (e.g., Engeström, 1999). Domain analyses carried out under the latter two perspectives increasingly reveal the importance of peoples' interacting with the technological environment noted in the introduction. Technology thus continually gives rise not only to new forms of representing and communicating extant information in terms of knowledge representations (KRs), but to new and often more complex tools and environments to which people must attune themselves, to create and transform information—all giving rise, in turn, to the kinds of capabilities we need to assess. Designing and troubleshooting computer networks is a prototypical example of an important domain that didn't even exist until recently.

In times of rapid economic, social, and political change, the existence and composition of domains will change rapidly. For example, prior to the digital revolution a common vocational track prepared individuals to work as office secretaries in a "typing pool" or as stenographers. These jobs have largely disappeared with the advent of personal computers and the ubiquity of typing skill in mature economies. These changes have socio-political consequences because the educational and professional constituents often vary in the abstractness or generalizability of the skill and knowledge they focus on. Professional training, staffing, and guild organizations often focus on supporting rapid change in work force skill needs, while educational organizations are often focused on more general educational shifts. Accordingly, periods of rapid societal change can increase the divergence of short term and long term foci and thereby increase friction in educational and assessment rhetoric. For example, in the current environment, there is friction between the conceptualization of skill and knowledge as a) narrower capabilities that define "workforce retraining" versus b) broader capabilities that "general education" is meant to develop. Assessment designers need conceptual models that can accommodate these types of variation in domain focus and proficiency models.

While domain analysis and its monitoring have traditionally been done via human analysis of job tasks, job requirements, and similar artifacts, there has been significant growth in the application of computer-based semantic analysis (Baayen, 2008; Biber, Conrad, & Reppen, 1998; Gries, 2009; Manning & Schuetze, 1999) to aid in the extraction of patterns in electronic data that may suggest shifts in domains or emergence of new domains. Such semantic analysis has historically been conducted by humans reading text, but as the artifacts of human activity (work products) become increasingly digital, the door is open for automated techniques to identify trends in new activity. In 2008 a white paper published by International Data Corporation (IDC) entitled "The Diverse and Exploding Digital Universe" argued that the digital universe (the size of all electronic data) was 10% larger than previously estimated, and that by 2011 it will be 10 times larger than it was in 2006 (IDC, 2008). A report by the National Academies notes that particle physics experiments conducted with the Large Hadron Collider at CERN are expected to generate 15 petabytes of data annually, thereby matching the amount of information stored in all U.S. academic and scientific libraries every two years (Committee on Ensuring the Utility and Integrity of Research Data in a Digital Age and National Academy of Sciences, 2009). These technological shifts in data collection will drive the need for new skills and methods for undertaking science in the computer age (e.g., Wolfram, 2002), and compatible new methods for revising and tracking changes to the structure and content of domains. As the core representations and understandings of domains evolve increasingly fast, challenges and opportunities for moving those understandings and representations into the educational and assessment world will continue to increase as well.

One method for addressing the need for unified understandings of domains is the application of web technologies for the consolidation and dis-

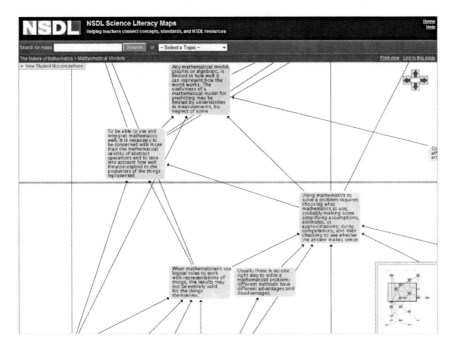

Figure 2.2 Science literacy map of the "Mathematical Models" domain. Interactive graphics available at http://strandmaps.nsdl.org.

tribution of domain models. Consider the digitization of the *Atlas of Science Literacy* (AAAS 2001; AAAS, 2007) provided by the National Science Digital Library (NSDL; http://strandmaps.nsdl.org/). These on-line representations communicate a number of important attributes of specific science concepts by placing them in a graphical space of grade level (vertical placement) and conceptual strand (horizontal placement), while indicating pre-requisite or supporting relationships with arrows (see Figure 2.2) The center panel is a detailed view of the subsection of the entire model that is depicted in the lower right panel. Each node in the model has hyperlinks to additional information and an overlay of relevant student misconceptions can be seen by using the pull-down menu in the upper left corner. As standards organizations evolve to use such distributed displays, the assessment community will benefit by having a united and reusable set of representations from which to carry out domain modeling and subsequent assessment artifacts.

DOMAIN MODELING

In domain modeling, designers organize information from domain analyses to describe relationships among capabilities, what we might see people

TABLE 2.1   Example of a "Claims and Evidence" Form

Claim 402: Develop a design that incorporates specified new device(s) into a network with minimum disruption to network operation

Representations to convey information to student (some or all to be presented to student):
Scenario (includes system requirements); building diagram; (existing) network diagram; existing configuration; physical network; simulation of network

Essential features (to be specified in task):
Timelines; device(s) to be added; characteristics of the network; location of utilities; telecommunications; distances; applications

Representations to capture information from student (i.e., potential work products):
Materials list; (final) network diagram; chart of IP addressing and subnet masking; cut sheet; number-base conversions worksheet; backup plan

Observable Features (i.e., evidence that can be identified from work products):
Re documentation: Completeness; accuracy
Re proposed solution: Practicality; cost effectiveness; timeliness; effective/appropriate use of existing assets; migration strategy
Re procedures: Efficiency; total time; down time

---

say, do, or make as evidence, and situations and features to evoke it—in short, the elements of assessment arguments. Graphical and tabular representations and schemas are constructed to convey these relationships, and prototypes may be used to fix ideas or test assumptions. Among the representational forms that have been used to implement ECD are "claims and evidence" worksheets, Toulmin diagrams for assessment arguments, and "design patterns" for constructing assessment arguments for some aspect of capabilities, such as design under constraints and model-based reasoning (Mislevy, Riconscente, & Rutstein, 2009). A sample of a "claims and evidence" form from a CNA curriculum regarding routing is shown in Table 2.1. These can serve as targets for creating specific tasks (multiple choice, written response, simulation, or actual-equipment tasks) or for determining what to seek evidence about in more complex tasks that encompass the specified claim as well as perhaps several other claims. The next section will give an example of a design pattern.

21ST CENTURY SKILLS

A first challenge for "assessing 21st century skills" lies in this area of domain analysis and modeling. When people use the phrase "21st century skills," just what capabilities are they referring to? What do we know about the development of those skills and the performance of those skills in real-world situations? The idea of 21st century skills is currently a rather amorphous theoretical construct suggesting new domains for occupational, educational, and personal activity. These domains are in need of more thorough analysis and modeling.

The term "21st century skills" has come to be associated with more broadly defined notions of communication, collaboration, and problem-solving—all of which remain important as environments change, but take forms shaped by the those environments. Fixing a Model-T is a substantially different cognitive activity from troubleshooting a computer network. There are, however, pervasive principles and structures that can be adduced to help design instruction and assessment today in both cases, and more importantly, ground students' learning so it can adapt to the situations of tomorrow (Schaafstal & Schraagen, 2000). Developing design patterns at this level can impart meaning to "21st century skills" in ways that can guide practical assessment development. A design pattern creates a design space to help task developers think through options and choices in designing tasks to evoke evidence about some targeted aspect of learners' capabilities, or to recognize and evaluate the evidence when as it arises in less structured assessments such as simulations and games.

Table 2.2 shows an abbreviated design pattern to support assessment design for troubleshooting, drawing on Wise-Rutstein's (2005) work. Three features of this design pattern are worth noting: It addresses troubleshooting at a level that guides assessment design across many domains for which its undergirding psychological perspective is appropriate; it guides designers' thinking through categories that help ensure that a coherent argument results; and it focuses on the nature of troubleshooting rather than on particular forms of evidence, and so conceptually unifies assessments that would use different task types for different purposes or in different contexts. Other examples of design patterns that stress interactive capabilities, whether in real-world or simulated environments, include experimental and observational investigation (Liu, Mislevy, Colker, Fried, & Zalles, 2010; Mislevy, et al., 2009), systems thinking (Cheng, Ructtinger, Fujii, & Mislevy, 2010), and a suite of design patterns for model-based reasoning that include model formation, use, revision, and inquiry cycles (Mislevy, Riconscente, & Rutstein, 2009).

THE EFFECT OF 21ST CENTURY TECHNOLOGY ON DOMAIN ANALYSIS AND DOMAIN MODELING

Not only has the current digital revolution changed the content of current constructs, it also affects how we may track and make sense of them. Specifically, technology has affected the practices of domain analysis and domain modeling by 1) changing the types of models of capabilities, environments, and performances we are likely to create, 2) providing new tools with which

TABLE 2.2   A Design Pattern to Support the Assessment of Troubleshooting

Attribute	Value(s)
Name	Troubleshooting in a finite physical system (Related: Troubleshooting in an open system; network troubleshooting)
Overview	Built on hypothetico-deductive approach, using Newell-Simon model; e.g., problem space, active path, strategies such as serial elimination and space-splitting. This design pattern concerns evoking or identifying direct evidence about aspects of these capabilities in a given context.
Central claims	Capabilities in a specified context/domain to iteratively troubleshoot finite systems: propose hypotheses for system behavior, propose tests, interpret results, update model of system, identify and remediate fault.
Additional knowledge that may be at issue	Knowledge of system components, their interrelationships, and functions; Familiarity with tools, tests, and knowledge representations; Self-regulatory skills in monitoring progress.
Characteristic features	Situation presents system operating in accordance with fault(s). There is a finite (possibly very large) space of system states (cf. medical diagnosis). Are procedures for testing and repairing.
Variable task features	Complexity of system/Complexity of problem. Scope: Full problem with interaction; problem segment with interaction; problem segment with no interaction (e.g., multiple-choice hypothesis generation, explanation, or choose/justify next step). Setting: Actual system, interactive simulation, non-interactive simulation, talk-aloud, static representations Type of fault: Single v. multiple; constant or intermittent. Kind / degree of support: Reference materials (e.g., circuit diagrams, repair manuals); Advise from colleagues, real or simulated. Collaborative work? (If so, also use design pattern for collaboration)
Potential performances and work products	Final state of system; identification of fault(s); trace & time stamps of actions; video of actions; talk-aloud protocol; explanations or selections of hypotheses, choice of tests, explanations of test results, effects on problem space; constructed or completed representations of system at key points.
Potential features of performance to evaluate	Regarding the final product: Successful identification of fault(s)? Successful remediation? Total cost / time / number of actions. Regarding performance: Efficiency of actions (e.g., space-splitting when possible or serial elimination, vs. redundant or irrelevant actions); systematic vs. haphazard sequences of action. Error recovery. Metacognitive: Quality of self monitoring; quality of explanations of hypotheses, interpretation, selected actions.
Selected references	Newell & Simon (1972): Foundational reference on human problem-solving. Jonassen & Hung (2006): Cognitive model of troubleshooting. Steinberg & Gitomer (1996): Example with aircraft hydraulics.

to analyze the domain, 3) allowing for the creation of digital representations, 4) providing means of collaboration around these representations, and 5) allowing for easier searching of these representations.

Writing from an economic-anthropological perspective, Perez (2003) has argued that technological revolutions not only change what we do, but the central metaphors that drive social discourse. For example, during the technological revolution of mass production (starting in approximately 1900) the core technologies sought efficiency through decomposition of work and use of hierarchical relationships. This led to educational distribution models based on mass production and organizational models in academia, business, and government centered on hierarchy. Following the more recent computer network revolution (starting with the use of the World Wide Web circa 1994), collaborative and computational networks have become a central metaphor in modern thought and discourse. Preceding this emphasis, many gains in experimental psychology were made through the information-processing revolution in psychology that arose from the "mind as a computer" metaphor (Anderson, 2009; Gardner, 1987). The new network metaphor has led to dramatic growth in the use of network representations (e.g., Barabasi, 2003) and analysis in the social and educational sciences (Freeman, 2004; Nooy, Mrvar, & Batagelj, 2005; Wasserman & Faust, 1994). These new metaphors affect our understanding of what it means to be proficient in a domain, how people become proficient, and how we assess their developing capabilities—and consequently the types of models we are likely to construct when representing a domain.

The growth of digital artifacts can accelerate the analysis and communication of domain understanding. For example, prior to the recent digital revolution, updates to standards by academic groups would have to be communicated by physical mail and verbal communication based on close personal and professional relationships. Access to new professional standards may have taken years as cycles of professional face-to-face meetings would serve as a core distribution methodology. Today instant communication via listserves, web sites, and RSS feeds allows for rapid promulgation of new information. This will likely lead to a dramatic increase in the rate and volume of research in the years ahead, thereby increasing the rate of change of the analysis and documentation of domains.

In addition to these more established technologies, newer interactive web technologies could encourage input and embellishment from large groups of interested parties, following models for wiki-nomics (Tapscott & Williams, 2008) or collective intelligence (e.g., Segaran, 2007). In such arrangements (wikipedia being the best known, but only a single variation) technology is leveraged to allow collaborative input and community evolution and resolution. These models have interesting economic dynamics (Benkler, 2007) that may have special advantages in certain highly collaborative educational environments where publishing was previously a bottleneck to not only the dissemination of knowledge but the collaborative construction of new knowledge.

One method of dealing with the growing profusion of curricular and assessment resources tied to models of a domain (for example, the plethora of state standards) is the use of detailed tagging associated with semantic web technologies. These tagging technologies support the machine-based search and aggregation of relevant information as well as the machine-based inference regarding associations implicit in the organization of the data. This means that not all relationships need to be made explicit, and that search is more forgivable and flexible and can be incorporated in new technologies driven by algorithmic requirements in addition to human search. Such systems can be seen, for example, in the Achievement Standards Network at http://www.jesandco.org/. In summary, 21st century technology has and will continue to impact the types of analyses and models we create and the methods we use to create, display, and analyze them.

THE CONCEPTUAL ASSESSMENT FRAMEWORK

Domain analysis and domain modeling serve as core inputs to what has been traditionally considered assessment activity as described in ECD as a series of conceptual models called the Conceptual Assessment Framework (CAF). It is in the CAF that the domain information is combined with information regarding particular goals, constraints, and logics to create a blueprint for an assessment.

Assessment design activity can be thought of as a series of questions such as "What are we measuring?" "How do we want to organize the world to collect evidence for the measurement?" "What are the conceptual linkages between observable evidence and abstract inferences?" Whereas domain modeling addressed these questions as integrated elements of an assessment argument, the CAF expresses answers in terms of specifications for the machinery through which the assessment is instantiated. The CAF is comprised of a number of pieces called *models* composed of objects, specifications, and processes to this end. Objects and specifications provide the blueprint for the operational aspects of work, including (a) the joint creation of assessments, tasks, and statistical models, (b) delivery and operation of the assessment, and (c) analysis of data fed back from the field. Implementing these objects and coordinating their interactions in terms of the four-process delivery system described in a following section brings the assessment to life. While domain modeling emphasized the interconnections among aspects of people's capabilities, situations, and behaviors, the CAF capitalizes on the separability of the objects that are used to instantiate

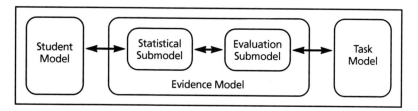

Figure 2.3 The central models of the Conceptual Assessment Framework.

an assessment. This becomes important in view of 21st century technology, as the models and their components can themselves be rendered in digital form. They are then amenable to assisted and automated methods of generation, manipulation, operation, and assembly (Mislevy, et al., 2010).

Figure 2.3 is a high-level schematic of the three central models in the CAF, and objects they contain. The specific elements they may contain in particular assessments include, for example, test specifications, item selection algorithms for adaptive testing, psychometric models, rubrics for raters or automated scoring routines, work product specifications, and task models. The CAF contains the core of the evidentiary-reasoning argument, from task design to observations to scoring to inferences about students.

THE STUDENT OR PROFICIENCY MODEL: WHAT ARE WE MEASURING?

The student model answers the question: What complex of knowledge, skills, or attributes (KSAs) should be assessed? A student model specifies a relevant configuration of the set of infinite configurations of skill and knowledge real students have, as seen from some perspective about skill and knowledge in the domain. These are the terms in which we want to determine evaluations, make decisions, or plan instruction. While the ECD literature sometimes refers to the elements of these models as Student Model Variables, in our work, we prefer a broader term and call them Proficiency Model Variables as part of proficiency models following Williamson, Almond, & Mislevy (2000). The number and nature of the proficiency model variables in an assessment depend on its purpose. A single variable characterizing overall proficiency might suffice in an assessment meant only to support a pass/fail decision or a broad characterization of progress at the end of a chapter. However, a more complex structure would be required to report proficiencies on multiple proficiency model variables (e.g., a networking assessment used to assess students' routing, configuration, and troubleshooting) as well as at diagnostic levels, to make instructional decisions, or to change the situation in a game- or simulation-based assessment (such as introducing on the fly a complication for a medical student performing well in a computerized patient management case). In this way, a proficiency model is likely to be a subset of the entities and relationships documented in the domain analysis stage, selected to align with a particular assessment goal and operationalized by the variables in a measurement model. Technically, the variables in a proficiency model are unobservable (latent) variables like those in psychometric models such as item response theory, latent class models, cognitive diagnosis models, and Bayesian inference networks. We will provide an example of the last of these shortly.

EVIDENCE MODELS: HOW ARE WE MEASURING IT?

After the key KSAs are instantiated in proficiency-model variables, evidence models are used to identify the behaviors or performances that reveal these constructs and their relationship to them. An evidence model embodies the argument about why and how our observations in a given task situation constitute evidence about student model variables.

The evidence model is composed of two parts: the evaluation submodel and the statistical submodel. The evaluation submodel answers the question of "what rules and procedures do we use to identify characteristics of work products as specific numeric or symbolic values, for summarization and reporting?" The outputs of these rules are called observable variables. The statistical submodel answers the question with "what weights and through what mechanisms do we want to combine this information from performances, as summarized by values of these observables, to update our belief about proficiency model variables, and at the same time understand and communicate our uncertainty about those values?"

The evaluation submodel is represented in its most simple and familiar forms by responses to multiple-choice items and raters' evaluations of open-ended responses. Both 21st Century skills and 21st Century technology are revolutionizing evaluation in assessment. We have noted that critical aspects of expertise are manifest in interactions with people and situations: apprehending, constructing and reasoning through representations that are adaptive and evolving, for example, and making choices and taking actions that create new situations. No longer is it simply a matter of a crisply defined task created solely by the assessor and a clearly separated response created solely by the examinee. Rather, the examinee's moves continuously create new situations that in turn engender further moves, often unique to every examinee who experiences the assessment. Qualities of the moves themselves, such as fluency, appropriateness, and effectiveness, are now targets of evaluation, as well as final products. A particular challenge is that making sense of an examinee's actions requires understanding key features of the situations as they evolve.

Assessments like these and evaluations of them were rare and costly when the performances were limited to live situations and evaluation was limited to human raters. A digital task environment, however, opens the door to automated data collection and evaluation. Technology in and of itself cannot determine what actions are important to capture, what to notice about them, and how to make sense of them; "data" is not the same thing as "evidence." The thinking is that domain modeling is essential to crafting automated scoring in digital environments (Bennett & Bejar, 1998). Williamson, Mislevy, and Bejar (2006) provide in-depth discussion of automated methods for evaluating complex performances, from the perspective of ECD.

The statistical submodel has been the sharp focus of the psychometric community for over 100 years. Approaches include classical test theory (Gulliksen, 1950/1987; Lord & Novick, 1968), generalizability theory (Brennan, 2001; Cronbach, Gleser, Nanda, & Rajaratnam, 1972), structural equation modeling (Kline, 2010), cognitive diagnosis models (Nichols, Chipman, & Brennan, 1995; Rupp, Templin, & Henson, 2010), item response theory (De Boeck & Wilson, 2004; Lord, 1980), and Bayesian Inference Networks (BNs) (Mislevy, 1994; Mislevy et al., 2003). Although all of these approaches are compatible with the ECD framework, Bayesian Inference Networks have been highlighted because their extensibility and graphical underpinning (both visually and computationally) align well with the central logic of ECD.

The networks are so named because they support the application of Bayes' theorem across complex networks by structuring the appropriate computations (Lauritzen & Spiegelhalter, 1988; Pearl, 1988). BNs properly and efficiently quantify and propagate the evidentiary import of observed data on unknown entities, thereby facilitating evidentiary reasoning under uncertainty as is warranted in psychometric and related applications (Almond, DiBello, Moulder, & Zapata-Rivera, 2007; Levy & Mislevy, 2004; Reye, 2004; Spiegelhalter, Dawid, Lauritzen, & Cowell, 1993). In assessment, a BN is constructed by modeling performance on tasks (as summarized by the observable variables from the evaluation submodel) as dependent on student capabilities (as summarized by the latent variables that comprise the proficiency model). Once data are collected, values for the observables are entered into the network and the distributions of the remaining variables are updated. This constitutes evidence accumulation in assessment, where the evidentiary impact of the observed data yields posterior distributions for unknown proficiency model variables (Mislevy & Gitomer, 1996; Mislevy & Levy, 2007).

BNs are a powerful statistical modeling approach that offers a number of advantages for evidence accumulation in assessment, particularly for innovative and complex assessment environments. Like other statistical modeling approaches to assessment, they can support modeling of tasks in terms of psychometric features (difficulty, discrimination) and probabilistic inferences about students. Two particular advantages allow BNs to operate on the cutting edge of evidence accumulation. The first is BN's flexibility for handling a variety of complexities that pose challenges to other statistical modeling approaches to evidence accumulation, including conditional dependence among observations, relationships between task features and students' capabilities, and multidimensional latent variable models where performance on tasks depends on multiple distinct though possibly related skills or other aspects of proficiency. This flexibility allows the analyst to specify a wide range of relationships reflecting theories of task performance and skill acquisition (Reye, 2004; VanLehn, 2008), including situations with multiple, confounded, and serially dependent observations. But the second advantage is more important in interactive digital environments. Using BNs to propagate the inferential force of observed data allows for the construction and piecing together of BN fragments in light of the features of an evolving situation and the examinee's actions up to that point. This capability uniquely supports dynamic and evolving assessment situations, from adaptive testing (Almond & Mislevy, 1999) to intelligent tutoring systems (VanLehn, 2008) and on-the-fly continuous assessment in multiplayer games (Shute, Hansen, & Almond, 2008).

TASK MODELS: WHERE DO WE MEASURE IT?

Task Models answer the question of how we structure the kinds of situations we need to obtain the kinds of evidence we need for the evidence models. This includes "What do we present to the examinee?" (the presentation material), and what is generated in response (the work products). They also answer the questions "what are the features of the tasks?" and "how are those features related to the presentation material and work products?"

Many 21st Century skills revolve around construction, communication, and interaction; they are enacted over time and across space, often in virtual environments, with cognitive and digital tools and representations. The capabilities for creating these environments for students to act in during assessment have arrived; we are able to build complex simulation environments that mirror or extend the real world. But this is not the same as saying we know how to leverage these environments to carry out assessment efficiently and validly. Building and making explicit assessment arguments in domain modeling goes a long way toward validity. Specifying the objects and processes to instantiate the arguments in re-usable, interoperable objects that match the assessment argument goes a long way toward efficiency. In designing simulation- and game-based assessment, for example, we want to build into task environments those features that require the targeted capabilities and provide affordances for students to enact their thinking—and we want to do this with code that we can re-use multiple times in many combinations with customizable surface characteristics. In the Cisco Networking Academy, for example, local instructors as well as test developers are provided a designer interface that allows them to easily create and share simulation tasks in the Packet Tracer environment (described in more detail below) using standard tools, representations, and affordances; automated scoring routines to identify features of final configurations are produced automatically for these tasks (Frezzo et al., 2010).

Important constituents of ECD task models are task model variables. These are features that task authors use to help structure their work in several ways, including effectively defining proficiency model variables, controlling difficulty, assembling tests to meet target specifications, and focusing the evidentiary value of a situation on particular aspects of skill (Mislevy, Steinberg, & Almond, 2003). The impact of different task features can be incorporated into the statistical submodels to improve the inferences about students in terms of proficiency model variables and/or to yield information that can be incorporated into assessment assembly to improve task construction and selection (De Boeck & Wilson, 2004).

THE EFFECT OF 21ST CENTURY TECHNOLOGY ON THE CAF

Psychometric advances in the statistical aspects of evidence models in the 20th century were largely predicated on logical and statistical independence of tasks. In addition, the evaluation submodels were largely predicated on fixed response scoring, and delivery models were restrictive in what could be provided. These limitations, together with a behavioral understanding of human activity, often contributed to assessment being constructed in highly atomized manner with little resemblance to the real-world tasks about which inferences to performance were being made.

The growing presence of digital experiences in day-to-day life and the emergence of interactive media and simulation for education and entertainment foreshadow the merging of digital tasks created for non-assessment uses becoming the basis for assessment inference moving forward. Indeed many common interfaces are equipped with built-in assessment systems as part of the daily experience. For example, Microsoft Word has an embedded evidence model that observes a user's typing and makes inferences about intended and actual spelling, and may make corrections to the text automatically or provide suggestions for alternate activity. This is a type of on-the-fly embedded assessment encountered as a non-assessment activity in day to day experience. Similarly, as we will discuss in the future directions section below, educational games contain many of the elements of evaluation of a work product and presentation of new tasks present in assessment. The difference between the assessment performance and the learning or work-based performance can often be reduced with digital assessment, compared to task design in physical modes.

From our perspective, these are examples of the fusion of "assessment driven tasks" and "daily-life-driven-tasks" enabled by the recording, storage, and manipulation of digital information. These requirements of recording, storage and manipulation have long been requirements of assessment inference but are now becoming wide standards for many activities in our digital lives. This opens the opportunity for what Behrens, Frezzo, Mislevy, Kroopnick, and Wise (2008) called "ubiquitous unobtrusive assessment" and what Shute (2011) calls "stealth assessment." As the world continues to evolve along these directions of increasingly digital interactions (Bell & Gemmell, 2009), assessment designers should continue to ask "do we need to collect new information, or is it occurring in the environment already?"

The keys to making use of voluminous digital information are recognizing, at a level of generality higher than the particulars of situations and actions, the patterns that signal cognitively important patterns—features of the situation, as well as features of the action. In troubleshooting, for example, what are essential features of the countless troubleshooting situations that admit to space-splitting, and what are essential features of action sequences in these situations that suggest that this is what the examinee has done? (See Steinberg & Gitomer, 1996 for answers to these questions in the context of troubleshooting aircraft hydraulics systems.)

ASSESSMENT IMPLEMENTATION AND DELIVERY: THE FOUR PROCESS MODEL

The delivery system used in the Networking Academy Program follows the Four Process architecture suggested in the ECD framework described by Almond, Steinberg, and Mislevy (2002). This view divides the delivery aspects of assessment into four core components, as illustrated in Figure 2.4. A fixed-form multiple-choice test may require a single trip around the cycle; a simulation-based task can require many interactions among the processes in the course of a performance; an intelligent tutoring system can jump out to instructional or practice models. The form of the logic, the processes, and messages have been specified out in the CAF models, which in turn have been developed to instantiate the assessment argument in domain analysis. (The relationships between the CAF models and the delivery system processes are delineated in Almond, Steinberg, & Mislevy, 2002.) In this way, we see the usually-hidden role that the pieces of machinery in an assessment play in reasoning.

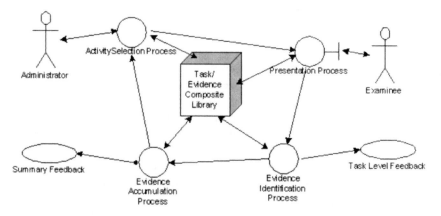

Figure 2.4 Processes in the assessment cycle (from Mislevy, Almond, & Lukas, 2004).

Activity or Task selection concerns the choices about what the examinee will be presented. This may be as simple as a rule to show the next question or may be based on a complex mathematical model of examinee knowledge and dispositional states. The next process is called *presentation*, which considers the display of information to the examinee and the capture of information from the examinee.

The result of the presentation process is a work product that must be examined and scored using rules derived from the evaluation submodel in the CAF. This process is called *response processing* or *evidence identification* and constitutes the third of the four processes. The ECD literature discusses the idea of looking for features in the work product and characterizing the work product in terms of one or more observable variables (note that work products, generally construed, can include process information, such as log files, captured screen actions, or video files of a performance). These observable variables characterize some aspect of the work, such as correctness, efficiency, or fluency, or more specific features such as whether a sequence of actions is consistent with space-splitting, or whether a router appropriately passes the messages it should allow to a particular computer and blocks the ones it should not allow. Most multiple choice questions are scored on a single observable of correctness. However, complexity is relatively easy to add even from this simple work product. For example, questions can be written with scoring rules such that if a student chooses option A, he or she may receive one point each for correctness and efficiency, while option B may represent an answer that receives one point for correctness and zero points for efficiency. The fourth process, *evidence accumulation*, is the process of combining information from all the observables and updating ability estimates in the student model through the statistical submodels in the CAF. If the assessment delivery has multiple phases, the activity selection process again decides what to do next.

Twenty-first century technology is influencing how assessments are delivered as conceptualized in the four-process model. Advances in computer-based semantic analysis and pattern matching allow for more complex evidence identification procedures. In both digital and physical systems, pattern recognition is used to map aspects of the work product to symbols representing quality or quantity of relevant aspects of the work product (i.e., values of observable variables). In physical scoring systems, however, the need for mechanical simplicity in scoring often drives backward up the ECD chain to constrain tasks to simplified formats consistent with simplified scoring, thereby constraining the kinds of evidence that can be obtained. In digital systems, we can program rules and algorithms to identify and process a wider variety of types of work products and apply scoring rules more flexibly.

Concomitant with this change in evidence identification are corresponding changes in evidence accumulation. The previous discussion of BNs as statistical submodels highlighted that BNs help us define how we gather evidence regarding proficiency model variables. They also are a sophisticated method of evidence accumulation that complements advances in computing technology to create adaptive learning and assessment tools. When a person completes a task in an adaptive assessment or intelligent tutoring situation, the resulting values for the observables that constitute evidence about proficiency are used to update the BN. This updates the estimates of the proficiency model variables of interest, including estimates of our uncertainty. These updated estimates can then be used to select the next task to present to the student. (See Mislevy & Gitomer (1996), VanLehn (2008), and Shute et al. (2008) for detailed descriptions of applications.)

AN APPLICATION OF ECD USING 21ST CENTURY TECHNOLOGY

One goal of the Cisco Networking Academy is to provide instructional support in order for students to become proficient networking professionals. Students need both a conceptual understanding of computer networking and the skills to apply this knowledge to real situations. Thus, hands-on practice and assessment on real equipment is an important component of the curricula. However, we also want to provide students with an opportunity to practice outside of class, explore in a low-risk environment, and build complex networks with more equipment than an average classroom has available.

To address these needs, Cisco has developed Packet Tracer (PT), a computer program that provides simulation, visualization, authoring, and assessment to support the teaching and learning of complex networking concepts (Frezzo et al., 2010). The PT software supports the authoring and distribution of network micro-worlds whose logic and activity are highly simulated at several levels of complexity, while also providing interfaces to support explanatory and assessment purposes. Numerous PT activities are pre-built into the current curricula (upward of 150 in some courses), instructors and students can construct their own activities, and students can explore problems on their own. For the purposes of this presentation we will focus on the affordances of PT that make it an effective assessment platform. Assessments in the Networking Academy fall into the categories of student initiated or instructor initiated. Student initiated assessments are primarily embedded in the curriculum and include quizzes, interactive activities, and PT challenge labs. These interactions provide feedback to the students to help their learning using a wide array of technologies including multiple-choice questions (in the quizzes) and complex simulations (in the challenge labs). Until recently, instructor initiated assessments consisted either of hands-on-exams with real networking equipment or multiple-choice exams in the online assessment system. As of 2010 this system additionally provides users with a variety of simulation-based end-of-chapter and end-of-course feedback and grading events. The assessment activity described below is called the Packet Tracer Skills Based Assessment (PT SBA). It integrates the flexibility and detailed feedback provided in the student-initiated assessments with the data collection, detailed reporting, and grade-book integration available in the more traditional instructor-initiated assessments. Examination of how the four process model described above is implemented with the PT demonstrates how technology makes these assessments possible.

TASK SELECTION

Task Selection is the process that is least automated in the current PT SBAs. Each assessment consists of one extensive network configuration or troubleshooting activity that may require up to one and a half hours of work across multiple sub-tasks. Access to the assessment is associated with a particular curricular unit, and it may be re-accessed repeatedly based on instructor authorization. PT assumes a task is selected for administration (by loading a network and task file) and that PT will act over the remaining three processes. In the future, it is possible that smaller tasks could be created and selected based on results of the previous tasks.

PRESENTATION

The rich interface and drag-and-drop interaction of PT is a hallmark of the software. It provides a deep (though imperfect) simulation of a broad range of networking devices and networking protocols including rich features set around the Cisco IOS. Instructions for tasks can be presented through HTML formatted text boxes that can be pre-authored and locked by any user. In this way PT is not simply a simulation tool, but actually a micro-world authoring and interaction tool with instructional and assessment affordances. One important differentiator between PT and many other instructional environments is its variable manager feature that allows the template creation of networks and the generation of random versions of the network based on ranges of values. Values can be generated by random selection from lists or numeric ranges in both the textboxes that describe the task or activity, as well as in values of much of the network data (e.g., IP addresses). This allows for the development of a large number of practice examples or isomorphic tasks to be generated at run time (Frezzo et al., 2010).

The micro-world environment in PT simulates a broad range of devices and networking protocols including a wide range of PC facilities covering communication cards, power functionality, web browsers, operating system configurations and so on. The particular devices, configurations, and problem states are determined by task authors guided by design patterns in order to address whatever proficiencies are targeted by the chapter, the course, or the instructional objective. When icons of the devices are touched in the simulator, more detailed pictures are presented with which the student can interact. A broad range of networking devices are simulated, including routers, switches, internet-based phones and video devices. Network management protocols are simulated from simple formats that may be used in a home to complex protocols used to manage portions of the internet.

Because the program provides assessment support to schools in over 160 countries with varying network bandwidth, there is a computational need to balance the size of a robust simulation engine with the need for a relatively small assessment definition package from the central web server. To accomplish this, the system is constructed to have the PT simulation program installed on the user's desktop before the assessment is initiated. This is usually non-problematic as the systems are generally pre-installed to support the curricular use of PT. At assessment run time, the assessment system sends the PT instance the micro-world definition file (a .pka file), which includes all the information necessary for the micro-world definition, and assessment scoring instructions (Figure 2.5). When the activity is submitted, the entire student network is relayed back to the server along with detailed

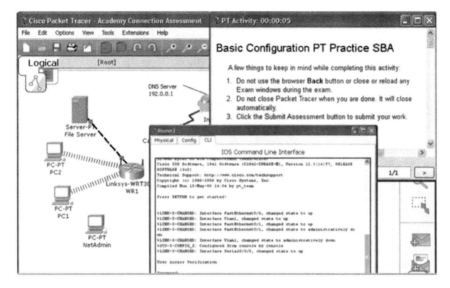

Figure 2.5 Screenshot of a Packet Tracer Skills-based Assessment.

log files and the results of the evidence identification work that was accomplished in the PT software.

EVIDENCE IDENTIFICATION/TASK SCORING

The approach taken in PT to assist with the authoring of scoring rules needed to be easy to use, comprehensive, and consistent with the flexibility of the ECD model. To accomplish this, PT provides an Activity Wizard that allows the construction of an Initial Network and an "Answer Network." The Initial Network is the starting state of the network micro-world. The Answer Network is the matching key created by the states of comparison network configured for scoring by providing the author with a comprehensive list of network states as depicted in the tree on the left side of Figure 2.6. The original state of the Answer Network provides a list of potential work product features of interest to the assessment designer. These are low-level features including how particular aspects of the device are configured, whether a cable is plugged in, and in what ways traffic on the network is occurring. By considering the purpose of the assessment and the relationship between work product features and signs of proficiency, the designer checks the boxes of all the features about which they would like to obtain data.

After indicating the features about which to create observable variables, the assessment designer edits the answer network values to create implied scoring rules. At the time of task completion, the target features of the

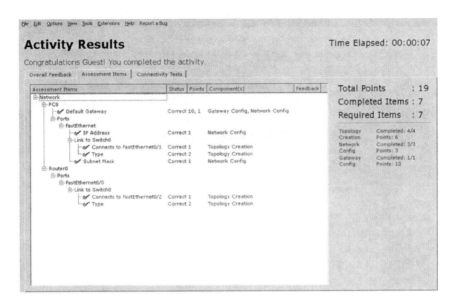

Figure 2.6 Packet Tracer Results screen showing features of Answer Network (left), observable values, component loading values, and components.

examinee's network are compared pair-wise with the corresponding features of the Answer Network. The comparisons used to generate observable variables may look for exact matches (answer network cable plugged in, examinee network cable plugged in) or may allow for evaluation of range of values (answer IP address between xx.xx.0 and xx.xx.100, examine network IP address xx.xx.50). This pattern matching is made flexible by both the use of the variable manager and the use of regular expressions in the evaluation clauses. In addition to answer network end-states, authors can also create network functionality tests. In other words, not only is the scoring automated, but the creation of algorithms necessary for automated scoring is itself automated, and driven by simple choices the author makes about which aspects of the work product to seek evidence. Areas of proficiency reporting associated with student model variables can also be specified and associated with observable summation as shown on the right side of Figure 2.6.

In the most basic interface, the Activity Wizard provides ease of use and structure to support basic assessment authoring; in addition, PT also gives instructors and other assessment designers direct access to many of the micro-world variables using a comprehensive macro language. By providing this custom programming layer, more detailed observable definition and combination schemes can be created from the network values. Recent versions of PT have also included the availability of a macro-language for directly accessing micro-world states, translating them into observable values and combining the lower level observables into higher order combinations.

While log files are not currently being evaluated by the PT scoring engine (see future directions below), they are captured and available for further review by students and instructors through the on-line grade book. This allows instructors and students to review the work of the student in detail and make custom decisions or discussions enabled by the assessment infrastructure. The files can also be exported to automated systems for analysis and evaluation. Another feature of evidence identification in the ECD framework is that it is the minimum requirement for providing feedback. After some aspects of the work products have been characterized in terms of observable variables, these variables can be used to trigger feedback to students. PT supports this by allowing the authoring and reporting of observable level feedback. That is to say, different strings can be presented to the student depending on whether a specific work product feature, or combination of features, is present or not. In the results window presented to the student (as seen in Figure 2.6), the values of the observed variables are communicated with the labels of "correct" and "incorrect" or any other value-specific string desired. For example, text identifying specific strategies or potential interpretations can be authored as well.

EVIDENCE ACCUMULATION

While Packet Tracer was not designed originally as an assessment and measurement tool, it has important features that support the facilitation of linkages from observables to variables called "components," which serve as proficiency model variables in the ECD framework. For each observable variable, PT allows the specification of multiple components to be associated with the observable variable and allows the specification of differential weights. In the ECD model this is described as a multiple-observable/ multiple-proficiency model variable architecture. Importantly, the different observable variables can provide information in multiple dimensions; for example, establishing communication between two routers can depend on a student's understanding on two dimensions: IP addressing and connectivity. Accordingly it is important to conceptualize the observable variables not simply as identifiers of correctness, but rather as pieces of information about a feature of performance that provides information for one or more proficiency model variables. In many traditional assessment systems each task generates one observable and updates exactly one proficiency model variable—a simplifying assumption at odds with the integrated use of multiple aspects of knowledge and skill that characterizes most problem solving in the real world. The primary limitation of the PT software in this area is that loadings between the observables and the components (proficiency estimates) are limited to standard algebraic functions found in common computer languages (which are thereby passed to the macro language). However, because PT's architecture allows communication of information to external systems, one possibility is that future versions could allow probabilistic updating using more complex algorithms including BN methods (Wainer, Dorans, Flaugher, Green & Mislevy, 2000).

As of fall 2010, after an extensive beta test period, the assessment is in the full production systems and approximately 2,000 PT SBA are being delivered each week across eight courses. The collection of observable values, logs, and final networks is providing a growing corpus of data with which to understand the variations in performance, missteps and expertise with which we plan to refine our scoring rules and reporting features. A survey of 141 instructors during the beta test period indicated an average satisfaction rating of 4.5 on a scale anchored by 1 = Very Dissatisfied, 3 = Neutral and 5 = Very Satisfied. A survey of 916 students indicated an average satisfaction score of 3.9, with students taking the exam at home showing significantly lower satisfaction than those taking the exam at school. This is likely a side effect of configuration and network dependency issues idiosyncratic to home networks. Analysis of the patterns of observables for each exam suggested patterns of performance consistent with expectation.

The feasibility of such a complex system was made possible because each system was designed with ECD conceptualization and orientation toward the four process delivery model. The scoring back-end of PT provides both the flexibility and support for task generation, evidence identification and evidence accumulation as well as the ability to communicate to other systems that might need to augment or replace one of the four processes. Integration with the core multiple choice assessment system and corresponding grade book was possible because that system had been written from a four process model perspective and included a four process model extension module that allows for robust extension of the system to performance based input systems such as PT (Behrens, Collison & DeMark, 2005). By creating systems under the view of common ECD architecture we are able to integrate new innovations over time, adding technologies that naturally promote re-use, efficiency and extensibility.

FUTURE DIRECTIONS, CURRENT LIMITATIONS

Despite the advances in the application of ECD to new assessment technologies, there remain both limitations and opportunities. This section will discuss three areas that present opportunity for future work and the Networking Academies' efforts in these areas.

Games and Embedded Assessment

The Packet Tracer Skills Based Assessments described in the previous section are clearly defined and understood as classroom assessments for students. This understanding does not come from the structure of the software or tasks but rather the control, uses, and implications of the activity (Frezzo et al., 2009). To provide high quality instructional and learning support while avoiding the constraints and costs of high stakes testing, we next sought to create an assessment tool that would move us toward the goal of "ubiquitous unobtrusive assessment" (Behrens et al., 2008). That is, we desire to build the affordances of assessment (tracking and feedback) into the fabric of the student daily activity. While a number of approaches to this could be taken, we decided to extend the micro-world infrastructure and ECD-based scoring system in PT to create a complex game like environment, thereby formalizing the work introduced in Behrens et al. (2008).

Games are seen as attractive potential learning tools because they engage and immerse players in ways that traditional school content does not, providing the context needed to encourage application of learning (Gee, 2003). Games often involve spontaneous learning and demonstration of concepts through play (Clark, Nelson, Sengupta, & D'Angelo, 2009), and they can elicit particular ways of thinking. Shaffer (2006) defines "epistemic frames" as the ways people in a given field decide what is worth knowing, agree on methods of adding new knowledge and standards of evidence, have concepts and representations to understand situations, and interact with each other and the world. When properly developed, epistemic games can engage people in thinking like doctors, or scientists, or network engineers.

Behrens et al. (2008) argued that simulation-based games themselves contain many parallels to assessment. For example, both games and assessments have the purpose of describing knowledge and skills in a quantifiable manner. Rules define what information is available and constraints around solution paths. The ECD four-process model that describes activity selection, presentation, response processing, and evidence accumulation in assessment can also be applied to simulation game scenarios (Behrens et al., 2008). Both assessment and simulation communities desire to create models of student (player) behavior and knowledge, and often use similar tools (e.g., BNs) to do so.

Given the promise of games in the assessment sphere, the question then becomes how to make this potential a reality. Shute, Ventura, Bauer, & Zapata-Rivera (2009) explore embedding formative assessment within games. They advocate for the use of unobtrusive measures of performance gathered while students maintain flow in the game to provide direct feedback on personal progress and/or modify the learning environment for the player. They introduce the term "stealth assessment" to describe embedded assessments so closely tied to the environment that they are invisible to the user. In the process of game play, students perform the very skills we would like to assess. It follows that we might capture their performance of these skills to provide information about students' knowledge, skills, and abilities. Shute et al. (2009) use the commercially available game Oblivion to demonstrate the use of ECD to assess creative problem solving. The paths users take through the game (for example, how they cross a river) serve as observable measures in task models that then inform evidence models and proficiency models, allowing for estimates of students' creative problem solving skills based on their game play.

The Cisco Networking Academy is in the early stages of experimenting with games as providers of assessment information. It recently released a networking and entrepreneurship game named Aspire (see Figure 2.7). The main idea of the game is that students are entrepreneurs who own small networking companies, and must make both business and technical decisions in the game. The Aspire system consists of a 2½-D interface that allows navigation, interaction with characters in the game, decision making and interaction (sometimes in the form of multiple choice questions) and complex scenarios that combine numerous task requirements. This interface is integrated with the PT software which renders and simulates the computer and networking devices and systems and provides the ECD-based scoring architecture. This provides a high degree of design and analysis re-use among PT, the PT SBA and the Aspire game. We are in the early stages of analyzing and working with the data from what early student reactions suggest is an engaging, stimulating, and informative tool.

Understanding Trace Data

The advent of computer-based simulations and gaming described above has brought with it the ability to capture highly detailed data as students progress through the environment. Data ranging in granularity all the way down to individual mouse clicks is available, creating vast stores of information. The challenge lies in how to determine which data are useful, and how to make use of this data in ways that will ultimately inform and improve student learning. These efforts fall primarily into the category of evidence identification. How do we take these work products and apply scoring rules that will provide meaningful information about students' knowledge, skills, and abilities?

In computer networking, one of the primary means of connecting networks is by programming routers and other network devices. In many contexts, these machines, which route data traffic such as your email or web page request, need to be programmed to be aware of the location it is in

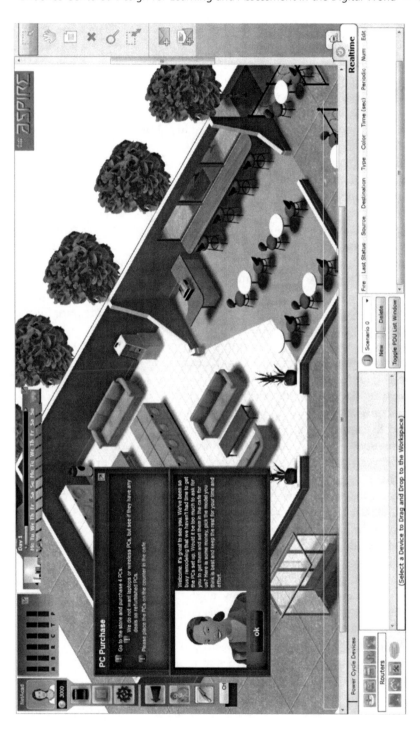

Figure 2.7 Screenshot of Aspire game.

and the rules required for giving or denying access. This programming pro-
duces logs of commands and is one of the work products of a PT SBA. We
will discuss ways we have explored analyzing these streams of commands,
and we believe the same concepts could be applied if, instead of each data
point being a command, it was a game location or mouse click. Of the many
ways to think about this trace data, we will briefly discuss three: thinking
about strings as words and sentences, thinking about strings as documents,
and thinking about strings as neighbors.

Thinking about strings as words and sentences leads us to the field of statistical natural language processing (NLP) (Manning & Schütze, 1999). If
we think of individual performances as text streams, it then raises questions
such as: can we understand the relationships between different elements in
the stream? Can we develop succinct descriptions of a performance? Can
we extend these techniques to help us with more broadly used techniques
such as clustering? DeMark and Behrens (2004) began this process with
router logs. This work has continued with the data from the PT SBAs. NLP
includes some common data techniques that have been helpful. For example, tokenization (or breaking the stream of data into meaningful segments) and creation of n-grams (groups of n tokens that occur together)
allow us to identify the commands that occur together. Using tokenization,
stemming, tagging, and other NLP techniques, we can examine command
use in the entire sample, as well as within novices or experts, and tie this
information back to the observables measured.

A second way to think about trace data is as texts in a corpus (Biber,
Conrad & Reppen, 1998). This may allow us to understand variability in
performances as a whole across individuals, describe similarity and dissimi-
larity between performances, cluster performances, and find the most informative dimensions of variation within and between performances. We
can cluster individuals based on the patterns and sequences of commands
(Gries, 2009). Ultimately, we believe this process will allow us to inform
instruction by identifying and suggesting strategies that successful and less
successful students employ.

A third way to think about trace data is as a network. In trace data, each
location, click, or command is in a sequence before some events and after
others. These could be thought of as neighbors, or members of a network,
and the tools of social network analysis employed to investigate the relationships (cf. De Nooy, Mrvar & Batagelj, 2005; Stevens, Johnson, & Soller,
2005). In router logs, there are different probabilities of commands occurring near each other. We can use visualization tools to help us understand
the networks. Figure 2.8 is a visual depiction of an entire exam's command
sequence from one individual. Based on this work, we can begin determining things like the average distance from one command to another,

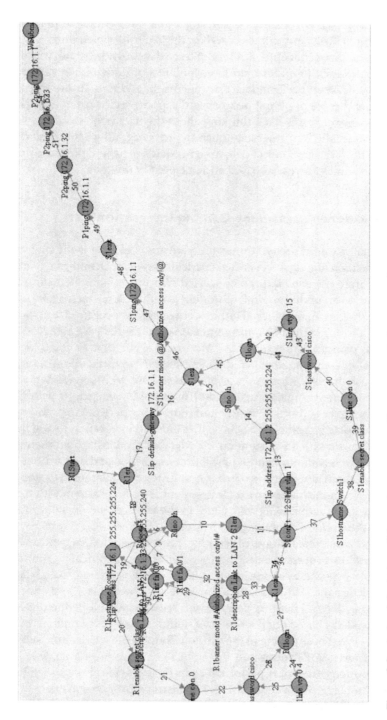

Figure 2.8 A visual depiction of the entire sequence of log commands for one student.

identifying salient features of networks that differentiate experts and novices, and cluster individuals based on these network elements.

These three conceptualizations of trace data provide us with various lenses through which to understand large amounts of student data gathered from computer-based performance assessments. In addition, future research may explore the use of neural network and support vector machine methodologies to examine this data, thinking about the data as observables. Consideration must also be given to automation processes and machine data learning given the large amounts of data under review. We believe there are numerous opportunities for research and advancement in this area.

Curriculum–Assessment–Gaming Integration

Finally, a third area of opportunity we are exploring is the integration of information and data. Very often curricula, assessment, and games are entirely separate projects, with no concerted effort to bring information from all sources to an understanding of student learning. Assessments are conducted by district, state, or national entities, curricula are produced and distributed by publishing companies, and games are produced by yet another set of companies or academic researchers. We would argue that to create a seamless flow of information about student learning, these three things should be integrated. In that effort, we are pursuing efforts to integrate data obtained from students using the curriculum (for example, practice PT activities), taking assessments (both formative and summative, performance and traditional), and playing games. We believe that with this integration we will be able to provide instructors and students with detailed feedback about their progress and make recommendations of resources, activities, and interactions that will further them along that progression while lowering the need to stop instruction for administratively driven assessment. This is consistent with the earlier discussion of embedding assessment in the fabric of the digital world. In this case, the world of digital on-line learning.

The conceptualization of learning progressions has helped us with this integration process. Learning progressions are empirically grounded and testable hypotheses about how a student's understanding and ability to use knowledge and skills in a targeted area develop over time (Corcoran, Mosher, & Rogat, 2009). Learning progressions are being developed in the Networking Academy based on: the results of statistical analyses of millions of student exams taken over the life of the previous four-course curriculum, subject matter expert (SME) input and the results of cognitive task analysis research into novice and expert performance in the curriculum domain (DeMark & Behrens, 2004; West et al., 2010). The learning progression analyses identify conceptual development of strands of increasing complexity/sophistication that we can then use to both develop curricula, assessments, and games and bring together data from these sources in a meaningful way.

We believe that the BNs described above provide a way to model performance on learning progressions using data from different sources. West et al. (2010) provide an example of the use of BNs to analyze progress on a single learning progression using only data from multiple choice tests. Future work will undertake the challenges of using data from multiple sources, modeling tasks that are influenced by multiple learning progressions, and modeling progression over time. The issue of modeling tasks that are influenced by multiple progressions is likely to be particularly important in the assessment of 21st century skills. In these assessments, there nearly always must be some content expertise that is needed to complete the question along with the 21st century skill of interest. For example, it is difficult to assess problem solving skills without a particular context for the assessment. So, it will be important to model both the level of the content learning progression and the 21st century skill progression of interest.

CONCLUDING OBSERVATIONS

A fundamental advantage of designing assessments in an ECD framework is that it is flexible enough to accommodate the affordances of new technologies and the demand to measure new domains while providing a unified framework to describe current practice across a wide range of assessment activities. We have seen major advances in assessment practice because of the availability of 21st century technology, we are glimpsing the beginnings of other changes, and there are surely still other developments that we cannot even guess at this time. Similarly, the domains we want to measure change as the demands of jobs and society change. The relevance of certain knowledge, skills, and abilities depends on the specific social, intellectual and physical contexts in which the educational and professional actors operate. Education seeks to prepare individuals for broad activity in society. Shifts in a society's understanding of itself will affect education, its desired outcomes, and by consequence, the measurement of those outcomes. We should aim to develop tools and systems not only to fit 21st century skills and technologies as we know them today, but to adapt to the changes in skills and technologies we will no doubt see before the turn of the 22nd century.

NOTES

John T. Behrens is Director, Network Academy Learning System Development. Dr. Behrens is also an Adjunct Assistant Research Professor in the Department of

Psychology at the University of Notre Dame, Notre Dame, IN. His research addresses the development and evaluation of e-learning and assessment tools that incorporate best practices in the computing, statistical, and cognitive sciences. JBehrens@cisco.com.

Robert J. Mislevy is Frederic M. Lord Chair in Measurement and Statistics at Educational Testing Service, and Professor Emeritus of Measurement, Statistics and Evaluation at the University of Maryland at College Park. His research applies developments in psychology, statistics, and technology to practical problems in educational assessment. RMislevy@umd.edu.

Kristen E. DiCerbo is an independent researcher who provides methodological consultation to the Network Academy program. Her research interests center on the use of interactive technologies to promote student learning and the use of assessment data to inform movement through learning progressions. KDiCerbo@cisco.com

Roy Levy is an Assistant Professor of Measurement and Statistical Analysis at Arizona State University. His research pursues methodological developments and applications of latent variable models and related statistical and psychometric methods to address persistent and emerging challenges in assessment, education research, and the social sciences. Roy.Levy@asu.edu.

REFERENCES

American Association for the Advancement of Science (AAAS). (2001). *Atlas of Science Literacy, Volume 1*. Washington, DC: Author.

American Association for the Advancement of Science (AAAS). (2007). *Atlas of Science Literacy, Volume 2*. Washington, DC: Author.

Almond, R. G., DiBello, L. V., Moulder, B., & Zapata-Rivera, J. D. (2007). Modeling diagnostic assessments with Bayesian networks. *Journal of Educational Measurement, 44*, 341–359.

Almond, R. G., & Mislevy, R. J. (1999). Graphical models and computerized adaptive testing. *Applied Psychological Measurement, 23*, 223–237.

Almond, R. G., Steinberg, L. S., & Mislevy, R. J. (2002). Enhancing the design and delivery of assessment systems: A four-process architecture [Electronic version]. *Journal of Technology, Learning, and Assessment, 5*.

Anderson, J. (2009). *Cognitive psychology and its implications* (7th ed.). New York: Worth Publishers.

Barabasi, A.-L. (2003). *Linked: How everything is connected to everything else*. New York: Plume.

Baayen, H. (2008). *Analyzing linguistic data: A practical introduction to statistics using R*. Cambridge: Cambridge University Press.

Behrens, J. T., Collison, T. A., & DeMark, S. F. (2005) The seven Cs of comprehensive assessment: Lessons learned from 40 million classroom exams in the Cisco Networking Academy Program. In S. Howell and M. Hricko (Eds.), *Online assessment and measurement: Case studies in higher education, K–12 and corporate*. (pp. 229–245). Hershey, PA: Information Science Publishing.

Behrens, J. T., Frezzo, D. C., Mislevy, R. J., Kroopnick, M., & Wise, D. (2008). Structural, functional, and semiotic symmetries in simulation-based games and assessments. In E. Baker, J. Dickieson, W. Wulfeck, & H. O'Neil (Eds.), *Assessment of problem solving using simulations* (pp. 59–80). New York: Earlbaum.

Behrens, J. T., Mislevy, R. J., Bauer, M., Williamson, D. M., & Levy R. (2004). Introduction to evidence centered design and lessons learned from its application in a global e-learning program. *The International Journal of Testing, 4,* 295–301.

Bell, G., & Gemmell, J. (2009). *Total recall: How the e-memory revolution will change everything.* New York: Dutton.

Benkler, Y. (2007). *The wealth of networks: How social production transforms markets and freedom.* New Haven, CT: Yale University Press.

Bennett, R. E., & Bejar, I. I. (1998). Validity and automated scoring: It's not only the scoring. *Educational Measurement: Issues and Practice, 17*(4), 9–17.

Biber, D., Conrad, S., & Reppen, R. (1998). *Corpus linguistics: Investigating language structure and use.* Cambridge: Cambridge University Press.

Boeck, P. D., & Wilson, M. (2004). *Explanatory item response models: A generalized linear and nonlinear approach.* New York: Springer.

Brennan, R. L. (2001). *Generalizability theory.* New York: Springer-Verlag.

Cheng, B. H., Ructtinger, L., Fujii, R., & Mislevy, R. (2010). *Assessing systems thinking and complexity in science (large-scale assessment technical report 7).* Menlo Park, CA: SRI International. Retrieved September 11, 2010 from http://ecd.sri.com/downloads/ECD_TR7_Systems_Thinking_FL.pdf

Clark, D., Nelson, B., Sengupta, P., & D'Angelo, C. (2009). *Rethinking science learning through digital games and simulations: Genres, examples, and evidence.* Paper presented at National Academies of Sciences Learning Science: Computer Games, Simulations, and Education conference.

Committee on Ensuring the Utility and Integrity of Research Data in a Digital Age and National Academy of Sciences. (2009). *Ensuring the integrity, accessibility, and stewardship of research data in the digital age.* Washington, DC: National Academies Press.

Corcoran, T., Mosher, F., & Rogat, A. (May 2009). Learning progressions in science: An evidence based approach to reform. Consortium for Policy Research in Education. *CPRE Research Report # RR-63. Center on Continuous Instructional Improvement,* Teachers College–Columbia University.

Cronbach, L. J., Gleser, G. C., Nanda, H., & Rajaratnam, N. (1972). *The dependability of behavioral measurements: Theory of generalizability for scores and profiles.* New York: Wiley.

De Boeck, P., & Wilson, M. (2004). *Explanatory item response models: A generalized linear and nonlinear approach.* New York: Springer.

De Nooy, W., Mrvar, A., & Batagelj, V. (2005). *Exploratory social network analysis with Pajek.* Cambridge: Cambridge University Press.

DeMark, S. F., & Behrens, J. T. (2004). Using statistical natural language processing for understanding complex responses to free-response tasks. *International Journal of Testing, 4,* 371–390.

Engeström, Y. (1999) Activity theory and individual and social transformation. In Y. Engeström, R. Miettinen, & R. Punamäki (Eds.), *Perspectives on activity theory* (pp. 19–38). Cambridge, UK: Cambridge University Press.

Freeman, L. C. (*2004*). *The development of social network analysis: A study in the sociology of science.* Vancouver: Empirical Press.

Frezzo, D. C., Behrens, J. T., & Mislevy, R. J. (2009b). Activity theory and assessment theory in the design and understanding of the packet tracer ecosystem. *International Journal of Learning and Media, 1*(2). doi:10.1162/ijlm.2009.0015

Frezzo, D. C., Behrens, J. T., & Mislevy, R. J. (2010). Design patterns for learning and assessment: Facilitating the introduction of a complex simulation-based learning environment into a community of instructors. *Journal of Science Education and Technology, 19*, 105–114.

Gardner, H. E. (1987). *The mind's new science: A history of the cognitive revolution.* New York: Basic Books.

Gee, J. P. (2003). *What video games have to teach us about learning and literacy.* New York: Palgrave/ Macmillan.

Gries, S. (2009). *Quantitative corpus linguistics with R: A practical introduction.* New York: Routledge.

Gulliksen, H. (1950/1987). *Theory of mental tests.* New York: Wiley. Reprint, Hillsdale, NJ: Erlbaum.

International Data Corporation. (2008). *The diverse and exploding digital universe.* Retrieved from http://www.emc.com/collateral/analyst-reports/diverse-exploding-digital-universe.pdf

Jonassen, D. H., & Hung, W. (2006). Learning to troubleshoot: A new theory-based design architecture. *Educational Psychology Review, 18,* 77–114

Kane, M., & Mitchell, R. (1996). *Implementing performance assessment: Promises, problems, and challenges.* Mahwah, NJ: Lawrence Erlbaum Associates.

Kline, R. B. (2010) *Principles and practice of structural equation modeling* (3rd ed.). New York: Guilford.

Lauritzen, S., & Spiegelhalter, D. (1988). Local computations with probabilities on graphical structures and their application to expert systems. *Journal of the Royal Statistical Society B, 50,* 157–224.

Levy, R., & Mislevy, R. J. (2004). Specifying and refining a measurement model for a computer-based interactive assessment. *International Journal of Testing, 4,* 333–369.

Levy, F., & Murnane, R. J. (2004). *The new division of labor: How computers are creating the next job market.* Princeton, NJ: Princeton University Press.

Liu, M., Mislevy, R., Colker, A. M., Fried, R., & Zalles, D. (2010). *A design pattern for experimental investigation (large-scale assessment technical report 8).* Menlo Park, CA: SRI International. Retrieved September 11, 2010 from http://ecd.sri.com/downloads/ECD_TR8_Experimental_Invest_FL.pdf

Lord, F. M. (1980) *Applications of item response theory to practical testing problems.* Hillsdale, NJ: Erlbaum.

Lord, F. M., & Novick, M. R. (1968). *Statistical theories of mental test scores.* Reading, MA: Addison-Wesley.

Mager, R. (1962). *Preparing instructional objectives.* Palo Alto, CA: Fearon Publishers.

Manning, C. D., & Schütze, H. (1999). *Foundations of statistical natural language processing.* Cambridge, MA: MIT Press.

Messick, S. (1994). The interplay of evidence and consequences in the validation of performance assessments. *Educational Researcher, 23*(2), 13–23.

Mislevy, R. J. (1994). Evidence and inference in educational assessment. *Psychometri-ka, 59*, 439–483.

Mislevy, R. J. (2006). Cognitive psychology and educational assessment. In R. L. Brennan (Ed.), *Educational Measurement* (4th ed.) (pp. 257–305). Phoenix, AZ: Greenwood.

Mislevy, R. J., Almond, R. G., & Lukas, J. (2004). A brief introduction to evidence-centered design. *CSE Technical Report 632.* Los Angeles: The National Center for Research on Evaluation, Standards, Student Testing (CRESST), Center for Studies in Education, UCLA.

Mislevy, R. J., Behrens, J. T., Bennett, R. E., Demark, S. F., Frezzo, D. C., Levy, R, et al. (2010). On the roles of external knowledge representations in assessment design. *Journal of Technology, Learning, and Assessment, 8*(2). Retrieved from http://escholarship.bc.edu/jtla/vol8/2

Mislevy, R. J., & Gitomer, D. H. (1996). The role of probability-based inference in an intelligent tutoring system. *User-Modeling and User-Adapted Interaction, 5*, 253–282

Mislevy, R. J., & Levy, R. (2007). Bayesian psychometric modeling from an evidence-centered design perspective. In C. R. Rao and S. Sinharay (Eds.), *Handbook of statistics, volume 26* (pp. 839–865). North-Holland: Elsevier.

Mislevy, R., Liu, M., Cho, Y., Fulkerson, D., Nichols, P., Zalles, D., et al. (2009). *A design pattern for observational investigation assessment tasks (large-scale assessment technical report 2)*. Menlo Park, CA: SRI International. Retrieved September 11, 2010 from http://ecd.sri.com/downloads/ECD_TR2_DesignPattern_for_ObservationalInvestFL.pdf

Mislevy, R. J., & Riconscente, M. M. (2006). Evidence-centered assessment design: Layers, concepts, and terminology. In S. Downing & T. Haladyna (Eds.), *Handbook of test development* (pp. 61–90). Mahwah, NJ: Erlbaum

Mislevy, R. J., Riconscente, M. M., & Rutstein, D. W. (2009). *Design patterns for assessing model-based reasoning (PADI-large systems technical report 6)*. Menlo Park, CA: SRI International. Retrieved September 11, 2010 from http://ecd.sri.com/downloads/ECD_TR6_Model-Based_Reasoning.pdf .

Mislevy, R. J., Steinberg, L. S., & Almond, R. G. (2002). *Design and analysis in task-based language assessment.* CRESST Technical Report 579. Retrieved from http://www.cse.ucla.edu/products/Reports/TR579.pdf

Mislevy, R. J., Steinberg, L. S., & Almond, R. G. (2003). On the structure of educational assessments. *Measurement: Interdisciplinary Research and Perspectives, 1*, 3–62.

Newell, A., & Simon, H. A. (1972). *Human problem solving.* Englewood Cliffs, NJ: Prentice-Hall.

Nichols, P. D., Chipman, S. F., & Brennan, R. L. (Eds.). (1995). *Cognitively diagnostic assessment.* Hillsdale, NJ: Erlbaum.

Nooy, W. D., Mrvar, A., & Batagelj, V. (2005). *Exploratory social network analysis with Pajek* (illustrated edition.). Cambridge: Cambridge University Press.

Pearl, J. (1988). *Probabilistic reasoning in intelligent systems: Networks of plausible inference.* San Mateo, CA: Kaufmann.

Perez, C. (2003). *Technological revolutions and financial capital: The dynamics of bubbles and golden ages.* Cheltenham, UK: Edward Elgar.

Porter, M. E., & Kramer, M. R. (December, 2002). The competitive advantage of corporate philanthropy. *Harvard Business Review* (pp. 5–16).

Reye, J. (*2004*). Student modeling based on belief *networks*. *International Journal of Artificial Intelligence in Education, 14*, 1–33.

Rupp, A. A., Templin, J., & Henson, R. J. (2010). Diagnostic measurement: Theory, methods, and applications. New York: Guilford.

Segaran, T. (2007). *Programming collective intelligence.* New York: O'Reilly Media.

Schaafstal, A., & Schraagen, J. M. (2000). Training of troubleshooting: A structured, task analytical approach. In J. M. Schraagen, S. F. Chipman, and V. L. Shalin (Eds.), *Cognitive task analysis* (pp. 57–70). Mahwah, NJ: Erlbaum.

Shaffer, D. W. (2006). Epistemic frames for epistemic games. *Computers & Education, 46*, 223–234.

Shute, V. J. (2011). Stealth assessment in computer-based games to support learning. In S. Tobias, & J. D. Fletcher (Eds.), *Computer games and instruction.* Charlotte, NC: Information Age Publishers.

Shute, V. J., & Psotka, J. (1996). Intelligent tutoring systems: Past, present, and future. In D. Jonassen (Ed.), *Handbook of research for educational communications and technology* (pp. 570–600). New York, NY: Macmillan.

Shute, V. J., Ventura, M., Bauer, M. I., & Zapata-Rivera, D. (2009). Melding the power of serious games and embedded assessment to monitor and foster learning: Flow and grow. In U. Ritterfeld, M. Cody, & P. Vorder, (Eds.), *Serious games: Mechanisms and effects* (pp. 295–321). Mahwah, NJ: Routledge, Taylor and Francis.

Spiegelhalter, D. J., Dawid, A. P., Lauritzen, S. L., & Cowell, R. G. (1993). Bayesian analysis in expert systems. *Statistical Science, 8,* 219–247.

Steinberg, L. S., & Gitomer, D. H. (1996). Intelligent tutoring and assessment built on an understanding of a technical problem-solving task. *Instructional Science, 24,* 223–258.

Stevens, R., Johnson, D. F. & Soller, A. (2005). Probabilities and predictions: Modeling the development of scientific problem-solving skills. *Cell Biology Education, 4,* 42–57.

Tapscott, D., & Williams, A. D. (2008). *Wikinomics: How mass collaboration changes everything.* New York: Portfolio.

Tekian, A., McGuire, C. H., & McGahie, W. C. (Eds.). (1999). *Innovative simulations for assessing professional competence.* Chicago: University of Illinois, Department of Medical Education.

VanLehn, K. (2008). Intelligent tutoring systems for continuous, embedded assessment. In C. A. Dwyer (Ed.), *The future of assessment: Shaping teaching and learning,* pp. 113–138. New York, NY: Erlbaum.

Wainer, H., Dorans, N. J., Flaugher, R., Green, B. F., & Mislevy, R. J. (2000). *Computerized adaptive testing: A primer.* New York: Routledge.

Wasserman, S., & Faust, K. (1994). *Social network analysis: Methods and applications.* Cambridge: Cambridge University Press.

West, P., Rutstein, D. W., Mislevy, R. J., Liu, J., Levy, R., DiCerbo, K. E., et al. (2010). *A Bayesian network approach to modeling learning progressions.* Los Angeles: The National Center for Research on Evaluation, Standards, Student Testing (CRESST), Center for Studies in Education, UCLA.

Wiley, D. E., & Haertel, E. H. (1996). Extended assessment tasks: Purposes, definitions, scoring, and accuracy. In M. B. Kane & R. Mitchell (Eds.), *Implementing performance assessment: Promises and challenges* (pp. 61–89). Mahwah, NJ: Lawrence Erlbaum Associates.

Williamson, D. M., Almond, R. G., & Mislevy, R. J. (2000). Model criticism of Bayesian networks with latent variables. *Uncertainty in Artificial Intelligence Proceedings 2000*, 634–643.

Williamson, D. M., Bauer, M., Steinberg, L. S., Mislevy, R. J., Behrens, J. T., & Demark, S. (2004). Design rationale for a complex performance assessment. *International Journal of Measurement, 4*, 333–369.

Williamson, D. M., Mislevy, R. J., & Bejar, I. I. (Eds.). (2006). *Automated scoring of complex performances in computer based testing.* Mahwah, NJ: Erlbaum Associates.

Wise-Rutstein, D. (2005, April). Design patterns for assessing troubleshooting in computer networks. Presented at the annual meeting of the American Education Research Association, San Francisco, CA.

Wolfram, S. (2002). *A new kind of science.* Champaign, IL: Wolfram Media.

CHAPTER 3

21ST CENTURY DYNAMIC ASSESSMENT

**Edys S. Quellmalz, Michael J. Timms, Barbara C. Buckley,
Jodi Davenport, Mark Loveland, and Matt D. Silberglitt**

INTRODUCTION

How can we assess the core knowledge and skills that students need to succeed in the 21st century? Researchers and practitioners have identified a variety of competencies, referred to as 21st century skills, information communication technology (ICT) skills, media literacy, cyberlearning, and new literacies. With the explosion of information in all fields comes the need for students to become adept at using knowledge, not just memorizing it. Students must be able to apply complex skills such as problem solving, critical thinking, creativity, communication, and collaboration across a range of problems in academic and practical contexts. Thus, assessments of 21st century skills must provide students opportunities to demonstrate competencies for acquiring, applying, and transferring knowledge. We can tap into these skills through dynamic assessments that expand how phenomena, information, and data can be represented and increase the number of ways learners can demonstrate their knowledge and skills. In addition, technology can support use of scaffolding during assessment tasks to monitor and promote learning progress. The challenges for K–12 educators and

Technology-Based Assessments for 21st Century Skills, pages 55–89

assessment developers are to create assessment tasks that allow students to demonstrate 21st century skills and to create evidence models for making inferences about student progress and proficiency.

In this chapter we focus on the design of dynamic assessments of cognitive learning in academic domains. We define 21st century dynamic assessment as assessments that capitalize on the affordances of technology to: (1) focus on complex, integrated knowledge structures and strategies; (2) provide rich, authentic task environments that represent significant, recurring problems; (3) offer interactive, immediate, customized, graduated scaffolding; and (4) analyze evidence of learning trajectories and proficiency. We synthesize research related to identifying significant 21st century target knowledge and skills, developing appropriate rich, interactive, assessment tasks, and eliciting evidence of development and achievement of 21st century skills that can inform teaching and benefit learning. We cite examples of assessments attempting to measure 21st century skills, then describe the SimScientists program as a case study for using technology-enhanced, dynamic assessments to measure complex science learning representing core 21st century skills. Specifically, we first describe how the evidence-centered design assessment framework has shaped the development of our assessments of 21st century skills. We address four key issues for educators wanting to assess these skills. First, what knowledge and skills do we want to assess? Second, what types of tasks and environments allow students to demonstrate proficiency in these skills? Third, what evidence models are required for making inferences about student progress and proficiency? We conclude with a discussion of the challenges we must address to realize the promises of dynamic assessment in the 21st century.

EVIDENCE-CENTERED DESIGN ASSESSMENT FRAMEWORK

The NRC report *Knowing What Students Know* presented advances in measurement science that integrate cognitive research findings into systematic test design frameworks (Pellegrino, Chudowsky, & Glaser 2001). Evidence-centered assessment design, described in depth in another chapter in this volume, is the process of creating assessments that meaningfully tap into specified targeted knowledge and skills. First, a *student model* specifies the domain knowledge and practices to be assessed. Then, a *task model* specifies the types of tasks or performances that will allow students to demonstrate the extent to which they can apply the competencies in the student model. Finally, the *evidence model* specifies the types of response summaries and scores that will indicate levels of proficiency (Messick, 1994; Mislevy, Steinberg, & Almond, 2003). Cognitively-principled assessment design for science, therefore, would begin with a student model derived from a theoretical framework of the kinds of enduring science knowledge structures and strategies that are expected of students in a domain, provide problems and environments in which students can carry out tasks that demonstrate their proficiency, and make explicit what and how evidence from these tasks is being analyzed to gauge progressing proficiency.

Although the evidence-centered design framework may seem intuitive, in practice many simulation-based learning programs fail to identify the specific knowledge and skills that are targeted, and few assessments allow students the opportunity to demonstrate their understanding of rich interconnected knowledge and their ability to employ complex problem solving skills. Even when the targeted knowledge and skills are made explicit, the majority of assessment instruments remain static, traditional test formats that fail to provide an environment for students to demonstrate their ability to acquire, apply, and transfer knowledge in new settings. Finally, the evidence models (how the task performances are related to proficiency) are typically "point-based" and do not reflect partial, developing understandings or common misconceptions.

What 21st Century Knowledge and Skills Do We Want to Assess?

Schemas

Many of the targeted knowledge and skills specified in 21st century frameworks are not new to educators. Decades of research in cognition, measurement and psychometrics stress the importance of targeting integrated knowledge structures and models in assessments (Pellegrino et al., 2001). Across academic and practical domains, research on the development of expertise indicates that experts have acquired large, organized, interconnected knowledge structures, called schemas, and well-honed, domain-specific problem-solving strategies (Bransford, Brown, & Cocking, 2000). For example, expert writers use different schema when composing persuasive versus narrative texts. Mathematicians use schema to identify types of problems and initiate appropriate solution routines and strategies. Scientists use schema represented in physical, mathematical, and conceptual models as tools for generating and testing hypotheses and to communicate about natural and designed systems (Nersessian, 2008).

Ability to Acquire and Apply Knowledge

21st century skills imply that students not only have knowledge, but also have the skills to acquire, apply and transfer schematic knowledge in new contexts. What are the components of these complex skills? Research on systems thinking and model-based learning suggest that effective learners form, use, evaluate, and revise their mental models of phenomena in a recursive process that results in more complete, accurate, and useful mental models (Gobert & Buckley, 2000). For example, students who participate in cycles of model-based reasoning build deeper conceptual understandings of core scientific principles and systems (Stewart, Cartier, & Passmore, 2005). Students with model-building proficiencies are able to interpret patterns in data and formulate general models to explain phenomena (Lehrer, Schauble, Strom, & Pligge, 2001). A growing body of research shows model-based reasoning to be a signature practice of the sciences, supporting how scientists create insights and understandings of nature through conceptual, physical, and computational modeling (Nersessian, 2008). Further, cognitive research shows that learners who internalize schemas of complex system organization—structure, functions, and emergent behaviors—can transfer this heuristic understanding across systems (e.g., Goldstone, 2006; Goldstone & Wilensky, 2008).

Thus, the framework for model-based learning provides a basis for identifying the domain knowledge and reasoning required for an integrated and extensible understanding of a system. Assessments can then be built around age-appropriate simulation models of the components, interactions, and emergent behaviors characteristic of all complex systems, as well as the particular instances of these in the system being studied (Buckley, in preparation).

What Types of Tasks and Environments Allow Students to Demonstrate Proficiency in 21st Century Skills?

Affordances of Simulation-Based Environments as Learning Platforms

Technologies are seen as tools that support schema formation and mental model construction by automating and augmenting performance on cognitively complex tasks (Norman, 1993). In the domain of science, core knowledge structures are represented in models of the world built by scientists (Hestenes, Wells, & Swackhamer, 1992; Stewart & Golubitsky, 1992). Science simulations provide dynamic representations of spatial, temporal, and causal phenomena in science systems, often not directly observable, that learners can explore and manipulate. In contrast to animations, where students view predetermined scenes and can only control viewing direction and pace, simulations adapt the dynamic displays in response to learner inputs. Key features of simulations include manipulation of structures and patterns that otherwise might not be visible or even conceivable, representations of time, scale, and causality, and the potential for generating and superimposing multiple physical and symbolic representations. Moreover, since simulations can illustrate content in multiple representational forms, simulations can inform students' mental models of concepts and principles and also reduce potentially confounding language demands. Simulations can present the opportunity for students to engage in the kinds of investigations that are familiar components of hands-on curricula as well as to explore problems iteratively and discover solutions that students might not have discovered in other modalities. Importantly, simulations also can make available realistic problem scenarios that are difficult or impossible to create in a typical classroom.

Numerous studies by multimedia researchers, cognitive psychologists, curriculum developers, and commercial companies illustrate the benefits of science simulations for student learning. Simulations can support knowledge integration and the development of deeper understanding of complex topics, such as genetics, environmental science, and physics (Hickey, Kindfield, Horwitz, & Christie, 2003; Horwitz, Gobert, Buckley, & Wilensky, 2007; Krajcik, Marx, Blumenfeld, Soloway, & Fishman, 2000; Doerr, 1996). For example, when Model-It was used in a large number of classrooms, positive learning outcomes based on pretest-posttest data were reported (Krajcik et al., 2000). After participating in the Connected Chemistry project, which used NetLogo to teach the concept of chemical equilibrium, students tended to rely more on conceptual approaches than on algorithmic approaches or rote facts during problem solving (Stieff & Wilensky, 2003). Seventh, eighth, and ninth grade students who completed the ThinkerTools curriculum performed better, on average, than high school students on basic physics problems and were able to apply their conceptual models for force and motion to solve realistic problems (White & Frederiksen, 1998). An implementation study of the use of *BioLogica* by students in eight high schools showed an increase in genetics content knowledge in specific areas, as well as an increase in genetics problem-solving skills (Buckley, Gerlits, Goldberg-Mansfield, & Swiniarski, 2004). Log files of student responses were analyzed to identify systematic (versus haphazard) inquiry performances, which correlated with overall learning gains (Buckley, Gobert, Horwitz, & O'Dwyer, 2010). At the middle school level, a simulation of an aquatic ecosystem was used to allow students to look beyond the surface structures and functions they could see when an aquarium served as a physical model. The simulation allowed students to create connections between the macro-level fish reproduction and the micro-level nutrification processes (Hmelo-Silver et al., 2008). Repenning and colleagues found that students using a collective simulation of multiple human systems significantly improved student learning about system facts, making connections, and applying knowledge about relationships between systems in new situations (Ioannidou et al., 2010). It appears that making the connections between system levels explicit benefits students' understanding; dynamic simulations are a productive way to make those connections salient (Slotta & Chi, 2006).

Simulations and 3D immersive environments have been proposed from a "connectionist" view of mental processing to allow for the development of "projective identities" (Gee, 2008a), which can be utilized in a virtual environment to promote embodiment and reveal student thinking and problem solving abilities (Gee, 2008b). Embodiment through the use of immersive technologies can utilize multiple perspectives to trigger powerful psychological associations and facilitate transfer, resulting in a greater sense of empowerment and higher student engagement (Dede, 2009; Dunleavy, Dede, & Mitchell, 2009). Digital and networking technologies can connect learners with peers and experts, helping to build knowledge and to reveal its progression. Other 21st century skills that can be measured through the use of technology include argumentation (Squire & Jan, 2007), cooperation (Oberholzer-Gee, Waldfogel, & White, 2010), collaboration (Hausmann, van de Sande, & VanLehn, 2008; Lim & Wang, 2005), and innovation (Gee, 2009).

Affordances of Simulation-Based Environments for Assessment

Given that simulations provide dynamic environments for learning in science, they can also support tasks that assess whether students are able to acquire, apply, and transfer knowledge through science investigations. Multimedia research suggests that when degrees of learner control and interactivity are variables, spatial representations allow students to create effective mental models and visualizations (Schwartz & Heiser, 2006). Rieber, Tzeng, and Tribble (2004) found that students who were given graphical feedback while using a simulation (laws of motion) that included short explanations far outperformed those given only textual information.

This interactive capability of simulations to provide contingent feedback and additional instruction in multiple modalities can be tapped in 21st century dynamic assessment task designs. Simulations are one resource for offering technology-enhanced ways to extend the 20th century methods of individually administered dynamic assessment tutorials. For example, Palincar, Brown and Campione (1991) developed a strategy of providing graduated prompts to scaffold completion of tasks. Their work built on Vygotsky's theory of the zone of proximal development between an individual's independent and guided performance (Vygotsky, 1987). Feuerstein and colleagues studied approaches for providing guidance during assessment (Feuerstein, Rand & Hoffman, 1979). Similarly, intelligent tutoring systems are providing graduated scaffolding in highly structured mathematics tasks, although primarily for instructional rather than assessment purposes (Feng & Heffernan, 2010).

In science, simulations can vastly expand feedback and coaching methods by offering and documenting types of graduated levels of graphical and textual feedback and coaching elicited by students' responses during simulation-based investigations. As in prior generations of dynamic assessment, types and levels of feedback and coaching are based on a student's response to assessment tasks carefully placed on a developmental continuum. 21st century dynamic assessments offer alternatives to labor intensive, one-on-one administration by using technology as the mechanism for administering the simulation-based assessments. The simulation program can link student responses to an underlying learning progression in order to offer appropriate levels of feedback and additional instruction designed to help move students along the task sequence. The assessment management infrastructure undergirding simulation-based assessments can be programmed to document the levels and amounts of help each student uses and to factor these into metrics for assessing and reporting learning progress. Moreover, such rich, dynamic, interactive assessment environments can vastly expand current conceptualizations of "adaptive testing." In sum, science simulations, in particular, open significant opportunities for the design of assessments of systems thinking, model-based reasoning, and scientific inquiry as advocated in national science standards, but seldom tapped in static, conventional tests (Quellmalz, DeBarger, Haertel, & Kreikemeier, 2005).

Affordances of Technology for Universal Design and Accommodations

Technology-based assessments can have many of the flexible presentation and response features recommended in Universal Design for Learning (UDL) guidelines by reducing language demands that may interfere with understanding information and directions in assessment tasks and with expressing understanding. Assessments can make use of the flexibility provided by digital technologies to implement recommendations in the Universal Design for Learning framework: (1) representing information in multiple formats and media, (2) providing multiple pathways for students' action and expression, and (3) providing multiple ways to engage students' interest and motivation (CAST, 2008). The visual, dynamic, and interactive features of simulations can make assessment tasks more accessible to a greater range of students (Pellegrino et al., 2001). Computer technology makes it possible to develop assessments reflecting UDL and to embed these assessments in instruction. However, to avoid invalid estimates of student achievement, students should have prior experience using the technology-based assessments.

If these innovative formats are to be used for instruction and assessment, the needs of *all* students must be considered, particularly access for students with disabilities. Accommodations currently provided for print-based assessments have parallels in digital formats. The most commonly requested accommodations are extended time, large print, and read-aloud. Extended time is important for a wide range of students, particularly those facing the additional cognitive demand of using the other accommodations. Large print has its parallel in digital assessments as a zoom feature that enlarges the screen. Text-to-speech (TTS) can replace read-aloud accommodations, useful for students with disabilities for whom print is a barrier to accessing the content of the assessments. TTS also has advantages for those English learners who may understand spoken English, but are not yet very proficient in written English (Kopriva, 2000). Thus, dynamic assessments can increase the opportunities for students to demonstrate proficiency in challenging science content and inquiry investigations for all students.

Affordances of Technology for Assessment Administration

Dynamic assessments allow for more flexibility in terms of when and where an assessment can be administered. Computer-based programs, such as SimScientists, offer on-demand access to assessments on a range of topics through classroom computers or a school's computer lab. Handheld technologies can increase the ability to deliver assessments in a wider range of spaces. Handhelds have been used in formal education to measure student learning in Jigsaw cooperative learning environments (Lai & Wu, 2006), inquiry-based science classrooms (Vonderwell, Sparrow, & Zachariah, 2005), outdoor learning spaces (Liu, Tan, & Chu, 2009), urban city centers (Morrison et al., 2009), class field trips (Weller, Bickar, & McGuinness, 2008), and historic and environmental sites (Klopfer & Squire, 2008). In addition to extending the temporal and geographic flexibility of administering assessments, handheld technologies also facilitate the collection of data and recording of student responses in these non-classroom environments (Patten, Sanchez, & Tangey, 2006).

Though formal education has been the focus of most technology-enhanced assessment development, digital technologies can also be used to measure learning in informal environments. Informal learning takes place in designed spaces (e.g., museums, science centers), natural environments, social settings, and in the home (NRC, 2009; NRC 2010). But how do we really know what people are learning in these environments? As paper and pencil are not appropriate in informal settings, many studies have examined ways that technology-based systems can assess how and what people are learning in informal spaces. Museums are developing electronic guide systems that deliver content and facilitate a museum visit, while also recording visitor responses in order to determine what they are learning (Bruce, 2010). These systems help museums to better understand how people learn from exhibits, help visitors connect to the museum space (Duff et al., 2009), and stimulate complex thinking about exhibit topics (Schmitt, Bach, Dubois, & Duranthon, 2010). Digital tools also enable education researchers to measure what people know about important topics that are not yet a part of established formal education curricula, such as nanotechnology (Crone, 2008) and climate change (Schultz & Shugart, 2007). In combination, the affordances of technology vastly expand what can be assessed and how, when, and where testing can occur.

What Evidence Models Are Appropriate for Assessing 21st Century Skills?

Increased Types of Evidence

Evidence models for the types of 21st century dynamic assessments envisioned in this chapter will be complex. There are several reasons for this. First, the number and range of constructs to be measured during assessment will increase. Future assessments will simultaneously be measuring a diverse set of variables such as the actions that students take in accomplishing the task at hand, numbers and types of coaching, responses to previous tasks, estimates of the difficulty of the tasks being undertaken, time taken to respond, and could even include biometric data such as emotional state (via video capture of expressions), galvanic skin response (via a wrist band) or posture (via a pressure pad on the chair) (Arroyo et al., 2009; D'Mello, Craig, & Graesser, 2009a, 2009b).

The actions and inputs that students make in response to complex tasks and items in the dynamic assessment process are gathered as raw data linked to different elements of each task. Raw data must be processed before being scored in the next stage of the assessment cycle. The response processing step identifies the essential features of the response that provide evidence about the student's current knowledge, skills, and capabilities for identified content and inquiry targets.

For example, the Framework and Specifications for the 2014 NAEP Technology and Engineering Literacy assessments propose that when students are engaged in a design task, a student's interaction with the tasks and tools in the scenarios will generate raw data. When processed, the student's choice of tools to accomplish a design task, how the tools were used, and the design outcome all become quantifiable evidence of student proficiency. Other evidence will come from the selected-response or constructed-response questions that students answer during scenarios that include multiple, scenario-based tasks or in sets of shorter discrete items.

Evidence models for 21st century skills will need to accommodate not only a greater number of variables, but also the diverse nature of these variables. In traditional assessments, the data are processed into ordered categories such as correct/incorrect for selected responses or a score of 0, 1, 2, or 3 for constructed responses. Measures have followed a pattern in which a higher ranking generally means that the student is doing better. But in dynamic assessments the measures are not necessarily ordered or linear. For some data in the evidence model, meeting a greater number of criteria might indicate higher achievement. However, greater values in the raw data will not always translate into higher scores. For example, a task may require students to test a system and make changes. Less knowledgeable students may test the system only once, failing to identify the optimal settings for the system. Slightly higher achieving students may use trial and error, testing the system many times in a non-systematic way. The highest achieving students may use a more strategic and therefore more efficient method. These students' responses would indicate higher achievement than students who had both fewer and greater numbers of tests. Thus, there need to be criteria for processing the response data in order to convert them to a form that is interpretable as part of the summary scoring.

The use of dynamic assessments for formative purposes presents another challenge for the evidence model. Formative assessments provide immediate feedback to students as they take the assessment, rather than waiting until a complete set of responses and actions are recorded. At the point that feedback needs to be given, we may have a very incomplete set of evidence on the current state of the student's knowledge and skills, and so traditional assessment methods that need evidence from many items to make reliable judgments have limited use. Methods for generating real-time feedback during dynamic assessments must rely on estimates of the state of student knowledge. In assessments meant to be used formatively, to intervene and adjust instruction, feedback can be accompanied by hints and coaching to provide additional instruction. The levels and amounts of coaching can become variables in analyzing developing proficiencies. This requires probability-based methods, which are discussed in the next section.

The desire to give immediate feedback to students will also push us to develop methods for interpreting written constructed responses, since we know from human-scoring of written responses that they provide deep insights into student thinking. Methods of Natural Language Processing are emerging that will enable the sort of interpretation and categorization needed to provide feedback to students in real time. There will be a growth of systems that can do this. Such technologies generally require that the system be "trained" by scoring hundreds of student responses with previously assigned scores (obtained by human scoring). Periodic checks by human scorers of subsequent computer scoring should also be instituted.

New Psychometrics Required for 21st Century Dynamic Assessments

Just as the diverse data types collected during dynamic assessments necessitate more complex evidence models, they also demand more sophisticated psychometric analysis methods. Historically, the field of educational psychometrics has grown up around the types of responses that are typical in paper-based, large-scale assessments: primarily multiple-choice and written response items. Over the years, the methods of analyzing these types of student responses have become increasingly sophisticated, progressing from Classical Test Theory to Item Response Modeling methods that can model different dimensions of students' responses and even dynamically adapt the assessment to the ability of the student during the assessment.

However, the complex tasks envisioned for 21st century dynamic assessments cannot easily be modeled using just Classical Test Theory (CTT) and Item Response Theory (IRT). The complex tasks in dynamic assessments lead to diverse sequences of actions that produce multiple measures, often gathered simultaneously, and may involve interpreting patterns of behavior across multiple tasks. The multidimensional nature of assessment in simulations makes CTT unsuitable as a measurement method because it cannot model different dimensions of a performance simultaneously. When the assessments also need to be made in real time as the student is still engaged in the task, as is the case for classroom-based formative assessments, the interpretations are often calculated based on very limited amounts of data. The types of measurement methods that better lend themselves to simulations are probability-based methods (like IRT and Bayes Nets) that can handle uncertainty about the current state of the learner, can provide immediate feedback during tasks (e.g., Model Tracing or rule-based methods like decision trees), and are able to model patterns of student behavior (e.g., Artificial Neural Networks and Bayes Nets). These methods are briefly described below.

Item response models have the advantage that they place estimates of student ability and item difficulty on the same linear scale, measured in logits (a logarithm of the odds scale). This means that the difference between a student's ability estimate and the item difficulty can be used to interpret student performance. Since both the estimates of student abilities and the estimates of item difficulty are expressed in logits, they can be meaningfully compared. IRT could be a useful methodology to use in determining how much help students need in solving problems in an intelligent learning environment by measuring the gap between item difficulty and current learner ability (Timms, 2007).

Bayes nets have been widely used in intelligent tutoring systems, and over the years their use in systems for assessment has grown. For examples, see Martin and VanLehn (1995); Mislevy and Gitomer (1996); Conati, Gernter, and VanLehn (2002); Behrens, Frezzo, Mislevy, Kroopnick, and Wise (2008) and the example given later in this chapter.

Artificial neural networks (ANNs) have been widely used in intelligent systems, especially those in which the system needs to learn from data. An ANN is an adaptive, most often nonlinear system that learns to perform a function (an input/output map) from data. In science education, the work of Stevens in a series of projects in IMMEX (Interactive MultiMedia Exercises) provides an example of the use of ANNs. A recent article (Cooper & Stevens, 2008) describes the use of ANNs to assess student metacognition in problem-solving in chemistry.

Model tracing was developed for cognitive tutors produced by the Pittsburgh Advanced Cognitive Tutors (PACT) center at Carnegie Mellon University. Model tracing works by comparing the student's solution of a problem to an expert system for the domain of interest. Production rules, or rules about knowledge and skills in a given domain are, in this system, based on the work of cognitive scientist John Anderson. His ACT-R model represents skill-based knowledge (Anderson, 1993; Anderson & Lebiere, 1998).

Rule-based methods employ some logic method to decide how to interpret a student action in order to provide immediate feedback during formative assessments. A simple example would be posing a multiple-choice question in which the distractors (wrong answer choices) were derived from known misconceptions in the content being assessed. The student's incorrect response could then be diagnosed and immediate action, such as coaching, can be taken. This type of diagnosis is the basis of the work of Minstrell and Kraus in their work with the DIAGNOSER software that assesses students' knowledge in science and diagnoses their understandings and misconceptions (Minstrell & Kraus, 2007).

The increased use of dynamic assessments will need to be accompanied by psychometric methods suited to the complex nature of thinking and reasoning to be measured and the complex types of tasks in which 21st century skill must be applied. The designs and analyses of 21st century skill progressions will require collaboration of cognitive scientists, domain experts, and measurement experts.

HOW CAN DYNAMIC ASSESSMENTS OF 21ST CENTURY SKILLS BE INTEGRATED INTO BALANCED, MULTILEVEL ASSESSMENT SYSTEMS?

A critical issue arising from a focus on assessment of 21st century skills is the integration of dynamic assessments into assessment systems operating in states and districts to determine student proficiencies. The National Research Council (NRC) has developed a Framework for Science Education. States have set rigorous standards for what students should know and be able to do. Yet, many states are still using traditional student outcome measures that are not tightly aligned with reform goals and do not document progress on challenging standards. State-level, large-scale tests typically favor breadth of content coverage over depth of reasoning. To address the need for stronger science testing methods, NSF funded the NRC project "Test Design for K–12 Science Assessment" to offer recommendations to states on their science assessment systems. In a report commissioned by that NRC project, Quellmalz and Moody (2004) proposed strategies for states to form collaboratives and use technology to create multilevel science assessment systems. They described how collaboratives can leverage resources, provide technology supports, and use assessment results at different levels of the system. Methodologies recommended in this report are applicable to non-science topics as well.

It is widely recognized that states must aim for balanced state assessment systems in which district, classroom and state tests are nested, mutually informative, and aligned (Pellegrino et al., 2001). Such assessment systems, like successful standards-based education, must be developmentally, horizontally, and vertically coherent (Wilson & Bertenthal, 2006). The *developmental coherence* of a system builds upon knowledge about how student understanding develops and the knowledge, abilities, and understandings that are needed for learning to proceed. The *horizontal coherence* of curriculum, instruction, and assessment arises from aligned learning goals and are mutually reinforcing. The *vertical coherence* of assessments at the classroom, school, district, and state can be forged with common goals for education as well as common purposes and methods of assessment.

The ideal model is based on alignment of assessments at each level with national and state standards based on a common set of design specifications for assessment tasks and items to be used at the various system levels (Quellmalz & Moody, 2004). Each level would employ assessment items and tasks that are common or parallel to those used at the other levels. Therefore, classroom assessments will use types of tasks and items parallel to those employed in district and state testing. In general, to serve formative, diagnostic purposes, classroom assessments would incorporate more items and complex assessment tasks than assessments developed for district and state summative, accountability purposes. The construction of assessments would vary for each level of the educational system, as would expectations for interpretation and use of the assessment results. However, the results would complement one another. While classroom assessments might provide immediate feedback to students and teachers about progress on a particular learning goal, statewide assessment would address proficiency on the learning goal, in the context of the larger set of related standards for all students.

Although less ideal, a more practical model may be needed where components of a system already exist such as those in multi-state collaboratives that already have unique state assessments and distinct design specifications. The newly funded Race to the Top assessment consortia have been funded to develop a range of assessment methods to test common core standards in English language arts and mathematics. In a balanced assessment model, vertical coherence is achieved through the use of reports that show the relationships among reporting categories at each level of the assessment system. Starting from a common set of standards, assessments at each level expand on the detail of inferences drawn at the level above. For example, at the state level, reports might describe achievement at the domain or sub-domain (strand) level. Within each strand, mastery of major topics might be reported at the district and school level. At the classroom level, progress toward mastery of these topics, along with immediate feedback to teachers and students, would still be possible.

Figure 3.1 shows how a report from multilevel assessments of science standards would connect related parts of the assessment system in either model.

Figure 3.1 Report from a multilevel assessment system for science.

WHAT EXAMPLES EXIST OF ASSESSMENTS
OF 21ST CENTURY SKILLS?

Assessments of 21st century skills require new open-ended, collaborative options for accessing, organizing, transforming, and communicating information. Programs, both small and large-scale, are beginning to explore the possibilities of dynamic, interactive tasks for obtaining evidence of learning achievement levels. Although the current accountability stakes and constraints tend to restrict a program's options, innovative designs are appearing in contemporary assessments. This new generation of assessments is moving beyond the use of technology for delivery and scoring of conventional item formats to harness technology that enables assessment of those aspects of cognition and performance that are complex and dynamic, and difficult or impossible to assess directly. Such work involves reconceptualizing assessment design and use, focusing in particular on relating, if not integrating, assessments more directly with learning environments. Some summative assessments are beginning to use interactive, scenario-based item sets, while curriculum-embedded assessments designed for formative purposes are beginning to use the affordances of technology to provide immediate, individualized feedback and graduated coaching during the assessment. The new generation of both summative and formative assessments will greatly expand the knowledge and processes targeted and the ways by which they are tested.

Summative Assessments

The majority of large-scale assessments are traditional paper and pencil tests, limited to multiple-choice format and open-ended items that require a written response. However, many knowledge domains and sub-domains are difficult to assess with traditional approaches. The potential for innovative assessment approaches is just now being considered. In English language arts assessments, for example, interactive, scenario-based tasks can address reading, writing, and discourse goals set within authentic problems. The 2011 NAEP for writing will employ computer-based prompts and word processing tools for students to compose a range of types of writing. Innovative dynamic assessments for English language arts could also offer students additional "tools of the trade" such as web search, highlighting, notepads, tables, and presentation tools to access, read, assemble, organize, transform, and represent information from multimedia resources composed of text, graphic, images, and video. Student responses could go beyond conventional item formats to include innovative computer-enabled formats that employ hot spots, highlighting, cut and paste capabilities, table entry, written text, and presentation software.

For math performance assessments, interactive dynamic tasks could present multimedia images, graphics, and symbols along with technology-based mathematics "tools of the trade" to search and find data and information, analyze data, interpret or create visualizations, and use simulations to run iterative solutions, transform representations (tables, graphs), select and present best evidence, and present, explain, and display processes and solutions (Quellmalz, 2009).

Science assessment methods are leading the way, since knowledge of causal, temporal, and dynamic relationships among components within physical, life, and Earth systems, as well as inquiry processes, such as conducting investigations and communicating results, are difficult to test with traditional item formats (Quellmalz & Haertel, 2004). Some states have tested inquiry skills with hands-on performance assessments, but there are many logistical and economic challenges related to equipment, implementation, and scoring of such assessments both in classrooms and on the large scale required for state testing (Sausner, 2004). In their efforts to improve the validity and authenticity of assessments, many large-scale assessment programs are considering innovative formats made feasible by recent developments in computer-based testing. Both the Program for International Student Assessment (PISA) and the National Assessment of Educational Progress (NAEP) include interactive, computer-based components. For NAEP, interactive components are part of assessments for science, writing, technology and engineering literacy. In Minnesota's state science tests, computer-based science assessments with innovative formats have been operational since 2008. In Utah, tryouts of Computer Innovative Items (CII) began in 2010. Along with increased opportunities to use technology in instruction and assessment, recent research and development of simulation-based assessments in science are providing evidence that simulations provide rich, real-world environments and test science knowledge and skills that tap the sorts of deep understanding that are difficult to test in paper format, or that are challenging to provide as hands-on tasks (Quellmalz, Timms, & Buckley, 2010).

Formative Assessments

The benefits of formative assessment in the classroom are well established (Black & Wiliam, 1998, 2009; Nicol & Macfarlane-Dick, 2006); how technologies can support the necessary features of formative assessment is an ever-evolving area of research. From intelligent tutors to simulation-based curricula to video games and virtual worlds, information technologies are well suited to supporting many of the data collection, complex analysis, and individualized feedback and scaffolding features needed for the formative use of assessments. Considerable work has gone into the development of education technology for the assessment *of* learning, or summative assessment, as described previously. Assessment *for* learning has a different set of requirements, necessitating a slightly different approach to the development of technology-based assessment tools (Stiggins, 2006). Formative assessments should include an emphasis on authenticity and complexity in the content and methods of assessment rather than reproduction of knowledge and reductive measurement, as is typical of traditional classroom testing. Additionally, dynamic assessments are designed to serve formative purposes by facilitating meaningful feedback to students on "how they are doing," providing additional scaffolding and instruction to bolster partial understandings, developing students' abilities to direct their own learning and evaluate their own progress, and supporting the learning of others (McDowell et al., 2006). As a result, effective formative assessment can promote collaborative learning, dialogue and discourse, and the social construction of knowledge within a discipline (Sambell, 2010).

Technology-based assessments can provide extensive opportunities to engage in the kinds of tasks that develop and demonstrate student learning, building confidence and capabilities before students are summatively assessed. Using immediate, individualized feedback and customized follow-on instruction, dynamic assessments can provide coaching and hints when an error is detected (Quellmalz & Silberglitt, 2010). When this feedback is graduated, students have multiple opportunities to confront their misconceptions with increasingly specific levels of coaching. The continuous use of this feedback has been found to help students revise their mental models of a given science system (Quellmalz & Silberglitt, 2010). In addition to improving student mental models, technology-enhanced assessments for formative uses has also been shown to motivate and focus student learning, promote dialogical discourse, and develop metacognitive skills (Beatty & Gerace, 2009). Feedback can also come in the form of reports at the end of assessments. Reports that provide the kinds of descriptive feedback that help students connect their success in the assessment to their efforts are more productive than reports in the form of grades; the latter can undermine learning and student motivation (Covington, 1999; Maehr & Midgley, 1996).

The capacity to track student learning progress is particularly valuable for monitoring students with Individualized Education Plans. Computer technology also makes it possible to embed assessments reflecting Universal Design for Learning (UDL) in learning and assessment activities, and has been found to level the playing field for English language learners and students with disabilities (Wang, 2005; Case, Brooks, Wang, & Young, 2005;

Twing & Dolan, 2008). In the SimScientists assessments, this goes beyond the usual focus on text to include graphical representations, simulation controls, and an investigation of what happens when enlarging text or graphics results in loss of contiguity. Tools already built into students' computers can allow multiple representations and multiple media (Twing & Dolan, 2008; Case, 2008). Through the National Instructional Materials Accessibility Standard (NIMAS) and digital formats such as the Digital Accessible Information System (Daisy Consortium, 2006) automated transformation of text into alternate formats can be achieved (Twing & Dolan, 2008).

Below we describe how the SimScientists program uses simulations to push the frontiers of formative and summative assessment of science systems.

A Case in Point: The SimScientists Program

Funded by NSF, IES, and OESE, projects in WestEd's SimScientists program (www.simscientists.org) conduct research and development on the benefits of simulations for promoting and assessing complex science learning by developing powerful exemplars of formative and benchmark assessments of "new science literacies." The exemplars assess systems thinking, model-based reasoning, inquiry practices, and students' abilities to use the multimedia tools of science (Quellmalz, Timms, & Buckley, 2009; Quellmalz & Haertel, 2008). The SimScientists projects build on a theoretical framework that integrates model-based learning and evidence-centered design principles.

Models of Science Systems and Model-based Reasoning

Model-based learning (Gobert & Buckley, 2000; Buckley, in press) involves the formation, use, evaluation and revision of one's mental models of phenomena through a recursive process that results in more complete, accurate and useful mental models. Ideally, mental models build structures and relationships that represent science systems—the system structures (spatial arrangement of components), the interactions of those components, and the behaviors or properties that emerge from those interactions. Simulation-based assessments provide opportunities for students to demonstrate not only their understanding of a system, but also their ability to reason about the system as they predict, investigate, evaluate and explain the functioning of the system.

Thus, the framework for model-based learning provides a basis for identifying the domain knowledge and reasoning required for an integrated and extensible understanding of a scientific system. Instruction, investigations, and assessments can be built around simulations that represent the components, interactions, and emergent behaviors characteristic of all complex systems, as well as the particular instances of these in the science system being studied.

SimScientists' assessment suites are composed of two or three curriculum-embedded assessments that the teacher inserts into a classroom instructional sequence at key points for formative purposes and a summative benchmark assessment at the end of the unit. The dynamic embedded assessments provide immediate feedback and graduated coaching as students interact with the simulations, reports on progress to students and teachers, and off-line classroom collaborative reflection activities to help the teacher adjust instruction based on results of the formative simulation-based assessment. The summative benchmark assessment presents tasks and items parallel to those in the embedded assessments, but without feedback and coaching, to gauge student proficiency at the end of the unit. Students may work on the embedded assessments in pairs, but must take the benchmark assessment individually. Teachers are supported through face-to-face professional development, along with print and web-based guidelines, a procedures manual, help files, and the SimScientists HelpDesk. Assessments are delivered and data collected by the SimScientists' Assessment Management System (AMS).

SimScientists Student Model: Specification of System Models and Targets

SimScientists simulation-based assessments are being designed to address national middle school science standards related to science systems in life, physical and earth science. Simulation environments include ecosystems, biodiversity, human body systems, atoms and molecules, force and motion, climate, and plate tectonics. The assessments are aligned with national science frameworks and will be aligned with the new NRC national science frameworks and standards.

Using evidence-centered design methods, the design of each assessment suite begins with analyses of the domain, standards, and curricula. From these analyses, we define the three levels (components, interactions, emergent behaviors) that we will use to model the science system based on the grade-level-appropriate science standards. Figure 3.2 presents the system model specified for the middle school assessment of ecosystems.

The model levels in Figure 3.2 are represented in terms of food for energy and building blocks for growth and maintenance, organisms and their roles in dyad interactions (producers/consumers, predator/prey), as well as in the food web (diagrams that represent the flow of matter and energy through ecosystems). The population changes that emerge from interactions among organisms and with abiotic factors in the environment are represented in models that include both the organism view and graphs of populations. The last column in Figure 3.2 lists inquiry targets or science

Model Levels: Generic		Content Targets	Inquiry Targets
Components and Roles	What are the components and behaviors of the system (at this level)? What are the "rules" of the system in general?	Every ecosystem has a similar pattern of organization with respect to the roles (producers, consumers, and decomposers) that organisms play in the movement of energy and matter through the system.	Use principles to identify role of organisms.
Interactions	How do the interactions influence the individual components?	Matter and energy flow through the ecosystem as individual organisms interact with each other. Food web diagrams indicate the feeding relationships among organisms in an ecosystem.	Observe interactions among organisms.
Emergent Behaviors	What is the overall state of the system that result from many interactions following specific rules?	Interactions between organisms and between organisms and the ecosystem's nonliving features cause the populations of the different organisms to change over time.	predict observe explain investigate

Figure 3.2 SimScientists system model and content and inquiry targets—middle school ecosystems.

practices assessed at each level. The model levels described above—components, interactions, and emergent behavior—are ubiquitous in all systems.

SimScientists Task Models: Embedded and Benchmark Assessments

The cognitive demands of the student model are determined by the complexity of the assessment tasks and items. SimScientists task difficulties are affected by how phenomena are represented and the types of thinking and reasoning students must use. In SimScientists assessments, we base designs on progressively more complex models of science systems. We reframe inquiry standards in terms of the science practices and model-based reasoning needed for students to demonstrate and extend their understanding while conducting investigations at each level of a system. A progression of tasks both develops and elicits students' understanding of the target models and inquiry skills. The tasks are designed to focus on inquiry and reasoning that resemble those of scientists as they create, observe, evaluate, and revise their models of phenomena. For example, we ask students to make observations to identify components and interactions, make predictions, design experiments, interpret data, evaluate their predictions, and explain the results and their reasoning. These are all key science practices. Cognition and multimedia learning research guide the design of student interactions with the simulations.

Curriculum-embedded formative assessment task models and evidence model. The dynamic assessment tasks designed to be used formatively must be sufficiently structured to enable targeted feedback and graduated coaching. Tasks that are too open make it difficult to provide useful feedback. Each task is usually part of a series of steps necessary to complete a more complex task. As students complete each step, they receive one of four levels of feedback and coaching. If correct, students receive confirmation and a restatement of the explanation. The first incorrect response triggers feedback to try again. The second incorrect response triggers feedback that restates the task and presents the rule or concept students need to apply to complete the task correctly. Feedback may also address common misconceptions. A third incorrect response triggers the correct explanation or action, and a worked example with detailed instructions for how to complete the task before students can move on. The examples shown in Figures 3.3 and 3.4 illustrate feedback and coaching provided in the dynamic embedded assessments for ecosystems.

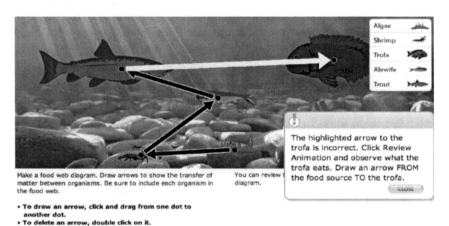

Figure 3.3 Screen shot of draw food web task with coaching.

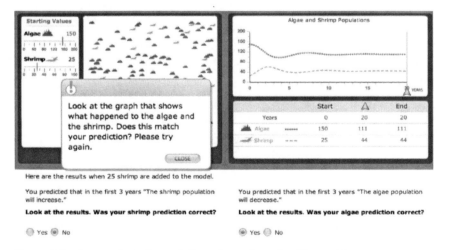

Figure 3.4 Screen shot of populations dynamics task with coaching.

In the task in Figure 3.3, students are asked to draw a food web showing the transfer of matter between organisms based on prior observations made of feeding behaviors in the novel ecosystem. When a student draws an incorrect arrow, a feedback box also coaches the student to observe the animation of feeding behaviors again and explains that the arrow should be drawn from the food source to each consumer.

Figure 3.4 shows feedback for a student asked to evaluate a prediction about emergent behaviors at the population level as depicted in the population graph. In this case, the student incorrectly evaluated his/her prediction and is coached to revisit whether the prediction and the data match and to try again.

When students have completed a dynamic embedded assessment, they receive a report on their progress (Figure 3.5). For both content and inquiry targets it describes the target knowledge or skill and the student's performance in terms of *on track, progressing,* or *needs help.* This is calculated based on the amount of help a student needed to complete the tasks related to that target.

After a class has completed a dynamic embedded assessment, the teacher accesses the Assessment Management System (AMS) to review student performances. The AMS provides a progress report for the whole class that summarizes this information and provides suggestions for grouping students into teams and groups based on their performances (Figure 3.6). Teachers are also encouraged to use their understanding of class dynamics to assign students to the suggested teams and groups.

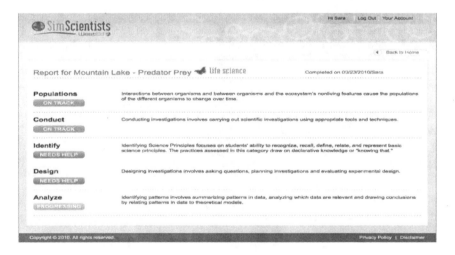

Figure 3.5 Student progress report for embedded assessment.

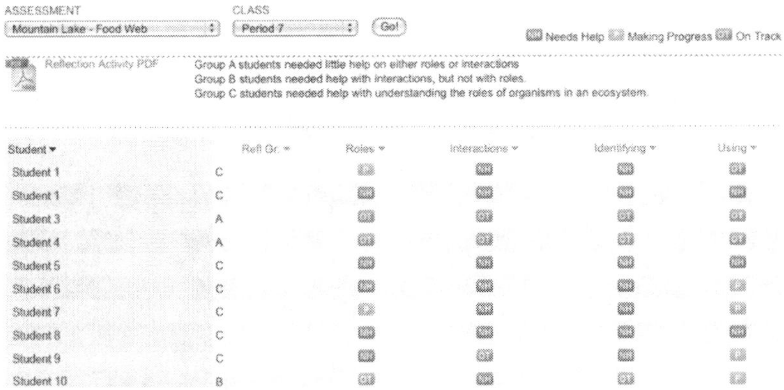

Figure 3.6 Class progress report for embedded assessment.

Embedded assessment reflection activities. An important component of the dynamic embedded assessment is an offline reflection activity designed to provide differentiated tasks and to engage students in scientific discourse as they apply their science content knowledge and inquiry skills to new, more complex ecosystems. Students are assigned to teams who are given tasks that address the content and inquiry targets with which they needed the most help. For example, one team might examine pictures of organisms eating behaviors to identify their roles as consumers. Another team might be responsible for identifying the producers. A third team might be responsible for drawing the arrows depicting the flow of energy and matter in the system. Small group work then feeds into a larger group task that requires a presentation to the class describing the roles of organisms in each ecosystem and the flow of matter and energy. Student peer assessment is promoted as the students as well as teachers evaluate the presentations using criteria for judging the evidence-base and clarity.

Summative, unit benchmark assessment task models and evidence model. Tasks and items parallel to those in the embedded assessment are administered in the benchmark assessment. Benchmark tasks often combine component tasks of the embedded assessments into integrated tasks. Importantly, benchmark assessments require transfer of understanding of the model to a novel ecosystem (Figure 3.7) and do not provide feedback and coaching.

The SimScientists benchmark assessments employ a Bayes net to determine the proficiency levels of students on each of the content and inquiry targets. A Bayes net is a probabilistic graphical model that represents a set of random variables and their conditional independencies via a directed acyclic graph. In a Bayes net, nodes represent random variables and the edges (links between the nodes) encode the conditional dependencies be-

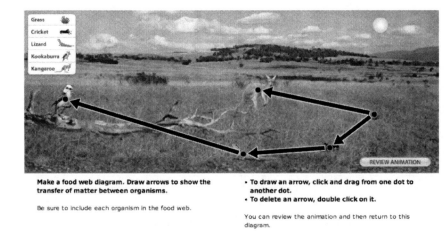

Make a food web diagram. Draw arrows to show the transfer of matter between organisms.

Be sure to include each organism in the food web.

• **To draw an arrow, click and drag from one dot to another dot.**
• **To delete an arrow, double click on it.**

You can review the animation and then return to this diagram.

Figure 3.7 Draw food web task in Benchmark assessment.

tween the variables. Across a series of nodes and edges a joint probability distribution can be specified over a set of discrete random variables. Figure 3.8 shows an example of a fragment of a Bayes Net used in the scoring of the ecosystems benchmark assessments in SimScientists. It shows how nodes in the network representing data gathered from student actions in the assessment (the lower two rows) provide information to assess the top-level variables of content knowledge and science inquiry skills represented in the upper two rows. Values for the edges are encoded, but not visible in this view.

Observable variables, that is responses that students gave and actions that they took in the simulation-based activities, are coded to the appropriate science content or science inquiry targets that they represent evidence of

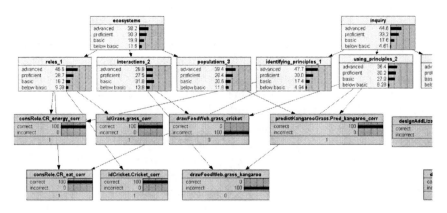

Figure 3.8 Fragment of a Bayes Net From the SimScientists Ecosystems Benchmark Assessment.

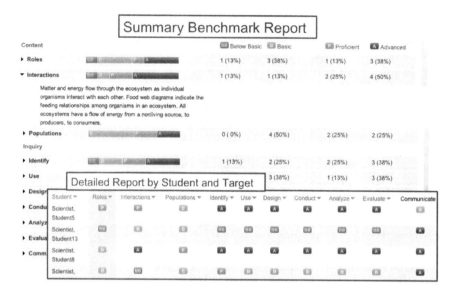

Figure 3.9 Benchmark reports for whole class and individual students.

in the student's performance. Using a scoring rubric provided in the assessment management system (AMS), teachers score students' written responses. These scores are added to the record of observable variables for each student's assessment file. When all observable variables for an assessment are gathered, the teacher uses the learning management system to initiate scoring, a process that sends the observable variables data to the Bayes net. The data updates the probability estimates for each student in each of the content and inquiry targets and the report to the student shows the category (advanced, proficient, basic or below basic) that has the highest probability of being applicable for that student on each content and inquiry target. Results of the summative unit benchmark assessments are reported by the AMS in four proficiency levels for the content and inquiry targets.

Data on SimScientists Assessment Quality, Utility, and Feasibility

SimScientists projects have documented the effectiveness, utility, feasibility, and technical quality of simulation-based science assessments designed for curriculum-embedded formative assessment purposes and for summative accountability purposes. Calipers I, a demonstration project funded by NSF, documented evidence of the technical quality (validity and reliability), feasibility, and utility of simulation-based summative benchmark assessments for two middle school science topics (Quellmalz, Timms, & Buckley, 2010). Alignments of the assessments with national science standards, as well as the accuracy of scientific content were confirmed by independent experts, including AAAS, and teacher reviews of the assessments. Teachers and students completed cognitive labs, thinking aloud as they responded to the simulation-based assessment tasks. The results provided construct validity evidence that the items elicited the intended science knowledge and skills. In-depth analysis of data from Calipers I demonstrated that simulation-based assessments can be developed to meet traditional psychometric measures for technical quality. An Item Response Theory (IRT) analysis of the response data from 109 students on the force and motion assessments and 81 students on the Ecosystems assessments showed that items functioned well overall. The mean reliability was .71 (Cronbach's Alpha), which for assessments that contain a mix of auto-scored, selected-response and human-scored constructed-response items, is within accepted usual ranges of reliability. The difficulty of the selected-response items ranged from .22 to .88, with a mean of .65, and the weighted mean square values of the items showed that all the items fit well to the science constructs being measured. In addition, by comparing the fit of one-dimensional and two-dimensional IRT models and testing if the difference was statistically significant using a Chi Square test with two degrees of freedom, it was shown that the assessment items in Calipers could be effectively used to measure two different dimensions of science learning (content knowledge and inquiry skills), and that this approach yielded a more accurate measure of student ability than treating the science content knowledge as a single dimension. Evidence of the discriminant validity was based on the overall pattern of student performance that followed the expected progression of scores for high achievers, medium achievers, and lower achievers. Follow-up teacher interviews provided strong and enthusiastic support for the utility and feasibility of the simulation-based assessments.

Similar research to that conducted in Calipers I is currently underway in the NSF-funded Calipers II project on the benefits of simulation-based *formative* assessments that are embedded in curriculum units. The technical quality of linked unit benchmark assessments is also being documented. Data collection on the feasibility, utility, reliability, and validity of the formative and summative assessment modules continues in Calipers II. To date, data have been collected for two science topics, including expert reviews by AAAS of scientific accuracy, alignments of the assessments with national science standards and representative curricula, cognitive laboratories with teachers and students, classroom pilot testing, classroom observations, and teacher surveys and interviews. Data from 28 think-aloud sessions have provided preliminary evidence of the construct validity of the assessment tasks for eliciting the intended knowledge and skills. Classroom observations detected some initial technical deployment challenges that were overcome. Observations also showed high student engagement. The embedded assessments took students about 15–30 minutes and the benchmark assessments took about 20–40 minutes to complete.

In a third project, *Integrating Simulation-Based Science Assessments into Balanced State Science Assessment Systems, an Enhanced Assessment Grant (EAG),* funded by the Office of Elementary and Secondary Education, six states are involved in a study in which we developed three types of computer-based accommodations (visual enlargement, text-to-speech and extended time) which were added to the Calipers II simulation-based formative and benchmark assessments for two topics: ecosystems and force and motion. We have pilot tested them in approximately 60 middle school classrooms with 6,000 students to determine if these richer, deeper forms of science assessment benefit student learning, profile student proficiencies in more depth, and can augment evidence of achievement of standards in a state science assessment system (Quellmalz & Moody, 2004). The resulting data set will allow item response model analyses of the performance of the assessment tasks and items to further establish the technical quality of the simulation-based assessments and examine how well they measure performances of students with disabilities and of EL students who use the accommodations. As of May 1, 2010, the assessments for ecosystems and force and motion have been implemented in three states by 55 teachers with 5,867 students in 39 schools in 28 districts. Two hundred eighteen students (5%) have used the accommodations (mostly the text-to-speech and extended time). Responses from the teachers to online teacher surveys indicated that, overall, teachers were able to use the assessments successfully in their instruction and that, with occasional assistance from the SimScientists help desk, were able to overcome technology challenges and complete the assessments. Teachers rated the quality and utility of the assessments highly. In addition, UCLA CRESST, the external evaluator, conducted nine case studies to evaluate use of the assessments in more depth. Data will be analyzed during the summer of 2010. Six states (NV, UT, NC, CT, MA, and VT) are participating on the project Design Panel to examine the potential of including the summative simulation-based unit benchmark science assessments in a state science assessment system. Utah is currently pilot testing short science simulation tasks for the online state science test. Data from this EAG project is providing strong evidence that the simulation-based embedded and benchmark assessments can be used on a large scale with diverse student populations and in school systems with varying technical infrastructures.

WHAT ARE THE CHALLENGES AND PROMISE
FOR THE FUTURE?

Challenges

Dynamic assessments of 21st century skills are on the increase, but still relatively rare. One problem is definitional. Frameworks for 21st century skills range across disciplinary, workplace, and societal domains. Debates continue about the relative value, practicality, and benefits of assessing generic skills versus domain-specific knowledge structures and strategies, individuals versus groups, technology tool operations, and methods for appraising less tractable constructs such as innovation, creativity, citizenship, and responsibility. Moreover, new and updated frameworks and standards present moving targets for assessment design. In this chapter, we have focused on 21st century cognitive constructs such as problem solving, communication, and collaboration as they apply in academic disciplines, particularly in model-based learning and reasoning in science.

Although rhetoric often calls for challenging, authentic complex tasks within which learners apply 21st century skills, the range of contexts and tasks in current assessment practice is quite limited. The high stakes typically associated with summative purposes tend to suppress innovation in favor of brief, highly structured assessment tasks targeting simple concepts and skills and collecting standard selected and constructed responses. Concomitantly, assessments intended for formative classroom uses tend to mirror the limited constructs and task designs in summative assessments. Too often, engaging, rich technology-based learning environments do not explicitly articulate learning goals, present dynamic embedded assessments to promote learning, or use the affordances of the technologies to gather evidence of attainment of those goals. Consequently, there are relatively few exemplars, some described in this volume, of rich, dynamic tasks designed to assess significant, specified 21st century skills.

At the same time, dynamic assessments produce extensive log files of learner responses. The assessment framework of evidence-centered design calls for specification at the outset of the data that will provide evidence of achievement of targeted knowledge and skills. However, many technology-based learning and assessment environments defer principled extraction of evidence of learning in favor of exploratory post hoc mining of log files. In this chapter, we assert that dynamic assessments must develop new evidence models and psychometric methods to extract data from complex assessment tasks that can be combined in various ways to characterize and monitor the progressive development of 21st century proficiencies.

Implementations of these novel dynamic assessments pose a number of challenges. Teachers and students are likely to require training and experience to take advantage of the new dynamic assessments. Students need to become familiar with the novel formats and their operations. Teachers need professional development on identifying appropriate places to use the assessments formatively within instruction, and on methods for implementing and interpreting them. Policymakers and the public need information on the purposes, features, and benefits of dynamic assessments.

A final challenge to scalability and sustainability of dynamic assessments is the cost of initial development, ongoing maintenance, updates, and changes in technology requirements and platforms. Considerable development costs of dynamic assessments may be defrayed by designs that allow the assessments to test standards addressed in multiple curricula and reusability of designs and components. Research must provide evidence that the benefits of dynamic assessments warrant the costs.

Promise

Dynamic assessments of 21st century skills promise to revolutionize the types of learning that can be assessed and the ways in which learning can be measured, promoted, and interpreted. Broad 21st century cognitive capabilities such as problem solving, inquiry, communication, collaboration, and tool use can be tested within rich, authentic, complex contexts and tasks. Learners can employ significant, extended strategic thinking and reasoning, using a range of technology "tools of the trade." Rich assessment tasks can present highly engaging 2D simulations and 3D virtual worlds in which collaboration and discourse play key roles in developing solutions and achieving goals. Assessment tasks can present scenarios that will both test and promote, through feedback and graduated coaching, the development of schema and mental models that learners can transfer across prototypical problems in academic and applied domains. Systems thinking and model-based reasoning can become manageable assessment targets. The dynamic nature of the new generation of assessments will further open the types of phenomena and environments that can be presented in assessment problems and the opportunities to document evidence of interest and engagement.

The distinctions between learning and assessment will become blurred as dynamic systems can provide immediate feedback and offer customized coaching and learning opportunities. Conceptions of adaptive testing can move from simple branching based on item difficulty statistics to multiple learning progressions based on cognitive analysis of the development of domain knowledge and skills. As we start to collect more and more evidence of learning and incorporate dynamic feedback and coaching into the assessments, they will become more like intelligent tutoring systems that can gauge and scaffold performance in rich, complex tasks. As these trends progress, we will see more blending of the methods from both the fields of educational measurement and of intelligent tutoring to form a hybrid system in which learning and assessment are blended in such a way that they are indistinguishable.

Dynamic assessments can be delivered by a variety of platforms, allowing for more flexibility in terms of when and where evidence of learning can be collected. Dynamic assessments can be administered on school-based computers and also by ever-changing mobile computing devices. Portability will enable assessments in informal environments in designed educational spaces such as museums or in distributed out-of-school learning communities. Dynamic environments are well on their way to fulfilling the promise to transform assessment of learning.

REFERENCES

Anderson, J. R. (1993). *The rules of the mind.* Hillsdale, NJ: Erlbaum.

Anderson, J. R., & Lebiere, C. (1998). *The atomic components of thought.* Mahwah, NJ: Lawrence Erlbaum Associates.

Arroyo, I., Woolf, B. P., Cooper, D. G., Burleson, W., Muldner, K., & Christopherson, R. (2009). *Emotion sensors go to school.* Paper presented at the International Conference of Artificial Intelligence in Education, Brighton, England.

Beatty, I., & Gerace, W. (2009). Technology-enhanced formative assessment: A research-based pedagogy for teaching science with classroom response technology. *Journal of Science Education and Technology, 18*(2), 146–162.

Behrens, J. T., Frezzo, D., Mislevy, R., Kroopnick, M., & Wise, D. (2008). Structural, functional, and semiotic symmetries in simulation-based games and assessments. In E. Baker, J. Dickieson, W. Wufleck & H. F. O'Neil (Eds.), *Assessment of problem solving using simulations* (pp. 59–80). New York: Lawrence Erlbaum Associates.

Black, P., & Wiliam, D. (1998). *Inside the black box: Raising standards through classroom assessment.* London, UK: King's College.

Black, P., & Wiliam, D. (2009). Developing the theory of formative assessment. *Educational Assessment, Evaluation and Accountability, 21*(1), 5–31.

Bransford, J. D., Brown, A. L., & Cocking, R. R. (2000). *How people learn: Brain, mind, experience, and school.* Washington, DC: National Academy Press.

Bruce, J. (2010). Innovative museum guide systems. Paper presented at the Designing Usable Systems: 2010.

Buckley, B. C. (in press). Model-based learning. In N. Seel (Ed.), *Encyclopedia of the sciences of learning.* New York: Springer Science.

Buckley, B. C. (in preparation). Supporting and assessing complex biology learning with computer-based simulations and representations. In D. Treagust & C.-Y. Tsui (Eds.), *Multiple representations in biological education.* New York: Springer Science.

Buckley, B. C., Gobert, J., Kindfield, A. C. H., Horwitz, P., Tinker, B., Gerlits, B., et al. (2004). Model-based teaching and learning with hypermodels: What do they learn? How do they learn? How do we know? *Journal of Science, Education and Technology, 13*(1), 23–41.

Buckley, B. C., Gobert, J., Horwitz, P., & O'Dwyer, L. (2010). Looking inside the black box: Assessing model-based learning and inquiry in Biologica. *International Journal of Learning Technologies, 5*(2).

Case, B. J. (2008). Accommodations to improve instruction, learning, and assessment. In R. Johnson, & M. Ross (Eds.), *Testing deaf students in an age of accountability*. Washington, DC: Gallaudet Research Institute.

Case, B. J., Brooks, T., Wang, S., & Young, M. (2005). *Administration mode comparability study*. San Antonio, TX: Harcourt Assessment, Inc.

CAST. (2008). *Universal design for learning guidelines version 1.0*. Wakefield, MA: Author.

Conati, C., Gernter, A., & VanLehn, K. (2002). Using bayesian networks to manage uncertainty in student modeling. *Journal of User Modeling and User-Adapted Interaction, 12*, 371–417.

Cooper, M. M., & Stevens, R. (2008). Reliable multi-method assessment of metacognition use in chemistry problem solving. *Chemistry Education Research and Practice, 9*, 18–24.

Covington, M. V. (1999). Caring about learning: The nature and nurturing of subject-matter appreciation. *Educational Psychologist, 34*(2), 127–136.

Crone, W. (2008). *Bringing nano to the public through informal science education*. Paper presented at the 2008 American Physical Society March meeting.

D'Mello, S. K., Craig, S. D., & Graesser, A. C. (2009a). Automatic detection of learner's affect from gross body language. *Applied Artificial Intelligence, 23*, 123–150.

D'Mello, S. K., Craig, S. D., & Graesser, A. C. (2009b). Multi-method assessment of affective experience and expression during deep learning. *International Journal of Learning Technology, 4*, 165–187.

Daisy Consortium. (2006). Digital accessible information system (DAISY). Available from http://www.daisy.org.

Dede, C. (2009). Immersive interfaces for engagement and learning. *Science, 323*(5910), 66–69.

Doerr, H. M. (1996). Integrating the study of trigonometry, vectors, and force through modeling. *School Science & Mathematics, 96*(8), 407.

Duff, W., Carter, J., Dallas, C., Howarth, L., Ross, S., Sheffield, R., & Tilson, C. (2009). *The changing museum environment in North America and the impact of technology on museum work*. Paper presented at Empowering users: An active role for user communities.

Dunleavy, M., Dede, C., & Mitchell, R. (2009). Affordances and limitations of immersive participatory augmented reality simulations for teaching and learning. *Journal of Science Education and Technology, 18*(1), 7–22.

Feng, M. & Heffernan, N. (2010) Can We Get Better Assessment From A Tutoring System Compared to Traditional Paper Testing? Can We Have Our Cake (Better Assessment) and Eat It too (Student Learning During the Test)?. Educational Data Mining, 2010.

Feuerstein, R., Rand, Y., & Hoffman, M. B. (1979). *The dynamic assessment of retarded performers: The Learning Potential Assessment Device*. Baltimore: University Park Press.

Gee, J. P. (2008a). What's a screen mean in a video game? Paper presented at the 7th international conference on Interaction design and children.

Gee, J. P. (2008b). Video games and embodiment. *Games and Culture, 3*(3–4), 253–263.

Gee, J. P. (2009). Pedagogy, education, and 21st century survival skills. *Journal of Virtual Worlds Research, 2*(1), 4–9.

Gobert, J. D., & Buckley, B. C. (2000). Introduction to model-based teaching and learning in science education. *International Journal of Science Education, 22*(9), 891–894.

Goldstone, R. L. (2006). The complex systems see-change in education. *The Journal of Learning Sciences, 15*, 35–43.

Goldstone, R. L., & Wilensky, U. (2008). Promoting transfer through complex systems principles. *Journal of the Learning Sciences, 17*, 465–516.

Hausmann, R., van de Sande, B., & VanLehn, K. (2008). Shall we explain? Augmenting learning from intelligent tutoring systems and peer collaboration. In B. P. Woolf, E. Aimeur, R. Nkambou & S. Lajoie (Eds.), *Intelligent tutoring systems* (pp. 636–645). New York: Springer.

Hestenes, D., Wells, M., & Swackhamer, G. (1992). Force concept inventory. *The Physics Teacher, 30*(March), 141–158.

Hickey, D. T., Kindfield, A. C. H., Horwitz, P., & Christie, M. A. T. (2003). Integrating curriculum, instruction, assessment, and evaluation in a technology-supported genetics learning environment. *American Educational Research Journal, 40*(2), 495–538.

Horwitz, P., Gobert, J., Buckley, B. C., & Wilensky, U. (2007). *Modeling across the curriculum annual report to NSF.* Concord, MA: The Concord Consortium.

Hmelo-Silver, C. E., Jordan, R., Liu, L. Gray, S., Demeter, M., Rugaber, S., Vattan, S., & Goel, A. (2008). Focusing on function: Thinking below the surface of complex science systems. *Science Scope.* Retrieved from http://dilab.gatech.edu/publications/Science-Scope-Paper.pdf

Ioannidou, A., Repenning, A., Webb, D., Keyser, D., Luhn, L., & Daetwyler, C. (2010). Mr. Vetro: A collective simulation for teaching health science. *International Journal of Computer-Supported Collaborative Learning, 5*(2), 141–166.

Klopfer, E., & Squire, K. (2008). Environmental detectives—the development of an augmented reality platform for environmental simulations. *Educational Technology Research & Development, 56*(2), 203–228.

Kopriva, R. (2000). *Ensuring accuracy in testing for English language learners.* Washington, DC: Council of Chief State School Officers.

Krajcik, J., Marx, R., Blumenfeld, P., Soloway, E., & Fishman, B. (2000). *Inquiry-based science supported by technology: Achievement and motivation among urban middle school students.* Paper presented at the American Educational Research Association, New Orleans, LA.

Lai, C. Y., & Wu, C. C. (2006). Using handhelds in a jigsaw cooperative learning environment. *Journal of Computer Assisted Learning, 22*(4), 284–297.

Lehrer, R., Schauble, L., Strom, D., & Pligge, M. (2001). Similarity of form and substance: Modeling material kind. In D. K. S. Carver (Ed.), *Cognition and instruction: 25 years of progress* (pp. 39–74). Mahwah, NJ: Lawrence Erlbaum Associates.

Lim, K. Y. T., & Wang, J. Y. Z. (2005). Collaborative handheld gaming in education. *Educational Media International, 42*(4), 351–359.

Liu, T.-Y., Tan, T.-H., & Chu, Y.-L. (2009). Outdoor natural science learning with an rfid-supported immersive ubiquitous learning environment. *Journal of Educational Technology & Society, 12*(4), 161–175.

Maehr, M. L. & Midgley, C. (1996) *Transforming school cultures.* Boulder, CO: Westview Press.

Martin, J., & VanLehn, K. (1995). Student assessment using Bayesian nets. *Journal of Human-Computer Studies, 42*(6), 575–591.

McDowell, L., Sambell, K., Bazin, V., Penlington, R., Wakelin, D., Wickes, H., & Smailes, J. (2006). *Assessment for learning: Current practice exemplars from the Centre for Excellence in Teaching and Learning in Assessment for Learning.* Available at http://www.northumbria.ac.uk/sd/central/ar/academy/cetl_afl/pubandpres/intpub/occasional/

Messick, S. (1994). The interplay of evidence and consequences in the validation of performance assessments. *Educational Researcher, 32,* 13–23.

Minstrell, J., & Kraus, P. A. (2007). *Applied research on implementing diagnostic instructional tools.* Seattle, WA: FACET Innovations.

Mislevy, R. J., & Gitomer, D. H. (1996). The role of probability-based inference in an intelligent tutoring system. *User-Modeling and User-Adapted Interaction, 5,* 253–282.

Mislevy, R. J., Steinberg, L. S., & Almond, R. G. (2003). On the structure of educational assessment (with discussion). *Measurement: Interdisciplinary Research and Perspective, 1*(1), 3–62.

Morrison, A., Oulasvirta, A., Peltonen, P., Lemmela, S., Jacucci, G., Reitmayr, G.,... Juustila, A. (2009). *Like bees around the hive: A comparative study of a mobile augmented reality map.* Paper presented at the 27th international conference on human factors in computing systems.

Nersessian, N. J. (2008). *Creating scientific concepts.* Cambridge, MA: MIT Press.

Nicol, D. J., & Macfarlane-Dick, D. (2006). Formative assessment and self-regulated learning: A model and seven principles of good feedback practice. *Studies in Higher Education, 31*(2), 199–218.

Norman, D.A. (1993). *Things that makes us smart.* Reading, MA; Adddison-Wesley.

NRC. (2009). *Learning Science in Informal Environments: People, Places, and Pursuits.* Washington, DC: The National Academies Press.

NRC. (2010). *Surrounded by Science: Learning Science in Informal Environments.* Washington, DC: The National Academies Press.

Oberholzer-Gee, F.,Waldfogel, J. & White, M. (2010). Friend or foe? Cooperation and learning in high-stakes games. *The Review of Economics and Statistics, 92*(1), 179–187.

Palincar, A. D., Brown, A. L. & Campone, J. (1991). Dynamic assessment. In H. L. Swanson (Ed.), *Handbook on the assessment of learning disabilities: theory, research, and practice* (pp. 75–95). Austin, TX: PRO-Ed.

Patten, B., Sanchez, I. A., & Tangey, B. (2006). Designing collaborative, constructionist and contextual applications for handheld devices. *Computers & Education, 46,* 294–308.

Pellegrino, J., Chudowsky, N., & Glaser, R. (2001). *Knowing what students know: The science and design of educational assessment.* Washington, DC: National Academy Press.

Quellmalz, E. S. (2009). Assessing new technological literacies. In F. Scheuermann & F. Pedro (Eds.), *Assessing the effects of ICT in education: Indicators, criteria, and benchmarks for international comparisons.* Luxembourg: European Union/OECD.

Quellmalz, E. S., DeBarger, A., Haertel, G., & Kreikemeier, P. (2005). *Validities of science inuqiry assessments: Final report.* Menlo Park, CA: SRI International.

Quellmalz, E. S., & Haertel, G. (2004). *Technology supports for state science assessment systems.* Paper commissioned by the National Research Council Committee on Test Design for K–12 Science Achievement.

Quellmalz, E. S., & Haertel, G. D. (2008). Assessing new literacies in science and mathematics. In J. D. J. Leu, J. Coiro, M. Knowbel, & C. Lankshear (Eds.), *Handbook of research on new literacies* (pp. 941–972). Mahwah, NJ: Erlbaum.

Quellmalz, E. S., & Moody, M. (2004). *Models for multi-level state science assessment systems.* Paper commissioned by the National Research Council Committee on Test Design for K–12 Science Achievement.

Quellmalz, E. S., & Silberglitt, M. S. (2010). *Integrating Simulation-Based Science Assessments into Balanced State Science Assessment Systems.* Paper presented at the annual meeting of the American Educational Research Association, Denver, CO.

Quellmalz, E. S., Timms, M. J., & Buckley, B. C. (2009). *Using science simulations to support powerful formative assessments of complex science learning.* Paper presented at the American Educational Research Association, San Diego, CA.

Quellmalz, E. S., Timms, M. J., & Buckley, B. C. (2010). The promise of simulation-based science assessment: The Calipers project. *International Journal of Learning Technologies, 5*(3), 243–265.

Rieber, L. P., Tzeng, S., & Tribble, K. (2004). Discovery learning, representation, and explanation within a computer-based simulation. *Computers and Education, 27*(1), 45–58.

Sambell, K. (2010). Enquiry-based learning and formative assessment environments: Student perspectives. *Practitioner Research in Higher Education, 4*(1), 52–61.

Sausner, R. (2004). Ready or not. District administration. Retrieved May 29th, 2007 from http://districtadministration.ccsct.com//page.cfm?p=832

Schwartz, D. L., & Heiser, J. (2006). Spatial representations and imagery in learning. In R. K. Sawyer (Ed.), *The Cambridge handbook of the learning sciences.* Cambridge: Cambridge University Press.

Schmitt, B., Bach, C., Dubois, E., & Duranthon, F. (2010). *Designing and evaluating advanced interactive experiences to increase visitor's stimulation in a museum.* Paper presented at the 1st Augmented Human International Conference.

Schultz, P., & Shugart, E. (2007). *Communicating with museum audiences about climate science: Contributions of Gene Rasmusson.* Presented at the Gene Rasmusson Symposium.

Slotta, J. D. & Chi, M. T. H. (2006). The impact of ontology training on conceptual change: Helping students understand the challenging topics in science. *Cognition and Instruction 24*(2), 261–289.

Squire, K. D., & Jan, M. (2007). Mad city mystery: Developing scientific argumentation skills with a place-based augmented reality game on handheld computers. *Journal of Science Education and Technology, 16*(1), 5–29.

Stewart, J., Cartier, J. L., & Passmore, C. M. (2005). Developing understanding through model-based inquiry. In M. S. Donovan & J. D. Bransford (Eds.), *How students learn* (pp. 515–565). Washington, DC: The National Academies Press.

Stewart, I., & Golubitsky, M. (1992). *Fearful symmetry: Is God a geometer?* Cambridge, MA: Blackwell Cambridge.

Stieff, M., & Wilensky, U. (2003). Connected chemistry—incorporating interactive simulations into the chemistry classroom. *Journal of Science Education and Technology, 12*(3), 285–302.

Stiggins, R. (2006). Assessment for Learning: A key to motivation and achievement. *Edge, 2*(2), 3–19.

Timms, M. J. (2007). *Using item response theory (IRT) to select hints in an ITS.* Paper presented at the Artificial Intelligence in Education, Marina del Ray, CA.

Twing, J. S. & Dolan, R. P. (2008). *UD-CBT guidelines.* Retrieved March 5th, 2008 from http://www.pearsonedmeasurement.com/cast/index.html

Vonderwell, S., Sparrow, K., & Zachariah, S. (2005). Using handheld computers and probeware in inquiry-based science education. *Journal of the Research Center for Educational Technology, 1*(2), 1–11.

Vygotsky, L. S. (1987). *The collected works of L.S. Vygotsky. Vol I.* New York: Plenum.

Wang, S. (2005). *Online or paper: Does delivery affect results?* San Antonio, TX: Harcourt Assessment, Inc.

Weller, A. M., Bickar, J. C., & McGuinness, P. (2008). Making field trips podtastic! Use of handheld wireless technology alleviates isolation and encourages collaboration. *Learning & Leading with Technology, 35*(6), 18–21.

White, B. Y., & Frederiksen, J. R. (1998). Inquiry, modeling, and metacognition: Making science accessible to all students. *Cognition and Instruction, 16*(1), 3–118.

Wilson, M. R., & Bertenthal, M. W. (Eds.). (2006). *Systems for state science assessment.* Washington, DC: The National Academies Press.

CHAPTER 4

WHERE STREAMS CONVERGE

Using Evidence-Centered Design
to Assess Quest to Learn

Valerie J. Shute and Robert J. Torres

INTRODUCTION

According to the recent National Educational Technology Plan (March, 2010), our education system needs a revolutionary transformation rather than evolutionary tinkering. In general, the plan urges our education system at all levels to: (a) be clear about the outcomes we seek; (b) collaborate to redesign structures and processes for effectiveness, efficiency, and flexibility; (c) continually monitor and measure our performance; and (d) hold ourselves accountable for progress and results every step of the way. With an eye toward those goals, this chapter describes an ongoing assessment of a transformative new school called Quest to Learn (Q2L). Q2L is an innovative, student-centered, games-based public school that opened in New York City in September 2009 for grades six through 12 (beginning with a sixth-grade cohort). It includes a dynamic and interdisciplinary curriculum, using design principles of games to create highly immersive learning experiences for students. The curriculum, like games, is immersive, participatory, allows for social engagement, and provides a challenge-based context for students to work within.

Technology-Based Assessments for 21st Century Skills, pages 91–124
Copyright © 2012 by Information Age Publishing
91

Basing the design of a school on games can certainly be construed as revolutionary. There are, however, some good reasons for this. For example, Gee (2008) has argued that game design has a lot to teach us about learning, and contemporary learning theory has something to teach us about designing better games and instructional environments. One link in place between these realms (i.e., games, learning, and instructional environments) is formative feedback—a critical part of any learning effort (e.g., Shute, 2008), and also a key component in good game design which adjusts challenges and gives feedback so that different players feel the game is challenging and their effort is paying off.

We believe that (a) learning is at its best when it is active, goal-oriented, contextualized, and interesting (e.g., Bransford, Brown, & Cocking, 2000; Bruner, 1961; Quinn, 2005; Vygotsky, 1978); and (b) learning environments should thus be interactive, provide ongoing feedback, grab and sustain attention, and have appropriate and adaptive levels of challenge—in other words, the features of good games. Along the same lines, Gee (2003) has argued that the secret of a good game is not its 3D graphics and other bells and whistles, but its underlying architecture where each level dances around the outer limits of the player's abilities, seeking at every point to be hard enough to be just doable. Similarly, psychologists (e.g., Falmagne, Cosyn, Doignon, & Thiery, 2003; Vygotsky, 1987) have long argued that the best instruction hovers at the boundary of a student's competence. More recent reports (e.g., Thai, Lowenstein, Ching, & Rejeski, 2009) contend that well-designed games can act as transformative digital learning tools to support the development of skills across a range of critical educational areas. In short—well designed games have the potential to support meaningful learning across a variety of content areas and domains.

So, Q2L is based on principles of game design, and is intended to enable *all* students, regardless of their academic or personal challenges, to contribute to the design and innovation necessary to meet the needs and demands of a global society. The school culture aims to foster deep curiosity for lifelong learning as well as a commitment to social responsibility, and respect for others and self. These are excellent goals, but as with any grand new idea, Q2L needs to be systematically evaluated—from the level of the whole school down to the individual (e.g., student, teacher). The obvious challenge is to figure out how to accurately infer the success of Quest to Learn when there is nothing comparable. Hence our driving questions are: How can we effectively capture the *critical goals/values* of Q2L so that we can develop and validate an objectives model, and how can we accurately assess the development of *important new competencies* that Q2L claims it is teaching its students?

Our main claim in this chapter is that evidence-centered design (ECD) (Mislevy, Steinberg, & Almond, 2003), originally developed as an approach for creating assessment tasks, can be expanded and employed for assessing Q2L—at both the school and student levels. This is possible because ECD allows for the collection and integration of both qualitative and quantitative data across multiple, situated contexts. That is, ECD allows us to synthesize information from disparate sources into a common framework, characterize its evidentiary value, and reason through often complex relations among what we observe and what we want to infer.

The organization of this chapter is as follows. First, we describe Quest to Learn relative to its theoretical foundation and unique pedagogy. Second, we overview our ongoing research project that is intended to identify and model important school-level variables (i.e., key goals/values of Q2L) and assess students on three 21st century competencies (i.e., systems thinking, teamwork, and time management). And third, we describe preliminary findings[1] and future research that can be conducted within Q2L.

QUEST TO LEARN

The School

A recent report called The Silent Epidemic (Bridgeland, DiIulio, & Morison, 2006) indicates that 81% of students who drop out of school say that school is not relevant to their lives. Q2L's designers are keenly aware of these realities and have drawn inspiration from digitally mediated and collaborative practices that mirror those in most professional industries from business, health and medicine to government and the arts. These practices are marked by participatory, co-creative processes and social engagements that exemplify what contemporary learning scientists have been saying for some time: that learning is not simply individualized, but a highly social, context-dependent and collaborative achievement (e.g., Bransford et al., 2000; Lave & Wenger, 1991; Vygotsky, 1978).

Led by the digital practices of today's kids, Q2L has been carefully designed to capitalize on those practices to engage students in deep forms of learning. Drawing from contemporary research and theories of learning as a socially and technologically-mediated endeavor, a design group at the Institute of Play made up of game designers, learning scientists, and content experts, has spent the past two years architecting Q2L, prior to its recent opening. Q2L was created in an attempt to change the conversation about school reform from one traditionally focused on ensuring students acquire numeracy, reading, and writing skills, to creating the conditions in which students are challenged to apply those skills to help solve the invention and innovation challenges necessary of our time. Indeed, Q2L—designed to serve as a lab for larger school reform efforts—was based on the belief that a core thrust of education in this century must be to engage learners (as is the purpose of most scientific and industry professions) in imagining, researching and prototyping the necessary inventions of our time. This represents a large departure from the historical purposes of K–12 schooling.

To meet this goal, Q2L uses a systems-thinking framework as a core curricular and pedagogical strategy within carefully designed game-like, immersive environments. By systems thinking we mean a holistic perspective that sees the world as increasingly interconnected and can be understood systemically, from elemental components to complex systems of activity (e.g., Assaraf & Orion, 2005; Barak & Williams, 2007; Forrester, 1994; Ossimitz, 2000; Salisbury, 1996). This broad definition includes social, natural, and technological systems that can be studied and understood as having certain cross-cutting commonalities, such as rules, goals, and particular behaviors. These game-based curricula are designed by teachers, professional game designers, curriculum directors, and other content experts to create 10-week "missions" (i.e., units of study) which are unique and create an immersive world in which students take on various identities, from cartographers to architects to nature ecologists, to solve design and systems-based problems.

The curriculum at Q2L is interdisciplinary. It follows national and local content standards, is design-focused (e.g., continually places students in the role of designer), and relevant to the culture of today's students. There are six critical features to the school's structure: (a) a systems-thinking and design-thinking focus, (b) a philosophy and practice of technology integration, (c) a blending of new literacies and traditional literacies in a set of interdisciplinary domains, (d) a game-based pedagogy, (e) an ecological and distributed approach to learning, and (f) an innovative approach to teacher development and curriculum design.

Upon its opening, Q2L welcomed an ethnically and economically diverse group of New York City sixth graders. Entry into the school is based on interest—students and families must attend an information session, but no student is denied admission based on merit or prior experiences in school. The inspiration for Q2L came from two observations: the huge gap that exists between traditional schooling and the digital practices of today's youth, and the alarming and unchanging rates of high school dropouts in the United States. For more information on the school, see www.q2l.org and also Torres, Rufo-Tepper, and Shapiro (in press).

Our Research Project

> *The strength of the pack is the wolf, and the strength of the wolf is the pack.*
> —Rudyard Kipling

We began an 18-month-long study to concur with the first days of the school opening in September 2009. The high-level purpose of our research is to define and refine a valid assessment approach designed to work across multiple levels—from the whole school down to specific students. We intend to establish the necessary models that will enable analysis of the efficacy of Q2L in relation to two systemic problems: (1) the need to recognize and support new competencies, and (2) student (dis)engagement relative to current, outdated educational systems.

New competencies are needed to effectively compete in our shrinking, interconnected world. We are being confronted with problems of enormous complexity and global ramifications (e.g., nuclear proliferation, global warming, and poverty). When faced with highly technical and complex problems, the ability to think creatively, critically, collaboratively, systemically, and then communicate effectively is essential. Learning and succeeding in a complex and dynamic world is not easily measured by multiple-choice responses on a simple knowledge test. Instead, solutions begin with re-thinking assessment, identifying new skills and standards relevant for the 21st century, and then figuring out how we can best assess students' acquisition of the new competencies.

Disengagement reflects the large gap between what students do for fun and what they're required to do in school. Most schools cover material that is deemed "important," but students are often unimpressed. These same kids, however, are highly motivated by what they do for fun (e.g., play games, participate in social networking sites). Recent reports (e.g., Ito et al., 2008; Palfrey & Gasser, 2008; Watkins, 2009) have documented not only the extensive worlds youth have created in digital spaces, but have highlighted the highly social, collaborative, and interest-based learning taking place in these digital environments. This mismatch between mandated school activities and what kids choose to do on their own is cause for concern regarding the motivational impact (or lack thereof) of school, but it needn't be the case. Imagine these two worlds united—as is the goal and reality of Q2L. Student engagement is strongly associated with academic achievement; thus, embedding school material within game-like environments has tremendous potential to increase learning, especially for disengaged students.

Before describing our research further, we turn for a moment to games-based learning, which is at the core of the Q2L intervention. Beyond simply using games to teach, Q2L advocates using the internal architecture of games to create game-like learning environments, whether they are analog or digital. Games instantiate constrained systems of activity (or worlds) in which players engage mediational tools (e.g., a racket in tennis, a written quest prompt in *World of Warcraft*), other players, and rule sets to achieve clearly defined winning (or goal) conditions. This requires players to enact specific game behaviors. These behaviors in the gaming world are called "core mechanics" players must perform to successfully move through a game.

Now, to suit the needs of the 21st century, learning environments should reflect "knowledge domains" or "discourse communities" that reflect the epistemology of real world professional and/or industry domains. That is, learners should be offered opportunities to apply the actual kinds of skills, knowledge and behaviors (i.e., core mechanics) needed to participate in the domain of, say, U.S. history, systems biology, or minimalist architecture. Learners should be offered genuine and ample opportunities to produce and iterate on content endemic to real knowledge domains, and they should also be offered communities of practice where they can collaborate and informally (or formally) share their work with a community of peers. Games enable such social networking, which, as we mentioned, is a core activity in the lives of today's youth. Furthermore, having an audience has been seen as a core driver of engagement of youth in online social networking sites (e.g., Ito et al., 2010). In summary, games are engaging spaces that foster the kinds of valuable new competencies (e.g., problem solving, critical thinking skills) we believe are important to succeed in the 21st century. Additionally, they permit one to try on various identities and may be structured in ways that transition smoothly to the real, complex world. For more on this topic, see Gee, 2010; Shute, Rieber, and Van Eck, in press.

Goals of the Research Project

The two main goals of this effort are to (a) *identify and model important school-level variables* (i.e., key objectives of Q2L based on the articulated goals of the designers, administrators and teachers), and (b) *identify and assess a set of key student-level variables* (i.e., important attributes related to success in the 21st century and aligned with the Q2L objectives).

Identified critical school objectives comprise a clear target toward which everything else related to the school should aim—such as valued student processes and outcomes. Modeling the competencies, and assessing and supporting students in relation to 21st century skills will allow students to grow in important new areas. Some examples of valued competencies at Q2L include the ability to function productively within multidisciplinary teams; identify and solve complex problems with innovative solutions; communicate effectively and persuasively; engage in deep exploration of various topics of interest; use technology efficiently; demonstrate intellectual curiosity; understand local and global system dynamics; engage in evidence-based reasoning, reflexivity, and ethical decision making; and work toward the development of a more just and peaceful world.

Data derived from our 18-month effort can also be used to enable Q2L faculty and staff to responsively revise and improve the school's processes to align student achievement and school goals. As we describe later in this chapter, relevant stakeholders can be notified about problems that arise, on any level (i.e., individual student, classroom/course, or school), providing the information necessary to nip problems in the bud, formatively speaking.

School Objectives Hierarchy. The first step of this 18-month effort was to identify the critical goals espoused and embodied by the school (i.e., what "success" and "failure" of the school would look like) and to structure that information into an evaluation hierarchy (i.e., a graphical model of the objectives/goals; see examples in the Appendix). This effort required about seven months of interviews, surveys, focus groups, and observations involving relevant stakeholders (e.g., directors of Q2L, teachers, administrators, curriculum designers, and students) and a critical study of the school's design documents (see Salen, Torres, Ruff-Tepper, Shapiro, Wolozin, in press) in an iterative design. Information gleaned from this effort was then arrayed in a hierarchical model—with "Q2L Success" as the uppermost goal (or "node"), followed by progressively more specific variables. For example, one dominant value that was voiced by a majority of respondents concerned the "culture" of Q2L, with one type of culture being "*establishing a cohesive and inclusive community.*" That variable was ultimately decomposed into more specific variables, such as: (a) appreciating diversity, (b) feeling of belonging, and (c) being physically and emotionally safe. Finally those variables can be further refined to measurable variables with associated rubrics—such as *appreciating diversity* being further specified to "respects other ethnic groups," and "values others' views/traditions."

The objectives hierarchy will serve as the basis for subsequent research/ evaluation efforts comprised of school, classroom, and student level assessments. The aim is to clearly describe and depict what is of value to the school and its extended community, while also establishing a framework to help in evaluating what works, what does not work, and why. In other words, we are teasing out and clearly specifying the important goals and values of Q2L in terms of what makes this school and its affiliated community unique, and then creating particular metrics and criteria, per goal by which to assess it (see Methods section for how we are accomplishing this via an evidence-based approach). Setting up the infrastructure to gather quantitative and qualitative data on identified values is thus a critical part of our research.

Assessing Student Competencies and Other Attributes. Concurrent with the school-goals analysis described above, we are also assessing student-level variables. This involves the administration of a set of assessments at 6-month intervals across the 18-month period to capture the current states of critical competencies and monitor their development over time. These are not your typical bubble-form assessments. Instead, they consist of engaging surveys, questionnaires, situation-judgment tasks, and performance tasks relating to selected competencies. (Note that authentic embedded assessments will eventually be built into the Q2L curriculum—outside the scope of this project). To counter concerns about comparative measures that may arise with innovative endeavors like Q2L, data are also being collected from traditional tests. This will enable us to match Q2L students with other public school students and compare academic achievement. We have currently identified two NYC middle schools in the same district as Q2L with demographically similar student populations.

We are assessing the following three competencies during the 18-month period: (1) systems thinking, (2) teamwork, and (3) time management. Each of these three competencies has its own set of variables. Figure 4.1 (4.1a, 4.1b, 4.1c) shows each of the three main variables and their prima-ry (first-level) nodes. The models were derived from the literature, based on theoretical and empirical support. For example, the three main nodes comprising systems thinking (Figure 4.1a) relative to Q2L are based on re-search reported by Ossimitz (2000), Richmond (1993), Shute et al. (2010), Sweeney and Sterman (2000; 2007), and Torres (2009).

Assessment instruments for each of these three competencies were de-signed, developed, and validated previously. Our assessment for systems thinking is based on the protocol employed by Sweeney and Sterman (2007). For the teamwork model (Figure 4.1b), we synthesized research described by the following: Rysavy and Sales (1991); Tindale, Stawiski, and Jacobs

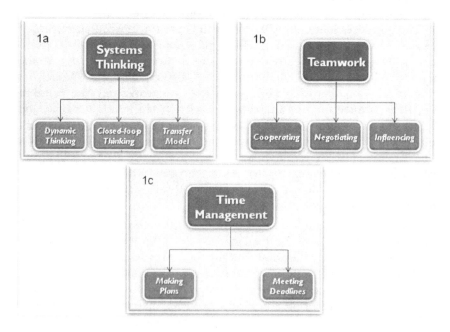

Figure 4.1   Three mini competency models for student assessment in Q2L.

(2008); Totten, Sills, Digby, and Russ (1991); Van den Bossche, Segers, and Kirschner (2006); and Zhuang, MacCann, Wang, Liu, and Roberts (2008). The three-factor solution shown in Figure 4.1b has been consistently reported for this variable relative to middle- and high-school students (see Zhuang et al., 2008). Finally, our time management model (Figure 4.1c) was based on the findings of Liu, Rijmen, MacCann, and Roberts (2009); MacCann, Duckworth, and Roberts (2009); MacCann, Shahani, Dipboye, and Phillips (1990); and Roberts, Schultze, and Minsky (2006). This two-factor solution has been reported relative to middle-school students.

The first research question related to student assessment asks: *Does the incoming cohort of 6th grade students at Q2L demonstrate improved performance over 18 months in the areas of systems thinking, teamwork, and time management skills?* These three competencies are supported (albeit implicitly) during the course of daily school activities (e.g., completing projects in small groups, analyzing games in terms of their underlying systems). In addition, we will be examining this cohort's academic achievement (i.e., mathematics and reading skills) in relation to a normative sample of NYC public school students. The associated research question is: *Do students in the Quest to Learn school perform comparably to matched students in other NYC public schools on standardized math and reading test scores?* We will be able to determine if Q2L is successfully supporting students' development of important new competencies as a function of its unique environment, while not sacrificing traditional (i.e., math and reading) academic achievements.

In relation to our first research question, we hypothesize that students will, on average, demonstrate improved performance in relation to the three focal competencies from initial (Time One, September 2009) to final (Time Four, March 2011) assessment. In terms of research question two, and in line with the premise of *primum non nocere* (first, do no harm), we hypothesize that students in the Quest to Learn school will do no worse than a comparable sample of students (normative data) from the New York City Public Schools.

METHODS

Measurements are not to provide numbers but insight.
—Ingrid Bucher

Evidence-Centered Design

Ensuring validity and reliability of the assessments is critical throughout the 18-month assessment project. Consequently, we are using an evidence-centered evaluation (ECE) approach to assess school-level goals, and evidence-centered design (ECD) to assess student-level variables.

Evidence-Centered Evaluation (ECE) for Assessing School Goals

ECE (Shute & Zapata-Rivera, 2008) represents an extension of evidence-centered design for assessments (Mislevy, Steinberg, & Almond, 2003) and involves an initial specification of various models—objectives, evidence, and data (see Figure 4.2). ECE can support the ongoing monitoring and diagnosis of Q2L variables across multiple levels. Furthermore, data can be aggregated up to the main "Q2L success" node (i.e., the top circle in the Q2L Objectives box in Figure 4.2), or disaggregated to class- or student-level data. This systematic evidence-based approach provides a way to lay out an evaluation complete with evidentiary arguments that explicitly link data to Q2L objectives. It is intended to eventually provide for ongoing monitoring of relevant indicators (captured, analyzed, and diagnosed) with increased validity for each of the main Q2L objectives as well as the constituent sub-goals.

Following the specification of the objectives model derived from extensive interviews, surveys, focus groups, document reviews, and observations conducted during the first seven months of this effort, the evidence model is ready to be crafted. The evidence model represents the statistical glue between the set of Q2L objectives (unobservables) and the wide collection of observable data or indicators (e.g., classroom observations, test scores, questionnaire responses, etc.). Statistical models, such as Bayesian nets, may be used for accumulating evidence across multiple sources (albeit this is outside the scope of our current project). Accumulation of evidence is accomplished by mapping the scoring or "evidence" rules to relevant nodes in the objectives model (see Evidence box in the middle of Figure 4.2). For each evidence model, we are defining the methods needed to elicit, score, and accumulate observations. Finally, for all observables, we will define the

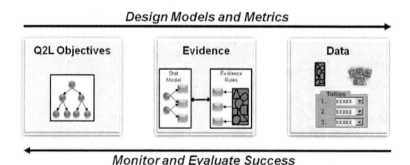

Figure 4.2 Three primary ECE models working in concert to evaluate Q2L goals.

characteristics of the data needed to satisfy evidentiary needs—in other words, what do these data look like, and how much information do they contribute toward the unobservable variables?

Reversing the flow (from right-to-left in Figure 4.2) enables us to diagnose the current state of success (e.g., low, medium, or high) per objective in the objectives model. Again, this involves using multiple sources of data to score, analyze, and combine evidence to infer probabilistic estimates of success (per node, and to what degree). The objectives model will always be up-to-date, providing the current state of the model at any point in time and at any level of interest. The beauty and power of this approach is that it can provide clear evidentiary arguments (from data to objectives) for data-driven decision making, transparency, and accountability purposes—all important aspects of the unique culture of Q2L. It can also provide timely alerts for relevant stakeholders regarding successes or perhaps more critically, *problems* that need immediate attention. That is, alerts may be established in the model, defined as cut-values, which could then trigger automatic emails to relevant stakeholders. A similar evidence-based approach is used for the student variables, discussed next.

Evidence-Centered Design (ECD) for Assessing Student Variables

To assess our selected competencies, we are using evidence-centered design as a way of reasoning about student performance (for more, see Behrens, Mislevy, DiCerbo, & Levy, this volume). ECD also provides a way of reasoning about assessment design, which may be used subsequent to our initial 18-month effort to develop additional assessments for Q2L on valuable competencies. To assess students' systems thinking, teamwork, and time management skills, we are using existing assessment instruments and protocols, as mentioned earlier.

The key idea of ECD (as with ECE described above) is to specify the structures and supporting rationales for the evidentiary argument of an assessment. By making the evidentiary argument explicit, it becomes easier to examine, share, and refine. Argument structures encompass, among other things, the claims (inferences) one wishes to make about a student, the observables (performance data) that provide support for those claims, the task performance situations that elicit the observables from the students, and rationales for linking it all together (for more, see Behrens et al., this volume; Shute, Hansen, & Almond, 2008; Shute et al., 2010). The three main models used in ECD for student assessment follow:

- *Competency Model*—A given assessment is meant to support inferences for some purpose, such as grading, providing diagnostic feedback, and so on. The competency model describes the knowledge, skills, and other attributes about which inferences are intended, context under which the ability is demonstrated, and the range and relations of competencies in the knowledge domain.

- *Evidence Model*—This defines the evidence that is needed to support the aforementioned claims. Evidence models describe what's to be scored, how to score it, and how to combine scores into claims. These models establish the boundaries of performance and identify observable actions that are within those boundaries.
- *Task/Activities Model*—The purpose of this model is to identify tasks, features of tasks, and/or activities that are able to elicit the evidence defined in the evidence model. Task models specify the inputs required to perform the observable actions as well as the work products that result from performing the observable actions.

Currently, we have competency models established for each of our main variables: systems thinking, teamwork, and time management skills (see Figure 4.1). Now, to determine how well a student is (or is not) acquiring/honing these skills, we collect relevant data that is disentangled and interpreted in valid and reliable ways. A good diagnostic system should be able to accurately infer competency estimates (i.e., levels of mastery) for a student on virtually any type of variable (e.g., demonstrating knowledge of a time delay within a given system, showing proper interpersonal skills during a collaborative effort, allocating time appropriately during a time-critical task). Again, this process begins with the design of an accurate and informative competency model that provides the basis for both specific (e.g., closed-loop thinking) and general (e.g., systems thinking) diagnoses to occur, as well as quantitative and qualitative data to be accumulated.

Information from students' interactions with specific tasks and with the environment in general can be analyzed to inform environmental affordances for competency development and the degrees to which students met those competencies. For example, we are able to correlate individual student gains in systems thinking with in situ student experiences in classrooms and other learning environments (e.g., afterschool, online), peer and student-teacher interactions, tasks assigned to students, and work they produce. Task-level diagnoses can provide local support to the student, via scoring rules and feedback. Competency-level estimates provide valuable information to the teacher to inform subsequent instruction, to the student to reflect on how well she is doing, and to Q2L administrators to see how well the school is achieving its goals of engendering student learning.

In all cases, interpretation of competency level is a function of the richness and relevance of the evidence collected. In a valid competency model, each piece of knowledge, skill, and ability is linked to more than one task or activity so that evidence of a student's performance can be accumulated in a number of different contexts and via a variety of ways. This represents converging streams of information.

Mixed-Model Design

A mixed-model research design employing both quantitative and qualitative approaches is being used for the research effort. More specifically, the research design may be characterized as exploratory, descriptive, qualitative, quantitative, as well as somewhat longitudinal in scope. This allows us to triangulate data in order to optimally inform our findings and conclusions.

School-level assessment began with a qualitative approach using semi-structured interviews to elicit participants' thoughts and beliefs about Q2L values and objectives. Content analysis was used to induce and generate dominant themes from the 500+ pages of transcripts that came from the individual interviews with each of the 16 Q2L stakeholders (i.e., teachers, game designers, curriculum designers, and administrators). All participants were interviewed for one and a half to two hours, and asked questions relating to their view of what is of value to Q2L, such as: How would you describe a successful teacher? How would you describe a successful student? What is Q2L's role in the community? What's the most important feature or function of Q2L?

Themes were induced from the full set of interviews, summarized in an 11-page "collective self portrait" document, and shared with all of the participants. Accompanying the collective self portrait document was a link to a short 10-item anonymous survey. The survey asked participants for their role at the school, as well as their thoughts about the content of the collective self portrait—whether it generally and accurately represented Q2L's goals/values, if it represented their particular views, and what may have been missing or off target. Each participant also rank ordered the themes in terms of their importance to Q2L (culture, systems thinking, design thinking, teamwork, resource management, and game-based pedagogy).

After analyzing the results from the surveys, we organized a series of focus groups to further flesh out the Q2L model. Moreover, we conducted (and continue to do so) bi-weekly observations in classrooms using two independent observers representing another stream of converging data (note that actions often speak louder than words). In addition to the interviews, surveys, focus group data, observations, and other data sources were analyzed for triangulation purposes, including extant Q2L design documents and mission statements. As explained earlier, the emergent themes were subsequently developed into an *objectives model* for our assessment of Q2L goals, and is currently being validated by relevant stakeholders. See the Preliminary Results section for a summary of the objectives, and the Appendix for the corresponding graphical models.

Student-level assessment is currently ongoing, and mostly quantitative, but partly qualitative. That is, we have been collecting and analyzing quantitative data from the N = 72 students' responses to assessments designed to measure systems thinking, teamwork, and time management skills. These assessments are being administered with formats and wording suitable for middle school students. In addition, we have been following students into some of the various places where they travel, physically and virtually, to access content. This includes locations inside and outside of school—such as various classrooms, the after-school program, the school's unique online social networking site, and the cafeteria. These observations are particularly important relative to our goal of determining how/why students are developing key competencies. Consequently, we developed and are concurrently using a qualitative observation protocol.[2] For instance, the protocol calls for two independent observers per site, who conduct observations bi-weekly. The main categories of what they are looking for include: (a) documenting the types of thinking skills that are afforded by each node across the learning ecology (e.g., for systems thinking, observations relate to the evidences of dynamic thinking, closed-loop thinking, and ability to transfer models to other situations across multiple learning environments); (b) recording the type and frequency of specialized language used within each domain/node; (c) noting the kinds of social activity evident per node; and (d) capturing other important information such as the learning tools used, identities afforded by each site, artifacts produced, shared norms, physical (or virtual) space, and time allocated per activity in a given location.

Assessment Tasks

As noted earlier, we are using existing instruments to assess our three focal competencies during this 18-month project. Systems thinking is being assessed using a modified version of the protocol described in Torres' recent (2009) dissertation on the topic, which in turn was based on the protocol described in Sweeney and Sterman (2007). There are 12 items in this assessment, with different examples of systems used across administrations (e.g., hunger/eating vs. predatory/prey relations).

Teamwork and time management skills are measured via instruments that have been designed, developed, and validated by the Educational Testing Service for use by middle school students (see, for example, MacCann, Duckworth, & Roberts, 2009; Wang, MacCann, Zhuang, Liu, & Roberts, 2009; Zhuang, MacCann, Wang, Liu, & Roberts, 2008). The first teamwork assessment contained 57 Likert-scale items and 12 scenario-based items, but subsequent administrations of the assessment used fewer items (i.e., 22 Likert-scale items with the strongest weights on the three focal factors—cooperating, negotiating, and influencing others, along with 12 scenario-based items). The first time management assessment contained 36 Likert-scale items, and subsequent administrations employed only 24 items (again, those weighting most strongly on the focal two factors—making plans and meeting deadlines).

Example items (with text boxes for entering constructed responses) from the systems thinking protocol include: How are hunger and eating related or connected to each other? If you just finished eating, what happens to your level of hunger over time? Can you think of another situation that feels or seems like the same as this? Rubrics have been adapted from Torres' (2009) and Sweeney and Sterman's (2007) research to score the responses. For instance, there are five levels for the systems thinking rubric (from 0 to 4). Each level contains a description as well as several exemplar responses for each of the three main variables: dynamic thinking, closed-loop thinking, and transfer of models (i.e., Level 0: Incorrect or non-applicable response; Level 1: Describes static interconnections; Level 2: Describes aspects of system structures and behaviors; Level 3: Demonstrates understanding of principles guiding system behaviors (though descriptions may be limited); and Level 4: Full utilization of systems intelligence, such as a description of a system at multiple levels.

Example items from the teamwork survey (with 5-point Likert-scale responses, from never to always) are: I don't have an opinion until all of the facts are known; I know how to make other students see things my way; I give in when arguing; I find it difficult to keep team members on task; and I am a good listener. Finally, some items from the time management survey (similarly on a 5-point Likert scale, from never to always) include: I have a messy room; I complete my homework on time; I put off tasks until the last minute; I keep my desk neat; I like routine; I do my homework as soon as I get home from school; and I lose things. Prior to data analysis, some items were reverse coded so that all items would be in the same direction (i.e., higher values equal more often or more positive).

The student assessments occur at six-month intervals, including the initial and final weeks of this 18-month period, yielding four different data collection times (i.e., September 2009, March 2010, September 2010, and March 2011). This enables us to capture the current levels of the competencies and monitor their development over time. The assessments take approximately 30 minutes per competency, and are administered during non-academic periods, staggered across two days (i.e., one on one day and two on the next) to attenuate fatigue.

Traditional achievement testing occurs as part of normal NY state requirements for sixth-grade students. We plan to compare achievement (mathematics and reading) scores at the end of the 18-month period between (a) Quest to Learn students, and (b) a group of comparable students from the two middle schools we've identified as part of the New York Public School System, matched demographically. All data are being collected and analyzed within the guidelines and with the approval of the FSU and NY DOE Institutional Review Boards.

PRELIMINARY FINDINGS

School Data

Figure 4.3 shows the primary variables or objectives comprising our Q2L model. These were found to define the core goals and values of Q2L and its learning system. Each of these will be briefly described, along with a selected quote from the interviews.

Culture. The theme of culture permeated the interview data, with a majority of participants posing it as a critical aspect defining the school's success. Overall, culture represents the social-emotional environment of the school, including various relationships among adults and students, and the rituals and procedures needed to support and promote a culture of kindness, inclusivity, and appreciation of diversity. Additionally, a school-wide focus of

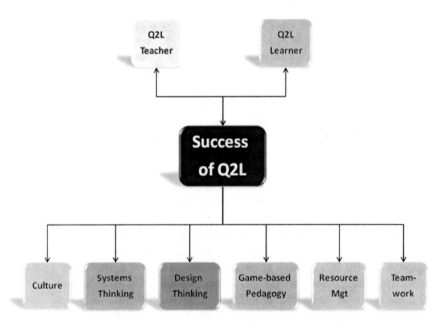

Figure 4.3 Overview of the primary Q2L goals.

systems thinking and design thinking are core thrusts that define a culture of innovation at Q2L. "*This attention to the cultivation of a community and culture is the number 1 thing right now—in order to be able to do all the other stuff. Because if you don't get that right, it actually doesn't matter all of the other stuff.*"

Systems Thinking. Generally, this competency represents a way of constructing meaning from an analysis of the whole and its parts. This involves, in part, the integration of new types of thinking, including dynamic thinking, closed-loop thinking, and the ability to transfer one model to another situation or phenomenon. Integration is achieved via specially-crafted missions and quests, specialist language used, opportunities for application across learning places, and effective assessment. "*If students can see how everything comes together, then there's nothing they can't understand. Many people get caught up in thinking in a very small scale, but everything is connected, so once you understand that nothing is by itself, then every time you learn something new, figure out where that fits in according to the system.*"

Design Thinking. This competency is supported when a person engages in opportunities to tinker (i.e., experiment and "mess around"), prototype models, play-test (to generate feedback), and redesign. Design thinking also requires opportunities to innovate around an idea or artifact after considering the historical context of that idea, possible new ways to iterate and gather feedback, and aesthetic coherence. "*Now we're designing experiences. Now we're designing environments. If we're designers, then we also iterate. If we're real designers, we look at how something happened and we can then consider it, step back, and go through a design process. How did that work? Why did that not work? How do we change it? So the whole process of teacher as designer and people who iterate on their work comes from this idea that we're worried about learning in context.*"

Game-based Pedagogy. Physical and virtual learning experiences are designed so that students step into situated and immersive spaces where there is a problem to solve. Environments are designed to be immersive contexts where students *learn to be* (historians, mathematicians) versus just *learn about* content knowledge. Learning to be requires that students employ behaviors and problem solving techniques endemic to the members of real-world knowledge domains (e.g., Gee & Shaffer, 2010). Students understand the purpose for solving problems and take specific and strategic actions to solve them. Problems are solved using both individually-driven strategies and in collaboration with others. "*It's a unique pedagogy. And within the vision, there's a responsibility on the teachers, the curriculum designers, and the game designers to take a child-centered and interest-driven approach and create something—create the mission, create the experience for the students to have that is immersive and takes their interests into account.*"

Managing Resources. At the highest level (i.e., administrative), this variable requires recognizing and strategically deploying policy-reform initiatives such as DOE waivers, managing communications, and crafting publications about Quest to Learn. At the learning level, this competency relates to the students' and teachers' abilities to synthesize and deploy the ever-increasing amounts of available information, as well as to effectively plan and meet deadlines. *"At the earlier levels of synthesis, it means being able to discern credible sources, to be able to deal in the large body of crazy amounts of information. What is correct? What is useful for me as a learner for my particular purpose? That even involves [figuring out] where to go look for things and when I go look, how do I determine whether it's credible, or useful, or good or bad? So it is about aggregating, remixing, and reformulating in a novel way."*

Teamwork. Students and staff collaborate, in various and changing configurations, to meet common goals, support and learn from each other, resolve conflicts, and solve problems. They are open to new ideas, help others, and continually reflect on their own actions and contributions to their teams. Effective communication is key to successful collaboration within teams. *"When you put different people together of different backgrounds and different qualifications and skills, then that's when you have innovation. So I think that's a model for our team, but it's also important for the school and for the students. Everybody has real different interests, and together we can make something new. And that moment when kids actually make something new and it's successful, it's like they're in heaven, really. It's just the best feeling!"*

Successful Teacher. A successful Quest to Learn teacher works closely and collaboratively with other staff and with students, experiments with games-based learning approaches to teaching and learning, is inquisitive about deep learning, has expertise in development and assessment, and is committed to educational change. With game designers and curriculum directors, Q2L teachers strive to design effective game-based and immersive learning environments. As a core strategy to developing innovative thinkers and inventors, teachers engage students in solving system and design-based problems. *"For teachers, there needs to be a huge amount of self-reflection, and really thoughtful tinkering, like coming up with a well thought out plan, testing it out, and then reflecting on how that goes. Playing around with their ideas, and then coming up with something new, and trying it out."*

Successful Learner. Successful Q2L learners develop emotional intelligence, and systemic design and reasoning skills. They learn to solve and innovate for complex 21st century problems, and to select and discern credible sources of information. They also become adept at using technological tools as research, design, and computational resources. Successful learners, *"seek out answers for questions that they're genuinely curious about, and can also understand, or at least see, and talk about the big picture, like why they're learning the things that they're learning, not just because it's what's next on the schedule. A successful learner enters the topic from their own point of interest... and is also curious enough to grab on to those connections, or maybe make up some of those connections, is persistent... and willing to work through challenges."*

We now turn our attention from the school level variables toward student level assessment.

Student Data

Assessments of the three competencies (systems thinking, teamwork, and time management) are scored upon completion. This includes a numeric value on the general competency (e.g., teamwork), as well as scores on sub-skills (e.g., teamwork consists of three sub-skills: cooperating, negotiating, and influencing others). If students are interested, they may view their scores and sub-scores. There is no evaluative feedback associated with any score. Because this is not an experimental study, and there are no explicit interventions (apart from the school itself), students may be informed that, like in games, they should try to score higher the next time around. Teachers, in turn, may use the assessment information to guide their teaching. For instance, if the teachers see that many of their students scored low on "cooperation," then he/she could create situations to facilitate teamwork and cooperation. Related research outside the scope of this project may observe teachers in the classroom to see what they do in response to obtaining scores from assessments (e.g., change lesson plans to bolster students' shortcomings, carry on as planned, etc.). Perhaps the ones who are more adaptive are also the more effective teachers.

Systems Thinking

Internal Reliability. The first question we examined was whether our 12-item, systems thinking assessment was a reliable tool, particularly since it (a) used a constructed response format, and (b) was administered with a paper-and-pencil format for administration one (September 2009) and an online format for administration two (March 2010). All subsequent administrations will be online. To determine the reliabilities of the two assessments (at different times and in different formats), we computed Cronbach's alpha for each administration: (a) for ST (time 1), $\alpha = .85$, and (b) for ST (time 2) $\alpha = .86$. Thus both ST assessments are similarly reliable.

Inter-rater Reliability. Given our use of two separate teams of scorers (i.e., two people in New York City, and two people at Florida State University), we needed to determine inter-rater reliability regarding the scores on the ST assessment. For administration 1, Kendall's $\tau = .83$ (and Spearman's $\rho = .87$). For administration 2, Kendall's $\tau = .86$ (and Spearman's $\rho = .96$). Scoring in the first administration was accomplished by the two teams independently scoring all $N = 72$ students' constructed responses using our 5-point (levels 0–4) rubric. Both teams (a) recorded their scores in an Excel spreadsheet, then (b) exchanged spreadsheets, and (c) highlighted scores that differed by > 2 points. The highlighted scores were then discussed and re-scored; in some cases converging on the same number, and in other cases changing to scores that differed by only one point. In the first administration of the ST assessment, this exchange-discuss-revise process required two full iterations until no scores were > 1 point different. By the time of the second administration, and using the same teams, only one iteration was required, with only a few discrepant scores requiring discussion.

Mean ST Differences from Time One to Time Two. Recall that we are interested in analyzing changes that may occur in terms of students' competencies over time at Q2L. We currently have data from two administrations, spaced six months apart. For the 12 questions in the ST assessment, we computed a single mean score for each person. The rubrics ranged from 0–4, where higher is better. For the first (September 2009) administration, $M = 0.78$; $SD = 0.50$; $N = 60$ (excluding cases with missing data). In March, $M = 1.02$; $SD = 0.58$; $N = 60$. Students showed significantly greater ST skills on the second, compared to the first, administration, $t_{59} = 3.31$; $p < .01$, suggesting growth of this competency, overall.

Teamwork

Internal Reliability. Similar to the ST assessment, our teamwork (TW) assessment was administered at time one in a paper-and-pencil format, and at time two online. This assessment contained 57 items for the first administration, then 22 items on the second. We computed Cronbach's alpha for each administration: (a) for TW (time one), $\alpha = .89$, and (b) for TW (time two) $\alpha = .83$. Thus both TW assessments are similarly reliable, which was encouraging because the shorter assessment (with 35 of the original 57 items removed) was found to be very reliable. (Note that the items were scored automatically; thus there was no need to compute an inter-rater reliability score.)

Construct Validity. The literature that we reviewed on this construct and for this age group (teenagers) indicated three distinct factors: (1) cooperating, (2) negotiating, and (3) influencing others (the latter also called "leadership" in the literature) (see Zhaung et al., 2008). We began by reverse coding three items (which had been phrased in an opposite manner from the construct—such as item 25, "I don't like working with others"), so all would be on the same scale. Next, we computed exploratory factor analyses (EFAs) using principal factor analysis with promax rotation for the student self-report scale. Table 4.1 shows our three-factor solution which cleanly matches the results described in the Zhaung et al. study. The item numbers are from the first administration, but the same set of 22 items were used in the second administration (and will be used in the third and fourth administrations as well).

Mean TW Differences from Time One to Time Two. For the items on the first TW assessment that matched the same 22 items on the second, we com-

TABLE 4.1 Factor Loadings of the Student Self-Report Teamwork Scale

	Factor		
	1	2	3
56. I am inspired by others' ideas and thoughts.	.82	.14	.19
55. I think that trading ideas among students leads to the best solutions.	.68	.19	.01
33. Feedback is important to me.	.61	.21	.37
23. I enjoy helping team members.	.60	−.02	.28
12. I am flexible when doing group projects.	.53	.16	.38
50. I know when to step in when an argument starts getting out of control.	.52	.07	.21
54. I learn from other students.	.49	−.04	.09
40. I find it easy to approach others.	.47	.18	.17
51. I'm influenced by other students' opinions.	.45	.04	.08
47. I believe that I'm a good leader.	.39	.79	.21
20. I like to be in charge of group projects.	.12	.79	.17
48. I can convince my peers about anything.	.03	.76	.31
49. I can fight for a cause that I believe in.	.23	.70	.25
5. I know how to make other students see things my way.	.03	.57	.14
35. During group assignments, I make demands on other students.	−.34	.39	−.12
39. I suggest different solutions to problems.	.24	.31	.62
27. I can make deals in any situation.	.14	.28	.61
42. I enjoy bringing team members together.	.46	.25	.58
34. I like to solve problems using different tactics.	.25	.18	.55
4. I don't have an opinion until all of the facts are known.	−.12	.04	.48
18. I like being responsible for projects.	.19	.10	.40
25. I like working with others.	.13	−.09	.36

Extraction Method: Principal Axis Factoring.
Rotation Method: Promax with Kaiser Normalization.
■ Cooperating ▨ Influencing Others ▨ Negotiating

puted a single mean score for each person. The scale ranged from "never" to "always," coded from 1 to 5, so higher was better, with 3 as the middle/ neutral value. For the first (September 2009) administration, $M = 3.39$ (a little above the mid-point of TW); $SD = 0.56$; $N = 47$ (excluding cases with missing data). In March, $M = 3.36$; $SD = 0.48$; $N = 47$, and, $t_{46} = 0.41$ (not significant). Thus students showed no overall difference in relation to their TW skills from the first to second administrations.

Time Management

Internal Reliability. Similar to the ST and TW assessments, our time management (TM) assessment was administered at time one in a paper-and-pencil format, and at time two online. This assessment contained 36

Likert-scale items for the first administration, and 24 items on the second. We computed Cronbach's alpha for each administration: (a) for TM (time one), $\alpha = .82$, and (b) for TM (time two) $\alpha = .82$. Thus both TM assessments are similarly reliable.

Construct Validity. The literature that we reviewed for this construct and age group (middle-school students) indicated two distinct factors comprising time management: (1) planning, and (2) meeting deadlines (see Liu et al., 2009, based on $N = 814$ students). We began by reverse coding several items so all items would be on the same scale. Next, we computed exploratory factor analyses (EFAs) using principal factor analysis with promax rotation for the student self-report scale. Table 4.2 shows our two-factor solution, which aligns with the structure described in the Liu et al. study.

TABLE 4.2 Factor Loadings of the Student Self-Report Time Management Scale

Item	F1	F2
12. Each day, I spend a few minutes planning what I am going to do tomorrow.	.69	.56
15. I like to make lists of things to do.	.69	.30
21. I have already planned all the things I am going to do tomorrow.	.66	.59
13. I mark dates that are important to me on a calendar.	.64	.17
22. I am early for practice (sports, music) or anything I might do after school.	.56	.22
7. I like to make schedules.	.55	.40
5. I like routine.	.49	.31
17. I keep my locker neat.	.47	.06
24. I know what I want to do next weekend.	.42	.28
8. I write tasks down so I won't forget to do them.	.41	.16
10. I use computers or cell phones to remind me of deadlines.	.37	.08
11. I know what is in my backpack.	.29	.19
18. I'm rarely late for breakfast.	.28	.11
4. I keep my desk neat.	.26	.03
9. When I am going somewhere, I am never late.	.16	.64
23. I am one of the first people to get to class.	.36	.63
6. I am never (or rarely) late for class.	–.05	.61
19. I finish tests with plenty of time to go over my answers.	.37	.60
2. I never put off tasks until the last minute.	.11	.55
20. I plan events ahead of time with my friends.	.41	.49
1. I complete my homework on time.	.36	.47
3. When I have to be somewhere, I arrive on time.	.44	.44
14. People never complain that I am late.	.03	.43
16. My teachers are glad that I'm never late for class.	.22	.29

▪ Making plans ▫ Meeting deadlines

The same 24 items will be used in the third and fourth administrations as well as this assessment.

Mean TM Differences from Time One to Time Two. For the items on the first TM assessment that matched the same 24 items on the second, we computed a single mean score for each person. The scale ranged from "never" to "always," coded from 1 to 5, so higher was better, like with TW. For the first (September 2009) administration, $M = 2.77$ (a little below the mid-point); $SD = 0.57$; $N = 54$ (excluding cases with missing data). In March, $M = 3.19$; $SD = 0.71$; $N = 54$. Students showed significant improvements on their time management skills after six months at Q2L ($t_{53} = 5.74$; $p < .01$.

This two-factor solution is not quite as clean as the results from the teamwork factor analysis. That is, two of the items load almost equally on the two factors (i.e., items 20 and one), and item three loads equally. While these data are preliminary and not definitive, we will likely remove item three from subsequent administrations of this survey.

DISCUSSION

Like games, which instantiate learning contexts, the goal of the Q2L learning model is to design rich learning environments and experiences that mirror discourse communities. In this way, the unit of analysis is not the individual alone (as is characteristic of schools and approaches to student assessment), but learner-in-context, considering not only her development, but the degrees to which the context (e.g., physical or virtual spaces, teachers, tasks, peers, tools) afford and mediate intended learning outcomes. The methodological problem we are tackling in this ongoing research concerns the best way to effectively conjoin the wealth of quantitative and qualitative data from this innovative new school (Q2L) to yield a clear, accurate, valid, and timely depiction of (a) the school's important goals/values, and (b) its support of students' acquisition of new competencies, in-situ. We have chosen to use evidence-centered design as our approach to modeling the school and assessing student competencies.

Again, our claim is that ECD is a very useful tool for capturing individual student data, and it allows us to correlate that data against qualitative data to understand students in context. Early results are encouraging. In relation to the school-level model (and its associated sub-models), within a couple of months we succeeded in inducing six main "themes" from the corpus of interview data. Interestingly, those same themes have remained in place across various exchanges with the participants (see Figure 4.3). Minor tweaking is ongoing with regard to the lowest-level "indicators" (i.e., the measurable variables). In terms of the student-level development of new competencies, we have seen some demonstrable student gains in just six months on two out of our three select competencies. We have also ascertained that our instruments are reliable and valid, even when shortened and administered online.

We are confident that our methodological approach is sound and can continue to bring together observational data (via Q2L's complex and distributed learning context) with quantitative data to allow us to make claims as to why learning happened or did not. Furthermore, we believe that this approach (and the particular models that we've developed) can be used to assess other game-based environments, and also be employed in other studies concerned with learning in context. A major concern (and stumbling block) for projects like this is how to best account for both context and hard learning data when assessing the effectiveness of the learning environment. The core of Q2L's innovation is its insistence that context is inseparable from learning, and that accounting for context effects is critical if we are to understand not only why kids learn or not, but to increasingly understand how to enable learning. Therefore given Q2L's insistence on the design and understanding of context (which should put overall education practices on notice since it's becoming increasingly clear that deep meaning making occurs in discourse communities like games), a qualitative and quantitative endeavor is crucial for capturing (1) learning (or discourses and their development) in situ, as well as (2) measurable data of school and student-level performance. Our ECD-based research and analysis program, integrating qualitative data (outside the scope of this chapter) with quantitative data is intended to give us insight into both situ learning and individual student learning.

In closing, we reiterate that this chapter represents our initial research efforts using ECD as our methodological approach to assessing Q2L. The processes that we've undertaken, as well as the data collected and analyzed to date, suggest that the approach is very fruitful for our purposes. It's important to note, however, that even when our 18-month project concludes, because it is "exploratory," there will remain a lot of important questions concerning the school and the individuals therein. The good news is that we have set up the infrastructure (e.g., competency, objective, evidence models) that can begin to answer these questions systematically and accurately about what works, what does not, and why, in ongoing, longitudinal studies spanning multiple years.

AUTHOR NOTES

We'd like to offer special thanks to Connie Yowell and the John D. and Catherine T. MacArthur foundation for funding this research, and Katie Salen who generously helped make this research happen and also spent quality time being interviewed herself. We are indebted to Loretta Wolozin for her awesome classroom observations and careful ST scoring, and to Oktay Donmez, Umit Tokac, and Lilian Torres for their marathon scoring efforts. We thank Jim Gee for his intellectual support, and Rim Razzouk and Marilyn McGhee for helping flesh out the culture model. Finally, we would like to thank all of the teachers, designers, and students at Q2L for welcoming us into their world, and Barbara Davis for her assistance with the interviews and induction of themes.

NOTES

1. This project began at the same time that Q2L opened in September, 2009 and will conclude March, 2011. Currently (as we are writing this chapter), we are about two thirds of the way into the 18-month research effort.
2. This protocol applies to observations of students, but also to observations of the teacher, as well as the physical characteristics of the classroom, to inform context.

APPENDIX:
QUEST TO LEARN SUCCESS MODEL (OBJECTIVES/GOALS)

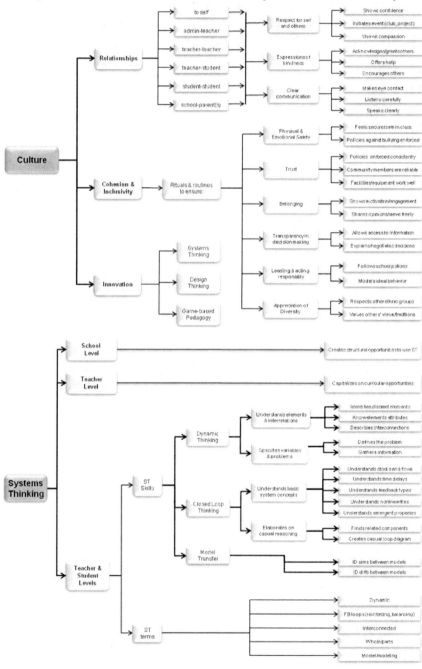

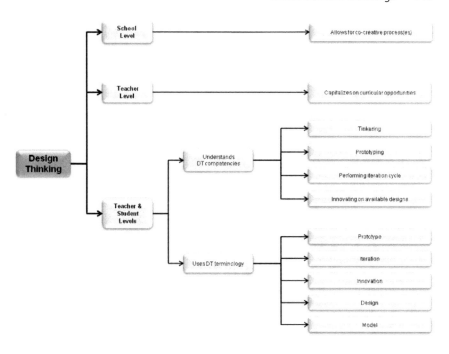

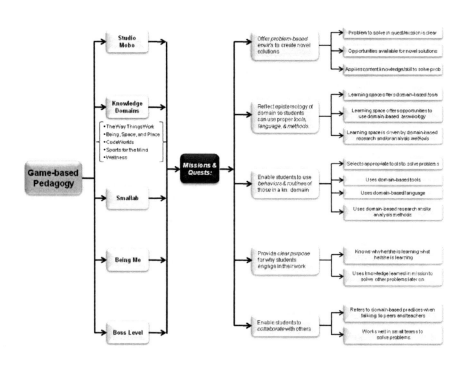

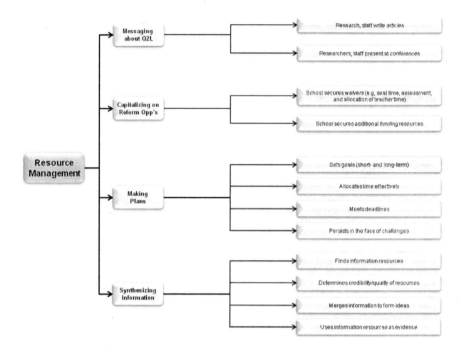

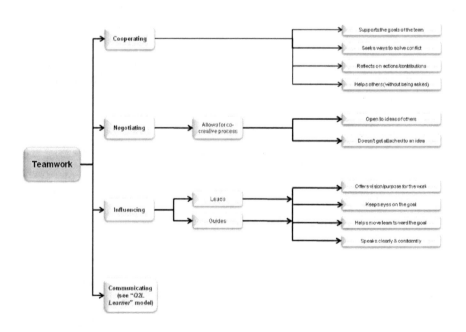

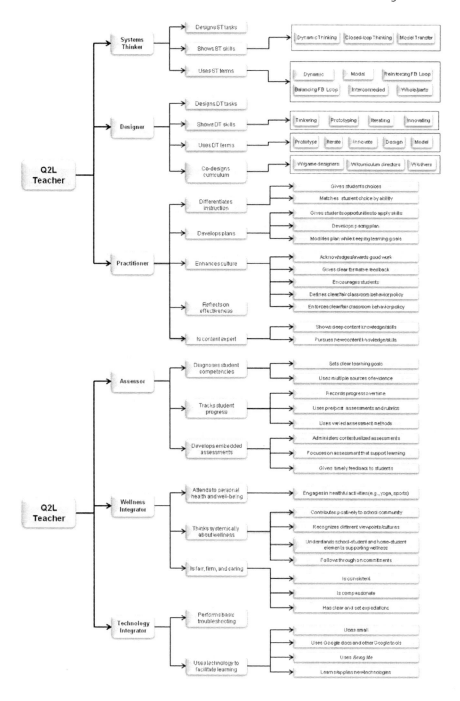

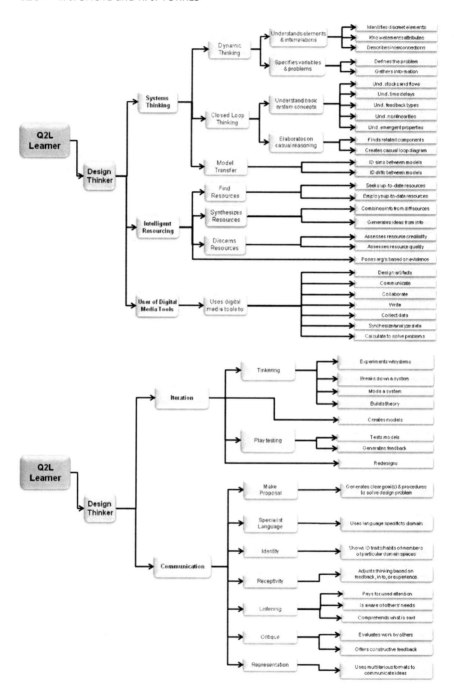

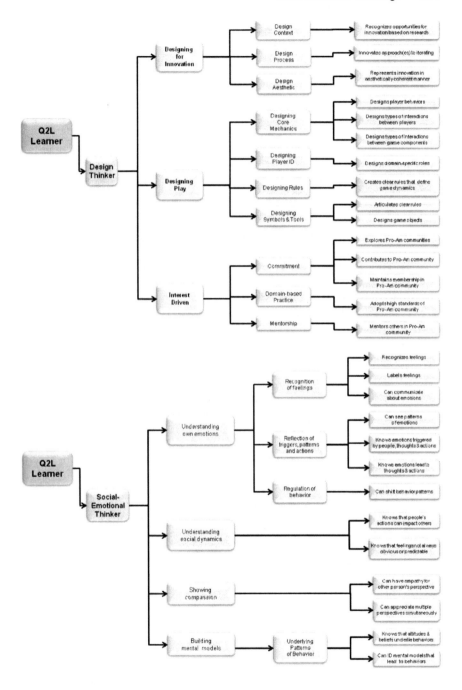

REFERENCES

Assaraf, O. B. -Z., & Orion, N. (2005). Development of system thinking skills in the context of earth system education. *Journal of Research in Science Teaching, 42*(5), 518–560.

Barak, M., & Williams, P. (2007). Learning elemental structures and dynamic processes in technological systems: A cognitive framework. *International Journal of Technology and Design Education, 17*(3), 323–340.

Behrens, J., Mislevy, R., DiCerbo, K., & Levy, R. (2011). Evidence centered design for learning and assessment in the digital world. In M. Mayrath, J. Clarke-Midura, D. H. Robinson, & G. Schraw (Eds.). *Technology-based assessments for 21st century skills: Theoretical and practical implications from modern research* (pp. 13–54). Charlotte, NC: Information Age.

Bransford, J., Brown, A., & Cocking, R. (2000). *How people learn: Brain, mind, and experience & school.* Washington, DC: National Academy Press.

Bridgeland, J., Dilulio, J., & Morrison, K. (2006, March). *The silent epidemic: Perspectives of high school dropouts.* A report by Civic Enterprises in association with Peter D. Hart Research Associates for the Bill & Melinda Gates Foundation. Retrieved May 10, 2010, from http://www.civicenterprises.net/pdfs/thesilen-tepidemic3-06.pdf

Bruner, J. S. (1961). The act of discovery. *Harvard Educational Review 31*(1), 21–32.

Falmagne, J. -C., Cosyn, E., Doignon, J. -P., & Thiery, N. (2003). The assessment of knowledge, in theory and in practice. In R. Missaoui & J. Schmidt (Eds.), *Lecture notes in computer science: Vol. 3874: 4th International conference on formal concept analysis* (pp. 61–79). New York: Springer-Verlag.

Forrester, J. W. (1994). System dynamics, systems thinking, and soft OR. *System Dynamics Review, 10*(2–3), 245–256.

Gee, J. P. (2003). What *video games have to teach us about learning and literacy.* New York: Palgrave/Macmillan.

Gee, J. P. (2008). Video games, learning, and "content." In C. Miller (Ed.), *Games: Purpose and potential in education* (pp. 43–54). Boston, MA: Springer.

Gee, J. P. (2010). Human action and social groups as the natural home of assessment: Thoughts on 21st century learning and assessment. In V. J. Shute & B. J. Becker (Eds.), *Innovative assessment for the 21st century: Supporting educational needs* (pp. 13–39). New York, NY: Springer-Verlag.

Gee, J. P., & Shaffer, D. W. (2010). *Looking where the light is bad: Video games and the future of assessment* (Epistemic Games Group Working Paper No. 2010-02). Madison: University of Wisconsin-Madison.

Ito, M., Horst, H., Bittanti, M., boyd, d., Herr-Stephenson, B., Lange, P. G., . . . Robinson, L. (2008). *Living and learning with new media: Summary of findings from the Digital Youth Project.* Chicago, IL: The John D. and Catherine T. MacArthur Foundation Reports on Digital Media and Learning.

Lave, J., & Wenger, E. (1991). *Situated learning: Legitimate peripheral participation.* Cambridge: Cambridge University Press.

Ito, M., Baumer, S., Bittanti, M., boyd, d., Cody, R., Herr-Stephenson, B., . . . Yardi, S. (2010). *Hanging out, messing around and geeking out: Kids living and learning with new media.* Cambridge, MA: MIT Press.

Liu, O. L., Rijmen, F., MacCann, C., & Roberts, R. D. (2009). Measuring time management abilities for middle school students. *Personality and Individual Differences, 47*, 174–179.

Macan, T. H., Shahani, C., Dipboye, R. L., & Phillips, A. P. (1990). College students' time management: Correlations with academic performance and stress. *Journal of Educational Psychology, 82*, 760–768.

MacCann, C., Duckworth, A. L., & Roberts, R. D. (2009) Empirical identification of the major facets of conscientiousness. *Learning and Individual Differences, 19*, 451–458.

Mislevy, R. J., Steinberg, L. S., & Almond, R. G. (2003). On the structure of educational assessments. *Measurement: Interdisciplinary Research and Perspectives, 1*(1), 3–62.

National Educational Technology Plan. (March, 2010). Retrieved May 9, 2010, from http://www.ed.gov/technology/netp-2010.

Ossimitz, G. (2000). *The development of systems thinking skills using system dynamics modeling tools.* Retrieved May 10, 2010, from http://wwwu.uni-klu.ac.at/gossimit/sdyn/gdm_eng.htm.

Palfrey, J., & Gasser, U. (2008). *Born digital: Understanding the first generation of digital natives.* New York: Basic Books.

Quinn, C. (2005). *Engaging learning: Designing e-learning simulation games.* San Francisco: Pfeiffer.

Richmond, B. (1993). Systems thinking: Critical thinking skills for the 1990s and beyond. *System Dynamics Review, 9*(2), 113–133.

Roberts, R. D., Schulze, R., & Minsky, J. (April, 2006). *The relation of time management dimensions to scholastic outcomes.* Presentation at 2006 Annual Meeting of the American Educational Research Association, San Francisco, CA.

Rysavy, D. M., & Sales, G. C. (1991). Cooperative learning in computer-based instruction. *Educational Technology Research & Development, 39*(2), 70–79.

Salen, K., Torres, R. J., Ruff-Tepper, R., Shapiro, A., & Wolozin, L., (in press). *A Quest to Learn planning document: Growing the school for digital kids.* MacArthur Foundation White Paper, Cambridge, MA: MIT Press.

Salisbury, D. F. (1996). *Five technologies for educational change: systems thinking, systems design, quality science, change management.* Englewood Cliffs, NJ: Educational Technology Publications.

Shute, V. J. (2008). Focus on formative feedback. *Review of Educational Research, 78*(1), 153–189.

Shute, V. J., Hansen, E. G., & Almond, R. G. (2008). You can't fatten a hog by weighing it—Or can you? Evaluating an assessment for learning system called ACED. *International Journal of Artificial Intelligence and Education, 18*(4), 289–316.

Shute, V. J., Rieber, L., & Van Eck, R. (in press). Games…and…Learning. To appear in R. Reiser & J. Dempsey (Eds.), *Trends and issues in instructional design and technology*, 3rd ed.). Upper Saddle River, NJ: Pearson Education, Inc.

Shute, V. J., Masduki, I., Donmez, O., Kim, Y. J., Dennen, V. P., Jeong, A. C., & Wang, C., -Y. (2010). Modeling 21st century knowledge and skills in game environments. In D. Ifenthaler, P. Pirnay-Dummer, & N. M. Seel (Eds.), *Computer-based diagnostics and systematic analysis of knowledge* (pp. 281–309). New York, NY: Springer-Verlag.

Shute, V. J. & Zapata-Rivera D. (2008). *Evidence-centered evaluation.* Unpublished document. Florida State University.

Sweeney, L. B., & Sterman, J. D. (2000). Bathtub dynamics: Initial results of a systems thinking inventory. *Systems Dynamics Review, 16*(4), 249–286.

Sweeney, L. B., & Sterman, J. D. (2007). Thinking about systems: Student and teacher conceptions of natural and social systems. *System Dynamics Review, 23*(2/3), 285–312.

Thai, A., Lowenstein, D., Ching, D., & Rejeski, D. (2009). *Game changer: Investing in digital play to advance children's learning and health.* New York, NY: The Joan Ganz Cooney Center at Sesame Workshop.

Tindale, R. S., Stawiski, S., & Jacobs, E. (2008). Shared cognition and group learning. In V. I. Sessa & M. London (Eds.), *Work group learning: Understanding, improving and assessing how groups learn in organizations* (pp. 73–90). New York: Lawrence Erlbaum Associates.

Torres, R. J. (2009, April). *Learning on a 21st century platform: Gamestar Mechanic as a means to game design and systems-thinking skills within a nodal ecology.* New York University: ProQuest Dissertations.

Torres, R. J., Rufo-Tepper, R., & Shapiro, A. (in press). Quest to Learn: A public school for today's digital kids. To appear in H. Gautchi & M. Manafy (Eds.), *How digital natives are transforming the way business is done today.* Medford, NJ: Cyberage Books.

Totten, S., Sills, T., Digby, A., & Russ, P. (1991). *Cooperative learning: A guide to research.* New York: Garland.

Van den Bossche, P., Segers, M., & Kirschner, P. A. (2006). Social and cognitive factors driving teamwork in collaborative learning environments. *Small Groups Research, 37,* 490–521.

Vygotsky, L. S. (1978). *Mind in society: The development of higher psychological processes.* Cambridge, MA: Harvard University Press. (Original work published in Russian in 1930)

Vygotsky, L. S. (1987). *The collected works of L. S. Vygotsky.* New York: Plenum.

Wang, L., MacCann, C., Zhuang, X., Liu, O. L., & Roberts, R. D. (2009). Assessing teamwork skills: A multi-method approach. *Canadian Journal of School Psychology, 24,* 108–124.

Watkins, S. C. (2009). *The young and the digital: What the migration to social-network sites, games, and anytime, anywhere media means for our future.* Boston: Beacon Press.

Zhuang, X., MacCann, C., Wang, L., Liu, O. L., & Roberts, R. D. (2008). *Development and validity evidence supporting a teamwork and collaboration assessment for high school students.* ETS Research Report, RR-08-50, Princeton, NJ.

CHAPTER 5

THINKING OUTSIDE THE BUBBLE

Virtual Performance Assessments for Measuring Complex Learning

**Jody Clarke-Midura, Jillianne Code,
Chris Dede, Michael Mayrath**
Harvard University

Nick Zap
Simon Fraser University

*I'm calling on our nation's governors and state education chiefs to develop
standards and assessments that don't simply measure whether students can fill
in a bubble on a test, but whether they possess 21st century skills like problem-solving
and critical thinking and entrepreneurship and creativity.*

—President Obama
Remarks to Hispanic Chamber of Commerce, March 10, 2009

Current assessment approaches are inadequate for determining how well
our students are developing sophisticated inquiry skills in science—a key
21st century capability for science, technology, engineering, and mathematics (STEM) careers. Research has documented that sophisticated,

Technology-Based Assessments for 21st Century Skills, pages 125–147
Copyright © 2012 by Information Age Publishing
125

higher-order thinking skills related to complex cognition, inquiry process-es, formulating scientific explanations, communicating scientific under-standing, and approaching novel situations, are difficult to measure with multiple choice or even with constructed-response paper-and-pencil items (National Research Council (NRC), 2006; Quellmalz & Haertel, 2004; Resnick & Resnick, 1992). These items also demonstrate limited sensitivity to discrepancies between inquiry and non-inquiry based science instruc-tion (Haertel, Lash, Javitz, & Quellmalz, 2006; Quellmalz, Kreikemeier, DeBarger, & Haertel, 2007). For example, Quellmalz et al. (2007) report that, on paper-and-pencil tests such as the National Assessment of Educa-tional Progress (NAEP), the Third International Math and Science Study (TIMSS), and New Standards Science Reference Exams (NSSRE), inquiry is not measured effectively. While some of these tests involve formats other than paper-and-pencil, the investigators note that, "even the hands-on per-formance tasks in these large-scale science tests are highly structured and relatively short (15–40 minutes), truncating the investigation strategies that can be measured" (Quellmalz et al., 2007, p. 1). Thus, despite the increas-ing focus of worldwide science standards on inquiry, current assessments continue to demonstrate misalignment and validity issues in the measure-ment of this domain.

Failure to adequately assess student inquiry skills and to diagnose indi-vidual issues around inquiry learning has led to a decline of the average American student's science achievement scores on an international scale (NRC, 2007; Songer, Kelcey, & Gotwals, 2009). For example, in the U.S., the 2009 National Assessment of Education Progress results reveal that a major-ity of the students who took the test received scores below proficient (U.S. Department of Education, 2011). On the 2006 Program for International Student Assessment (PISA), American fifteen year olds' average science lit-eracy score was significantly below the international average and placed U.S. students in the bottom third of participating nations (Organization for Economic Co-operation and Development (OECD), 2007). The PISA specifically focuses on higher-order cognitive skills required for science in-quiry, such as the use of scientific knowledge to identify questions, acquire new knowledge, explain new phenomena, and draw evidence-based conclu-sions (OECD, 2007). American students also performed the lowest in areas around problem solving aspects of inquiry (OECD, 2007). This is alarming because key reports on economic development in the context of globaliza-tion identify inquiry and complex reasoning as critical skills for competing in our knowledge-based economy (NRC, 2006; President's Council of Advi-sors on Science and Technology (PCAST), 2010). In order to address these deficiencies, we need comprehensive assessment systems that link cognitive models of inquiry learning to both content standards and assessments. Such a comprehensive system should take into account advances in research on cognition (how students learn inquiry), advances in measurement models, and advances in technology. The purpose of this chapter is to illustrate how advances in technology are creating opportunities for designing assessments of 21st century skills. The technology we focus on is immersive virtual environments (IVEs).

IVEs enable the creation and measurement of authentic, situated performances characteristic of how students learn inquiry (NRC, 2005). IVEs are three-dimensional (3D) environments, either single or multi-user, where digitized participants engage in virtual activities and experiences. Each participant takes on the identity of an avatar, a virtual persona that can move around the 3D environment. These immersive "worlds" enable students to engage in inquiry practices in a context that is more reflective of how a scientist does inquiry. Research has documented the effective, practical use of this interactive medium for offering students opportunities to engage in authentic inquiry practices (Clarke & Dede, 2009), suggesting that IVEs offer a promising opportunity for assessment.

In this chapter, we present a case study of the Virtual Performance Assessment (VPA) Project. The VPA project exemplifies the potential of VPAs as a dynamic model for student assessment using IVEs to assess science inquiry processes of middle school students for summative assessment and accountability purposes. In the following sections, we first set the context by discussing the importance of reliable and valid assessments of science inquiry content and skills. We then provide a historical perspective that examines both the promise and challenge of multiple-choice and performance-based assessments for measuring inquiry. Then we discuss the Virtual Performance Assessment Project that illustrates how IVEs have the potential to overcome current assessment challenges.

THE IMPORTANCE OF 21ST CENTURY
SCIENCE CONTENT AND SKILLS

Numerous reports on U.S. competitiveness in the emerging global economy emphasize sophisticated thinking skills and knowledge of science and technical content. The application of information technology to the very core of business operations has caused a profound change in the needed skills and talents of workers (OECD, 2007; PCAST, 2010; U.S. Department of Education (USDE), 2010). Markets in today's knowledge-driven economy are rewarding those who have both high educational achievement and technical skill (Task Force on the Future of American Innovation, 2005; PCAST, 2010). Tomorrow's workers must be prepared to shift jobs and careers more frequently, be flexible and adaptable in acquiring job skills, and synthesize a dynamic mix of job-derived and education-based knowledge on business processes and problems (Friedman, 2005; PCAST, 2010). Linking economic development, educational evolution, workforce development, and strengthened social services is essential to meeting this challenge (National Academy of Science, 2006; PCAST, 2010). The worker of the 21st century must have science and mathematics skills, creativity, fluency in information and communication technologies, and the ability to solve complex problems (Business-Higher Education Forum, 2005; PCAST, 2010). A consistent theme in recent reports and frameworks on education in America is that science, technology, engineering and mathematics (STEM) drives innovation, and students must attain more advanced educational outcomes in science. Thus, the future personal economic security and well-being of American workers is tied to STEM educational achievement and 21st century skills (Federal Reserve Bank of Dallas, 2004; PCAST, 2010).

The vision of the knowledge, skills, and abilities required in science education is expanding as global economic competition increases and becomes a fundamental challenge facing the U.S. over the next decade (USDE, 2010). As a result, the National Education Technology Plan (NETP) (USDE, 2010) calls for immediate action to ensure that today's American students are learning 21st century skills that will foster both innovation and economic prosperity. One recommendation in the Plan focuses specifically on developing sophisticated forms of technology-based assessment: "*2.3 Conduct research and development that explores how embedded assessment technologies, such as simulations, collaboration environments, virtual worlds, games, and cognitive tutors, can be used to engage and motivate learners while assessing complex skills*" (USDE, 2010). Congress is now considering various forms of legislation and funding to strengthen science education and assessment.

During the summer of 2010, the National Research Council released a public draft of their conceptual framework for new science education standards, *A Framework for Science Education* (NRC, 2010). A primary emphasis in this new framework is that learning about science and engineering involves the integration of both knowledge of scientific explanations (i.e., content knowledge) and the practices needed to engage in scientific inquiry and engineering design. Other national and international science frameworks such as the *Science Framework for the 2011 National Assessment of Educational Progress* (National Assessment Governing Board, 2010), *College Board Standards for College Success* (College Board, 2009), and the *Programme for International Student Assessment* (OECD, 2007), all place emphasis on science practices and performances, thus placing scientific inquiry as a major standard in most policy doctrines (American Association for the Advancement of Science (AAAS), 1990; American Association for the Advancement of Science (AAAS), 1993; NRC, 1996). Coherent assessment systems that are capable of measuring student attainments from this type of learning experience that are both reliable and valid—and that are practical at scale in classroom settings—are a vital aspect of improvement in science education. Current standardized assessments have not been able to accomplish this goal despite decades of refinements. These issues are not limited to America, as all nations now must strive to prepare their next generations for a technology-based and globalized workplace.

HISTORICAL PERSPECTIVE ON THE VALUE AND CHALLENGES OF PERFORMANCE ASSESSMENTS

Despite the focus of worldwide science standards on inquiry, multiple-choice assessments continue to dominate assessment practice in this domain despite misalignment and validity issues. As mentioned previously, numerous studies have shown that higher order thinking skills related to sophisticated cognition (e.g., inquiry processes, formulating scientific explanations, communicating scientific understanding, approaches to novel situations) are difficult to measure with multiple choice or even with constructed-response paper-and-pencil items (NRC, 2006; Quellmalz & Haertel, 2004; Resnick & Resnick, 1992). Alignment studies of national assessments have shown that inquiry is not measured effectively (Haertel et al., 2006). Thus, the research community has looked for better measures of inquiry, such as "hands-on" performance assessments.

Research on alternatives to multiple-choice tests for measuring inquiry has a history. In the decade preceding the passing of No Child Left Behind Act of 2002 (NCLB; Public Law 110-107), there was a movement that advocated for alternative performance measures that provided a more direct measure than multiple choice tests of students' conceptual understanding and higher-level skills like problem solving (Linn, 1994). Studies, primarily based on hands-on performance assessments, were conducted to assess the reliability and construct validity of these alternate assessments. These studies focused on the feasibility (i.e., cost effectiveness and practicality) of using these types of measures on a large scale (Linn, 2000). Research findings indicated that these alternate assessments were more transparent to the content being measured and valuable for providing formative, diagnostic feedback to teachers about ongoing student attainment (Frederiksen & Collins, 1989). However, there were several limitations to their use as summative assessments for accountability. Research on hands-on performance assessments in accountability settings found that they:

- are cost-prohibitive when compared to multiple choice tests (Stecher & Klein, 1997);
- contain task sampling variability (Shavelson, Baxter, & Gao, 1993);

- contain occasion-sampling variability (Cronbach, Linn, Brennan, & Haertel, 1997); and
- have limited validity (Linn, Baker, & Dunbar, 1991).

Hands-on performance assessments suffered technical, resource, and reliability problems that undercut both their validity and their practicality (Shavelson, Baxtor, & Gao, 1993; Cronbach et al., 1997; Shavelson, Ruiz-Primo, & Wiley, 1999; Webb, Schlackman, & Sugrue, 2000; Haertel et al., 2006). Research conducted by Shavelson and his colleagues on computer-based tasks had similar findings when it came to looking at the reliability and validity of the measures (Baxter, 1995; Baxter & Shavelson, 1994; Pine, Baxter, Shavelson, 1993; Shavelson, Baxter, Pine, 1991; Rosenquist, Shavelson, & Ruiz-Primo, 2000). One interesting result of these studies was that the hands-on and computer-based investigations were not tapping the same knowledge (Shavelson, Baxter, Pine, 1991). At the time, recommendations were to create multiple measures that could be triangulated. This recommendation is still applicable today.

CURRENT ATTEMPTS TO EXPAND ASSESSMENTS

In order to meet the requirements of NCLB, it is recommended that states develop a variety of assessment strategies (including performance assessments) that collectively fulfill said requirements (NRC, 2006). Following these recommendations, NAEP published their framework for establishing a new science assessment in 2009 (National Assessment Governing Board, 2010) that calls for multiple modes of assessment, including interactive computer assessments. The report cites four reasons for re-thinking the assessment framework: 1) publication of national standards for science literacy since the previous framework, 2) advances in both science and cognitive research, 3) growth in national and international science assessments, and 4) increases in innovative assessment approaches. We add a fifth reason: development in education technology research. Unlike in the 1990s, technology now has the capability to provide rich learning experiences, if designed correctly. Further, in addition to research on the pedagogical affordances of technology-based learning environments (NRC, 2001; NRC, 2000; Dede, 2009), research on video games has grown from the study of arcade games (Loftus & Loftus, 1983) to numerous books (e.g., Gee, 2003), journals (e.g., Gamestudies, http://gamestudies.org/1101), academic programs (Gamasutra, 2010), and even a school "that uses the underlying design principles of games to create academically challenging, immersive, game-like learning experiences for students" (Quest to Learn, 2010). Advances in the technology and videogame industries have made technology more accessible, reliable, and cost effective for schools.

EXISTING RESEARCH ON VIRTUAL ENVIRONMENTS FOR LEARNING SCIENTIFIC INQUIRY

Sophisticated educational media, such as single-user and multi-user virtual environments, extend the nature of the performance challenges presented and the knowledge and cognitive processes assessed. These simulated contexts provide rich environments in which participants interact with digital objects and tools, such as historical photographs or virtual microscopes. Moreover, this interface facilitates novel forms of communication between students and computer-based agents, using media such as text chat and virtual gestures (Clarke, Dede, & Dieterle, 2008). This type of "mediated immersion" (pervasive experiences within a digitally enhanced context) enables instructional designers to create curricula that are intermediate in complexity between the real world and structured exercises in K–12 classrooms. These new technologies allow instructional designers to construct both individual and shared simulated experiences otherwise impossible in school settings (Dede, 2009).

In September 2009, the NRC held a workshop on games and simulations in science education; the full report will be published in spring, 2011. The white papers from this research conference urge further studies to determine the full potential of collaborative, immersive simulations to support assessment (Quellmalz & Pellegrino, 2009), as well as virtual worlds that interweave assessment with engagement and learning (Clark, Nelson, Sengupta, & D'Angelo, 2009). Rigorous, empirically based research studies are needed to explore this potential.

RESEARCH ON MULTI-USER VIRTUAL ENVIRONMENTS

For almost a decade, our research team has studied the feasibility and practicality of using Immersive Virtual Environments to increase student achievement in scientific inquiry (Clarke, Dede, Ketelhut, & Nelson, 2006; Dede, 2009; Nelson, Ketelhut, Clarke, & Dede, 2005). In this research, we have studied how virtual environments enable students to do authentic inquiry and engage in the processes of science. Our first series of studies, funded by NSF from 1999 through 2009, were on *River City*. The *River City* curriculum was a multi-user immersive virtual environment designed to teach middle school science (Clarke, et al., 2006). The curriculum was centered on skills of hypothesis formation and experimental design, as well as on content related to national standards and assessments in biology and ecology. We worked with over 200 teachers and more than 20,000 students. We conducted a series of quasi-experimental design studies to determine if virtual environments can simulate real world experimentation and provide students with engaging, meaningful learning experiences that increase achievement in scientific inquiry. Using conventional paper-and-pencil, item-based measures, our results from a series of research studies showed that these virtual environments enable students to engage in authentic inquiry tasks including problem finding and experimental design, and also increase students' engagement and self-efficacy (Clarke & Dede, 2007; Clarke et al., 2006; Ketelhut, 2007; Nelson, 2007; Nelson et al., 2005). However, we found that students' performance on multiple choice pre-post-tests did not necessarily reflect learning that we saw via interviews, observations, summative essays, and analyses of log file data that capture students' activity as they interact with the environment (Clarke, 2006; Ketelhut & Dede, 2006; Ketelhut et al., 2007). To further examine this issue, we built rich case studies of student learning in which we triangulated and compared different data sources, both qualitative and quantitative in order to illustrate and understand students' inquiry learning (Clarke, 2006; Clarke & Dede, 2005, 2007; Ketelhut et al., 2007). A finding from our experience was that paper-and-pencil item-based assessments, even after extensive refinement, did not fully capture students' learning of inquiry skills.

Overall, our and others' studies of these virtual environments (Barab, Thomas, Dodge, Carteaux, & Tuzun, 2004; Neulight, Kafai, Kao, Foley, & Galas, 2007) have led us to argue that this immersive and experiential medium is a potential platform for providing both single and multi-user virtual performance assessments. The fact that this medium underlies rapidly growing entertainment applications and environments such as multi-player Internet games (e.g., *World of Warcraft, America's Army*) and "virtual places" (e.g., Second Life) ensures the continuing evolution of sophisticated capabilities and authoring systems for these immersive virtual environments. Further, our immersive virtual environments and similar interactive, immersive media enable the collection of very rich data streams about individual learners that provide better ways to assess inquiry processes (Clarke, 2009; Clarke-Midura, Mayrath, & Dede, 2010; Ketelhut et al., 2007). We believe that these streams of "active" behavioral data on student performances can be utilized in the development of virtual assessments. While research on game-like simulations for fostering student learning is starting to proliferate, studying the potential of this medium for summative assessments of student learning in a standardized fashion is still in its infancy.

AFFORDANCES OF VIRTUAL PERFORMANCE ASSESSMENTS

The findings from the 1990s about performance assessments are largely due to the intrinsic constraints of paper-based measures, coupled with the limited capabilities of virtual assessments created based on what computers and telecommunications could accomplish more than a decade ago. We believe that virtual performance assessments face fewer threats from generalizability and efficiency concerns than traditional performance assessments. By alleviating dependence issues that arise from a student incorrectly answering on a sub-component of the task (i.e., via simply putting the student on the right track after a wrong answer or a certain time limit), comparable generalizability can be demonstrated with significantly fewer tasks than traditional performance assessments. In addition, because virtual situations are more easily and uniformly replicated, virtual performance assessments may not encounter the significant error from the test occasion in traditional performance assessments (Cronbach et al., 1997).

Developing virtual assessments will be more cost-effective for schools, easier to administer and score, and can address task and occasion sampling variability through design. For example, as opposed to kits of tasks that contain items and objects, virtual performance assessments enable automated and standardized delivery via a web-based application. By making the tasks independent, we can design assessments with a larger number of tasks, thus increasing the overall reliability of the instrument.

ADVANTAGES OF VIRTUAL PERFORMANCE ASSESSMENTS

Virtual performance assessments based on immersive environments have several advantages. First, virtual assessments alleviate the need for extensive training for administering tasks. Since the entire experience is conducted online, the environment can be very controlled from beginning to end. In contrast, it is difficult to standardize the administration of paper-based performance assessments, and extensive training is required to administer the tasks. With virtual assessments, we can ensure standardization by delivering instruction automatically via the technology. A second advantage is that virtual assessments alleviate the need for providing materials and kits for hands-on tasks. Everything is inside the virtual environment. Third, performance assessments are easier to administer and require very little, if any, training of teachers. Scoring is done behind the scenes—there is no need for raters or training of raters. Fourth, virtual assessments alleviate safety issues and inequity due to lack of resources. Fifth, the digital objects, architectures, agents, and contexts produced in these assessments—and curricula—can be shared to bring down development costs. Finally, virtual assessments enable the design of assessments that involve simulations access to large data sets: GIS map visualizations, ability to compare and contrast visualizations of different data, and ability to perform computations on data. Virtual assessments will allow us to include visualization of data and information, including phenomena that can't be observed with the naked eye or even in real time. In our work in developing virtual inquiry curricula, we developed the ability to simulate the passing of time, to allow students to collect data as it changes over time, and to conduct experiments where time can be fast-forwarded. These capabilities allow for rich learning experiences and the ability to conduct experiments that may take too much time to use for learning or assessment purposes.

The potential to develop assessments that can condense time and experiments within a class period opens new doors for assessing inquiry and students' ability to conduct empirical investigations. For example, virtual assessments can allow for interactive speeds (slow, fast, rewind) and the ability to show change over time quickly, repeat steps, or vary parameters. The advances in technologies for teaching concepts like Newtonian physics could also be used to assess students' understanding of such concepts.

VIRTUAL PERFORMANCE ASSESSMENT PROJECT

With funding from the Institute of Education Sciences (IES), the Virtual Performance Assessment Project at the Harvard Graduate School of Education is developing and studying the feasibility of immersive virtual performance assessments to assess scientific inquiry of middle school students as a standardized component of an accountability program (see http://vpa.gse.harvard.edu). The goal is to provide states with reliable and valid technology-based performance assessments linked to state and NSES academic standards around science content and inquiry processes, extending capabilities to conduct rigorous randomized studies that provide empirical data on student academic achievement in middle school science.

In order to provide evidence that our assessment measures students' core concepts, we used the Evidence Centered Design framework (ECD) (Mislevy & Haertel, 2006; Mislevy & Rahman, 2009) and conducted a series of validity studies that provide evidence on construct validity. As mentioned in other chapters in this volume (i.e., Behrens et al., Chapter Two), this framework is a multi-step process meant to ensure construct validity during the design. ECD requires the designers to articulate every aspect of the assessment from the knowledge, skills, and abilities that they are measuring to the types of evidence that will allow one to make claims about what students know. ECD creates an evidentiary argument in which observable variables generate evidence that allows for inferences to be made about what a student knows (Mislevy, Steinberg, & Almond, 2003).

The first step in the ECD process is to conduct a domain analysis. We compiled research on inquiry learning, specifically focusing on cognitive models and frameworks for middle grades (sixth through eighth). From these models and frameworks, we developed knowledge, skills, and abilities (KSAs) that would provide competencies of understanding. We sent these KSAs for expert review and revised them based on feedback. Following are examples of some of the KSAs we are measuring:

- Student develops a scientific explanation of what is happening in the virtual world that includes: 1. a claim about the phenomena, 2. the evidence (either empirical or observations), 3. reasoning that links claims with evidence.
- Student modifies claims or predictions based on new data either collected or provided.
- Student gathers data that help explain or provide evidence to answer the question being asked (or claim being made).
- Student identifies causal relationships between variables that explain what is causing the problem.
- Student determines which data from a specific investigation can be used as evidence to address a scientific question or to support a prediction or an explanation, and distinguish credible data from noncredible data in terms of quality.
- Student evaluates alternate explanations by rating the strength of different claim-evidence-reasoning pairings using the data they collected or data provided.
- Student provides evidence that supports and/or refutes his or her claim in an explanation of what is happening in the virtual world.

In addition, we used the Principled Assessment Designs for Inquiry (PADI) system, an architecture for creating assessments for science inquiry based on the ECD framework (Kennedy, 2005; Mislevy & Rahman, 2009). PADI is used to create design templates that can be used to develop additional assessments of the same KSAs. The templates detail the knowledge, skills, abilities being measured and then links the KSAs to the observable variables, evidence, and student model. Through the process of articulating the exact details of what is being measured and how it is being measured, it is very easy to link the KSAs to evidence of student learning.

As a part of our implementation of the ECD framework, we have extended its application to include an examination of learning trajectories as opposed to individual test items. This was done so that ECD can be used with

VPAs to measure student performance situated within an immersive narrative (e.g., students gathering data, identifying problems, making claims, and using data as evidence). To assist us with operationalizing this process, PADI provides design architecture for creating assessment templates for science inquiry within the ECD framework.

Within each of these PADI templates, we have detailed the KSAs we are measuring and then linked these KSAs to specific observable tasks within the VPAs that represent each of the science inquiry processes (see Figure 5.1). Linking KSAs like this provides a measure of validity that research has found often lacking in performance assessments (e.g., Linn et al., 1991). Using the ECD Framework, we have determined the constructs tapped by the assessment and selected interactions, or superobservables (Mislevy et al., 2003; Almond, 2009), that were later used. Some of the superobserv-

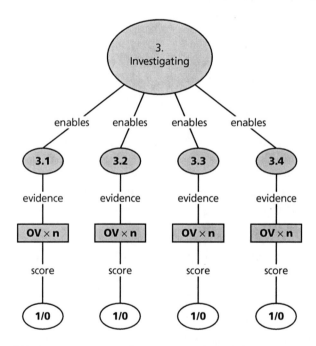

Figure 5.1 This figure represents the representation of the larger construct, Investigating and how it is broken down into KSAs (3.1: Student gathers data that help explain or provide evidence to justify the claim being made. 3.2: Student determines which data from a specific investigation can be used as evidence to address an explanation. 3.3: Student distinguishes credible data from non-credible data in terms of quality. 3.4: Student is able to gather data after the experiment that will provide the evidence needed to prove or disprove whether the causal relationship was true). OVxn: Observational variables, or superobservables (Almond, 2009; Mislevy, Steinberg, & Almond, 2003), associated with each KSA.

ables were used in every assessment so that we are able to associate them with parallel forms of the assessments. After piloting, the discrimination of interactions in each assessment were reviewed using point-biserial analysis to determine whether they required modification. Our research questions enable further validation of these VPA designs.

DESCRIPTION OF THE ASSESSMENT

Traditional assessments often focus on individual test items and rely on student affirmation as a response that indicates knowledge. In our VPAs, we base the evaluation of student performance on measurements captured as in-world interactions. These interactions allow us to assess what students know and do not know about science inquiry and problem solving. As a part of the inquiry progression embedded within the VPAs, students are required to make a series of choices as a part of an ongoing narrative. Similar to the Choose Your Own Adventure books (Chooseco, 1977–2011) where readers construct their own narrative through a series of choices, students in our VPAs experience the interactive outcomes of their choices. The focus of the VPAs is not on the attainment of a single right answer, but rather on the result of a series choices that students make. The series of interactions result in rich observations that enable us to make a fine distinction of students' understanding of the various facets of inquiry discussed earlier.

To illustrate this further, the following is a brief description of a VPA and how educators use it in the classroom.

> It is May, and students in Ms. Jones' 8th grade science class have to take their achievement tests. She logs into the VPA teacher's portal and creates accounts for her students, selecting the initial assessment she wants them to take. When class starts, the students sit at individual computers and login to begin their simulated experience.

> Arielle sits at her computer and logs into the student portal. She opens the assessment and is immediately allowed to choose what her avatar looks like (see Figure 5.2). She selects an avatar and enters the world.

The ability for students to choose their own avatar is a design decision that we hope will provide students with a sense of autonomy for the experience.

> The camera slowly provides an aerial view of the world to orient Arielle to the problem space. Arielle sees that there is a village and what appears to be farms with ponds. The camera then focuses in on a multi-colored frog with six legs. Arielle wonders, "What could be causing this frog to have six legs?" The assessment begins. A scientist and farmers who have just discovered this mutated frog greet Arielle. The farmers all offer competing hypotheses for why the frog is

Figure 5.2 An example of a VPA avatar selection screen.

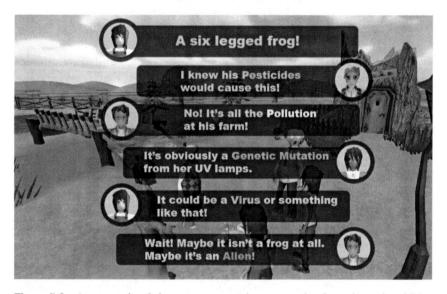

Figure 5.3 An example of characters presenting competing hypotheses in a VPA.

mutated (Figure 5.3). The scientist turns to Arielle's avatar and tells her that she must conduct an investigation and come up with her own theory and back it up with evidence. He asks her if she thinks any of the hypotheses are plausible.

Having the characters present competing hypotheses sets up the context of the assessment. This question also allows us to identify in the assess-

Figure 5.4 Setting up the problem.

ment any misconceptions or prior knowledge that students may bring to the problem. Research has shown that this is an important part of science inquiry that is often overlooked in assessments (Sadler, 1998).

> The scientist shows Arielle a science lab and tells her to come find him when she is ready. Arielle inspects the six-legged frog and puts it in her backpack to investigate in the lab. She then walks around the village and sets out to explore the farms.

At this point in the assessment, Arielle has a choice. She could have gone to the lab and accessed information there such as research articles. However, she chose to go explore. This choice is recorded on the back-end. We are recording students' choices that are then compiled into patterns. These patterns are then built and compared to profiles of students' inquiry knowledge established during our cognitive task analyses.

Because of this, the assessment has a built-in framework that enables us to examine students' intent and interpret their actions.

> Before entering the first farm, she is asked by the farmer what she is planning to do there. At the first farm, Arielle says she plans to collect a water sample. She enters the farm and collects a sample of the water. She also picks up a frog and a tadpole to take back to the lab and run some tests. She finds a research article and starts reading it. It contains information on tadpoles and viruses, so she puts it in her backpack and decides to visit another farm. At this point, Arielle has collected five pieces of data. Her backpack will only allow her to hold eight pieces of data at a time (see Figure 5.5).

Figure 5.5 An example of the VPA backpack containing a limited number of items.

Arielle must make a choice about what data she thinks is the most important or that she wants to investigate first. If students were allowed to pick up every piece of data in the world then it would be difficult to make inferences about their knowledge of what data is important evidence in the investigation. If students were asked to evaluate a piece of data every time they collected it, then the task would become boring. Thus, the design is requiring students to make a choice through actions. She can go to the lab at any times to run tests on the data (e.g., water tests, blood test, genetic test). Any piece of discarded data from the backpack will go back into the world and can be picked back up at any time (given there is space in the backpack).

> Arielle has collected eight pieces of data from two farms. She does not want to discard any data and decides to go to the lab to run some tests. She arrives at the lab and examines the water samples. Her tests show that the lab water and water from one of the farms contains pesticides. However, one of the farms has clean water. She runs genetic tests on the two frogs she collected and sees that they are the same. She notes that both of the frogs have high counts of white blood cells. She decides that she needs more evidence and goes to collect water samples from the other two ponds. At this point, Arielle has spent her time collecting data and running tests.

> At the computer on her left, Maria has been tackling the assessment differently. As soon as Maria spoke with the scientist she decided to go to the science lab. She examined the research that was available on frogs and tadpoles. She read about viruses and genetic mutations in frogs and decided to go gather data to determine which is the cause. She goes to each of the four farms and

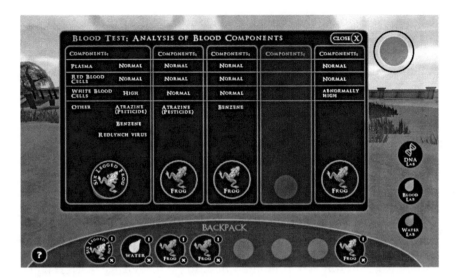

Figure 5.6   An example of a VPA lab.

collects a tadpole and a frog to run tests on. She gets back to lab and finds that all of the frogs have similar genetic make up. However, two of the tadpoles have small tails. She notes that a frog from the same farm also has a virus in its blood. She looks up the virus in the research documents and believes she has found evidence. She speaks to the scientist and builds a claim for why the frog is mutated, including evidence and then reasoning.

After class, Ms. Jones reviews the reporting tool to see the diagnoses the assessment provides about what each student knows and does not know about the various sub-skills involved in science inquiry. The tool presents data at both the individual and class level, and Ms. Jones finds that, while the majority of students are strong in providing evidence, they are weak in reasoning from evidence. However, only a few of the students took Maria's approach and went to the research first to seek information on the problem. The rest of the class spent time exploring and gathering data and then analyzing it first. Some of the students did not even use the research. Some only collected one or two pieces of data before they attempted to make a claim.

The goal of VPA is for students to make choices based on sound science inquiry skills that advance the theory that they are attempting to build. In VPAs, a student's measure of science inquiry performance is based on his or her in-world actions. Students' actions and choices are given a range of scores and weightings that contribute to an ongoing student model of science inquiry. They are temporally evaluated based on past, present, and future actions. In other words, a choice is evaluated in terms of the previous actions, their actual choice within the context of the available choices, and the outcome of their choice that sets the stage for the next set of actions. For example, if a character asks a student what they think the problem is and the student responds that they think the mutant frog is a result of pollution, the character will ask the student to provide evidence for their claim. The evidence that a student gives will be weighted and evaluated based on their prior actions (data that they have previously collected) and by what they choose to present as evidence.

CONCLUSION

In this chapter, we discussed VPAs as a new model for re-conceptualizing the assessment of higher order skills, including creative problem solving and inquiry. The VPAs we are developing are based on over 20 years of research on assessment design, cognition, technology, and videogame design. A case study was presented describing the Virtual Performance Assessment Project and how numerous technology platforms are being integrated to innovate a new performance measure of middle school students' scientific inquiry knowledge, skills, and abilities. At the heart of the VPA project is Evidence Centered Design. ECD allows the researchers to create an assessment argument and improve construct validity by linking multiple components of the student's work products to observable variables to KSAs to the measurement model and ultimately the student model with a proficiency score for a specific KSA. Such frameworks and assessment templates allow the field to design better assessments that are more reflective of how students learn, as opposed to having students select from four or five options.

We are at a confluence in time where we have capabilities to design comprehensive assessment systems around cognitive models of student learning. While the research we presented here is around summative assessments, we see great potential for formative and classroom based assessments using ECD and IVEs. As technology advances, the capabilities for designing learning and assessment environments will evolve. The rapid, continual evolution in personal technology products, such as tablets, phones and mobile devices is already opening the door to new methods of assessment. For example, multi-touchscreen interfaces allow for precise measurement of a student's ability to trace a letter or number using his or her fingers. We are at an exciting time in assessment where we have the research, technology, and policy support to create innovative assessments that move beyond multiple-choice. However, it is important that the field remains focused on developing quality assessment systems that document validity and reliability across multiple domains and interfaces.

REFERENCES

Alexander, L. (2010). ESA: 300 Schools Now Offer Game Design Programs. Gamasutra, August 16, 2010. Retrieved from http://www.gamasutra.com/view/news/29930/ESA_300_Schools_Now_Offer_Game_Design_Programs.php

Almond, R. G. (2009). Bayesian network models for local dependence among observable outcome variables. *Journal of Educational and Behavioral Statistics, 34*(4), 491–521.

American Association for the Advancement of Science (AAAS). (1990). *Science for all Americans.* New York: Oxford University Press.

American Association for the Advancement of Science (AAAS). (1993). *Benchmarks for science literacy: A Project 2061 report.* New York: Oxford University Press.

Barab, S., Thomas, M., Dodge, T., Carteaux, R., & Tuzun, H. (2004). Making learning fun: Quest Atlantis, a game without guns. *Educational Technology Research & Development, 53*(1), 86–108.

Baxter, G. P. (1995). Using computer simulations to assess hands-on science learning. *Journal of Science Education and Technology, 4*(1), 21–27.

Baxter, G. P., & Shavelson, R. J. (1994). Science performance assessments: Benchmarks and surrogates. *International Journal of Educational Research, 21*(3), 279–298.

Business-Higher Education Forum. (2005). A commitment to America's future: Responding to the crisis in mathematics & science education. Washington, DC: Author.

Chooseco. (1977–2011). Choose Your Own Adventure. Retrieved January 30, 2011, from http://www.cyoa.com/public/index.html

Clark, D. B., Nelson, B., Sengupta, P., & D'Angelo, C. M. (2009). *Rethinking science learning through digital games and simulations: Genres, examples, and evidence.* Invited Topic Paper in the Proceedings of The National Academies Board on Science Education Workshop on Learning Science: Computer Games, Simulations, and Education. Washington, DC: The National Academies Press.

Clarke, J. (2006). *Making learning meaningful.* Qualifying paper submitted to the Harvard Graduate School of Education. Cambridge, MA.

Clarke, J., Dede, C., Ketelhut, D. J., & Nelson, B. (2006) A design-based research strategy to promote scalability for educational innovations. *Educational Technology, 46*(3), 27–36.

Clarke, J., & Dede, C. (2005). Making learning meaningful: An exploratory study of using multi-user environments (MUVEs) in middle school science. Paper presented at the American Educational Research Association Conference, Montreal, Canada.

Clarke, J., & Dede, C. (2007). *MUVEs as a powerful way to study situated learning. The proceedings of conference for computer supported collaborative learning (CSCL).* Mahwah, NJ: Erlbaum.

Clarke, J., Dede, C., & Dieterle, E. (2008). Immersive learning environments in K–12 education. *International Handbook of Information Technology in Education.* Springer, 901–907.

Clarke, J. (2009). Exploring the compexity of inquiry learning in an open-ended problem space. Unpublished Doctoral Dissertation, Harvard University, Cambridge, MA.

Clarke, J., & Dede, C. (2009). Design for scalability: A case study of the River City curriculum. *Journal of Science Education and Technology, 18*(4), 353–365.

Clarke-Midura, J. Mayrath, M., & Dede, C. (2010). Designing immersive virtual environments for assessing inquiry. Paper presented at American Education Research Association Conference, 2010. Denver, Colorado.

College Board. (2009). *Science College Board Standards for College Success.* New York, NY: The College Board.

Cronbach, L. J., Linn, R. L., Brennan, R. L., & Haertel, E. H. (1997). Generalizability analysis for performance assessments of student achievement or school effectiveness. *Educational and Psychological Measurement, 57*(3), 373–399.

Dede, C. (2009). Immersive interfaces for engagement and learning. *Science, 323*(5910), 66–69.

Federal Reserve Bank of Dallas (2004). What d'ya know? Lifetime learning in pursuit of the American dream. Dallas, TX. Retrieved from http://dallasfed.org/fed/annual/2004/ar04b.cfm

Frederiksen, J. R., & Collins, A. , (1989). A systems approach to educational testing. *Educational Researcher, 18*(9), 27–32.

Friedman, T. H. (2005). *The world is flat.* New York: Farrar, Straus and Giroux.

Gee, J. P. (2003). *What video games have to teach us about learning and literacy.* New York: Palgrave Macmillan.

Haertel, G., Lash, A., Javitz, H., & Quellmalz, E. (2006). An instructional sensitivity study of science inquiry items from three large-scale science examinations. Paper presented at the Annual Meeting of the American Educational Research Association, San Francisco, CA.

Kennedy, C. (2005). Constructing PADI measurement models for the BEAR Scoring Engine (PADI Technical Report 7). Menlo Park, CA: SRI International.

Ketelhut, D. J. (2007). The impact of student self-efficacy on scientific inquiry skills: An exploratory investigation in River City, a multi-user virtual environment. *The Journal of Science Education and Technology, 16*(1), 99–111.

Ketelhut, D. J., & Dede, C. (2006). Assessing inquiry learning. Paper presented at the National Association of Research in Science Teaching, San Francisco, CA.

Ketelhut, D. J., Dede, C., Clarke, J., & Nelson, B. (2007). Studying situated learning in a multi-user virtual environment. In E. Baker & J. Dickieson & W. Wulfeck & H. O'Neil (Eds.), *Assessment of problem solving using simulations* (pp. 37–58). Mahwah, NJ: Erlbaum.

Linn, R. L. (1994). Performance assessment: Policy promises and technical measurement standards. *Educational Researcher, 23*(9), 4–14.

Linn, R. L. (2000). Assessments and accountability. *Educational Researcher, 29*(2), 4–16.

Linn, R. L., Baker, E. L., & Dunbar, S. B. (1991). Complex performance-based assessment: Expectations and validation criteria. *Educational Researcher, 20*(8), 5–21.

Loftus, G. R., & Loftus, E. F. (1983). *Mind at play: The psychology of video games.* New York: Basic Books.

Mislevy, R., & Haertel, G. (2006). Implications of evidence centered design for educational testing, *PADI Technical Report 17*. Menlo Park, CA: SRI Interantional.

Mislevy, R., & Rahman, T. (2009). Design pattern for assessing cause and effect reasoning in reading comprehension, *PADI Technical Report 20*. Menlo Park, CA: SRI Interantional.

Mislevy, R., Steinberg, L. S., & Almond, R. G. (2003). On the structure of educational assessment. *Measurement: Interdisciplinary Research & Perspective, 1*(1), 3–62.

National Academy of Science. (2006). *Rising above the gathering storm: Energizing and employing America for a brighter economic future*. NAP: Washington, DC.

National Assessment Governing Board (NAGB). (2010). Science framework for the 2011 national assessment of educational progress. Washington, DC: Author.

National Research Council (NRC). (1996). *National science education standards*. Washington, DC: National Academies Press.

National Research Council. (2000). *How people learn: Brain, mind, experience, and school: Expanded edition*. Committee on Learning Research and Educational Practice, M. S. Donovan, J. D. Bransford, & J. W. Pellegrino (Eds.). Washington, DC: The National Academies Press.

National Research Council. (2001). *Knowing what students know: The science and design of educational assessment*. The Science and Design of Educational Assessment Committee on the Foundations of Assessment, J. W. Pellegrino, N. Chudowsky, & R. Glaser (Eds.). Board on Testing and Assessment Center for Education Division of Behavioral and Social Sciences and Education National Research Council. Washington, DC: National Academies Press.

National Research Council. (2005). *How students learn: History, mathematics, and science in the classroom*. Committee on How People Learn, A Targeted Report for Teachers, M. S. Donovan and J. D. Bransford (Eds.). Division of Behavioral and Social Sciences and Education. Washington, DC: The National Academies Press.

National Research Council (NRC). (2006). *Systems for state science assessment*. Washington, DC: The National Academies Press.

National Research Council. (2007). *Taking science to school: Learning and teaching science in grades K–8*. Committee on Science Learning, Kindergarten Through Eighth Grade, R. A. Duschl, H. A. Schweingruber, & A. W. Shouse (Eds.). Board on Science Education, Center for Education. Division of Behavioral and Social Sciences and Education. Washington, DC: The National Academies Press.

National Research Council (NRC). (2010). A framework for science education: Preliminary public draft. Retrieved December 12, 2010, from http://www7.nationalacademies.org/bose/Standards_Framework_Homepage.html

National Research Council (NRC). (2011). *Learning science through computer games and simulations*. Washington, DC: The National Academies Press.

Nelson, B. (2007). Exploring the use of individualized, reflective guidance in an educational multi-user virtual environment. *The Journal of Science Education and Technology, 16*(1) 83–97.

Nelson, B., Ketelhut, D.J., Clarke, J., Bowman, C., & Dede, C. (2005). Design-based research strategies for developing a scientific inquiry curriculum in a multi-user virtual environment. *Educational Technology, 45*(1), 21–27.

Neulight, N., Kafai, Y. B., Kao, L., Foley, B., & Galas, C. (2007). Children's learning about infectious disease through participation in a virtual epidemic. *Journal of Science Education and Technology 16*(1), 47–58.

Organisation for Economic Co-operation and Development (OECD). (2007). *PISA 2006: Science competencies for tomorrow's world. Volume 1: Analysis.* Paris: OECD.

Pine, J., Baxter, G. P., & Shavelson, R. J. (1993). Assessments for hands-on elementary science curricula. *MSTA Journal, 39*(2), 5–19.

President's Council of Advisors on Science and Technology (PCAST). (2010). *Prepare and inspire: K–12 education in science, technology, engineering, and math (STEM) for America's future.* Washington, DC: Executive Office of the President.

Quellmalz, E., & Haertel, G. (2004). Technology supports for state science assessment systems. Paper commissioned by the National Research Council Committee on Test Design for K–12 Science Achievement. Washington, DC: National Research Council.

Quellmalz, E., Kreikemeier, P., DeBarger, A. H., & Haertel, G. (2007). *A study of the alignment of the NAEP, TIMSS, and New Standards Science Assessments with the inquiry abilities in the National Science Education Standards.* Paper presented at the Annual Meeting of the American Educational Research Association, Chicago, IL.

Quellmalz, E., & Pellegrino, J. W. (2009). Technology and testing. *Science, 323*(5910), 75–79.

Quest to Learn (2010). Retrieved September, 2010 from http://q2l.org/

Resnick, L. B., & Resnick, D. P. (1992). Assessing the thinking curriculum: New tools for educational reform. In B. Gifford & M. O'Connor (Eds.), *Changing assessments: alternative views of aptitude, achievement, and instruction* (pp. 37–75). Norwell, MA: Kluwer Academic Publishers.

Rosenquist, A., Shavelson, R. J., & Ruiz-Primo, M. A. (2000). *On the "exchangeability" of hands-on and computer simulation science performance assessments.* (CSE Technical Report 531). Los Angeles, CA: National Center for Research on Evaluation, Standards, and Student Testing.

Sadler, P. M. (1998). Psychometric models of student conceptions in science: Reconciling qualitative studies and distracter-driven assessment instruments. *Journal of Research in Science Teaching, 35*(3), 265–296.

Shavelson, R. J., Baxter, G. P., & Gao, X. (1993). Sampling variability of performance assessments. *Journal of Educational Measurement, 30*(3), 215–232.

Shavelson, R. J., Baxter, G. P., & Pine, J. (1991). Performance assessment in science. *Applied Measurement in Education, 4*(4), 347–362.

Shavelson, R. J., Ruiz-Primo, M. A., & Wiley, E. (1999). Note on sources of sample variability in science performance assessments. *Journal of Educational Measurement, 36*(1), 59–69.

Songer, NB., Kelcey, B., & Gotwals, A. (2009). How and when does complex reasoning occur? Empirically driven development of a learning progression focused on complex reasoning about biodiversity. *Journal of Research in Science Teaching, 46*(4), 610–633.

Stecher, B. M., & Klein, S. P. (1997). The cost of science performance assessments in large-scale testing programs. *Educational Evaluation and Policy Analysis, 19*(1), 1–14.

Task Force on the Future of American Innovation. (2005). The knowledge economy: Is the United States losing its competitive edge? (Benchmarks of Our Innovation Future). T. F. o. t. F. o. A. Innovation. Retrieved from http://www.futureofinnovation.org/PDF/Benchmarks.pdf

U.S. Department of Education (USDE). (2010). National education technology plan 2010. Washington, DC: Author.

U.S. Department of Education (USDE). (2011). The nation's report card. Washington, DC: Author.

Webb, N. M., Schlackman, J., & Sugrue, B. (2000). The dependability and interchangeability of assessment methods in science. *Applied Measurement in Education, 13*(3), 277–301.

CHAPTER 6

EXPLORING THE ROLE OF GAMES IN EDUCATIONAL ASSESSMENT

Diego Zapata-Rivera and Malcolm Bauer
Educational Testing Service

ABSTRACT

This chapter describes the characteristics of games and how they can be applied to the design of innovative assessment tasks for formative and summative purposes. Examples of current educational games and game-like assessment tasks in mathematics, science, and English language learning are used to illustrate some of these concepts. We argue that the inclusion of some aspects from gaming technology may have a positive effect in the development of innovative assessment systems (e.g., by supporting the development of highly engaging assessment tasks). However, integrating game elements as part of assessment tasks is a complex process that needs to take into account not only the engaging or motivational aspects of the activity but also the quality criteria that are needed according to the type of assessment that is being developed.

Technology-Based Assessments for 21st Century Skills, pages 149–171

INTRODUCTION

Educators have long recognized the ability of games, particularly immersive, narrative-based games, to capture the attention and imagination of students. Many authors (e.g., Barab et al., 2007; Gee, 2003; Prensky, 2001; Shaffer, 2006; Squire 2002) posit that online games represent an educational breakthrough that could transform how people learn in and outside the classroom. In general, large formal educational systems, like those that exist in the public school systems in the U.S. and elsewhere seem resistant to change, so the question becomes in what ways can these new technologies be integrated into the current education system in order to improve it?

In this chapter, we explore opportunities for technology—and specifically game technology—to have a positive effect on aspects of an education system aimed at achieving specific goals such as preparing children to be skilled members of the workforce and to be informed and productive citizens (Banathy, 1992). We argue that to achieve these particular goals, several conditions need to exist: (a) students need to be motivated to learn, (b) students need to be provided with appropriate learning opportunities, and (c) an *assessment system* that provides educational stakeholders with information needed to keep the education system functioning appropriately should be in place. This assessment system should be able to support decision-making by different educational stakeholders at different levels of granularity (e.g., Frederiksen & Collins, 1989). For example, it should provide information directly to students and those directly facilitating their learning (teachers, other students, parents, etc.) to support instructional decisions, as well as feedback to support resource allocation decisions by administrators at local, state, and federal levels.

In order to meet the educational demands of an evolving society, new comprehensive assessment systems have been implemented around the world with positive results (Darling-Hammond & Pecheone, 2010). For example, in countries such as the United Kingdom, Singapore, Hong Kong and Australia, the assessment system focuses on central concepts in the disciplines and students using knowledge to solve authentic problems, and demonstrating higher order skills. These assessment systems provide students with multiple opportunities to demonstrate their knowledge and skills through the use of classroom embedded assessments that take a variety of forms (e.g., open ended questions, giving oral presentations or creating portfolios of student work). These assessment systems often include end-of-course assessments (summative assessments) and embedded periodic classroom assessments aimed at guiding instruction (formative assessments). Comprehensive assessment systems are integrated with standards, curriculum and instruction, and teacher professional development. Assessment results provided by these systems are used by different educational stakeholders at the individual/student-, classroom-, school-, district-, state- and national levels (Darling-Hammond, 2010).

ETS's Cognitively Based Assessment of, for, and as Learning (CBAL) research project (Bennett & Gitomer, 2009) is an example of an assessment system that includes summative, formative, and teacher professional development components. Each of these components has clear goals and supporting tools. These components complement each other in order to provide educational stakeholders with the information they need to make decisions (e.g., Underwood, Zapata-Rivera, & VanWinkle, 2010; Zapata-Rivera, VanWinkle, & Zwick, 2010).

In this chapter, we argue that some properties of games can enhance different components of a comprehensive assessment system. Although the idea of game technologies may generate some skepticism, especially when used in the context of assessment, we will show that there is room for these types of game-like elements in educational assessment. We examine game technologies in relation to the components of a comprehensive assessment system. Examples from prior research in the area are used to illustrate some of the concepts. These examples include: English ABLE (Zapata-Rivera, VanWinkle, Shute, Underwood, & Bauer, 2007), English and Math ABLE (EM ABLE) (Zapata-Rivera, VanWinkle, Doyle, Buteux, & Bauer, 2009), and an interactive student score report in the area of CBAL mathematics (Zapata-Rivera, 2009).

GAMES

Juul (2005) defines games as "a rule-based formal system with a variable and quantifiable outcome, where different values are assigned different variables, the player exerts effort in order to influence the outcome, the player feels attached to the outcome, and the consequences of the activity are optional and negotiable" (p. 36). Although not all games fit this definition, it covers the main components found in a variety of games. Crawford (1982) describes four general characteristics of video games: representation (games subjectively model external situations), interaction (the player influences the world represented in the game and gets meaningful responses), conflict (there are obstacles in the game that get in the way of the player achieving the goal), and safety (players can experiment with different strategies in a controlled environment).

Educational games share many features of conventional games. Researchers have reported some common game elements that influence player motivation include challenge, control, and fantasy (Lepper & Malone, 1987; Malone, 1981; Rieber, 1996). Educational games, like conventional games, can create a continuous cycle of cognitive disequilibrium and resolution

(Van Eck, 2006). Engaged players may experience a state of "flow" (Csik-szentmihalyi, 1990). Serious games, for example, are immersive environments that are explicitly intended to educate or train. Casual games, on the contrary, can be immersive but not necessarily educational (Carey, 2006).

Klopfer, Osterweil and Salen (2009) comment that "by offering challenges that seem worth attempting, games channel players' efforts, while still affording them the freedom needed to manage their individual experience in ways that are self-directed and beneficial to their own development" (p. 5). All these elements may make playing games a highly engaging activity. Teachers and researchers have used games in classrooms as motivational tools to familiarize students with the content area and help students develop domain knowledge and skills in immersive, interactive, graphical environments (e.g., Squire & Jenkins, 2003; Lepper & Malone, 1987).

Games share some characteristics with simulations and micro worlds. Hogle (1996) views games as cognitive tools and points out that while research on games has focused mainly on psychomotor and motivation issues, research on microworlds has dealt with conceptual and cognitive issues. Research on simulations has involved work on both motivation and cognitive aspects of their use. The use of simulations in assessment is an area that has received great attention, especially in the area of science assessment (e.g., Bennett, Persky, Weiss, & Jenkins, 2007; Quellmalz & Pellegrino, 2009).

The global economy demands from students a set of skills and knowledge that are not emphasized in the current education system (Dede, 2007). Some of these demands include creativity, fluency in information and communication technologies, ability to solve complex problems, collaboration, adaptability, systems-thinking, interpretative analysis, plan formulation and execution, entrepreneurial spirit, and leadership. These skills have been called 21st century skills. New technologies, including video games, can play an instrumental role in transforming current educational and assessment practices by facilitating the creation of environments where students can acquire and demonstrate 21st century skills (e.g., Federation of American Scientists, 2006). For example, multiplayer games can be used to support communication and collaborative problem-solving (Dede, 2007). Klopfer et al. (2009) argue that assessment systems should be able to measure student understanding of certain concepts and progress on particular skills as they play the game (e.g., knowledge of science concepts in Quest Atlantis). Games are also often instances of multimedia-based learning systems. Substantial research exists on exploring barriers and supports for learning within these systems (e.g., Mayer & Moreno, 2003).

Next we describe the role of games in the creation of tools for formative assessment. These tools involve the use of game-like elements and embedded assessment. We also discuss some considerations that need to be taken into account when designing summative assessments that are compatible with these new types of tools.

GAMES AND ASSESSMENT

Games have potential for improving how formative assessment is performed. Games can engage students in meaningful tasks that, if designed appropriately, will produce valuable information for teachers and students. One of the main challenges is to create engaging gaming scenarios that can be used as assessment tasks while satisfying assessment quality criteria (e.g., fairness, validity, and reliability considerations).

Although the issues discussed in this section have a direct application to the area of formative assessment, to some extent some of these issues are also relevant to summative assessment.

There are many issues that need to be taken into account when considering the integration of games elements in the development of assessment tasks. These issues include:

- *Introduction of construct irrelevant content and skills.* When designing interactive gaming activities, it is easy to introduce content and interactions that impose requirements on knowledge, skill, or other attributes (KSA) that are not part of the construct (i.e., the KSAs that we are not trying to measure). That is, authenticity added by the context of a game may also impose demands on irrelevant KSAs (Messick, 1994). Designers need to explore the implications for the type of information that will be gathered and used as evidence of students' performance on the KSAs that are part of the construct.
- *Interaction issues.* The nature of interaction in games may be at odds with how people are expected to perform on an assessment task. Making sense of issues such as exploring behavior, pacing, and trying to game the system is challenging and has a direct link to the quality of evidence that is collected about student behavior. The environment can lend itself to interactions that may not be logical or expected. Capturing the types of behaviors that will be used as evidence and limiting other types of behaviors (e.g., gaming the system or repeatedly exploring visual or sound effects) without making the game dull or repetitive is a challenging activity.
- *Demands on working memory.* Related to both the issues of construct irrelevant variance (i.e., when the "test contains excess reliable variance that is irrelevant to the interpreted construct"; Messick, 1989, p. 34) and interaction is the issue of demands that game-like assessments place upon students' working memory. By designing

assessments with higher levels of interactivity and engagement, it is easy to increase cognitive processing demands in a way that reduces the quality of the measurement of the assessment. These types of demands or cognitive load are perhaps best expressed by the work of Sweller (1999), Mayer and Moreno (2003) and Mayer (2005). For example, Mayer and Moreno (2003) define three kinds of demands:[1] (1) *essential processing* demands that are aimed at use of working memory for selecting, organizing, and integrating information related to the core learning goals or assessment needs (i.e., demands that *are* construct relevant); (2) *incidental processing* demands are aimed at use of working memory for selecting, organizing, and integrating information not directly related to the core learning goals or assessment needs (i.e., demands that are *not* construct relevant); and (3) *representational holding*, which describes the task demands for maintaining information in working memory (i.e., demands that *may or may not be* construct-relevant depending upon the nature of the construct). There are many design strategies that can be used to address cognitive load in the design of game-like assessments. Mayer and Moreno (2003) propose a dual processing theory for images and sounds in multimedia learning systems and provide nine research based ways to reduce cognitive load.

- *Accessibility issues.* Games that make use of rich, immersive graphical environments can impose great visual, motor, auditory, and other demands on the player to just be able to interact in the environment (e.g., sophisticated navigation controls). Moreover, creating environments that do not make use of some of these technological advances (e.g., a 3D immersive environment) may negatively affect student engagement, especially for students who are used to interacting with these types of games. Parallel environments that do not impose the same visual, motor and auditory demands without changing the construct need to be developed for particular groups of students (e.g., students with visual disabilities). In addition, new types of assistive technologies that can be integrated into these gaming environments may be required (e.g., Supalo et al., 2006). We have explored some of these issues by applying an argument-based approach to analyzing accessibility issues of a game activity designed around a commercial game (Hansen & Zapata-Rivera, 2010). We have found that a clear assessment argument that takes into account two kinds of KSAs—(a) focal (construct related) and (b) nonfocal (non-construct related) but demanded to enable access to the activity as intended—is instrumental in designing accessible assessment activities.

- *Tutorials and familiarization.* Although the majority of students have played some sort of video game in their lives, students will need support to understand how to navigate and interact with the graphical environment. Lack of familiarity with navigation controls may negatively influence student performance and student motivation (e.g., Lim, Nonis, & Hedberg, 2006). The use of tutorials and demos can support this familiarization process. The tutorial can also be used as an engagement element (e.g., Armstrong & Georgas, 2006).

- *Type and amount of feedback.* Feedback is a key component of formative assessments. Research shows that interactive computer applications that provide immediate, task-level feedback to students can positively contribute to student learning (e.g., Hattie & Timperley, 2007; Shute, 2008). Black and Wiliam (1998) review the literature on classroom formative assessment and show evidence supporting the provision of frequent feedback to students in order to improve student learning. Students in this approach are considered active participants working with teachers to implement formative strategies in the classroom. Shute (2008) reviews research on formative feedback and identifies the characteristics of effective formative feedback for specific situations (e.g., multidimensional, nonevaluative, supportive, timely, specific, and credible). Depending on the purpose of the assessment (i.e., formative or summative), different types of feedback need to be available. Immediate feedback that results from a direct manipulation of objects in the game can provide useful information to guide exploration or refine interaction strategies. Availability of feedback may influence motivation and the quality of the evidence produced by the system. Measurement models need to take into account the type of feedback that has been provided to students when interpreting the data gathered during their interaction with the assessment system (e.g., one way of measuring the effects of feedback is by varying the difficulty of the activity based on the feedback provided).

- *Re-playing, number of attempts and revisions.* As in the case of feedback, measurement models need to handle the number of attempts and revisions. This could be done by comparing the outcomes of consecutive actions/events or by interpreting a subset of actions. Based on the type of assessment, operational constraints (e.g., time) may impose a limit in the number of attempts allowed before moving to the next scenario.

- *Handling dependencies among actions.* Dependencies among actions/events can be complex to model and interpret. Assumptions of conditional independence required by some measurement models may not hold in complex interactive scenarios. Designing scenarios carefully in order to minimize dependencies will help reduce the complexity of measurement models. Using data mining techniques to support evidence identification can also help with this issue.

Some of these issues are currently being explored. We expect that in the future new measurement models will be developed in order to address some of these challenges. We expect that as these new assessment systems become available, they will have an important role to play as part of a comprehensive assessment system. The following sections present several examples of how game elements have been integrated into various educational assessment tools, including two assessment-based gaming environments— English ABLE (Zapata-Rivera et al., 2007), English and Math ABLE (EM ABLE) (Zapata-Rivera et al., 2009), and an interactive student score report.

ASSESSMENT-BASED GAMING ENVIRONMENTS

Assessment-based gaming environments were developed by applying the principles of Evidence Centered Design (ECD) (Mislevy, Steinberg, & Almond, 2003). ECD is a methodology for assessment design that emphasizes a logical and explicit representation of an evidence-based chain of reasoning from tasks to proficiencies. ECD helps us design assessments that can respond to the following questions posed by Messick (1994):

- What complex of knowledge, skills, or other attributes should be assessed?
- What behaviors or performances should reveal those constructs?
- What tasks or situations should elicit those behaviors?

The main goal of applying ECD principles is to design assessment-based, interactive, gaming scenarios that can be used to help students learn the content while at the same time help the system capture valid assessment information to adapt its behavior. These gaming environments can provide teachers and students with estimates of student performance on valued skills.

A major goal of assessment-based gaming environments is to provide adaptive gaming scenarios that can be used to help students learn and provide valid assessment information to students and teachers. These gaming scenarios are composed of various interactive activities (i.e., assessment tasks). Each scenario has an underlying storyline aimed at defining: (a) the behavior to be observed (student task-related decisions to navigate the task) and (b) the interactive activities needed to elicit such behaviors. Creating such scenarios requires input from an interdisciplinary team including users (i.e., students or players), domain experts (e.g., teachers and researchers), assessment specialists, and experts in interactive systems design.

The development process of these assessment-based gaming environments encompasses the following activities: (a) gathering domain knowledge information; (b) designing initial competency and evidence models; (c) selecting initial competencies and required evidence to focus on; (d) brainstorming about scenarios and activities that can be used to elicit desired behavior; (e) describing scenarios and activities; this activity includes: defining the role of the student, the role of the teacher, the role of the virtual characters or pedagogical agents (e.g., Biswas, Schwartz, Bransford, & TAG-V, 2001; Chan & Baskin, 1990; Graesser, Person, Harter, & TRG, 2001), the level of feedback or scaffolding, the assessment activities to be administered in particular situations, the work products for each activity, and the evidence rules for the activity; (f) updating task models, competency and evidence models; and (g) iterating until all the target competences have been covered. Once a scenario is described, interactive design experts and system developers create a prototype, pilot test it with users, and make changes based on the feedback that is gathered. More information about this process is provided by Zapata-Rivera et al. (2009).

Next we describe two assessment-based gaming environments that make use of game components (e.g., virtual characters or pedagogical agents, immediate feedback or scaffolding, scores, points and knowledge/power levels).

English ABLE

English ABLE (Assessment-Based Learning Environment) uses assessment information to support student learning of English grammar. English ABLE draws upon a database of TOEFL® CBT tasks to create new packages of enhanced tasks that are linked to particular component English language skills. In English ABLE, players help a *virtual student* learn English by correcting this student's writing from a notebook of facts/sentences based on TOEFL® tasks. The player can see how much the student knows about various English grammar components by looking at the virtual student's *knowledge levels*. To make the game more compelling, virtual students are able to express basic emotions, which are triggered by a list of predefined rules that take into account recent student performance on particular tasks. A character named Dr. Grammar provides *adaptive instructional feedback* (i.e., rules, procedures, examples and definitions) based on the student model. Figure 6.1 shows a screenshot of English ABLE.

English ABLE implements a Bayesian student model that divides English grammar into three main categories: use, form, and meaning. The Bayesian model is used to capture and propagate evidence of student knowledge regarding some aspects of English grammar, including sentence-level gram-

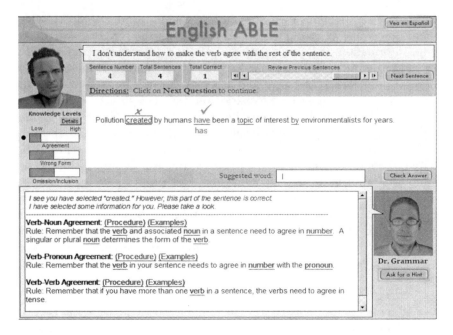

Figure 6.1 English ABLE. The player helps a virtual student (Jorge) correct his writing while receiving feedback from a virtual professor (Dr. Grammar).

matical concepts (e.g., agreement) as well as word-level concepts (e.g., individual parts of speech). Tasks are linked to grammar concepts using IRT (Item Response Theory) task parameters (Zapata-Rivera et al., 2007).

English ABLE showcases an indirectly visible Bayesian student model (Zapata-Rivera, 2007). In this approach the student model is seen through the eyes of the virtual student. That is, as the player makes progress through the game by helping the virtual student correct his written notes, the Bayesian student model is used to accumulate evidence and produce knowledge levels (see upper-left area in Figure 6.1). These *knowledge levels* are assigned to the virtual character in the game but actually represent the player's current knowledge level based on his/her performance in the game.

EM ABLE

EM ABLE (English and Math ABLE) models both English language and math competencies. It combines game elements (e.g., immediate feedback, sound effects, and progress indicators: points and power levels, pedagogical agents and various forms of scaffolding). The game starts when the student chooses and customizes a student character with which to play the game. The student also selects a friend to accompany the character while playing the game. The student's mission is to help his/her student character interact in the EM (English-Math) "city." The student character is invited to participate in various activities (e.g., a pizza party). Each activity provides an integrated learning and assessment scenario for the student. As part of each activity, the student character interacts with virtual people who provide guidance, feedback, and, at the same time, administer embedded assessment tasks to the learner related to predefined vocabulary and math proficiencies. Evidence of student knowledge is obtained through the student's interaction with these characters and his/her performance on various math and vocabulary activities. Activities vary in difficulty based on the student's prior performance and include short, text-based dialogues using a virtual cell phone (i.e., conversations) as well as math completion tasks (i.e., math activities). As the learner advances in the game, he or she accumulates points for his/her student character.

Figure 6.2 shows a screenshot of EM ABLE. In this figure, Frankie (a virtual friend) asks Miguel for help finding out what kind of pizza each person wants. This figure also shows Miguel's virtual cell phone, math and

Figure 6.2 EM ABLE. The player's character (Miguel) helps a virtual friend (Frankie) prepare a pizza party.

language point indicators, and a map of the game, which shows the current location of Miguel in the game (i.e., Frankie's apartment).

After finding out what each person wants, the player takes a picture of the resulting graphical representation and sends it to Frankie's Mom, who will order the pizzas. Then, Miguel and Frankie receive cell phone call from Frankie's Mom asking them to produce a numerical representation of the order using fractions. Figure 6.3 shows part of a dialogue between the player and Frankie's Mom.

EM ABLE also implements a Bayesian student model. Knowledge-level estimates (called "power levels") are continuously updated based upon performance and are visible to the learner through his/her virtual cell phone. These power levels are externalized as progress bars (one for vocabulary and one for math) and are referred to as the character's "knowledge levels." These power levels are available for inspection through the *Status* button of the virtual cell phone.

Both English ABLE and EM ABLE have been evaluated with real students. Initial results have been positive. Students find the games engaging and teachers appreciate the opportunity to witness what is going on in the game through teacher reports that include information about student performance and knowledge-level estimates (Zapata-Rivera et al., 2007, 2009).

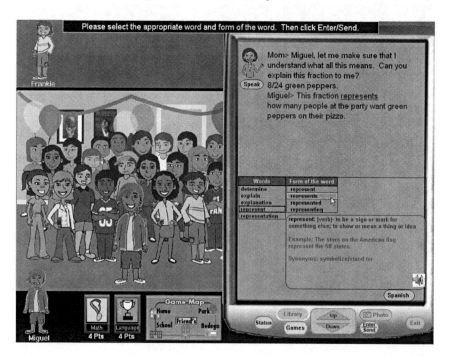

Figure 6.3 EM ABLE. The player chats with Frankie's Mom about the pizza order.

Integrating Game Elements into English ABLE and EM-ABLE

Several game elements are common to both English ABLE and EM ABLE. This section elaborates on how some of these game elements are integrated into these systems.

- *Immediate and adaptive feedback.* In both English ABLE and EM ABLE immediate feedback is available based on the current state of the internal Bayesian student model. In English ABLE, for example, Dr. Grammar offers immediate verification feedback (e.g., "I see you have selected 'created.' However, this part of the sentence is correct." See Figure 6.1) and additional adaptive instructional feedback (i.e., grammatical rules, procedures, examples and definitions). Feedback is not handcrafted at the item level but instead is keyed to grammatical categories, students' native language, and estimated skill level. The amount and type of information presented to the student varies according to the student's knowledge level (i.e., intermediate students receive more detailed information compared to intermediate-advanced and advanced students). In the case of EM ABLE, feedback is embedded in the written dialogues with other characters (e.g., Frankie and his mom in Figure 6.2) and also appears on the box at the top of Figure 6.2. These assessment based environments are intended to be used for formative purposes. Feedback is used to help students make progress in the game and facilitate student learning. Feedback provided is taken into account when adding evidence to the student model. That is, answering a question when hints have been provided makes the item easier. The difficulty of the task is changed in the model accordingly to reflect this issue.
- *Pedagogical agents.* Virtual characters in these assessment-based games are pedagogical agents. They provide feedback via rules that are triggered based on the current state of the student model. Some of these characters can express basic emotions (Zapata-Rivera et al., 2007). For example, in Figure 6.1 Jorge (the virtual character) appears confused and expresses it ("I don't understand how to make the verb agree with the rest of the sentence"). The presence of these characters make the assessment-based gaming environment more engaging while providing another way of interacting with the student and gathering evidence of particular KSAs (e.g., written conversations with characters in EM ABLE are used as evidence of students' knowledge of vocabulary and mathematics).

- *Points.* While "knowledge levels" (called "power levels" in EM ABLE) are estimates of the student's proficiency that fluctuate according to the student's performance, points earned never decrease (i.e., points either stay the same or increase as the student correctly answers questions in the game). EM ABLE includes mathematics and language points. These two indicators of progress can be used in different ways (e.g., teachers may be more interested in knowing how much progress a student has made on a particular skill, as opposed to the number of points the student has accumulated).

- *Visible student models.* Visible Bayesian student models serve as progress/state indicators. Using these indicators, students see how their KSAs (or the virtual character's KSAs, in the case of English ABLE) are changing based on their performance in the game. This is another element of engagement that may be used to explore self-reflection and other metacognitive skills.

- *Number of attempts and revisions.* Students are allowed to try again for a limited number of times. However, as in the case of hints, this is taken into account when adding evidence to the student model. Trying several times changes the difficulty of the item. In some cases, depending on the number of attempts, no points are given to the student.

- *Navigation.* In EM ABLE, a map is used to provide students with location information. This map provides students with a sense of where in the game they are and information about where they will go next. In English ABLE, the current grammatical category is presented in the knowledge levels area. The total number of sentences per each grammatical category is also presented. Even though in these games navigation is adapted based on the student model, students can choose to visit a particular place (e.g., a different grammatical category in English ABLE or a part of the city in EM ABLE). Having freedom to explore in the game makes it more interesting to students. Each area of the game provides opportunities to elicit evidence of students' KSAs.

- *Sound.* Sound is used to provide feedback on particular events in the game (e.g., points earned and cell phone calls in EM ABLE). In addition, sound is used to help students with reading difficulties (Mom's speak button) and pronunciation of words (speaker icon when selecting words to complete sentences in EM ABLE). The use of sound has been useful in facilitating the interaction of English language learners in the game.

- *Goals and storyline.* In both cases (English ABLE and EM ABLE), students are told a story that creates a meaningful context for their interaction. This story provides students with a clear goal to accomplish in the assessment-based gaming environment. In English ABLE, the student's goal is to help the virtual character (Jorge or Carmen) achieve a high level on each of the knowledge level categories by correcting his/her sentences. In EM ABLE, the student's goal is to collect the maximum number of points possible while increasing his/her power levels. This is achieved by helping a virtual friend solve a variety of embedded problems that are connected to the main story and are presented to the student as he/she visits different places in the EM city.

* *Customizing characters.* Before students start to interact with EM ABLE, the student chooses his/her virtual character from a list of predefined characters with a wide range of ethnicities. Then, the student selects a face, clothing, and "bling" (or accessories) for the character. The student also types in a name for the character. Students responded positively to this activity. This activity provided students with an engaging first interaction with the game.

An area of educational assessment in which game technologies can make a positive impact is score reporting for students. Score reports are usually designed for parents and are not always of interest to students. The next section describes the application of gaming elements into a new interactive score report for students.

AN INTERACTIVE STUDENT SCORE REPORT

Score reports should not only communicate assessment information to particular audiences effectively, but also foster communication among teachers, students, and parents. For example, students and teachers can use score report information to engage in an instructional dialogue aimed at increasing students' knowledge awareness, and at the same time teachers can gather additional evidence of students' knowledge in particular domain areas. Teachers can also use score report information to share student performance information with parents or guardians and help them become more involved in the learning process (Zapata-Rivera, Underwood, & Bauer, 2005).

Thinking of helping students become active participants in their learning process (e.g., Black & Wiliam, 1998; Assessment Reform Group, 1999, 2002) and considering their score reporting needs, we designed and evaluated a new interactive, game-like student score report. In this game the score report has been covered by six doors. The goal of this game activity is to uncover the score report. Doors are opened by answering a series of questions which currently deal with assessing students' understanding of the different sections of the score report (these questions about the score report can be modified to support a different goal). As students make progress, immediate feedback is provided to them based on their responses. After having uncovered the score report, students write about their performance and propose an action plan. This activity is aimed at facilitating student understanding of score report information and improving student engagement (Zapata-Rivera, 2009).

Figure 6.4 shows a character providing immediate feedback to students based on their responses. It also shows the door indicator and navigation buttons at the top of the screen. Figure 6.5 shows the uncovered score report. The four main sections of the score report are visible: identifying information (Your Space; upper-left area), purpose and use (top middle area), what you did on test three and a summary of performance on test three tasks (right side), and overall performance results based on the current test as well as past tests (bottom-left area). Figure 6.6 shows a dialogue box that prompts the student to provide ideas for improving his/her performance. The student also has the option of sharing this plan with the teacher or parents/guardians.

Results of a usability study with eight local middle school students showed that students find the activity engaging and the contents of the score report clear. Students made suggestions aimed at improving the look and feel of the interactive score report (e.g., using popular cartoon characters and raising the prominence of the cartoon character). Students appreciated

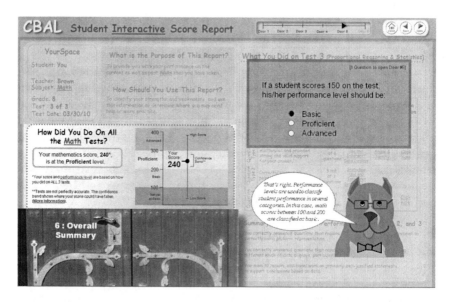

Figure 6.4 How did you do on all the math tests? (Door 5; Immediate Feedback).

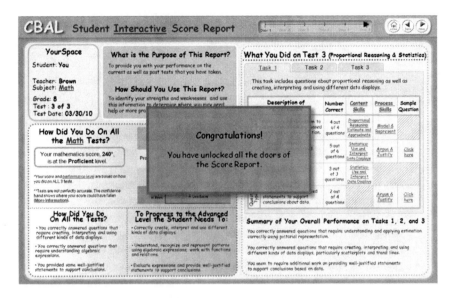

Figure 6.5 Uncovered score report.

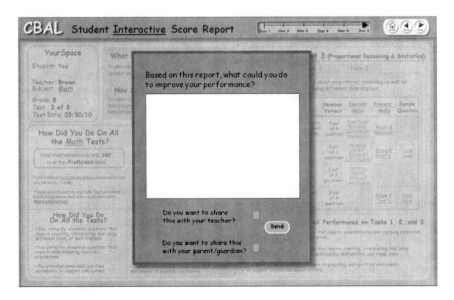

Figure 6.6 Writing and sharing an action plan.

the opportunity to share their own improvement plan with the teacher or parents/guardians.

Integrating Game Elements into the Interactive Score Report

The game elements in the interactive student score report include:

- *Uncovering the score report (storyline).* This activity serves two different purposes: it provides students with a familiar activity that guides their interaction with the score report and it focuses their attention to particular areas of the score report. Questions aimed at eliciting student understanding of particular areas of the score report are presented according to the door (area) that is being explored.
- *Immediate feedback to students.* A virtual dog is used to provide directions and feedback to students about their understanding of the report. This feedback includes verification feedback and hints tailored to help students find the correct answers. When all the options have been tried, the correct answer is provided to the students. The dog is also used to introduce students to the game activity as part of an initial tutorial. In addition, the score report includes links to additional information (e.g., definitions, statistical terms and sample test questions) that can be used to answer some of the questions. Data gathered is currently being used to explore usability aspects of the score report (Zapata-Rivera, 2009).
- *Navigation.* Students can either follow a sequential order when uncovering sections of the report (default navigation sequence) or explore the sections of the report in any order that they desire.

DISCUSSION

The examples presented in the previous section describe how game elements can be integrated into assessment components, in this case educational, assessment-based games for formative purposes and for student score reports. These are just some examples of the types of educational games that are available. Other examples are the DimensionU educational games (Math, Literacy, Science and History; Tabula Digita, 2010), which provide teachers with information regarding student performance on the games. These games have been shown to improve student math performance and motivation when compared to traditional classroom instruction (Kebritchi, 2007).

We expect that new games will have a better integration among content, game and assessment elements. Some researchers have been working on the development of embedded (stealth) assessments components that can be used to assess student learning in games (e.g., Shute, Masduki, & Donmez, in press; Shute, Ventura, Bauer, & Zapata-Rivera, 2009). These games will be able to provide teachers and other educational stakeholders with valid assessment information through the use of assessment activities seamlessly embedded in the game.

Work in this area should explore models for integrating these innovative assessment systems into comprehensive assessment systems. Issues related to alignment with all the components of the comprehensive assessment system will need to be taken into consideration. As new interactive tasks continue to be used for formative assessment purposes, compatible summative assessments are expected to be developed.

ACKNOWLEDGEMENTS

We would like to acknowledge the members of our development team: Janet Stumper, Thomas Florek, Waverely VanWinkle and Meg Vezzu for their hard work and the teachers and students who participated in the development and evaluation of these systems. Finally, we would like to thank Eric Hansen, Brian Young, and one anonymous reviewer for providing insightful comments on a previous version of this manuscript.

NOTE

1. Interpretations of these demands using assessment terms have been added.

REFERENCES

Armstrong, A., & Georgas, H. (2006). Using interactive technology to teach information literacy concepts to undergraduate students. *Reference Services Review, 34*(4), 491–497.

Assessment Reform Group. (1999). Assessment for learning: Beyond the black box. Retrieved from http://www.assessment-reform-group.org/AssessInsides.pdf

Assessment Reform Group. (2002). Assessment for learning: 10 principles: research-based principles to guide classroom practice. Retrieved from http://www.assessment-reform-group.org/CIE3.PDF

Banathy, B. H. (1992). *A systems view of education: Concepts and principles for effective practice.* Englewood Cliffs, NJ: Educational Technology Publications.

Barab, S., Dodge, T., Tuzun, H., Job-Sluder, K., Jackson, C., Arici, A.,...Heiselt, C. (2007). The Quest Atlantis Project: A socially-responsive play space for learning. In B. E. Shelton & D. Wiley (Eds.), *The educational design and use of simulation computer games* (pp. 159–186). Rotterdam, The Netherlands: Sense Publishers.

Bennett, R. E., & Gitomer, D. H. (2009). Transforming K–12 assessment: Integrating accountability testing, formative assessment and professional support. In C. Wyatt-Smith & J. Cumming (Eds.), *Educational assessment in the 21st century* (pp. 43–62). New York: Springer.

Bennett, R. E., Persky, H., Weiss, A., & Jenkins, F. (2007). Problem-Solving in technology rich environments: A report from the NAEP technology-based assessment project. NCES 2007-466, U.S. Department of Education, National Center for Educational Statistics, U.S. Government Printing Office, Washington, DC.

Biswas, G., Schwartz, D., Bransford, J., & the Teachable Agent Group at Vanderbilt (TAG-V) (2001). Technology support for complex problem solving: From SAD environments to AI. In K. D. Forbus & P. J. Feltovich (Eds.), *Smart machines in education: The coming revolution in educational technology* (pp. 71–97). Menlo Park, CA: AAAI/MIT Press.

Black, P., & Wiliam, D. (1998). Assessment and classroom learning. *Assessment in Education, 5*(1), 7–74.

Carey, R. (2006). Serious game engine shootout: A comparative analysis of technology for serious game development. Retrieved March 23, 2007, from http://seriousgamessource.com/features/feature_022107_shootout_1.php

Chan, T. W., & Baskin, A. B. (1990). Learning companion systems. In C. Frasson, & G. Gauthier (Eds.). *Intelligent tutoring systems: At the crossroads of AI and* education (pp. 6–33). Norwood, NJ: Ablex Pub.

Crawford, C. (1982). The art of computer game design. Retrieved April 20, 2010, from http://www.vancouver.wsu.edu/fac/peabody/game-book/ACGD.pdf

Csikszentmihalyi, M. (1990). *Flow: The psychology of optical experience.* New York: Harper Perrennial.

Darling-Hammond, L., & Pecheone, R. (2010). Developing an internationally comparable balanced assessment system that supports high-quality learning. Retrieved from http://www.k12center.org/publications.html.

Darling-Hammond, L. (2010). Performance counts: Assessment systems that support high-quality learning. Washington, DC: The Council of Chief State School Officers. Retrieved on May 20, 2010 from http://flareassessment.org/resources/Paper_Assessment_DarlingHammond.pdf

Dede, C. (2007). Transforming education for the 21st Century: New pedagogies that help all students attain sophisticated learning outcomes. Harvard University: Commissioned by the NCSU Friday Institute. Retrieved on April 20, 2010 from http://tdhahwiki.wikispaces.com/file/view/Dede_21stC-skills_semi-final.pdf

Federation of American Scientists. (2006). Summit on educational games—Harnessing the power of video games for learning. Retrieved on January 20, 2010 from http://fas.org/gamesummit/Resources/Summit%20on%20Educational%20Games.pdf

Frederiksen, J. R., & Collins, A. (1989). A systems approach to educational testing. *Educational Researcher, 18*, 27–32

Gee, J. P. (2003). *What video games have to teach us about learning and literacy.* New York: Palgrave Macmillan.

Graesser, A. C., Person, N., Harter, D., & TRG. (2001). Teaching tactics and dialog in AutoTutor. *International Journal of Artificial Intelligence in Education, 12*, 257–279.

Hansen, E. G., & Zapata-Rivera, D. (2010). Evidence centered design (ECD) for a game-based assessment-for-learning (AfL) system for diverse students to learn mathematics. Presentation at the annual meeting of the National Council on Measurement in Education (NCME) on May 3, 2010 in Denver, Colorado.

Hattie, J., & Timperley, H. (2007). The power of feedback. *Review of Educational Research. 77*(1), 81–112.

Hogle, J. (1996). Considering games as cognitive tools: In search of effective "edutainment." Retrieved on January 20, 2010 from http://twinpinefarm.com/pdfs/games.pdf

Juul, J. (2005). *Half-real: Video games between real rules and fictional worlds.* Cambridge, MA: The MIT Press.

Kebritchi, M. (2007). The effects of modern math video games on student math achievement and math course motivation. Unpublished dissertation. College of Education, Department of Educational Technology, Research and Leadership. University of Central Florida.

Klopfer, E., Osterweil, S., & Salen, K. (2009). Moving learning games forward. Cambridge, MA: The Education Arcade, MIT. Retrieved on December 20, 2009 from http://education.mit.edu/papers/MovingLearningGamesForward_EdArcade.pdf

Lepper, M. R., & Malone, T. W. (1987). Intrinsic motivation and instructional effectiveness in computer-based education. In R. E. Snow & M. J. Farr (Eds.), *Aptitude, learning, and instruction: Vol. 3. Conative and affective process analyses* (pp. 255–286). Hillsdale, NJ: Lawrence Erlbaum.

Lim, C. P., Nonis, D., & Hedberg, J. (2006). Gaming in a 3-D multiuser virtual environment: engaging students in Science lessons. *British Journal of Educational Technology, 37*(2), 211–231.

Malone, T. W. (1981) Toward a theory of intrinsically motivating instruction, *Cognitive Science, 4*, 333–370.

Mayer, R. E. (2005). Cognitive theory of multimedia learning. In R. E. Mayer (Ed.), *Cambridge handbook of multimedia learning* (pp. 31–48). New York: Cambridge University Press.

Mayer, R.E., & Moreno, R. (2003). Nine ways to reduce cognitive load in multimedia learning. *Educational Psychologist, 38*(1), 43–52.

Messick, S. (1989). Validity. In R. Linn (Ed.), *Educational measurement* (3rd ed.). Washington, DC: American Council on Education.

Messick, S. (1994). The interplay of evidence and consequences in the validation of performance assessments. *Educational Researcher, 23*(2), 13–23.

Mislevy, R. J., Steinberg, L. S., & Almond, R. G. (2003). On the structure of educational assessment (with discussion). *Measurement: Interdisciplinary Research and Perspective, 1*, 3–62.

Prensky, M. (2001). *Digital game based learning.* New York: McGraw Hill.

Quellmalz, E. S., & Pellegrino, J. W. (2009). Technology and testing. *Science, 323*(5910), 75–79.

Rieber, L. P. (1996). Seriously considering play: Designing interactive learning environments based on the blending of microworlds, simulations, and games. *Educational Technology Research & Development. 44*(2), 43–58.

Shaffer, D. W. (2006). *How computers help children learn.* Basingstoke: Palgrave Macmillan.

Shute, V. (2008). Focus on formative feedback. *Review of Educational Research, 78*(1), 153–189.

Shute, V. J., Masduki, I., & Donmez, O. (in press). Modeling and assessing systems thinking skill in an immersive game environment. To appear in a Special Issue on: The future of adaptive tutoring and personalized instruction, in *Technology, Instruction, Cognition, and Learning.*

Shute, V. J., Ventura, M., Bauer, M. I., & Zapata-Rivera, D. (2009). Melding the power of serious games and embedded assessment to monitor and foster learning: Flow and grow. In U. Ritterfeld, M. J. Cody, & P. Vorderer (Eds.), *The social science of serious games: Theories and applications* (pp. 295–321). Philadelphia, PA: Routledge/LEA.

Squire, K. (2002). Cultural framing of computer/video games. *Game Studies, 2*(1). Retrieved on January 20, 2010 from http://www.gamestudies.org/0102/squire/

Squire, K., & Jenkins, H. (2003). Harnessing the power of games in education. Retrieved on November 20, 2009 from http://website.education.wisc.edu/kdsquire/manuscripts/insight.pdf

Supalo, C., Mallouk, T., Musser, A., Han, J., Briody, E., McArtor, C., . . . Kreuter, R. (2006). Seeing chemistry through sound: A submersible audible light sensor for observing reactions in real time. *Assistive Technology Outcomes and Benefits, 3*(1), 110–116.

Sweller, J. (1999). *Instructional design in technical areas.* Camberwell, Australia: ACER Press.

Tabula Digita. (2010). DimensionU. Retrieved on April 2, 2010 from www.dimensionu.com

Underwood, J. S., Zapata-Rivera, D., & VanWinkle, W. (2010). An evidence-centered approach to using assessment data for policymakers. *ETS Research Rep. No. RR-10-03.* Princeton, NJ: ETS.

Van Eck, R. (2006). Digital game-based learning: It's not just the digital natives who are restless. *Educause Review, 41*(2).

Zapata-Rivera, D. (2007). Indirectly visible Bayesian student models. In K. B. Laskey, S. M. Mahoney, & J. A. Goldsmith (Eds.), *Proceedings of the 5th UAI Bayesian modelling applications workshop, CEUR workshop proceedings, 268* (online). Retrieved from http://sunsite.informatik.rwth-aachen.de/Publications/CEUR-WS/Vol–268/paper11.pdf

Zapata-Rivera, D. (2009). Experimentally evaluating alternative report designs for CBAL: Math and writing. Princeton, NJ: ETS Internal Report.

Zapata-Rivera, D., Underwood, J. S., & Bauer, M. (2005). Advanced reporting systems in assessment environments. In J. Kay, A. Lum, & D. Zapata-Rivera

(Eds.), *AIED'05 Workshop on learner modelling for reflection, to support learner control, metacognition and improved communication between teachers and learners* (pp. 23–32). Amsterdam: IOS Press.

Zapata-Rivera, D., VanWinkle, W., & Zwick, R. (2010). Exploring effective communication and appropriate use of assessment results through teacher score reports. Paper presented at the annual meeting of the National Council on Measurement in Education (NCME).

Zapata-Rivera, D., VanWinkle, W., Shute, V., Underwood, J., & Bauer, M. (2007). English ABLE. *Artificial Intelligence in Education, 158*, 323–330

Zapata-Rivera, D., VanWinkle, W., Doyle, B., Buteux, A., & Bauer, M. (2009). Combining learning and assessment in assessment-based gaming environments: A case study from a New York City school. *Journal: Interactive Technology and Smart Education, 6*(3), 173–188.

CHAPTER 7

A TECHNOLOGY FOR ASSESSING MULTIPLE SOURCE COMPREHENSION

An Essential Skill of the 21st Century

**Susan R. Goldman, Kimberly Lawless, James Pellegrino,
and Flori Manning**
University of Illinois at Chicago

Jason Braasch
University of Poitiers, France

Kimberley Gomez
University of California, Los Angeles

ABSTRACT

Success in today's knowledge society requires the use of multiple sources of information to accomplish personal and professional goals. However, little is known about how young adolescents select, analyze, and synthesize multiple sources to address inquiry tasks. Using evidence-centered design we

Technology-Based Assessments for 21st Century Skills, pages 173–209

173

have constructed and tested web-based assessment activities for the selection of useful sources and for the analysis and synthesis of information across text sets. The activities are contextualized in science or history inquiry topics. The assessment activities are designed to provide formative information about student performance that can be used to plan instruction. The design process and the analyses of student performance on these activities are highlighting the unique challenges and opportunities of multiple source comprehension situations.

Two contexts serve to frame the contents of this chapter and its combined focus on technology, literacy, and assessment. The first context is very broad and considers the ways in which educators and researchers should be thinking about technology and its intersection with the processes of teaching, learning, and assessment in K–16+ education. To frame these issues we briefly discuss aspects of the vision put forth earlier this year in the National Educational Technology Plan (NETP) (U.S. Department of Education, 2010). The second context is more specific and focuses on a particular set of 21st century competencies that fall under the general heading of digital literacy. The specific focus is on understanding and assessing the knowledge and skills associated with the process of multiple source comprehension. We consider each of these framing contexts in turn as a way to situate the significance of the R&D work described in the remainder of this chapter.

THE NETP VISION FOR TECHNOLOGY AND EDUCATION

The U.S. Congress has mandated the creation of a NETP on roughly a five-year cycle. Prior iterations of the plan have been influential in policymaking at federal, state, and local levels, providing advocacy and guidance for decisions about how funds should be expended and how technology can be employed to best support the nation's education goals. For good reason, earlier plans focused on issues of gaining broad and equitable access to technology. Such an approach made sense as they were developed during an era that saw the rise of the Internet as a public utility and the rapid spread of powerful multimedia computers. The 2010 NETP, however, takes a different stance than the three prior plans because it arrives at a time when access to the Internet is nearly ubiquitous, growing numbers of people carry powerful connected computing devices in their pockets, and our knowledge of how people learn, from both psychological and neuroscience perspectives, is rapidly expanding (e.g., Bransford, Brown, Cocking, Donovan, & Pellegrino, 2000; Sawyer, 2006). Simultaneously, the education system faces unprecedented challenges in terms of student diversity (cognitive, developmental, socioeconomic, linguistic, etc.) and strained budgets.

In this climate, the 2010 NETP differs from its predecessors by focusing on core components of the educational system rather than technology per se.

The majority of the plan addresses current perspectives on *learning, assessment,* and *teaching,* as well as needed directions for *future research.* Furthermore, the plan thinks broadly about education, considering learning in both formal and informal contexts, across learners' entire lifetimes. The NETP urges policy makers to focus on grand challenge problems in educational research and development. "Grand challenge problems" are important problems that require bringing together a community of scientists, researchers, practitioners, and policy makers to work toward their solution. One of the four grand challenge problems highlighted in the NETP is "*Design and validate an integrated system for designing and implementing valid, reliable, and cost-effective assessments of complex aspects of 21st century expertise and competencies across academic disciplines*" (U.S. Department of Education, 2010, n.p.)

The model of 21st century learning described in the NETP that gives rise to the aforementioned assessment grand challenge requires new and better ways to *measure what matters*; diagnose strengths and weaknesses in the course of learning when there is still time to improve student performance; and involve multiple stakeholders in the process of designing, conducting, and using assessment. In all these activities, technology-based assessments can provide data to drive decisions on the basis of what is best for each and every student and that in aggregate will lead to continuous improvement across our entire education system. Among its recommendations to create more productive assessment systems for education, the NETP advocates for the following:

- Design, develop, and adopt assessments that give students, educators, and other stakeholders timely and actionable feedback about student learning to improve achievement and instructional practices.
- Build the capacity of educators and educational institutions to use technology to improve assessment materials and processes for both formative and summative uses.

For more than a decade, assessment has constituted one of the most controversial issues in education with respect to matters of theory, design, implementation, and educational policy (see e.g., Pellegrino, Chudowsky, & Glaser, 2001). Many of the arguments surround what we assess, how we assess, and the ways in which information derived from assessments is used to shape educational practice. As argued in various sources (e.g., Quellmalz & Pellegrino, 2009), new technologies provide opportunities to shift our assessment systems from a primary focus on summative and accountability practices to one focused instead on formative uses in which assessment information becomes an integral part of the teaching and learning process. But it is not simply a matter of using technology to shift how we assess students, nor the uses to which we put the information. Most importantly, it is a matter of careful consideration of what can and should become the targets for assessment—the types of knowledge and skill that arise in a 21st century digital world and that are essential for academic and personal success. It is the confluence of method, use, and content that offers the greatest chance for a dramatic shift in the productive integration of assessment into the processes of teaching and learning.

With assessments in place that assess the full range of expertise and competencies reflected in standards, student learning data can be collected and used to continually improve learning outcomes and productivity. For example, such data could be used to create a system of interconnected feedback for students, educators, parents, school leaders, and district administrators. For this to work, relevant data must be made available to the right people at the right time and in the right form. Educators and leaders at all levels of our education system also must be provided with support—tools and training—that can help them manage the assessment process, analyze data, and take appropriate action. This leads us then to the next major topic for consideration—those aspects of literacy that are appropriate and useful in a world dominated by digital content.

DIGITAL LITERACY IN THE 21ST CENTURY

Technological developments in just the first decade of the 21st century have made it impossible to ignore the changing face of literacy. Both the omnipresent access to online information resources and the unprecedented rate at which these resources have grown and continue to grow have focused attention on aspects of literacy beyond those associated with reading traditional print sources: search, evaluation, and integration of information across multiple sources. Although one can argue whether these are truly "new literacies" (New London Group, 1996), it is beyond argument that to be literate in the 21st century means being able to operate in electronic environments to address questions and solve problems that arise in academic, personal, interpersonal, and occupational contexts. Doing so means knowing how to locate relevant sources of information; evaluate sources for reliability, relevance, and quality; analyze the content of each source; and synthesize within and across multiple sources (Coiro, 2009; Coiro & Dobler, 2007; Goldman, 2010; Lawless, Goldman, Gomez, Manning, & Braasch, in press). Furthermore, Web 2.0 with its interactive capabilities increases the likelihood of collaboration and teamwork in carrying out these activities. In sum, technology-based digital environments not only make information *available* in multiple formats (e.g., audio and video as well as print) but enable answers and solutions to be produced in a range of formats. Recognition of this reality is beginning to appear in documents such as the recent Common Core Standards for English Language Arts (Council of Chief State School Officers (CCSSO) and the National Governors Association (NGA), 2010).

At the same time, extant data suggest that formal educational settings are providing very limited opportunities to acquire the literacy skills needed for success in the digital age (Goldman et al., 2011). A few research studies have examined upper-level high school students and college freshmen and reveal that these students use rudimentary approaches to locating, evaluating, and integrating information from multiple sources. For example, students often use imprecise key words in initial searches and have difficulty refining these for more targeted searches (Henry, 2006; Recker, Walker & Lawless, 2003; Wallace, Kupperman, & Kracjik, 2000). In addition, it has been demonstrated that learners' strategies for selecting from among a set of sources prioritize content overlap between the topic of the task and the information source, with limited attention devoted to evaluating the credibility or reliability of the information by examining the author, where the information was published, or the type of publication (Braasch et al., 2009; Britt & Anglinksas, 2002; Coiro & Doubler, 2007; Rouet, Favart, Britt, & Perfetti, 1997; Wineburg, 1991). However, other research indicates that sensitivity to the reliability of information sources is associated with better memory and learning of the information (Kim & Millis, 2006; Stadtler & Bromme, 2007; Strømsø, Bråten, & Britt, 2010; Wiley et al., 2009). When it comes to analyzing and synthesizing within and across information sources, the research indicates that learners have difficulty differentiating claims from evidence and conclusions (Brem, Russell, & Weems, 2001; Korpan, Bisanz, Bisanz, & Henderson, 1997; Norris & Phillips, 1994; Phillips & Norris, 1999) and tend to approach the different information sources separately and uncritically (Foltz, Britt, & Perfetti, 1996; Greene, 1993, 1994; Rouet, Britt, Mason, & Perfetti, 1996). When information from multiple sources is present in a response, evidence of conceptual integration is difficult to find (Goldman et al., 2011; Mateos & Solé, 2009).

It is important to note, however, that a few recently published studies indicate that both sourcing and integration are amenable to opportunities to learn. For example, several studies demonstrate that providing learners with instructions to evaluate sources and the basis for doing so increase sensitivity to differences in reliability (Britt & Anglinksas, 2002; Stadtler & Bromme, 2007; Wiley et al., 2009). Other studies demonstrate that making the connections among information sources more apparent through graphical overviews has a positive effect on cross-source intertextual connections (Salmerón, Baccino, Cañas, Madrid, & Fajardo, 2009;

Salmerón, Gil, Bråten, & Strømsø, 2010). Typically, however, the impact of such supports is found to interact with prior knowledge and epistemological orientation toward the topic as well as the type of task the learner is attempting to do (Bråten, Britt, Strømsø, & Rouet, in press; Bråten & Strømsø, 2006, 2010; Gil, Braten, Vidal-Abarca & Strømsø, 2010; Lawless, Schrader, & Mayall, 2007; Sanchez & Garcia, 2009).

The foregoing research findings stand in marked contrast to youths' involvement with digital media, largely in out-of-school settings. Indeed, youth are often much more actively engaged with digital media in out-of-school contexts than in in-school contexts (Lenhart, Rainie, & Lewis, 2001; Perez, 2009). The ethnographic studies of Digital Youth conducted over a three-year period by Ito and colleagues (Ito et al., 2009) indicate the existence of a robust youth culture built around online games, social networking sites, and mobile texting and communication devices. And often they are multitasking multiple forms of input at the same time (Lenhart, Hitlin, & Madden, 2005). The rapidity with which digital youth are becoming functionally literate in multimodal and multi-source contexts outside of school emphasizes the gap between what happens in formal educational settings and what happens outside of school. And their mastery of these skills belies the notion that multiple source activities are too complex for middle and high school students. As the gap between in-school and out-of-school literacy practices widens, society runs the risk of creating a youth culture that increasingly views school as irrelevant to what matters outside of school and to future career paths.

It appears then that from a number of perspectives it is important to bring a greater awareness of, and emphasis on, providing instructional support for acquiring the literacies demanded by the technology-based digital world of the 21st century. There are several challenges to address if this is to happen. First, educational practitioners need a better sense of the competencies, knowledge, and skills that need to be supported. Second, they need instructional techniques and materials that can be used to support them. Third, they need to know what knowledge and skills learners bring to the instructional situation and what progress they are making as a result of engaging in instruction. We take the position that high quality assessments, especially those intended to be used formatively, can address the first and third challenges and are thus critical to creating opportunities for youth to engage with 21st century literacies. Formative assessments can define the knowledge and skills that are involved and specify the performances that indicate that they are present. Good formative assessments make clear what students should know and be able to do and what we would take as evidence that they know and can do it (Pellegrino, Chudowsky, & Glaser, 2001). They make this clear to teachers, students, parents, and other stakeholders. This brings us to a consideration of the third section of this chapter: Our work on the assessment of a specific subset of 21st century literacies: multiple source comprehension.

THE ASSESSMENT OF MULTIPLE SOURCE COMPREHENSION

We approached the definition of 21st century skills in literacy from the standpoint of being able to use information from multiple sources of information to achieve a functional goal, such as answering an inquiry question or solving some problem. Too often comprehension is siloed as a goal in and of itself without practical relevance or connection to the world in which we live. Perhaps that is why over half of the adult population does not read well enough to meet their own health needs (Berkman, et al., 2004). Thus in the assessment context we developed, students are using source texts to accomplish a specific purpose, consistent with the increased emphasis on functional reading (OECD 2002, 2004, 2006).

Our approach to assessing multiple source comprehension relied on the formulation of assessment put forth in the National Research Council report *Knowing what students know* (Pellegrino, Chudowsky, & Glaser, 2001). According to that report, assessment is a process of reasoning from evidence—that is, conclusions about what a student knows or has learned are based on evidence of that knowledge or learning that can be externalized through some sort of observable performance. For quality assessments, three components of the reasoning process have to be aligned: (1) a model of how students represent knowledge and the skills they must appropriate to develop competence; (2) the observations that provide evidence in the form of student performance; and 3) the process for interpreting the evidence with respect to the model of competence. The Evidence-Centered Design (ECD) approach (Mislevy, Steinberg, & Almond, 2003) provides a systematic way to specify the model, the evidence, and the interpretation and is the conceptual design process we used to develop our assessment of multiple source comprehension.

In embarking on the assessment development process, we first constrained the type of multiple source comprehension that we wanted to assess by focusing on situations in which students were using multiple sources to answer an inquiry question in history or science. Historians and scientists routinely use multiple text sources to address questions in their fields to generate new theories, data, explanations, and knowledge claims (Bazerman, 1985; Berkencotter & Huckin, 1995; Goldman, 2004; Perfetti, Britt, & Georgi, 1995; Shanahan & Shanahan, 2008; VanSledright, 2002; Wineburg, 1991, 1994). In doing so they evaluate the credibility of the information source, the reliability of the data, and the strength of the evidence supporting various claims. However, the importance of each of these processes and the criteria used in the evaluation process are not the same across the two disciplines (Lee & Spratley, 2010; Moje & O'Brien, 2001; Shanahan & Shanahan, 2008). From an instructional viewpoint, both domains involve both information look-up (close-ended questions) and more extended inquiry projects (open-ended questions) (Stahl, Hynd, Britton, McNish & Bosquet, 1996; Wade & Moje, 2000; Williams & Gomez, 2002). Thus, developing multiple source comprehension assessment in these two disciplines allows us to specify a general set of knowledge and skills for engaging with multiple sources as well as realize the specification of the observations and the interpretation of the performance in the context of the practices of the different disciplines.

In the section that follows, we discuss the process we undertook in the development of our assessment across the three components of ECD. We purposely have allocated more discussion to the section detailing the development of the student model, because it is this step that is most often neglected in the development of assessments. That is to say, often researchers and evaluators jump prematurely past the specification of *what* must be assessed into *how* something will be assessed. One of the main purposes of the ECD approach is to prevent jumping to the design of assessment tasks that appear to have "face validity" without specifying in some detail the actual construct to be measured and the forms of evidence that specific tasks need to provide to support inferences about student competence. As we illustrate below, this process of specifying a domain model for purposes of designing valid assessment tasks is both challenging and laborious.

Evidence-Centered Design of Multiple Source Comprehension for Inquiry

The ECD process begins with a clear specification of the knowledge and skills that define competence in the domain of interest. This domain model becomes the basis for developing the student model. The student model is derived by creating claims regarding student performance (e.g., *The student can determine what information is relevant to the inquiry problem*) and the evidence in the student performance that is needed to support the claim. The task model defines the characteristics of the activities in which students will engage and thereby generate observations that speak to specific knowledge and skills in the student model. The interpretive model concerns how to appropriately "fit" the student model and the observations together; that is, how to use the observations as evidence for particular claims. In other words, the ECD approach provides conceptual guidance to defining what needs to be assessed, how to assess it, and how to make sense of that which is assessed.

The Domain Model

In developing our multiple source comprehension assessment, we based the domain model on extant theories, analyses, and empirical findings in library and information sciences, discourse comprehension, and literacy practices used by scientists and historians when reading in their fields. This led us to an initial student model illustrated in Figure 7.1. The model consists of five components that constitute groups of knowledge and skills that are relevant to successfully using multiple sources to address inquiry questions.

Interpreting the task is the process whereby the learner comes to understand the objectives, limitations, and boundaries of the task or problem and the kind of information that is relevant to addressing it. It may involve students posing their own question or responding to questions posed by others. One issue is the degree to which learners interpret tasks and adopt task goals that reflect the intended task as conceived of by the task creator. Indeed, students, including college undergraduates, often simplify open-ended, inquiry questions by turning them into close-ended questions for which they seek a single answer, often using a single source (Kuhlthau, 1993; Marchionini, 1995; Wallace, Kupperman, & Krajcik, 2000; Wiley et al., 2009). As such, correct uptake of a task is critical to any inquiry activity.

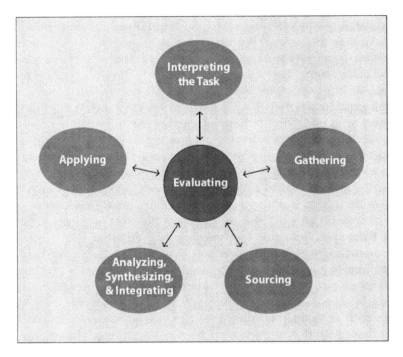

Figure 7.1   A six component multiple source comprehension model.

Gathering refers to processes associated with finding information that can be used to address the task. Learners might brainstorm various possible sources and how to locate them. Efficiency in this process involves a preliminary screening and may contribute to refining, altering, or substituting a new problem or question.

Sourcing and selecting refers to processes associated with determining the usefulness of sources for accomplishing the task based on initial screening of information sources that result from the gathering phase. This phase, ideally, reflects efforts to use information about a source, including its topic (indicated in title or brief summary), who wrote it, and when it was published to determine an initial estimation of its usefulness. It also involves estimating if one has sufficient information to address the problem. Decisions about sourcing and selecting may undergo revision as deeper analysis of the sources occurs.

Analyzing, synthesizing, and integrating information within sources and across multiple sources constitutes the processes of determining what information is in a source and whether it is relevant to the task. Some sources may contain information that is relevant and useful as well as information that is not. The learner has to critically evaluate the content from this perspective. Synthesis refers to determining how information from individual sources relates to the information in other sources; it involves comparison and contrast to determine whether and how information is consistent or conflicting. In the course of analysis, synthesis, and efforts to integrate information to address the task, the learner may determine that more sources are needed or some that looked relevant upon initial screening are not.

Applying information to accomplish the task requires that learners put the information together in a form that meets the constraints of the task. Learners must make decisions about whether the information adequately addresses the problem or question and how to "assemble" the information. Learners' knowledge of the norms and conventions for communicating disciplinary content play an important role in this phase.

Finally, *evaluation* plays a central role throughout multiple source comprehension in that it occurs within each component. In addition, evaluation also serves an executive coordination function by governing movement from one component to another (see Figure 7.1). Within each component, evaluation plays a key role in regulating the processes of that component (e.g., deciding when enough sources have been gathered, or which are relevant). However, the components are also interdependent in that the kinds of sources one gathers might necessitate a re-interpretation of the task, or upon evaluating the relevance of gathered sources, one might determine that more sources need to be gathered. In other words, evaluation occurs within each component and is critical to the coordination among the components. Our use of evaluation is consistent with metacognitive aspects of reading multiple sources (Azevedo & Cromley, 2004; Coiro & Doubler, 2007; Cromley & Azevedo, 2009).

The Student Model

Once the six overarching components in the domain model were identified, we developed the student model by unpacking each of the components in Figure 7.1 through a process of answering the question "What is meant by each component?" in terms of the claims about the knowledge and skills that a "competent" student would possess and therefore be able to demonstrate (Mislevy et al., 2003). This is an iterative process that ends when the claims specify skills and knowledge that are amenable to the development of task models of observable performances that can be used to provide the critical forms of evidence relevant to specific claims. Table 7.1 shows an abridged version of this unpacking for the Sourcing/Selecting

TABLE 7.1   Example of the Unpacking Process for Sourcing/Selection Component with Accompanying Claim and Evidence Statements

Subcomponent	Claim Statement Stem: The student makes use of …	Evidence Statement Stem: The work includes information …
Relevance	content information during the sourcing process	about the relevance of the content for answering the inquiry question
Reliability	attributes of the source information during the sourcing process	about the importance of source attributes
Source Attributes		
Author	author information in the sourcing process	about the credibility of the author or efforts to determine credibility of the author
Venue	publishing location in the sourcing process	about the credibility of the publication location or efforts to determine where something was published and the credibility of it
Currency/Date	publication relative to the content of the task in the sourcing process	indicating attention to date of publication in relation to task
Type	differences among kinds of resources (e.g., primary vs. secondary; fiction vs. nonfiction; opinion piece/editorial vs. news story) relative to their utility for completing the task	about differences among kinds of resources and their appropriateness for the task

component. The first column lists subcomponents of Sourcing/Selecting, the second illustrates the nature of Claim Statements, and the third illustrates Evidence Statements and their relationship to the claims.

What the subcomponents indicate is that sourcing involves determining the relevance of a source—is the content related to answering the question or solving the problem, as well as the "reliability" of the source. "Reliability" refers to the amount and type of bias or perspective attributable to the information in a source. Various attributes of an information source provide important cues to reliability and are important in guiding how learners interpret and evaluate the information with respect to its usefulness for their task. For example, in history knowing something about the author and the time frame of a document is informative with respect to the perspective that might be reflected in the document. That is, a British officer writing about the Boston Tea Party would be expected to have a different perspective on the event than a citizen living in Boston who was paying the tariff on tea. Journal entries or personal letters describing the event might be expected to reflect these differences in perspective, and a learner might therefore expect differences in the accounts. In science, the date and whether an article is published in a peer-reviewed journal are important to evaluating the quality of the data. Instrumentation available in the 21st century makes the collection of certain kinds of data more precise than would have been possible with the instrumentation 60 years ago. Differences in precision of the data might be very important for explaining discrepancies between data sets. The importance of an attribute in determining usefulness would be expected to fluctuate depending on the discipline and task context. We engaged in a similar process for unpacking all of the components shown in Figure 7.1. The results are depicted in Figure 7.2.

The Task Model

Moving from the claim-evidence student model to actual assessments of components and subcomponents involves developing task models that make it possible to gather the kind of evidence described in the third column of Table 7.1. The task model defines the context in which the "work" is produced as well as other relevant design features of the task situation used to collect the observations. In other words, the task model describes the situations and tasks that could be used to elicit student work that can provide observations that warrant statements about specific skills or knowledge as specified in a claim. A good task model is basically a template that isolates various attributes that can be manipulated to create multiple functionally equivalent tasks. We use the sourcing component as a context for illustrating how a task model is specified.

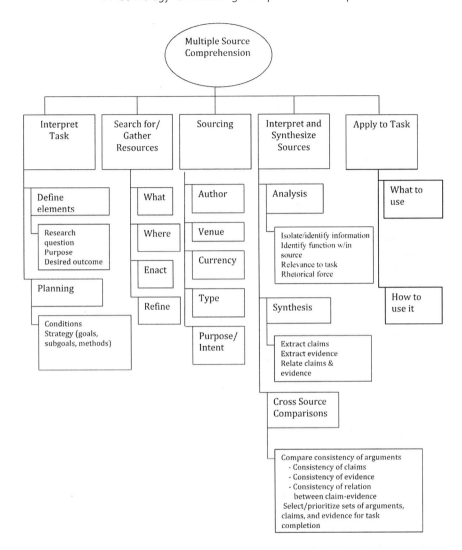

Figure 7.2 The Domain Model components and Student Model subcomponents.

The task model for sourcing represents the structure and features of sourcing task situations in terms of six parameters: 1) source, 2) work product, 3) context, 4) medium, 5) scaffolding, and 6) instructions. The source parameter defines the specific attributes of the texts that need to be specified when designing a sourcing task (e.g., relevance of content, author information, venue of publication, type of publication, etc). The source parameter also delineates some additional considerations that must be taken into account, such as the total number of sources that must be examined.

The work product parameter represents the type of work product students must produce, such as Likert rating, forced-choice yes/no response, essay, and so on. The context parameter indicates the type and amount of contextualization present for a given task and includes attributes such as the presence/absence of cover story in the task. The medium parameter denotes the medium on which a task is performed (e.g., computer or paper and pencil). The scaffolding parameter characterizes the type and degrees of scaffolding provided in the task. Finally, the instruction parameter designates the specific attributes of the instructions provided to students (e.g., where they appear, how much detail is provided and how explicit they are). In this way, the task model makes the process of assessment task design transparent because all the attributes of an assessment task situation are explicitly specified or explicitly marked as unspecified. This process, in turn, constrains the interpretation of the data the assessment task yields.

It was apparent to us that developing task models and actual task situations to assess each of the components shown in Figures 7.1 and 7.2 was more than we were going to be able to do. We decided to specifically focus task model development on just two of the components: Sourcing/Selection and Analysis, Synthesis & Integration. We prioritized these two because they seemed to us to most distinguish single source from multiple source comprehension and to constitute the core knowledge and skills important for multiple source comprehension in an electronic age (Coiro & Doubler, 2007; Goldman et al., 2010).

The Interpretive Model

The interpretive model relates the observations to the student model, indicating what the observations made in an assessment task situation imply for claims about associated knowledge and skills. The interpretive model includes the rules used for scoring or evaluating responses and is shaped by the purpose of the assessment.[1] That is, our interest was in creating a low-stakes assessment situation that would yield information that could help teachers plan multiple source comprehension instruction. As such, the interpretive model was geared toward defining what students *were* doing in the assessment task situation and what that implied about "next steps" in instruction relative to the specific subcomponent tapped by the particular assessment task. We discuss some assessment task situations and how we identified and scored subcomponents in that task in more detail in subsequent sections. Had we been developing a summative assessment for purposes of ranking students, the interpretation of the observed performances would have proceeded differently. The goal of the interpretation model in the context of formative assessment is to provide teachers with information useful to instructional decision-making. We thus attempted to develop interpretive models that reflected different performance profiles that had implications for instructional focus. For example, as will be elaborated below, if students were using information from only one information source in responding to the inquiry question, that would imply a different instructional strategy than one appropriate for students who were pulling in information from more than one source but doing so in a list format.

In the section of the paper that follows, we illustrate how we created tasks and materials to assess two components of the domain model for multiple source comprehension: Sourcing/Selecting sources and Analysis and Synthesis of Information Sources. We have implemented this process for two history topics (Immigration to Chicago and Civil Rights in the 60s) and two science topics (climate change and threats to the fresh water supply). We use the Immigration to Chicago topic to illustrate implementation.

SOURCING/SELECTING AND ANALYSIS AND SYNTHESIS

The assessment development work in which we have been engaged is designed to provide formative assessment information to teachers of middle school students, beginning with grade five (approximately 11 years old) and extending to grade eight (approximately 14 years old). We developed our student model to reflect the competencies of a proficient multiple source comprehender, but our task models defined parameters within which students in this age/grade range might be able to demonstrate mastery. This meant defining the number of sources and difficulty levels of the sources as well as identifying content that students in this age range would be sufficiently familiar with so that prior knowledge would not severely hamper performance. The topic that is used to illustrate the assessment of sourcing/selection and analysis/synthesis is the movement of people to Chicago between 1830 and 1930, transforming it from a small town of 100 people in 1830 to a metropolis of over 3 million people in 1930. The overall inquiry task for students was to address the question "Why did so many people move to Chicago between 1830 and 1930?"

The Sourcing/Selection Task Situation

In the domain model, the Sourcing component operates on sources that have been returned through an initial searching and gathering process. For example, one might submit a keyword or two to a Google search to gather an initial set of sources. The items among the list of sources "returned" vary in their utility for completing the task. Sourcing, as we have defined it in our domain model, refers to processes of "filtering" the items in the list of sources and selecting a subset for further, more in-depth examination. In our design, the Sourcing/Selection Task situation defines useful sources as those that are relevant to the topic and task and that are trustworthy. The source topic along with the attribute subcomponents shown in Figure 7.2 provide information important to determining relevance and trustworthiness. The task situation for Sourcing consisted of three activities to assess students' skill at each of these: Relevance Judgments, Trustworthiness Judgments, and Usefulness Ranking. Students received a score for each of these activities. The task model specified the basic characteristics of the set of sources: The set of eight needed to reflect a range of relevance and trustworthiness but were modified versions of authentic sources found through Google searches. The information about each source was similar to what might be present in a bibliographic reference and abstract of an article: For each source, there was a title, a 25-word summary describing the content, date and publication venue, author information, and type of publication.

The set of eight sources was rated by an independent set of expert judges (members of the research team not involved in generating the sources but familiar with criteria for reliability in history). According to the expert ratings, two of the eight sources were not relevant, three were highly relevant, and three were somewhat relevant. This basic design of the source set constitutes the task model enabling the replication of the activity for additional inquiry topics.

In the Chicago Immigration task, the students were introduced to the inquiry question "Why did so many people come to Chicago between 1830 and 1930?" and were told they were going to decide on the usefulness of eight sources for answering this question. They were further told that sources were useful if they were relevant to the task and trustworthy. They then completed three activities: Relevance Judgments, Trustworthiness Judgments, and Usefulness Rankings.

The first activity—Relevance Judgments—was designed to assess whether or not students could effectively discriminate relevant from irrelevant sources of information based on the content summary and title of each source. In order to help ensure that we were assessing students' skills at determining whether a source was relevant and not simply their knowledge of the definition of relevance, the instructions defined relevance in the context of the assessment activity. Figure 7.3 is a screen shot from our web-based selection task in which we define relevance and provide students with two questions to think about in making the judgment. We purposively used the word relevance to make connection with academic language and disciplinary vocabulary. All information was audio recorded so there was voice over for each screen.

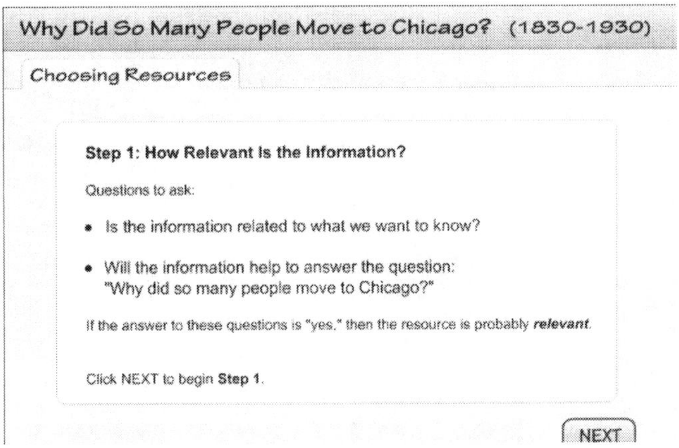

Why Did So Many People Move to Chicago? (1830-1930)

Choosing Resources

Step 1: How Relevant Is the Information?

Questions to ask:

- Is the information related to what we want to know?

- Will the information help to answer the question:
  "Why did so many people move to Chicago?"

If the answer to these questions is "yes," then the resource is probably *relevant*.

Click NEXT to begin **Step 1**.

NEXT

Figure 7.3 Screen shot from assessment application: Criteria for determining Relevance.

Students saw the title of each of the eight sources and clicked on the source to see the summary and make the rating. Using a three-point Likert-type scale (1 = highly relevant, 2 = somewhat relevant, 3 = not relevant) students judged the relevance of the content of eight sources of information in relation to the Chicago inquiry question. A sample screen for this judgment is shown in Figure 7.4.

Once all eight sources had been rated the student was shown the result and had an opportunity to revise any of the relevance judgments before proceeding to the second selection activity, trustworthiness judgment.

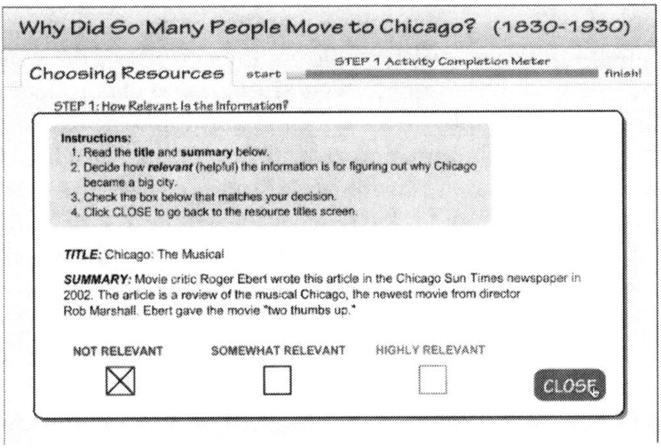

Why Did So Many People Move to Chicago? (1830-1930)

Choosing Resources   start   STEP 1 Activity Completion Meter   finish!

STEP 1: How Relevant Is the Information?

Instructions:
1. Read the **title** and **summary** below.
2. Decide how *relevant* (helpful) the information is for figuring out why Chicago became a big city.
3. Check the box below that matches your decision.
4. Click CLOSE to go back to the resource titles screen.

TITLE: Chicago: The Musical

SUMMARY: Movie critic Roger Ebert wrote this article in the Chicago Sun Times newspaper in 2002. The article is a review of the musical Chicago, the newest movie from director Rob Marshall. Ebert gave the movie "two thumbs up."

NOT RELEVANT   SOMEWHAT RELEVANT   HIGHLY RELEVANT

☒   ☐   ☐   CLOSE

Figure 7.4 Screen shot of Relevance Judgment.

Figure 7.5 Screen shot: Introduction to the Trustworthiness Judgment.

Sources that a student rated as "highly relevant" or "somewhat relevant" were retained for further examination for trustworthiness. Students make no additional judgments about sources that they had deemed "not relevant." Figure 7.5 shows the introduction to the trustworthiness judgment.

In the second activity the students are asked to rate the trustworthiness of any source they judged relevant by considering and rating four source attributes (author, type, publication date, and publication source). Hence this task requires students to think about things such as the credibility of the author, the reliability of the information and its currency. Students need to carefully attend to the source attributes in the context of the content and the inquiry question. For example, a geese migration expert may be highly credible in his/her field, but does not have any apparent expertise in historical trends in human population growth. Students make a holistic rating of trustworthiness and then provide an indication of whether each source attribute was helpful or not in deciding trustworthiness. Again, the holistic rating is three-point, Likert-type scale indicating highly trustworthy, somewhat trustworthy, and not trustworthy. The screens for these decisions are shown in Figure 7.6.

Only sources rated as "highly trustworthy" or "somewhat trustworthy" move forward to the Usefulness ranking activity. For this activity, students are asked to rank order the sources they rated as relevant and trustworthy

Why Did So Many People Move to Chicago? (1830-1930)

Choosing Resources   start   STEP 2 Activity Completion Meter   finish!

STEP 2: How Much Should I Trust It?

The Chicago Stockyards Are the Perfect Job
Michael Armour states his opinion that the stockyards are a good place for new immigrants to find work in Chicago. There are a large number of jobs helping to prepare and package meat, and the pay is good.

Instructions:
1. Read the details listed below about this resource.
2. Check the box that tells how much you can trust this resource.
3. After you decide how much you can trust it, you will get a new set of boxes where you will decide whether each the details below were helpful in making your decision.
4. Click CLOSE to go back to the resource titles screen.

Author:
Michael Armour, founder of Armour Meats

Date published:
April 29, 1925

Type:
Newspaper editorial

Who published it:
Chicago Tribune (newspaper)

Now make a decision about this *resource's* trustworthiness:

Not Trustworthy   Somewhat Trustworthy   Highly Trustworthy

CLOSE

(a)

Why Did So Many People Move to Chicago? (1830-1930)

Choosing Resources   start   STEP 2 Activity Completion Meter   finish!

STEP 2: How Much Should I Trust It?

The Chicago Stockyards Are the Perfect Job
Michael Armour states his opinion that the stockyards are a good place for new immigrants to find work in Chicago. There are a large number of jobs helping to prepare and package meat, and the pay is good.

Instructions:
1. Read the details listed below about this resource.
2. Check the box that tells how much you can trust this resource.
3. After you decide how much you can trust it, you will get a new set of boxes where you will decide whether each the details below were helpful in making your decision.
4. Click CLOSE to go back to the resource titles screen.

Not Helpful   Helpful

Author:
Michael Armour, founder of Armour Meats

Date published:
April 29, 1925

Type:
Newspaper editorial

Who published it:
Chicago Tribune (newspaper)

This is the decision you made about this resource:

Not Trustworthy   Somewhat Trustworthy   Highly Trustworthy

Now check the boxes that tell whether each detail above was *helpful* for deciding the resource's trustworthiness.

CLOSE

(b)

Figure 7.6   Screen Shots of (a) overall Trustworthiness judgment, and (b) judgment about importance of each attribute to making the judgment.

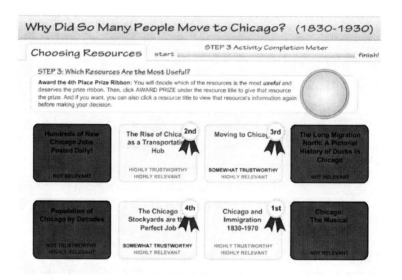

Figure 7.7   Screen Shot of the Usefulness Ranking activity.

in terms of overall usefulness in answering the inquiry question, "Why did Chicago became a big city?" This task is accomplished by having the student assign a first place "award ribbon" to the source they thought was most useful. The students continued to award 2nd, 3rd,... nth place ribbons to sources until they had assigned a ribbon to each of their relevant and trustworthy sources (see Figure 7.7).

Elsewhere we have discussed the details of the statistical and analytic techniques that we used to convert the judgment and rating data into scores that allowed us to characterize performance on the usefulness task and how the relevance and trustworthiness judgments related to the overall usefulness decision (Lawless et al., in press). For present purposes, we simply summarize the main findings that have now been replicated over several samples of students across grades five through eight.

Some students were very good at distinguishing useful from not useful sources, while others were not. For example, in a sample of 64 fifth grade students, 26 students met the criteria for good discrimination of useful from not useful sources, while 23 met the criteria for poor discrimination of sources (Braasch, et al., 2009; Lawless et al., in press). Students who performed at higher levels as compared to those performing at lower levels on the usefulness ranking task also performed at higher levels on the relevance judgment task; however, performance on trustworthiness judgments did not differ significantly. Pilot trials on the trustworthiness task using an open-ended response format replicated the attribute selection data found in the forced-choice format shown in Figure 7.6. The similar pattern across the two response formats suggests that the results are not an artifact of the response format.

One finding emerging across several samples of fifth to eighth grade students who have participated in the selection task is that those students who perform at higher levels on the usefulness judgments are also more efficient in terms of making use of attribute information. That is, they pay more attention to attribute information for relevant sources than for irrelevant. In contrast, those who perform at lower levels spend time on the attributes for all sources. Thus most students seem to know that source features such as author, date, and so on are important to consider, but students less proficient at this task are more unsure of when or why they are important to consider. Interestingly, when contrasted, the group of students who performed better on this task does not significantly differ on their performance on the district administered, standardized reading achievement test from students who performed poorly on sourcing. Thus, sourcing/selection—in particular the relevance judgment subcomponent of this task—appears to be tapping skills and knowledge not tapped by traditional assessments of reading comprehension.

The Analysis and Synthesis Task Situation

The task model for analysis and synthesis specifies the use of information from three source texts for a complete answer. The content of the texts was based on a consideration of the factors that historians typically discuss to account for the movement of people from place to place. These are *push* factors that encourage people to leave their current location, *pull* factors that draw people to a new location, and *enabling* factors that make it possible for people to get from their current location to new locations. Because we were interested in synthesis of information across texts, the task model specified that each text deal with one of the factors, but include some overlap in vocabulary that would assist learners in seeing the connections across the push, pull, and enabling factors. Thus, one text dealt with *push* factors (Titled: *The Search for a Better Life* and was about the inability of farming to support families), a second with *pull* factors (Titled: *Chicago: Center of Industry* was about industrialization in Chicago and availability of jobs for unskilled labor), and the third with *enabling* factors (Titled: *Chicago: Transportation Hub of the Midwest* was about rail and water transportation enabling the movement of people and goods into and out of Chicago). The text set was constrained to have minimal but some surface level connections in the form of overlapping words. The information and ideas in the three texts complemented rather than contradicted each other.

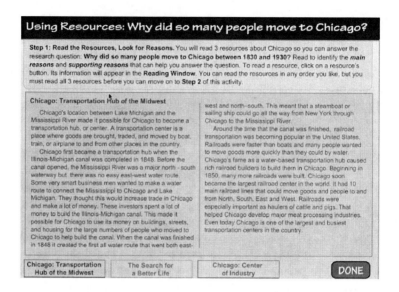

Figure 7.8 Screenshot of Synthesis Task Reading Instructions.

This task is designed to assess skills at using information from multiple texts to address the inquiry question, and we wanted to ensure that students began with a good understanding that this is what was intended in the task definition. Thus, the assessment itself provided scaffolding that defined using multiple resources as a jigsaw puzzle: The answer comes from many sources and you have to fit the reasons you find together like pieces in a jigsaw puzzle to answer the question. Students were instructed to read each source so they could find the main and supporting reasons to answer the inquiry question. The screenshot in Figure 7.8 shows the reading instructions for the Chicago task and the text conveying the *enabling* factors.

After reading the texts, students moved on to write their responses to the essay question. The writing screen had two sections: one for writing and one for bringing up the individual texts again. Thus, the texts were available to students during the writing portion of the assessment. Students were free to edit their writing. Log files enabled us to capture timing and sequence information during reading and writing portions of the assessment.

The interpretive model for the analysis and synthesis task specified a means of examining the essays for evidence that students: (1) were selectively including or summarizing information from the individual texts consistent with what was most relevant to the inquiry question (analysis); and (2) were connecting the information across the three texts and the relationships that were being captured in these connections (e.g., push-pull; enable movement, etc.) (synthesis). To conduct these examinations of the data, we created content structures for each text that specified which phrases or

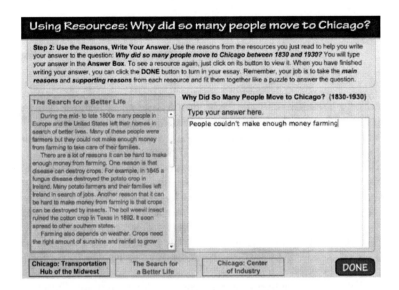

Figure 7.9 Screenshot of the Writing Phase of the Synthesis task.

sentences provided main, supporting, or detail information with respect to the theme/title of the text. A main idea was defined as the main reason(s) that supported the theme of the specific text. In the case of the *pull* factors text, these were statements about the growth of jobs in Chicago due to the emergence of three major industries. Supporting ideas were defined as information that showed that the three industries developed and had needs for people to fill various kinds of jobs. Details were ideas that elaborated the supporting ideas in a variety of ways (e.g., providing specific examples of a more general supporting idea). These content structures are similar to what Kintsch refers to as the *textbase* representation (Kintsch, 1994; Goldman, 2004). Box 7.1 presents the content structure for the *pull* factor text used with the Chicago task.

We mapped the student essay content to the content structure template to look at evidence of selective inclusion of information relevant to the inquiry question. In other words, the content structure mapping is a proxy indicator of students' skill at analyzing individual texts, identifying, and including in their responses the relevant, useful information as opposed to "just any" information from the text. In the case of the Chicago text set, evidence of "better" task-relevant selection would be reflected in a preference for the main ideas and/or supporting ideas over the details in the *push* and *pull* texts but for increased inclusion of details relative to main and supporting ideas in the enabling text. This was so because inquiry task-relevant information in the enabling text was conveyed in what were considered to be details given the theme of that text. Thus, the task model specified that

---

**BOX 7.1: CONTENT STRUCTURE OF *PULL* FACTOR TEXT:
CHICAGO: CENTER OF INDUSTRY**

Chicago: Center of Industry

In Chicago between 1830 and 1930, businesses grew a lot so they needed people to fill many different kinds of jobs. The jobs were mainly in three kinds of businesses: the railroad industry, meat processing, and retail stores that sold things to people.

The railroad industry provided many kinds of jobs. *Some businesses hired people to build the railroad cars. By the 1850s there were a half dozen companies making railroad cars.* One of the most famous was the Pullman Company, started by George Pullman. He invented the sleeping car. *Another important job was building and repairing the railroad tracks. Other people lifted and moved large crates and machines. All of these jobs needed skills that were not hard to learn* so people from Europe who had recently come to Chicago often filled these jobs. *The engineers who drove the trains had to know a lot more to get hired.*

By 1900, large numbers of people were working in the meat processing industry. *The railroads brought more and more cattle and pigs to Chicago so they could be turned into food and other products. To handle the load, the Union Stockyards opened in 1865. Meat processing factories in large numbers sprung up right next to it. Butchers cut the cattle and pigs into the meat* people bought in grocery stores. *The butchers had special skills. The factories also made other things like soap, glue and shoe polish. Most of these jobs required little skill and were easy to learn. For this reason, many people who came to Chicago without work skills or not speaking English could find work.* But the conditions in the factories were not very pleasant. They smelled bad and were very noisy.

During this same period of time, many retail stores opened and hired salespeople. *For example, Marshall Field opened his department store in 1863 and located it in the middle of downtown. People took jobs selling clothing and household items like sheets and towels. Other stores such as Montgomery Ward and Sears were in Chicago* but they mostly sold things through the mail.

Bold font: Main Ideas; *Italic font: Supporting ideas;* Smaller font size: Details

---

one text in the set have the property that the thematic content structure needed to be ignored to some degree in a search for information that was most relevant to the inquiry question (see Goldman, 1997 for a discussion of repurposing text information).

Evidence of synthesis required that students make connections across texts using inference processes such as cause-effect, if-then, super set—subset, and related forms of logical reasoning. These connections were not provided in the text set but constitute the construction of a "Situations model" or "Documents model" (Goldman, 2004; Perfetti, Rouet, &

Britt, 1999; Rouet 2006). Students could hypothetically make any number of cross-text, as well as within-text, connections, but only a subset of these might actually be relevant to addressing the inquiry question. To guide our decision making with respect to whether inferences present in the essays should be taken as indicators of cross-text synthesis, we constructed an "expert historian's" "situations model" that expressed the claims and support for them within each text as well as the inferences and connections across texts that expressed logical relations among the push, pull, and enabling factors relevant to answering the inquiry question, *Why did so many people come to Chicago between 1830 and 1930?* in the case of the Chicago topic. Thus, the situations model for the Chicago topic shown in Figure 7.10 captures claims and evidence for the push, pull, or enabling factors from each text (the rectangular and circular nodes in Figure 7.10), intra- and intertextual links, and links to the inquiry question. The content of the student essays were mapped against this representation.

We have explored a number of analytic strategies for summarizing the mappings between student essays and the textbase and situations model representations to provide formative information regarding the skills reflected among groups of students. To make claims about analysis, for example, we looked at the percentage of main, supporting, and detail elements

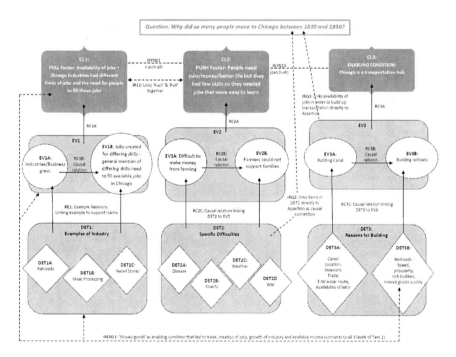

Figure 7.10   Situations Model for the Chicago task.

of each text that were included in the essays of 111 fifth grade students. The data patterns support evidence of analysis: Students were more likely to select main and supporting information from the *pull* or *push* texts than from the *enabling* text but were more likely to select details from the *enabling* text. This pattern is consistent with predictions about relevance of information in the texts based on the content structure and situations model representations. There was also some evidence that students understood that they were to use information from more than a single text to answer the inquiry question: 81% of the students included information from more than one text and 40% included information from all three texts. However, the mappings to the situations model indicated that inferences that reflected true synthesizing links were not that common. The overwhelming tendency was for sequential "blocks" of information from each source to be "listed" in the essay. Box 7.2 provides a contrast between a "blocked" essay and one that reflects greater presence of synthesis. To summarize, the most sophisticated essays reflected selection of the task-relevant information drawn from each of the texts with connecting links that signaled the integration of information across the texts.

BOX 7.2:   THREE ESSAYS THAT INCLUDED INFORMATION FROM MULTIPLE TEXT SOURCES BUT REFLECT DIFFERENT DEGREES OF CROSS-TEXT SYNTHESIS.

Example 1: Essay in "blocked" format. There is information from each text in the essay but each is simply enumerated as a reason with no inferential connections across the texts.

A lot of people came to Chicago and now I will write why did so many people come to Chicago.

The first reason I will tell is because of the jobs. Many new busines were opened in Chicago and they needed workers. People were coming from Europe and many other contries to work and earn some money. *The second reason is because* people were searching an better life. Many of these people were farmers but they could not make enough money from farming to take care of their families. And was a hard time for them. *And third reason is* because of transportation. A transportation center is a place where goods are brought, traded, and moved by boat, train, or airplane to and from other places in the country. Chicago soon became the largest railroad center in the world. It had 10 main railroad lines that could move goods and people to and from north, south, east, and west.

I think those and more other reason's were good to come to Chicago and a lot came here because of these reasons why people came to Chicago. (364)

Example 2: Explicit Connections synthesize push and pull factors

Why did so many people come to Chicago between 1830 and 1930? I believe so many people came to Chicago between 1830–1930 because businesses grew a lot. So because that happened they needed people to fill many different kinds of jobs. All of these jobs needed skills that were not heard to learn. This give people from Europe to come to Chicago to fill these jobs. The(y) was searching for a better life. They just knew how to farm. They did (not) have many other skills. Chicago job had little skills so they went to Chicago. For this little reason, many people who came to Chicago without work skills or not speaking English could find work. Some of the people came to help build the canal. **And said the want to stay in Chicago. Before people came to stay in Chicago it was businesses. So the people would be poor and homeless because they would have a job. So it wasn't a lot of people there because it was small businesses. Small businesses could have a lot of people work there.** *So that is why so many people move to Chicago. (54r)*

Example 3: Explicit Connections synthesize push, pull and enabling factors

Why did so many people come to Chicago is because farmers kept losing their crops. Reason one is that disease can destroy crops. For example a fungus disease destroyed the potato crop in Ireland. Another reason is insects can also destroy crops. And because of this farmers a losing a lot of money so they are moving Chicago. *In Chicago between* 1830 and 1930, businesses grew a lot so they needed people to fill many different jobs. Since that happened I think that's why so many people came to Chicago. By 1900, large numbers of people were working in the meat processing industry. Chicago's location between Lake Michigan and the Mississippi River made it possible for Chicago to become a transportation hub, or center. Chicago first became a transportation hub when the Illinois-Michigan canal was completed in 1848.

So many people also came to Chicago because there are so many jobs especially the farmers came because their crops were being destroyed so they moved here for better jobs. *That's why people came to Chicago. (309- Explicit Integration)*

Sources and Types of Information in the Essays are indicated by the following different fonts:

Industry text

Better Life text

Transportation text

Prior Knowledge

Inferences (any font) are underlined

Inquiry question or rhetorical metastatements

With a larger data set (247 essays across grades five through eight) we were able to consider multiple indicators of synthesis to identify groups of students who performed similarly with respect to their essays. Using a cluster analytic approach, nine variables were submitted as the dependent vector of scores for each student. All of these variables were determined through experimenter-coding of the essays. As this stage, the data were required to be hand coded as we were working on refining our coding rubrics. As we move forward the intent is to automate this coding to be conducted by a computer. Five of the coded variables were elements of the situations model that represented the presence of different kinds of cross-textual connections in students' essays. The other four variables represented: the number of times students linked text content back to the inquiry question, the number of elaboration (non-synthesis) inferences they made, essay word count, and the amount of time spent on the writing portion of the task. Because this selection of input variables contained variables that were both continuous and categorical, a two-step cluster algorithm was performed on the data (Norusis, 2010). To determine which number of possible clusters is most appropriate based on the data, each possible solution is compared using the Schwarz Bayesian Criterion (BIC) as the clustering criterion. The results of the analysis yielded three distinct clusters of students. Based on their profiles across variables, we dubbed the three groups *Satisficers* (50%), *Selectors* (36%), and *Synthesizers* (13%).

- *Satisficers* produced the shortest essays, spent the least time writing, included the least amount of presented information, and did not relate content across texts. Approximately one-third of the essays included information from only one text, another third from two, and the remainder from three.
- *Selectors* produced the longest essays, spent the most time writing, included the most information from the texts, but did not relate content across texts, even though 77% of the essays included information from three texts. None of the two or three text essays included synthesizing inferences. Basically, students copied information from the texts with little to no transformation. Changes reflected selective deletion of information.
- *Synthesizers* connected information across texts, usually relating the push and pull factors. Whether the essays included information from two texts (22%) or from three (77%), all of the essays included at least two synthesizing inferences. Essay length, time spent writing, and amount of information from the presented texts were all lower than those of the Selectors but higher than those of the Satisficers.

As with the selection task, there were no clear relationships between either the text based codes or the cluster membership and performance on standardized reading achievement scores. This finding suggests that skill at answering multiple-choice questions on short passages is not capturing the same knowledge and skills needed to read to answer an inquiry question involving multiple sources of information.

We have used the same task models to develop formative assessments of Sourcing and Analysis/Synthesis for three other topics. We are replicating the basic results that we obtained with the Chicago topic. However, some interesting disciplinary differences are emerging that we think are indicative of the nature of inquiry questions in history and at least certain areas of science. In history, explanations are sought of events that occurred; what is in dispute (typically) is the causes that explain why the event occurred. In contrast, there are many health and environmental sciences issues where the issue is not why a particular event occurred but whether it will occur. This difference has potential implications for the task model and the topic areas in both history and science where parallel models for the two content areas make sense and where they need to be different because the fundamental nature of the inquiry is different.

To summarize our illustration of the application of the ECD process, we illustrated the use of the ECD approach for two particular task situations and demonstrated that they produced a range of performance within and across grades five through eight and shed some light on multiple source comprehension. It is noteworthy that performance on neither the sourcing nor the synthesizing task were significantly related to performance on district-administered reading achievement tests. Thus, the work to date has been very encouraging with respect to elucidating and developing assessments of knowledge and skills that are specific to *multiple* source comprehension.

SUMMARY AND CONCLUSIONS

Our goals for this chapter were threefold: (1) describe elements of a model for multiple source comprehension, (2) illustrate how an evidence-centered design approach could be used productively to develop assessments of student competence, and (3) situate the work in the context of a 21st century web-enabled digital world where technology is a central component of the educative process. We will briefly consider each of these three topic areas in summing up and discussing implications and future directions for the work.

A major premise guiding the lines of inquiry described above is that multiple source comprehension is a significant and challenging aspect of contemporary literacy in formal educational settings as well as outside of school. In a world where it is commonplace to hear someone say they will "Google it" there is a paucity of information about the efficacy of that process, especially judging whether the results are being used productively to address a significant personal, intellectual, or educational question. The evidence that exists on how individuals search for information, how they evaluate what they have found, and how they make sense of and use that information to solve a problem or answer a question suggests that individual skill in engaging in the elements of this complex comprehension process is highly variable. In addition, educators have a ways to go in determining how well students can perform such tasks and in how to assist them. We have begun a line of work that is designed to provide the sorts of formative assessments that can influence instructional decision making and increase the likelihood that instruction will be differentiated to meet students where they are and enhance outcomes through a more sensitive processes of monitoring strengths and weaknesses over time.

We provided two examples of the application of this ECD approach to the production of formative assessments of two important multiple source comprehension components: Sourcing and Analysis/Synthesis. In describing these as well as the other components of the larger multiple source comprehension process, we have attempted to show how the use of an evidence-centered design approach to assessment development is extremely productive since it forces a detailed articulation of a cognitive model of the target domain. Not only does ECD lead to the generation of valid and potentially useful assessments, it is also very useful for theory development. By systematically unpacking the components of the model to identify the claims one wants to make about student competence and the forms of evidence that would provide warrants for those claims, the assumptions about cognition are articulated in a form such that the "constructs" are operationally defined. This can support the design of tasks and a measurement approach where the inferences about student competence are transparent and readily defended. Such a connection among cognition-observation-interpretation is at the heart of the reasoning from an evidence model of assessment described in *Knowing What Students Know* (Pellegrino, Chudowsky & Glaser, 2001).

Nevertheless, there is much more work to be done in that we have taken only the initial steps toward the development of a comprehensive formative assessment of multiple source comprehension. Although we explicated the many types of knowledge and skills that constitute a full model of multiple source comprehension, we have only scratched the surface in investigating but two of the components. The task situations we have used reflect but one task model of each component. Thus we have tapped a fairly limited range of the situations and work products that students might be called on to produce in multiple source comprehension situations. For example, the text sets were of one particular genre and contained no conflicting information. Other task models for analysis and synthesis might include multiple genres, different points of view on the part of the authors, and contradictions in accounts or explanations. Inferences about students' knowledge and skills relevant to analysis and synthesis under these different task models would be expected to differ from those drawn within the constraints of the task model that we used in this initial work.

It should be clear from the description of the tasks developed and implemented to date for the two different content areas of history and science that there is much work still left to be done in developing assessments. The same can be said of elaboration of the theory of multiple source comprehension. Such work includes extending the development of task models to include other types of texts as well as conducting measurement studies that apply statistical machinery such as generalizability theory (e.g., Shavelson & Webb, 1991) to estimate component sources of variance. Ultimately, the goal is to use the tasks productively in a measurement approach that includes obtaining performance measures that can be used formatively for instructional guidance. Future developments include refinement of the evidence/measurement model as well as automated coding of constructed responses.

We envision carrying out such work under Project READI as part of the Institute of Education Sciences network on *Reading for Understanding* (Goldman, et al., 2009). Thus, it is useful to situate this work in the context of arguments about the nature of reading comprehension and its assessment. For quite some time there has been discontent with the assessment of reading comprehension beyond the most basic levels. This has been especially true in the context of large-scale standardized tests used for summative assessment and accountability purposes. Multiple critiques exist and include: (a) a failure to take into account the structure of the texts to be understood, (b) issues of content knowledge, disciplinary genres, and disciplinary differences in forms of reasoning and argumentation, as well as (c) the limited forms of text processing and comprehension required to answer typical standardized test questions. Perhaps it is not surprising that the recently issued Common Core Standards for English Language Arts take several of these factors into account in describing the nature of the competence expected of students across the three to twelve grade span. There is even allusion to the types of multiple source comprehension skills described in this chapter. Indicative of the disconnect between past work in defining and assessing reading comprehension and the present research is our evidence of the lack of a relationship between scores on standardized reading tests and performance on the components of multiple source comprehension. Such data certainly suggest that the latter are distinct from single source reading as currently measured.

Finally, it is worth situating the research and development effort in the broader NETP context with which we opened this chapter. Two things can be highlighted relative to the goals and objectives spelled out in NETP for assessment and its integration with teaching and learning: (1) *measuring what matters* and (2) developing technology-enabled assessments that can provide instructionally useful information for teachers and students. Our claim is that what we are assessing is one aspect of the competencies that matter in a digital world dominated by the web and ubiquitous access to multiple sources of information known to vary in quality, utility, and truth value. Understanding what components of literacy are required in such a world of information, how to assess them, and how to use that information to assist students in becoming effective comprehenders for educational and everyday uses seems to us an important and worthwhile endeavor in keeping with the goals of NETP. Similarly, we are trying to harness the very same technologies that give rise to the comprehension process to effectively and seamlessly assess what students are doing in navigating the digital resource world. The goal is to provide that information to their teachers and others as part of a continuous improvement process. In addition to these goals for the assessments we are developing, we see them as a tool for introducing teachers to the kinds of knowledge, skills, and competencies that are required for literacy in the technological age. We have designed them to be relatively seamless with the kinds of tasks teachers might use for instructional purposes. Indeed, the task instructions for the assessments provide the initial steps of potential instructional units designed to develop sourcing or analysis and synthesis of texts and across multiple texts. As such, they might well be embedded within ongoing instructional activities. Thus, while we have a ways to go in attaining the goals described in NETP, hopefully we are at least on the right path.

ACKNOWLEDGMENTS

The authors gratefully acknowledge the contributions of Yasuhiro Ozuru, Kimberly Richards, Rachel Doherty, Rebecca Penzik, and Kristen Rutkowski in the conduct and analyses of assessment data reported herein. The assessment project described in this article is funded, in part, by the Institute for Education Sciences, U.S. Department of Education (Grant R305G050091). Any opinions, findings, and conclusions or recommendations expressed in this material are those of the authors and do not necessarily reflect the views of the sponsoring organization.

NOTE

1. Our use of the term Interpretive Model most closely matches the evaluation component of the Evidence Model described by Mislevy & Haertel (2006) and is focused on the evidence rules for determining the salient features of student work to be derived from the tasks and that form the basis for claims about student competence. For our present purposes we did not attempt to develop a formal measurement model that is considered by Mislevy & Haertel (2006) as the second major component of the Evidence Model.

REFERENCES

Azevedo, R., & Cromley, J. G. (2004). Does training on self-regulated learning facilitate students' learning with hypermedia. *Journal of Educational Psychology, 96*, 523–535.

Bazerman, C. (1985). Physicists reading physics: Schema-laden purposes and purpose-laden schema. *Written Communication, 2*(1), 3–23.

Berkenkotter, C., & Huckin, T. N. (1995). *Genre knowledge in disciplinary communication: Cognition/culture/power.* Hillsdale, N. J.: Lawrence Erlbaum Associates.

Berkman, N. D., DeWalt, D. A., Pignone, M. P., Sheridan, S. L., Lohr, K. N., Lux, L., Sutton, S. F., Swinson, T., Bonito, A. J. (2004). *Literacy and health outcomes. Evidence report/technology assessment No. 87* (AHRQ Publication No. 04-E007-2). Rockville, MD: Agency for Healthcare Research and Quality.

Braasch, J. L. G., Lawless, K. A., Goldman, S. R., Manning, F., Gomez, K.W., & MacLeod, S. (2009). Evaluating search results: An empirical analysis of middle school students' use of source attributes to select useful sources. *Journal of Educational Computing Research, 41*(1), 63–82.

Bransford, J. D., Brown, A. L., Cocking, R. R., Donovan, M. S., & Pellegrino, J. W. (Eds.). (2000). *How people learn: Brain, mind, experience, and school* (Expanded ed.). Washington, DC: National Academy Press.

Bråten, I., Britt, M. A., Strømsø, H., & Rouet, J. F. (in press). The role of epistemic beliefs in the comprehension of multiple expository texts: Towards an integrated model. *Educational Psychologist.*

Bråten, I., & Strømsø, H. (2006). Effects of personal epistemology on the understanding of multiple texts. *Reading Psychology, 27*, 457–484.

Bråten, I., & Strømsø, H. (2010). Effects of task instruction and personal epistemology on the understanding of multiple texts about climate change. *Discourse Processes: A Multidisciplinary Journal, 47*(1), 1–31.

Brem, S. K., Russell, J., & Weems, L. (2001). Science on the Web: Student evaluations of scientific arguments. *Discourse Processes, 32*, 191–213.

Britt, M. A., & Aglinskas, C. (2002). Improving student's ability to use source information. *Cognition & Instruction, 20*(40), 485–522.

Coiro, J. (2009). Rethinking Online Reading Assessment. *Educational Leadership, 66*(6), 59–63.

Coiro, J. & Dobler, E. (2007). Exploring the online reading comprehension strategies used by sixth-grade skilled readers to search for and locate information on the Internet. *Reading Research Quarterly, 42*(2), 214–257.

Council of Chief State School Officers (CCSSO) and the National Governors Association (NGA). (2010). *The Common Core State Standards for English language arts & literacy in history/social studies, science, and technical subjects.* Retrieved July, 16, 2010 from http://www.corestandards.org/the-standards/english-language-arts-standards

Cromley, J., & Azevedo, R. (2009). Locating information within extended hypermedia. *Educational Technology Research & Development, 57*(3), 287–313.

Foltz, P. W., Britt, M. A., & Perfetti, C. A. (1996). Reasoning from multiple texts: An automatic analysis of readers' situation models. In G. W. Cottrell (Ed.), *Proceedings of the 18th annual Cognitive Science Society* (pp. 110–115). Mahwah, NJ: Erlbaum.

Gil, L., Braten, I., Vidal-Abarca, E., & Stromso, H. I. (2010). Understanding and integrating multiple science texts: Summary tasks are sometimes better than argument tasks. *Reading Psychology, 31*(1), 30–68.

Goldman, S. R. (1997). Learning from text: Reflections on the past and suggestions for the future. *Discourse Process, 23,* 357–398.

Goldman, S. R. (2004). Cognitive aspects of constructing meaning through and across multiple texts. In N. Shuart-Ferris & D. M. Bloome (Eds.), *Uses of intertextuality in classroom and educational research* (pp. 313–347). Greenwich, CT: Information Age Publishing.

Goldman, S. R., et al. (2009). *Reading for understanding across grades 6 through 12: Evidence-based argumentation for disciplinary learning.* Funded July, 2010 by the Institute of Education Sciences, U.S. Department of Education, Grant # R305F100007.

Goldman, S. R., with Lawless, K. A., Gomez, K. W., Braasch, J. L. G., MacLeod, S., & Manning, F. (2010). Literacy in the digital world: Comprehending and learning from multiple sources. In M. G. McKeown & L. Kucan (Eds.), *Bringing reading researchers to life* (pp. 257–284). NY: Guilford.

Goldman, S. R., Ozuru, Y., Braasch, J., Manning, F., Lawless, K. Gomez, K., & Slanovits, M. (2011). Literacies for learning: A multiple source comprehension illustration. In N. L. Stein & S. W. Raudenbush (Eds.), *Developmental science goes to school: Implications for policy and practice* (pp. 30–44). New York: Routledge.

Greene, S. (1993). The role of task in the development of academic thinking through reading and writing in a college history course. *Research in the Teaching of English, 27,* 46–75.

Greene, S. (1994). Students as authors in the study of history. In G. Leinhardt, I. Beck, & K. Stainton (Eds.), *Teaching and learning history* (pp. 133–168). Hillsdale, NJ: Lawrence Erlbaum.

Henry, L. A. (2006). SEARCHing for an answer: The critical role of new literacies while reading on the Internet. *The Reading Teacher, 59,* 614–627.

Ito, M., Baumer, S., Bittanti, M., Boyd, D., Cody, R., Herr-Stephenson, B., ... Tripp, L. (2009). *Hanging out, messing around, and geeking out: Kids living and learning with new media.* Cambridge, MA: MIT Press.

Kim, H. J. J., & Millis, K. (2006). The influence of sourcing and relatedness on event integration. *Discourse Processes, 41*(1), 51–65.

Kintsch, W. (1994). Text comprehension, memory, and learning. *American Psychologist, 49*(4), 294–303.

Korpan, C. A., Bisanz, G. L., Bisanz, J., & Henderson, J. (1997). Assessing scientific literacy: Evaluation of scientific news briefs. *Science Education 81,* 515–532.

Kuhlthau, C. C. (1993). *Seeking meaning.* Santa Barbara, CA: ABC-Clio.

Lawless, K. A., Goldman, S., R., Gomez, K., Manning, F., & Braasch, J. (in press). Assessing multiple source comprehension through Evidence Centered Design. In J. P. Sabatini & E. R. Albro (Eds.), *Assessing reading in the 21st century: Aligning and applying advances in the reading and measurement sciences.* Lanham, MD: Rowman & Littlefield Publishing.

Lawless, K. A., Schrader, P. G., & Mayall, H. J. (2007). Acquisition of information online: Knowledge, navigation and learning outcomes. *Journal of Literacy Research, 39*(3), 289–306.

Lee, C. D., & Spratley, A. (2010). *Reading in the disciplines: The challenges of adolescent literacy.* New York, NY: Carnegie Corporation of New York.

Lenhart, A., Hitlin, P. & Madden, M. (2005). Teens and technology: Youth are leading the transition to a fully wired and mobile nation. *Pew Internet & American Life Project.* Retrieved July 10, 2010 from http://www.pewinternet.org/Reports/2005/Teens-and-Technology.aspx

Lenhart, A., Rainie, L., & Lewis, O. (2001). Teenage life online: The rise of the Instant-Message generation and the Internet's impact on friendships and family relationships. *Pew Internet & American Life Project.* Retrieved July 10, 2010 from http://www.pewinternet.org/Reports/2001/Teenage-Life-Online.aspx

Mateos, M., & Solé, I. (2009). Synthesising information from various texts: A study of procedures and products at different educational levels. *European Journal of Psychology of Education—EJPE (Instituto Superior De Psicologia Aplicada), 24*(4), 435–451.

Marchionini, G. (1995). *Information seeking in electronic environments.* Cambridge, UK: Cambridge University Press.

Mislevy, R. J., & Haertel, G. (2006). Implications for evidence-centered design for educational assessment. Educational Measurement: Issues and Practice, 25, 6–20.

Mislevy, R. J., Steinberg, L., & Almond, R (2003). On the structure of educational assessments. *Measurement: Interdisciplinary Research and Perspective, 1,* 3–67.

Moje, E. B., & O'Brien, D. G. (Eds.). (2001). *Constructions of literacy: Studies of teaching and learning in and out of secondary classrooms.* Mahwah, NJ: Erlbaum.

New London Group. (1996). A pedagogy of multiliteracies: Designing social futures. *Harvard Educational Review, 66,* 60–92.

Norris, S. P., & Phillips, L. M. (1994). Interpreting pragmatic meaning when reading popular reports of science. *Journal of Research in Science Teaching, 31,* 947–967.

Norusis, M. J. (2010). *PASW statistics 18 statistical procedures companion.* Upper Saddle River, NJ: Pearson.

Organization for Economic Co-Operation and Development (OECD). (2002). *Reading for change: Performance and engagement across countries.* Paris: OECD Publications.

Organization for Economic Co-Operation and Development (OECD). (2004). *Learning for tomorrow's world: First results from PISA 2003*. Paris: Author.

Organization for Economic Co-Operation and Development (OECD). (2006). Assessing scientific, reading and mathematical literacy: A framework for PISA 2006. Paris: Author.

Pellegrino, J. W., Chudowsky, N., & Glaser, R. (2001). *Knowing what students know: The science and design of educational assessment*. Washington, DC: National Academy Press.

Perez, S. (2009). Who's online and what are they doing? *Pew Internet and American Life Project*. Retrieved July, 10, 2010 from http://pewinternet.org/Media-Mentions/2009/Whos-Online-and-What-Are-They-Doing-There.aspx

Perfetti, C. A., Britt, M. A., & Georgi, M. C. (1995). *Text-based learning and reasoning: Studies in history*. Hillsdale, NJ: Erlbaum.

Perfetti, C. A., Rouet, J. -F., & Britt, M. A. (1999). Towards a theory of documents representation. In H. van Oostendorp & S. R. Goldman (Eds.), *The construction of mental representations during reading*. Mahwah, NJ: Erlbaum.

Phillips, L. M., & Norris, S. P. (1999). Interpreting popular reports of science: what happens when the reader's world meets the world on paper? *International Journal of Science Education, 21,* 317–327.

Quellmalz, E., & Pellegrino, J. W. (2009). Technology and testing. *Science, 323,* 75–79.

Recker, M., Walker, A., & Lawless, K. (2003). What do you recommend? Implementation and analyses of collaborative information filtering of web resources for education. *Instructional Science, 31*(4–5), 299–316.

Rouet, J. F. (2006). *The skills of document use: From text comprehension to web-based learning*. Mahwah, NJ: Erlbaum.

Rouet, J. F., Britt, M. A., Mason, R. A., & Perfetti, C. A. (1996). Using multiple sources of evidence to reason about history. *Journal of Educational Psychology, 88,* 478–493.

Rouet, J. F., Favart, M., Britt, M. A., & Perfetti, C. A. (1997). Studying and using multiple documents in history: Effects of discipline expertise. *Cognition & Instruction, 15,* 85–106.

Salmerón, L., Baccino, T., Cañas, J. J., Madrid R. I., & Fajardo, I. (2009). Do graphical overviews facilitate or hinder comprehension in hypertext?, *Computers & Education 53,* 1308–1319.

Salmeron, L., Gil, L., Bråten, I., & Strømsø, H. (2010). Comprehension effects of signaling relationships between documents in search engines. *Computers in Human Behavior, 26*(3), 419–426.

Sanchez, E., & Garcia, J. R. (2009). The relation of knowledge of textual integration devices to expository text comprehension under different assessment conditions. *Reading and Writing: An Interdisciplinary Journal, 22*(9), 1081–1108.

Sawyer, R. K. (Editor). (2006). *Cambridge handbook of the learning sciences*. New York: Cambridge University Press.

Shanahan, T., & Shanahan, C. (2008). Teaching disciplinary literacy to adolescents: Rethinking content-area literacy. *Harvard Educational Review, 78*(1), 40–59.

Shavelson, R. J., & Webb, N. M. (1991). *Generalizability theory: A primer*. Newbury Park, CA: Sage Publications.

Stadtler, M., & Bromme, R. (2007). Dealing with multiple documents on the WWW: The role of metacognition in the formation of documents models. *Computer-Supported Collaborative Learning,* (2), 191–210.

Stahl, S. A., Hynd, C. R., Britton, B., McNish, M., & Bosquet, D. (1996). What happens when student read multiple source documents in History? *Reading Research Quarterly, 31,* 430–456.

Strømsø, H. I., Bråten, I., & Britt, M. (2010). Reading multiple texts about climate change: The relationship between memory for sources and text comprehension. *Learning and Instruction, 20*(3), 192–204.

U.S. Department of Education. (2010). *Transforming American education: Learning powered by technology.* Washington, DC: U.S. Department of Education. Available online at http://www.ed.gov/technology/netp-2010

VanSledright, B. A. (2002). Confronting history's interpretive paradox while teaching fifth graders to investigate the past. *American Educational Research Journal, 39,* 1089–1115.

Wade, S. E., & Moje, E. B. (2000). The role of text in classroom learning. In M. L. Kamil, P. B. Mosenthal, P. D. Pearson, & R. Barr (Eds.), *Handbook of reading research: Volume III* (pp. 609–627). Mahwah, NJ: Erlbaum.

Wallace, R. M., Kupperman, J., & Krajcik, J. (2000). Science on the Web: Students online in a sixth-grade classroom. *Journal of the Learning Sciences, 9,* 75–105.

Wiley, J., Goldman, S. R., Graesser, A. C, Sanchez, C. A., Ash, I. K., & Hemmerich, J. A. (2009). Source evaluation, comprehension, and learning in Internet science inquiry tasks, *American Educational Research Journal, 46*(4), 1060–1106.

Williams, K. & Gomez, L. (2002). Presumptive literacies in technology-integrated science curriculum. In G. Stahl (Ed.), *Computer support for collaborative learning: foundations for a CSCL community* (pp. 599–600). Mahwah, NJ: Lawrence Erlbaum.

Wineburg, S. S. (1994). The cognitive representation of historical texts. In G. Leinhardt, I. L. Beck, & C. Stainton (Eds.), *Teaching and learning in history* (pp. 85–135). Hillsdale, NJ: Lawrence Erlbaum Associates, Inc.

Wineburg S. S. (1991). Historical problem solving: a study of the cognitive processes used in the evaluation of documentary and pictorial evidence. *Journal of Educational Psychology, 83,* 73–87.

CHAPTER 8

THE RIGHT KIND OF GATE

Computer Games and the Future of Assessment

David Williamson Shaffer[1]
University of Wisconsin-Madison

James Paul Gee
Arizona State University

ABSTRACT

In the past we have referred to games as good "learning engines." Here we argue that games are good learning engines because they are first good *assessment engines*, and that games require the kind of thinking that we need in the 21st century. They use actual learning as the basis for assessment. They test not only current knowledge and skills, but also preparation for future learning. They measure 21st century skills like collaboration, innovation, production, and design by tracking many different kinds of information about a student, over time. Thus we suggest that the road to better schools starts by making the tests in school more like the games that students are already playing out of school.

Technology-Based Assessments for 21st Century Skills, pages 211–227

INTRODUCTION

We have argued in previous work that computer games are good for learning (Gee, 2003, 2007; Shaffer, 2007). Computer games can create virtual worlds where players solve simulations of real-world problems and in the process learn real-world skills, knowledge, and values. Parents and teachers can use commercial games to stimulate discussions of important social, intellectual, and academic subjects. But most of all, places where people learn—schools, corporate training centers, summer camps, or living rooms—should become more game-like.

Good games focus on problem solving. They provide a good mix of practice and guidance. They use language and introduce complex concepts when they are needed—and thus when those tools can best be used and understood. They provide extensive time on task, but players are motivated to spend that time because games provide a sequence of challenges that gradually increase in difficulty, so players are constantly working at the cutting (and most exciting) edge of their abilities.[2] These are all things that any good learning environment should have, and commercial games have to use them for commercial reasons: if players couldn't learn to play commercial games—and eventually master them—no one would buy them (Gee, 2003, 2007).

These good principles for learning are even more important in the 21st century, where students need to learn to work with others and with digital tools to produce and not just to consume knowledge. They need 21st century skills like collaboration, innovation, production, and design. Digital technologies—including games—are letting young people produce products and knowledge and to participate in learning communities as never before. Through the Internet young people are becoming amateurs with professional level skills in areas like digital storytelling, fan fiction, graphic arts, machninma, game design, digital photography, robotics, and so on (Leadbeater & Miller, 2004).

Computers have changed learning. More and more they are being used by privileged families to accelerate their children's skills in literacy, history, civics, and math, science, and technology. But the same changes haven't happened in schools.

THE PROBLEM WITH TESTING, NOW

The reason we have not yet entered the 21st century in our classrooms is simple: assessment.

Our standardized tests, coupled with our accountability policies, force teachers to teach to out-of-date tests. The curriculum is based on reading from text books and listening to teachers talking on drill and practice, rather than on doing, exploring, and developing deep understanding of complex topics and issues. Classes focus on facts and formulas that learners need to pass standardized tests, even though when people learn that way they have a very hard time applying what they "know" to solve real problems (Gardner, 1991; Gee, 2004).

Part of the problem is that in our schools right now, learning and assessment are quite separate things. A teacher teaches for weeks and months, but the judgment of how well student and teacher have done is made on one day, on a test that knows nothing about the development of the learner. It is an assessment that captures one small snapshot in time of what a student can do. Based on that small slice of time, students, teachers, schools, and neighborhoods are graded. Decisions are made that affect funding, careers, and futures.

If we are going to succeed in introducing the new ways of learning that computers make possible, first we have to radically transform assessment. Only when teachers, parents, educators, and policy makers look at testing and assessment in new ways will they look at learning in new ways. We've been designing *games for learning* when we should have been designing *games for testing*.

WHAT'S IN A GATE?

The idea of designing games for testing is less radical—far less radical, in fact—than it sounds. To see why, let us examine some of the features that any Good Assessment for Twentyfirstcentury Education (GATE) would have to possess.[3] We argue that three fundamental properties of assessment need to change in the 21st century: *what* is assessed, *how* the assessment takes place, and the *purpose* of assessment in the first place.

What We Assess

The single biggest problem with standardized tests today is that they are built around facts and information in and for themselves, rather than around problem solving. When students master facts and information in isolation they often can write them down on a test, but they cannot reliably use them in the real world (Chi, Feltovich, & Glaser, 1981; Gardner, 1991; Gee, 2007). Any GATE would have to be built around central problems in an academic domain (like algebra, civics, or biology) or a real-world profession (like medicine, engineering, or law)—any place where central concepts in 21st century thinking are put to work in solving complex real-world problems.

In assessing students' problem solving skills, a GATE would also have to assess 21st century skills. There are now lists of such skills (Partnership for 21st Century Skills, 2004), often including things like innovation, collaboration, civic engagement, critical thinking, systems thinking, technical skills, ability to produce with digital media, and so on, but nearly all of those lists include, at a minimum, collaboration, innovation, production, and design.

Moreover, a GATE would not just tell us what students know and can do *now*. Knowledge and skills change and transform themselves quickly in the modern world, so a GATE would have to provide information about how instruction has helped students be ready to learn more *later on*: that is, how well prepared students are to learn more in the same or a related area in the future. A GATE needs to include resources that let students learn during the test, so we can assess what Bransford and Schwartz (1999) and others have described as *preparation for future learning*. Recent work has shown that choices students make on problem solving can tell us a great deal about their ability to learn new material later on, and this makes sense: certain choices in a domain show that someone understands problem solving at a basic level well enough to succeed at higher levels (Schwartz & Arena, 2009). So a GATE would assess whether learners can make good choices and understand the consequences of their choices.

In other words, a GATE would *test whether students make the kind of choices that experts do in a domain as they work with other people to solve complex problems of innovation, production, and design.*

How We Assess

In order to test whether students are making good decisions while problem solving, a GATE will have to track multiple variables. Learning in any domain is a complex phenomenon. For example, successful reading for content (say, in social studies) requires at a minimum skills in decoding text, domain vocabulary, and interpretive skills. These different abilities have to work together in sophisticated ways. Learners with a problem in reading do not all have the same problem, and often the problem is an interaction between two or more different variables. So a GATE has to be able to track how a student's decisions and actions are related to his or her overall development—and thus needs to clearly explain its theory of how the domain being learned works, and how learning and instruction work best.

Since decisions and actions unfold over time, a GATE would also have to be developmental: it would provide information relevant to students' learning and growth at different points. However, it is difficult to measure how a student's decisions and actions are related to his or her overall development based on "one-off" measurement events, like our current tests. Instead, we need measurements that show what students can do over time and tell us about the course of their development and how it can be improved. Any GATE should tell us about the different paths that students can take to mastering a domain, and also tell us where any student is on one of those paths.

To do this, a GATE needs to integrate assessment with learning. Digital media make it possible to collect large volumes of information, and to organize that information in real time. In a world where we can collect copious information and visualize it in different ways, the distinction between formative and summative assessment begins to disappear. We will be using much the same information to help learners and to judge the success of programs, processes, and practices for learning. To accomplish this, a GATE should be part of the learning space. That is, students shouldn't have to "step outside" for separate assessment events. When diagnostic learning tasks continually assess the development of learners, we get a portrait of problem solving decisions in real time. We can provide feedback to customize learning, and we can probe the strengths and weaknesses of students' thinking.

Why We Assess

All of which points to what is perhaps the most significant point: we need to rethink why we assess students in the first place. In the world that the No Child Left Behind testing regime has created, assessment is largely about punishing teachers. But continuous assessments of multiple data sources about complex problem solving and 21st century skills would be more about giving teachers, parents, students, and other stakeholders useful and actionable information. Any GATE should yield information—and organize that information—in ways that help teachers, parents, students, administrators, or policy makers to take appropriate actions to improve instruction and learning.

Most important in that regard, any GATE has to deal with one of the deepest problems with our current assessments: they treat all learners as if they have had the same opportunity to learn—the same experiences relevant to learning—and judge them all alike. They are oriented to the "status" of each learner in the sense that we assess whether each learner has reached a level of performance labeled something like "proficient." We do not measure growth, only whether or not a student has mastered some set of skills, no matter how small or long a trip this was for the child. And we hold teachers accountable in such terms, regardless of the progress their students have made, making judgments only about how many of their students have reached a certain level.

This is clearly problematic. On a reading test, for example, some children have experienced the content of the passages on the test in other books they have read, media they have watched, or on trips to the zoo or other educational locations. So they can answer some of the questions on the test—whether a tiger is larger than an elephant, for example—based on background knowledge, while other children cannot. Some children have heard parents use school-based vocabulary many times—Latinate words like "process" and "establish" for instance—while others have not. A GATE would have to take into account the fact that some children have not had the same experiences as others and provide missing resources before or during the assessment. After all, what we care about is less whether a child has passed point X in their development than what they are capable of doing next. We care about what they are capable of doing in a world where they have to solve complex problems with collaborators and technologies, not whether they remember the relative sizes of two species of mammals.

Imagine, if you will, two students. One comes from a family that has provided many learning experiences outside of school. This student starts the school year working at the 11th grade level and finishes at the 12th grade level. A second student comes from a family that does not (and perhaps can not) provide many enrichment experiences. She starts the school year working at the 7th grade level and finishes at the 11th grade level. The first child is a year "ahead" of the second in terms of her "level" of performance. However, with the appropriate resources, the second child made up four grade levels in a single year. The question is: which of these students would you want to hire? The choice seems obvious if what we care about is how well students take advantage of opportunities and use resources, rather than simply measuring what resources were already made available to them.

What We Need

In other words, we need to break the mold in our schools and introduce a new paradigm for teaching and learning, focused on real world problem solving and 21st century skills like collaboration, innovation, production, and design. To break out of the old paradigm of teaching to standardized tests of basic facts and skills we need new assessments that:

1. Change what we test by focusing on complex problem solving, 21st century skills like collaboration, innovation, production, and design, and evaluating students' preparation for future learning;
2. Change how the assessment takes place by tracking many different kinds of information about a student, over time, and integrate assessment with learning; and

3. Change the purpose of assessment from sorting students and punishing "underperforming" teachers and schools to providing students, administrators, parents and teachers with feedback they can use to make decisions that support good learning, and that account for the fact that different students have had different opportunities to learn inside school and out.

That is surely a very different view of assessment than we currently have. However, to get an assessment system for the 21st century, we *don't* have to reinvent the wheel.

GAMES AS ASSESSMENTS

We don't have to reinvent the wheel because games are already an exemplary platform for assessment. They have much to teach us about 21st century assessment, and they can lead us to design a transformative assessment system that has the potential to usher in a new paradigm for teaching and learning.

Too often today designers of learning in and out of school first think about how the learning ought to work—that is, what the curriculum and pedagogy will be—and then worry about how to assess the learning. To be clear, we include ourselves (or at least our past selves!) in that group.

But games take just the opposite approach. They worry first about how to test and challenge a player in an effective way. The learning design then follows from the assessment.

Consider, for example, some of the key properties of games, and how they create the conditions of a GATE:

1. *Games are built around problem solving*, and on the choices and actions players take to solve problems. So players have to use facts, information, and other representations (like graphs, diagrams, maps, and models) in the context of making consequential decisions.
2. *Games inherently require and assess a set of 21st century skills.* Many modern computer games require players to solve problems collaboratively with other people. In a game like *World of WarCraft*, a team of five players constitutes what modern workplaces call a "cross-functional" team, composed of people with deep and special expertise in different areas who can understand and integrate with each of the other team member's specialties. Games place a premium on a player's ability to create, innovate, and produce. Players are pushed to find their own solutions to challenging *boss levels*,[4] and often share these solutions with other players on fan forums. Many games today come

with the software by which the game was made, so players can modify (mod) the game, designing their own levels and scenarios, becoming designers as well as players. Finally, players have to figure out and model the rule system of a game in order to use it. In a game like *Civilization*, the player must map out a complex set of relationships among variables within a civilization and across civilizations. In turn, the player must use this model based reasoning and systems thinking to his or her advantage in the game.

3. *Games assess whether a player is ready for future challenges.* Boss levels do not just assess what a player knows and can do—that is, they don't just measure a player's mastery of the previous level. They also are designed to see if players are prepared for the greater challenges ahead. Good boss levels test whether the player is ready and prepared to learn, and learn well, on the next level.

4. *Games collect information about players on many dimensions.* They track multiple variables and relate them back to players in clear and actionable ways. In a game like *Civilization*, the game keeps track of how players deal with problems across time: issues in the economy, industry, technology, military, environment, religion, diplomacy, and governance of a civilization. The game tracks how the player's decisions and actions in all these spheres are related to his or her overall development and success.

5. *Games track information across time.* Games are designed in terms of levels. Each level demands players have mastered the skills on an earlier level, and demands that they learn new skills on the new level. That is, levels are deliberately designed to model the development of the player as the game proceeds.

6. *Games integrate learning and assessment.* In a game, learning and assessment are, in many ways, inseparable, and it is often hard to tell where one ends and the other begins. Every action a player takes and every choice a player makes has consequences. The player is given feedback about what worked and what did not. The player's actions and choices across a game as a whole are tracked and the player is informed in various ways as to how he or she is progressing. Results are always apparent. But such information does not only help, mentor, and develop learners. All the information the game does or could track and give back to the player as helpful feedback is also just the sort of information that could give us a deeply nuanced evaluation of the player and his or her learning.

7. *Games provide information that players can use to get better at the game.* The information a game gives a player, level by level—or when the player gets graphs and diagrams in a real-time-strategy game like *Rise of Nations*—is not used primarily to sort the player against other play-

ers;[5] rather the information is meant to be acted on, and so is presented in ways that make it actionable. It is the sort of information that allows players—and would allow people who wanted to mentor them—to make decisions about what to do next to get better, have more success, and develop. When a player finishes a level of an action game like *Darksiders*, the player knows whether he or she should repeat the level to get better, practice certain skills with more care in the next level, or try a new approach to the game. When a player gets feedback from a real-time strategy game like *Age of Empires*, he or she knows what went well and what went poorly in the last session of play, and has ideas about specific things to try next.

8. *Games have to be equitable.* To market a game successfully, game designers need to make games so that poor people and rich people, minorities and non-minorities, and players with little experience and players with lots of experience can play them. After all, the game industry is a business, and it cannot afford to cater only to the best players (although it cannot afford to lose them either). Games have traditionally not done a very good job at inviting girls and women in, but this is being remedied. The majority of players of the best selling game of all time, *The Sims*, are girls and women. The game industry is well aware that how much experience a player has already had with games or games of a certain type will predict a good deal about how well that player plays a new game of the same type. So games take this into consideration and offer different resources and different rewards for different sorts of players. Games resource players with less experience differently than they do more experienced players. They offer tutorials, advice and hints, lower difficulty levels, the ability to replay levels and so on. Sometimes they adjust the difficulty of the game on the fly, making it easier or harder based on how well the player is doing moment by moment.

Deep down, games do not just "have good assessments built into them." Games are nothing *but* good assessment. The player is always being tested, given feedback, and challenged to get better. Good game design starts with the question: How will the player be tested? The design follows from that: How can we help the player pass the test? How will we know the player has passed the test? If the player can pass one test, what's the next test he or she should be able to pass on the way to mastery? How do we know the test is fair?[6] These questions lead games to incorporate good learning designs precisely because they have first incorporated good assessment designs.

Good games achieve good learning because they do not set out, first and foremost, to teach. They set out to assess, and their approach to assessment leads to good teaching and learning.

THREE POSSIBLE SOLUTIONS

The fact that games are based, fundamentally, on the kind of assessments we need to promote 21st century learning has three immediate—and very dramatic—consequences, for games and for learning.

Adopt Game Principles

The first, and perhaps most evident, is that designers of 21st century assessments can learn a lot from games. Too much of the work currently being done on digital tools for assessment takes the same old standardized tests as a model: finding ways to make them cheaper, to use question banks more effectively, to make them more time-efficient by skipping questions a student is likely to get right, to make it harder to cheat, and so on.

Games offer a radically different example for assessment designers to build from: a kind of working model of what a 21st century test can look like. Designers can look for guidance to see how games offer hints or provide just-in-time resources to struggling students. They can look at how feedback is presented in games to help students and teachers use assessment as a constructive tool—that is, how to present feedback that can actually help students learn from the test. They can look at how games capture and use multiple sources of data over long periods of time to get information about a student's work. And perhaps most of all, they can look at games to see an example of how to present students with complex problems that require collaboration, systems thinking, and creativity to solve.

In other words, games can provide educators with an example of assessments that are *standardized*—in the sense that every player who opens a box or logs onto a game's website gets the *same game*—but that are about more than basic facts and basic skills.

But there is a more transformative consequence of the fact that games are good examples of 21st century assessment: Namely, that we can—and should—use games instead of traditional tests to assess what students know.

Using Existing Games as Assessments

The simplest way to use games as assessments is to have students play existing games and use their performance in the games (or perhaps their ability to explain what they did in the game and why) as a test of how well they understand a domain of knowledge.

For example, consider the game *Civilization*.[7] *Civilization* is a strategy game in which players build an empire starting from a Stone Age settlement. They make strategic decisions to invest in technological development or agriculture, and to use a combination of trade, diplomacy, religious conversion, and warfare with their neighbors. The game is based on historically accurate information about advances in technology, religion, warfare, and the arts, and takes a materialist-determinist approach to history, like the one presented by Jared Diamond in his Pulitzer Prize-winning book *Guns, Germs, and Steel* (Diamond, 2005). To do well in the game, players have to understand how geographical location, ease of trade, and access to raw materials create conditions for the successful growth of a civilization—and they have to be able to demonstrate that understanding in action. The game provides a wealth of information about how well a player has done in building his or her civilization and about the strengths and weaknesses of the strategies the players has chosen.

The game is realistic enough that advanced players develop better strategies by reading up on world history. So one can imagine a teacher asking students to play *Civilization* not to learn history (although that would surely be a good outcome), but to test how well they understand history. This might involve not just asking students to play the game and produce their scores, but also to provide an annotated explanation of what they did during the game and why—which is what advanced players in the game already do.[8] The fact that games like *Civilization* can be modified by players means that teachers or curriculum developers could produce scenarios customized to a particular content area, and also that students could be asked to design scenarios as part of their assessment.

There are, of course, two obvious drawbacks to such an approach. The first (and less significant) is that some work would need to be done to adapt a commercial game to serve as an assessment instrument, including a significant investment in determining the reliability of the measures used in the game, methods for ensuring that the test scenarios are not distributed in advance, and other criteria for assessments that would have to be met. In other words, a commercial game could be the core of an assessment tool, but the tool would have to be built to use the game in that way. But that is only to say that more research and development would be needed before a commercial game could be part of an assessment system.

The more significant issue is that, because the demands of the commercial marketplace differ in some ways from our assessment needs, there are not necessarily commercial games out there that meet every testing need.

Fortunately, that presents a possible solution: Develop a game system, game engine, and approach to educational gaming that can serve as a framework for creating assessment games.

Designing Games for Assessment

In what follows, we describe one system of developing games that can be used as 21st century assessments, and we do so by describing one particular game. It is a game we have written about elsewhere (Shaffer, 2007; Shaffer & Gee, 2005), and we present it as an example of the *kind* of assessment system we need to create. But we want to emphasize that there are other examples that we could have chosen as well.

We argued above that 21st century assessments have to be built around central problems in an academic domain or a real-world profession. The profession of urban planning is a good example of what we mean.

Urban planning is a domain of practice traditionally taught at the post-secondary level, but it is the kind of innovative and creative thinking that students need in the 21st century. Work in urban planning calls for some of the same skills and knowledge that are in the National Science Education Standards (National Research Council, 1995): things like understanding systems, order, and organization; evolution and equilibrium; and form and function in natural systems. Land use models that urban planners work with combine geographic features and other information into interactive visual models of complex systems. They show how land use decisions affect key environmental, economic, and social indicators: pollution, tax revenue, and acreage of wildlife habitat and so on. These models show the interaction between ecological and social systems in a local community that let planners explore, propose, and justify solutions to complex ecological and economic issues.

In the game *Urban Science*, players work as urban planners to create proposals for the development of the north side of Madison, Wisconsin, an area adjacent to a large wetland known as Cherokee Marsh. This development project raises a number of economic and ecological issues around wetland ecology and conservation. Not surprisingly, while working on plans for development near the Cherokee Marsh, players of *Urban Science* have to investigate, analyze, understand, and communicate about scientific issues: local species, their life cycle, and their habitat; the role of wetlands in the local ecological system; and specific pollutants, their sources, and their impacts.

To be successful in the game, players have to use and develop skills and knowledge from state science and environmental science standards. They have to learn and use concepts in ecology, such as systems thinking and sustainability. They have to value civic thinking, and use technology and scientific understanding to develop innovative solutions to real problems facing the city. They have to solve complex problems using the mathematics, communications, and science skills of urban planners (Bagley & Shaffer, 2009; Beckett & Shaffer, 2005; Shaffer, 2007).

Previous studies of *Urban Science* have focused on whether players developed these kinds of 21st century skills from playing the game. In one study, for example, middle school students used knowledge, skills, and values from ecology and urban planning more after playing the game than they did before playing (Bagley & Shaffer, 2009). Other studies have looked at whether games like *Urban Science* develop skills, interests, and motivation that can help players do better in science and other school subjects. For example, because players communicate with adult mentors in games like *Urban Science*, some become more comfortable talking with their teachers and talking in class (Shaffer, 2007).

What would it take, then, to use a game like *Urban Science* to assess whether students are learning anything useful in their classes? To answer that question, we would need to be able to measure the kind of 21st century thinking that is happening in the game, and show that the game can collect and report information that will help students, teachers, parents, and others decide whether teaching has been effective and where individual students still need help.

Research in the last two decades that suggests that learning to solve complex problems comes from being part of a community of practice: a group of people who share similar ways of solving problems (Hutchins, 1995; Lave & Wenger, 1991; Shaffer, 2006). A community of practice shares a common body of knowledge and set of skills, but also a system of values that determines when and how those skills and that knowledge should be employed, and a set of processes through which such decisions are made. And, of course, such a community also has a shared identity. In previous work we have described this collection of skills, knowledge, identity, values and epistemology of a community as its *epistemic frame* (Shaffer, 2007).

Thus, we can look at what urban planners say and do in their work, find the relevant skills, knowledge, identity, values and epistemology, and create a model of the way planners think about problems: a model that describes what it means "to solve problems the way an urban planner does." And we can do the same thing in the game Urban Science:

1. Look at what players say and do in their work in the game;
2. Find the relevant skills, knowledge, identity, values and epistemology from urban planning;
3. Create a model of the way the players think about problems in the game; and
4. Compare that to how real planners think.

Consider, for example, a player in *Urban Science*. Let's call her Sarah. We could determine the epistemic frame of urban planning that Sarah has at any point in the game. We could also determine the frame of the group or groups that Sarah has worked with. In fact, we could determine the frame of all of the parts of the game (including other players) that Sarah saw while playing. We could, from studies of real urban planners (or by having real planners play the game), construct a *reference frame* of how real planners solve problems.

A mathematical modeling technique, *epistemic network analysis* (ENA), can measure the similarities and differences between these ways of thinking—that is, between these epistemic frames (Shaffer et al., 2009). So we might ask, for example: How close did Sarah's frame get to the reference frame of real planners? That is, we could measure how much Sarah learned to think like a planner. We could see the path over time of Sarah's frame development in the game, and compare it to experts, or other players. We could ask whether Sarah's frame was more likely to become like a real planner's if the frame of the players she worked with had frames that became more like a planner's. That is, we could quantify one of the most elusive concepts in education, *opportunity to learn* (Darling-Hammond, 2006), by looking at how players do in the game compared to the context in which they were being tested.

In other words, we could use *Urban Science* to show conclusively how well Sarah was thinking like a planner—and give feedback about what areas she still needed to work on. In this sense, we call *Urban Science* an *epistemic game*: that is, a game based on the way of thinking (the epistemic frame) of some important community in the real world (Shaffer, 2007). In a similar way, we could imagine creating a whole host of games that could test how well students are able to think like journalists, architects, mathematicians, historians, engineers, physicists, doctors, biologists, and so on. And these epistemic games could test whether students can solve complex problems using 21st century skills.

CONCLUSION

We want to reiterate that epistemic games like *Urban Science* are just one example of how learning games can—and should—be used as assessment games. Games support and require the kind of learning that we need in the 21st century—and so they have the potential to usher in the new paradigm that we need, to develop the skills students need. It is in this sense that we suggest that instead of building games for learning we should be tackling the more difficult—but more fundamental—problem of assessment.

There is a good reason why the field of educational computer games (and educational technology more generally) has been looking at learning: Those of us who study educational games needed time to experiment with and to understand the kind of learning that computers make possible. But we all know what happens when we try to bring good games for learning into schools. Parents and teachers rightly ask: Will this help my children do well on the tests they need to pass?

What would happen, however, if students were tested—and schools judged—not by how well they perform on our current tests, but on whether they could solve real-world problems the way real-world professionals do? That is, what would happen if we used games—well designed games—as the new GATE through which students have to pass?

Assessments drive the learning in which a system will engage. Today's standardized assessments, coupled with a punitive accountability model, encourage and support a skill-and-drill system of learning that does not lead to problem solving, innovation, or preparation for future learning.

We are arguing that games can be an assessment system, too. That system would also drive teaching and learning, but it would drive schools where we want them and need them to be: toward a new paradigm.

There is a great deal of research and policy work today concerned with how to change our standardized testing system and how to build deeper, more authentic forms of assessment. All of that work suggests that any change will be contentious and difficult to achieve (Abell & Lederman, 2007). But we believe that one way to achieve a system-wide change is to provide assessment and accountability tools that demand better forms of learning—and that properly designed games can do a better job of showing us where learners are in a course of development towards mastery than can any standard paper-and-pencil test.

They can do this because games use actual learning as the basis for assessment: their assessments are built on solving problems and facing challenges. They test not only current knowledge and skills, but also preparation for future learning. They measure 21st century skills like collaboration, innovation, production, and design by tracking many different kinds of information about a student, over time. They can account for the fact that different students have had different opportunities to learn inside school and out. And they can provide students, administrators, parents and teachers with feedback they can use to make decisions that support good learning.

A game like *Urban Science* can be a completely new kind of standardized test. It is standardized in the sense that every player can have an experience designed in advance. It is a test in the sense that it can return a score (or scores) that indicates how well a player has done in the game. But it is a test that measures not the basic facts and basic skills of our current testing regime, but the kind of thinking that we value in the 21st century.

The road to better schools starts by making the tests in school more like the games that students are already playing out of school.

ACKNOWLEDGEMENTS

This work was funded in part by the MacArthur Foundation and by the National Science Foundation through grants REC-0347000, DUE-091934, DRL-0918409, and DRL-0946372. The opinions, findings, and conclusions do not reflect the views of the funding agencies, cooperating institutions, or other individuals.

NOTES

1. David Williamson Shaffer is Professor of Learning Science at the University of Wisconsin-Madison. James Paul Gee is the Mary Lou Fulton Presidential Professor of Learning Studies at Arizona State University. They are equal co-authors with names listed in reverse alphabetical order by middle name.
2. Experiences of this kind, that provide experiences that are neither too hard (and thus frustrating) or too easy (and thus boring) induce what psychologists and game designers refer to as a "flow state" of high excitement and focus, which, of course, explains why good games (like good books or good movies) can be so compelling. (Csikszentmihalyi, 1996; Gee, 2007).
3. We're describing this briefly here, but this summary of principles for 21st Century Assessment is based on a series of discussions funded by the Macarthur Foundation in their 21st Century Learning and Assessment Project (PI: James Paul Gee) over several years that have brought together some of the best current research on the problem of assessment in the new century.
4. "Boss battles" at the end of a level in a game are often used to assess whether the player has mastered the skills of the level just finished, and whether he or she is prepared for learning the more demanding challenge of the next level.
5. Some websites do use that information to create player rankings; but games can be played without reference to those external resources.
6. *Fair* is a term of art for players, meaning that the test/challenge has not been artificially constructed to help the player lose rather than win.
7. Our description of the educational potential of *Civilization* is based, in part, on the work of Squire, who has studied the use of the game in classrooms and after school clubs (Squire, 2004).
8. This approach of creating annotated walk-throughs of game play is used on the fan website Apolyton University, where advanced players share scenarios organized into courses on strategy games (including *Civilization*) and history more generally.

REFERENCES

Abell, S. K., & Lederman, N. G. (2007). *Research on science education.* Mahwah, NJ: Lawrence Erlbaum Associates, Inc.

Bagley, E. A. S., & Shaffer, D. W. (2009). When people get in the way: Promoting civic thinking through epistemic gameplay. *International Journal of Gaming and Computer-Mediated Simulations, 1*(1), 36–52.

Beckett, K. L., & Shaffer, D. W. (2005). Augmented by reality: The pedagogical praxis of urban planning as a pathway to ecological thinking. *Journal of Educational Computing Research, 33*(1), 31–52.

Bransford, J. D., & Schwartz, D. L. (1999). Rethinking transfer: A simple proposal with multiple implications. In A. Iran-Nejad & P. D. Pearson (Eds.), *Review of research in education*, Vol. 24 (pp. 61–101). Washington DC: American Educational Research Association.

Chi, M., Feltovich, P., & Glaser, R. (1981). Categorization and representation of physics problems by experts and novices. *Cognitive Science, 5*(2), 121–152.

Csikszentmihalyi, M. (1996). *Creativity: Flow and the psychology of discovery and invention.* New York: Harper Perennial.

Darling-Hammond, L. (2006). Securing the right to learn: Policy and practice for powerful teaching and learning. *Educational Researcher, 35*(7), 13–24.

Diamond, J. M. (2005). *Guns, germs, and steel : the fates of human societies.* New York: Norton.

Gardner, H. (1991). *The unschooled mind: How children think and how schools should teach.* New York: Basic Books.

Gee, J. P. (2003). *What video games have to teach us about learning and literacy.* New York: Palgrave/Macmillan.

Gee, J. P. (2004). *Situated language and learning: A critique of traditional schooling.* London: Routledge.

Gee, J. P. (2007). *Good video games and good learning: Collected essays on video games, learning and literacy.* New York: Peter Lang.

Hutchins, E. (1995). *Cognition in the wild.* Cambridge, MA: MIT Press.

Lave, J., & Wenger, E. (1991). *Situated learning: Legitimate peripheral participation.* Cambridge, MA: Cambridge University Press.

Leadbeater, C., & Miller, P. (2004). *The Pro-Am revolution: How enthusiasts are changing our society and economy.* London: Demos.

National Research Council. (1995). *National science education standards.* Washington, DC: National Academy Press.

Partnership for 21st Century Skills. (2004). *21st century readiness for every child.* Tucson, AZ.

Schwartz, D. L., & Arena, D. (2009). Choice-based assessments for the digital age. Stanford University. Retrieved from http://aaalab.stanford.edu/papers/ChoiceSchwartzArenaAUGUST232009.pdf

Shaffer, D. W. (2006). Epistemic frames for epistemic games. *Computers and Education, 46*(3), 223.

Shaffer, D. W. (2007). *How computer games help children learn.* New York: Palgrave.

Shaffer, D. W., & Gee, J. P. (2005). *Before every child is left behind: How epistemic games can solve the coming crisis in education.* (Working Paper): University of Wisconsin-Madison, Wisconsin Center of Education Research.

Shaffer, D. W., Hatfield, D., Svarovsky, G., Nash, P., Nulty, A., Bagley, E.,... Mislevy, R. (2009). Epistemic network analysis: A prototype for 21st Century assessment of learning. *The International Journal of Learning and Media, 1*(2), 33–53.

Squire, K. D. (2004). Sid Meier's Civilization III. *Simulations and Gaming, 35*(1).

CHAPTER 9

THE BEST AND FUTURE USES OF ASSESSMENT IN GAMES

Eva L. Baker, Gregory K. W. K. Chung, and Girlie C. Delacruz
University of California, Los Angeles

INTRODUCTION

The purpose of this chapter is to explore the use of games and how assessment practices can be developed to improve and document the effects of games on players. Can assessment be designed into games in more integral ways so to improve the learning value of the game, without disrupting the experience for the player? In this chapter, we discuss assessment of games. To provide a rationale for our approach, we describe a common argument for use of games for learning. We then address contexts of players, the individual differences of students, constraints on instructional settings, and educational policy changes as they contribute to the argument for games as an intervention. We further describe why valid assessment is needed. When evidence of games can be garnered to show effectiveness, they provide a cost-contained option to improve achievement quality and equity. Equity may be achieved because individuals wish to attain mastery and will exert different levels of effort to do so. In our analysis, we briefly discuss the shortcomings of typical game assessment as we see them. Moving to the essential step of architecture of assessment in game settings, we describe relation-

Technology-Based Assessments for 21st Century Skills, pages 229–248
Copyright © 2012 by Information Age Publishing
229

ships of learning goals, cognitive demands, and domain and task features. We illustrate the use of external representation of content and skill components, ontologies, and how this structure can be used to presage or later establish validity arguments. We provide a set of examples illustrating the specification process. Finally, we discuss future technologies and how they may affect assessment and validity of findings.

WHY GAMES FOR LEARNING?

The motivation to use games for learning purposes lies in their potential to support multiple learning outcomes, adapt to individual needs, and focus attention in order to increase and to maintain learners' engagement in the relevant tasks. Presumably, well-designed games will be able to address key elements understood to influence learning and performance, in addition to nuances of assessment. These include the following: (a) managing learners' attention throughout the game to concentrate on relevant content and skills, (b) accommodating complex and diverse approaches to learning processes, (c) embedding many trials with high levels of relevant interactivity and feedback, (d) creating a sense of enjoyment and intense engagement ("flow" or "presence"), (e) providing adaptive challenge, (f) attaining desired learning outcomes, and (g) influencing learners' self-efficacy and other affective constructs (e.g., de Freitas, 2006; Kirriemuir & McFarlane, 2003; O'Neil, Wainess, & Baker, 2005). This is a long list of features and may be augmented by considering the specific types of content, skill development, or creative problem solving games may engender. In any case, these are relevant for the evaluation of game processes and effects. Assessment, as we use it, however, focuses on students' learning, processing, and performance during and following the game experience(s).

In this chapter, we focus on games that are intended to support, develop, and even teach particular skills. For the most part, these games are designed to help individuals acquire specified, desired education and training outcomes, such as greater algebra expertise, cultural sensitivity, or procedural learning (Chung & Delacruz, in-press; Johnson & Valente, 2009; Koenig, Lee, Iseli, & Wainess, 2009), and games have been used with some success in the military, typically as orienting or practice environments (Shilling, Zyda, & Wardynski, 2002).

Game Players

When we consider the full range of games in use in our society at present, one unalterable fact is clear: no matter what the game, players display different levels of skill and interest. These variations are key in the analysis of adaptive, game-based assessment. Some players show extraordinary talent, physical adeptness, strategy, knowledge and expertise as appropriate. Players of most games, even when they have clear motivation to excel, may demonstrate skills well below target levels, and as a group, show a wide range of proficiency in any one game. In recreational games, those which are, for the most part, voluntary, players who are slow to improve may shift from game to game, in order to find those that seem to promise more success. In learning sports, this search is analogous to moving from basketball to baseball, or changing position within a sport, for instance, from pitcher to outfielder. In technology-supported games, choices are limited by a number of constraints: access to games and appropriate devices; available time and timing with regard to learning goals; levels of game-playing expertise; and source of motivation, whether self-challenge, escape, competition, or exploration. No doubt the orientation to games of students has rapidly shifted as games have increased in popularity and have become less novel.

School Context

In school learning, and in learning games themselves, choices for most students are rapidly expanding through the use of small applications (Apps) that can be used on mobile platforms such as phones and tablets. There are many other opportunities to apply games to meet important achievement shortfalls that cannot be well handled through other means, in adult and in school-based learning, for elementary, secondary, and post secondary settings. Virtual environments, and other simulated settings provide high fidelity to emulate real world experience. In addition, the range of scenarios exposed to individuals in a relatively compressed time in a game or simulation would not be obtained in the real world, even over vastly extended periods.

As games increase in sophistication, involving richer media and demanding more complex knowledge, the games must also incorporate 21st century skills, including communication, problem-solving, teamwork, situation awareness, and meta-cognition to be meaningful (Delacruz, Chung, & Baker, 2009; Holyoak, 1995; Morrison & Fletcher, 2002; O'Neil & Perez, 2008). So, when games also involve the collaborative (or competitive) engagement of other players, skills such as strategy, collaboration, and self-management come into play as outcomes. Clearly, the surface attraction of games is only part of the solution. Games need sufficient appeal to sustain engagement until outcomes are met. But students must voluntarily play *and* learn. Although preference data suggest students often prefer to play games, in schools (Arici, 2008; Project Tomorrow, 2010), they may choose to do so to escape reutilized, repetitive teaching practices. Our goal is to construct games and to share the technology that will lead to motivated play engaging critical learning outcomes.

Games, whether used in classrooms, less formal educational settings, unsupervised homework, or in free time, can be designed to redress gaps or misunderstandings in content and skills, either as the learner progresses from stage to stage in a particular skill set, or to extend and enrich learning.

Educational Policy Context

Focused learning games have found international purchase because many ministries have long adopted test-based systems, only in place in the last two decades in the United States. If fixed criteria are in place for students to achieve, for instance, on examinations, games may be used to extend time of learner engagement, by differentiating instruction for those who need additional exposure and practice, and to introduce or fortify new ideas in the classroom. Valid assessment of these games matters because tests serve as a policy and management lever, and bring with them sanctions for institutions and individuals. Moreover, the focus on testing has resulted in some countries in predictable differences in performance among different cultural or socio economic groups (OECD, 2009). Also in some countries, notably the United States, there is a wide range of performance found within any particular classroom. Games may be ways of raising performance for lower achieving students in a manner that does not overburden individual teacher's ability to adapt instruction to sometimes wide variation in student achievement. Because discretionary spending for schools is predicted to be lower in some countries in the near future, games may be an economical option to achieve quality and equity in performance, when compared to costs of additional teachers, better teacher preparation, or professional development for practicing teachers.

Fewer incentives given to teachers, such as desirable public pensions, may very well shift the burden of real teaching to replicable technology-based artifacts obtained through the web. The path of current policies may enable the acceptance of game-like alternatives that could combine deep knowledge of subject matter, interesting pedagogy, and adaptive learning strategies. Furthermore, shifting the burden of learning from teachers to the student should prepare them, when appropriately monitored, to become adept at learning content and skills beyond those specified in the curriculum.

As games become accepted as tools to support learning and instruction in formal educational and training settings, an increasingly important question is how does one design the "proof" that illustrates accomplishments whether it is found in performance on watershed examinations, college, or on the job?

EVALUATING THE EFFECTIVENESS OF GAMES

In education, the term "effectiveness" has many nuances, ranging from whether an implementation should be purchased because its claims have been verified or more formal inferences documenting whether students or institutions have met their goals within the time and cost allowed. Any game must be evaluated on its merits, and it may be helpful to review key evaluation functions in which game assessment is embedded. Most commonly, these are called summative and formative evaluation and in general serve different functions. Summative evaluation is comparative (Scriven, 1991) and uses procedures to judge the intervention on achieved students performance by comparing posttest or post or retention performances to pretest results. Effectiveness is also gauged by comparing the intervention to plausible alternatives, such as another game, simulation, a particular curriculum, alternative experiential options, or in the worst methodological case, poorly defined "conventional practice." Minimum characteristics for summative evaluation are the use of common outcome measures, to make fair comparisons, controlled administration conditions (or at least as well described procedures), and sufficient statistical controls, through randomization of participants, adjustments based on their characteristics and power analyses to secure sample sizes sufficient to support inferences. In addition, side effects or negative unanticipated outcomes are also a feature of summative evaluations and may be discerned by interview, questionnaire, observation, focus groups, or other qualitative measures.

Formative evaluation in contrast, has two different and somewhat related functions (Airasian & Jones, 1993; Baker, 1974; Black & Wiliam, 1998; Crooks, 1988; Kluger & DeNisi, 1996; Markle, 1967; National Research Council, 2001, 2003; Natriello, 1987; Nyquist, 2003; Scriven, 1967; Wiliam, Lee, Harrison, & Black, 2004). The first is to provide the developers with information during the piloting and revisions of the game in order to improve the final product. The users of the information are the game-design team. Here effectiveness may be inferred from comparisons of revised to earlier versions of the game using the same statistical controls. However, because development, in the game world in particular, occurs at breakneck speed, more informal, qualitative approaches are often used. For instance, students may be asked during game play to think aloud as they contemplate and execute moves, receive feedback and so on. Focus groups, and other interview or observation settings are often used to identify when the game is not "working." At a minimal level, developers may play the game themselves, and realize the game is not commanding their attention or has features that interfere with engagement or desired thinking. It is best, of course, that this type of developmental testing occurs using the target group of learners who are at the "right" spot in learning the desired goals, but pinpointing pilot-user expertise is not a simple matter. Another option here is to compare experts in the subject matter who are competent at game play with novices who do not know the content in depth and who may be less comfortable with games. Differences in these groups can lead to inferences about where and how the game might be revised to be more effective. Clearly formative evaluation is limited by the time and cost available for revision, and sometimes goals of games are shortchanged or dropped when adequate levels of achievement are not obtained within constraints. When games are to be embedded in particular settings, such as part of a curriculum, it is essential that the games be tried there, with multiple teachers, if the teacher has a role to assist and support students in the same content and skills (de Freitas, 2006; Mitchell & Savill-Smith, 2004; Sandford, Ulicsak, Facer, & Rudd, 2006).

The second aspect of formative evaluation actually occurs when the game itself is used and targets the continuous play of the learners. Here the attention is on whether the learner is successful at interim tasks, where the shortfalls lay, and how they may be remedied. In the ideal case, the game mechanic itself would be omniscient with regard to potential and errors and these could be remedied as part of the design. Whether the game should mirror instructional behavior in its use of formative assessment (Wiliam, 2006, 2010) of players is not resolved. In classrooms, feedback and specific help or instruction to assist the learner usually follows diagnostic information. Formative assessment is used for diagnostic purposes and the game monitor may simply shunt the student to experiences where areas of deficiency are experienced and desired behaviors are supported. In cruder version, students receive explicit feedback on why they have lost points, and may be guided or incented to help to enable the learning to quickly understand where knowledge and skills need to be improved (Delacruz, 2010). Formative assessment during game play allows a well-designed game to adapt to patterns and needs of individual students. In both sorts of evaluation, the details of assessment are key and not a casual afterthought. The evaluation requires detailed explication of goals and an analytic model of learning.

Whether for formative or summative purposes, good assessment practices are essential. They must be an intrinsic part of the game design; for instance, the basis for giving points, leveling up, and other forms of progress or awards must be tied to the desired performance needed at various stages of the game as well as its conclusion (Baker, Chung, & Delacruz, 2008; Baker & Delacruz, 2008a, 2008b). If a game is to facilitate knowledge and skill acquisition, retention, and transfer within and outside of supervised classroom settings, assessments become necessary to develop a high-functioning, highly effective implementation. In the next section we describe an assessment design architecture that specifies the general properties that underlie well-designed assessments: (a) focusing on the cognitive demands with respect to what it means to be successful both in the game and in the larger learning context, (b) representing the domain explicitly to ensure adequate sampling of important concepts and other knowledge elements, and (c) specifying the relationship between students' responses (e.g., their game play; their response on a test) to the learning outcomes of interest.

ASSESSMENT DESIGN ARCHITECTURE

Validity Concerns

Learning games are intended to cause learning and therefore the standards for their use are higher than other, more discretionary implementations. Without lapsing into an extended argument about validity, let it be said that evidence of the game's effectiveness should be obtained and available to users. Whether teachers carry the majority of the instructional weight, and the game serves as a practice environment could be discerned from the documentary effectiveness. In other cases, it would be possible to demonstrate the range of settings and types of learners that have been effectively engaged and have enabled students to reach criterion. If validity depends upon the argument one can make with available evidence to support claims and uses, it is important that the range of potential application options be described and at least some of them tested. Is the game a stand-alone activity, intended to introduce, expand and support learning independently? Does it need to be used with supervision? Is it to be integrated, perhaps after student deficiencies have been identified by a teacher or an assessment, in the on-going curriculum as a means of differentiating instruction? Is there evidence that students, on their own time, will persist in using the game and acquiring greater skill? And if the game itself is to be used as the assessment, what assessment properties would the game need to attend to? All of these are validity questions, requiring different levels of research designs and evidence of both positive and unexpected negative outcomes.

Current and State of the Art Assessment of Games

Typically, the game's scoring mechanism, such as the number of contacts made, obstacles overcome, and so on, provides the sense of an evaluation of performance, and when summarized, scores can be understood to represent a competitive position in a distribution of players or proficiency along some continuum of performance. However, what is counted rarely relates directly to the grander cognitive or domain aspects intended to be taught in the game. Rather, these points are used for motivational purposes (e.g., provide just the right amount of challenge), not for measurement ones. We are interested in understanding and instrumenting the process of learning so that a learning model(s) may superimpose on a click stream or other tabulated interface contacts. Performance can be described as it meets, surpasses, or deviates from optimal paths toward proficiency. Identifying what events are relevant requires a tight (conceptual) coupling among the set of goals of learning, purpose of assessment, student behaviors, student responses, task design, and assessment design. Data capture within the game includes at various levels of summary behaviors systematically chosen to align with the learning objectives of the game and how the assessment information will be used. External models fused with induction (Chung & Baker, 2003) provide the most efficient way of using event-driven information to examine online processes, in order to make sense of massive trails of data. The signal to noise ratio in highly instrumented environments, such as pilot cockpits or land-based sensors has been documented as a losing proposition. Thus, the models described below and procedures we recommend must apply to much of the new and unforeseen technology, under the assumption that it will provide even more massive and granular information about student behaviors.

Assessment Architecture for Now and the Future

The first step in designing an assessment is to clearly identify the learning objectives of the game. A key step of the process is to detail the learning outcomes at a level of specificity that can support the design process for all those involved. For example, it is not useful to simply say the game will target "fractions" or even "the adding of fractions." Rather, a more detailed description of the learning outcomes should be specified. The concept of "adding fractions" needs to be further defined by the fundamental principles of which adding fractions are an instance. If we want students to learn underlying principles, rather than rote procedures, and we do for transfer and generalization, the assessment architecture must then specify all the relevant concepts to principle (e.g., the size of a rational number is relative to how one unit is defined and that in mathematics, the unit is understood to be one of some particular quantity, intervals, areas, volumes, etc.).

Cognitive Demands

Once the learning outcomes have been specified, the cognitive demands of the task set must be identified. Cognitive demands involve the range of thinking skills that are required for success. These skills may function as largely domain independent—for instance, the ability to construct a topic sentence in a range of subjects; or they may be dependent upon the content domain in which they reside—for instance, trouble-shooting options for electrical power malfunction. While there are numerous groups set to define the canonical list of cognitive demands, we have used a set for some years to structure its assessment research. They include problem solving, communication, conceptual, procedural, and systemic understanding of the target domain, metacognition, and situation awareness (Baker, 2009). For example, in mathematics, conceptual understanding may require that students are able to recognize instances of a concept, generate examples, or be able to move among multiple representations of information. Computational fluency would be defined as the ability to compute mathematical problems at speed and with few or no errors. Specifying the cognitive demands serves the purpose of identifying how to operationalize the specified learning outcomes into cognitive and behavioral descriptions that will be used in the domain representation. They may be thought of as the rules, such as problem solving strategies or reasoning.

Domain Representation

The domain representation explicates the domain by depicting in network form key ideas or major principles, supporting or prerequisite knowledge, and their relationships. A network is a flexible representation that is able to depict relationships among concepts, where the relationships may be of different types (e.g., causal, temporal). Structures that are inherently "messy" are more easily represented with networks than other representations (e.g., matrix, table, tree). It is one view of the universe of what is to be learned. We use the technical term "ontology" to describe such representations. Assessment development occurs in part by assuring that the domain represented is sampled sufficiently and in enough formats to estimate the players' proficiencies as at various points in the game the domain representation may call out probable errors, or confusable concepts. Its referential use is for the designers of the game to help assure that key elements of learning have been included, and omissions have been deliberate. Although the principal uses of representations are in design of assessment and game learning experiences, other functions may also be served. For instance, the representation, or domain map can be given to instructors or to students as a job aid to provide an overview of what is to be learned (at the levels of standards or within a particular game implementation). Often the details of the domain may be obscured and information given at a larger grain size to facilitate understanding. It is clear that instructional options for teachers and technologies operate at different levels of specificity.

In most of our work, we have kept content domain representation and cognitive demands separate. We have representations that combine the two, for instance, showing how problem solving, situation awareness, and communication demands interact with problems of ship protection (Koenig et al., 2009). Because this situation involves well-bounded procedural problems, it made sense to integrate cognition and content domains. When addressing large skill sets, such as the understanding and problem solving associated with algebra or genetics, it is not feasible to integrate cognitive demands and content in one domain representation because of the complexity of the display. We have undertaken two different remedies for this problem. First, we are in the process of developing ontologies for domain independent cognitive demands—for example, problem solving, and testing their utility as they are embedded explicitly in a domain ontology (Mayer, in process). Second, we have moved the domain representations to serve as a meta-tagged system for the design of assessments and learning. In this system, it is possible to approach the database from a variety of perspectives, with given trajectories relevant to content sequence, cognitive development, prerequisites, linguistic requirements, and task elements. Such a system incorporates data from game play, uses Bayesian approaches to manage individual performance, and can be sampled to provide formative or summative snapshots.

While we are enthusiastic about the use of ontologies, they have certain limitations. They tend to represent present state of the world, as they are compiled through expert elicitation and integration of formal documents. They may be socially defined by the sample of experts selected. Although they are represented in two dimensions as a network, there is scant empirical evidence to infer that moving right to left or from the bottom to the top is the preferred sequence. Because the cost and complexity of identifying effective alternative sequences is prohibitive, given different student entry status and background features, each trajectory must itself be verified, at least through formative assessment processes. The data from multiple paths then can be mapped on to the ontology to allow future users to understand what seems to work under specific conditions and which paths usually lead to oblivion.

Task Specification

In any assessment, task specifications identify how the behavior of the learner will be obtained and how inferences about understanding or other competencies will be made. Minimally, they include materials or environments with which the learners are expected to interact, typically as problems or features of the game narrative or scenarios, and the range of actions that might be taken by the game players at any particular point. Finally, independent of the purpose of the assessment (e.g., certify proficiency, improve individual's effective paths, or revision of the game overall), the task specifications include both an explicit scoring model that links learning to advancement in the game and access to additional tools, awards, or other incentives. Specifications will also aid in classifying performance into levels of attainment and give one basis for which a validity argument can be established and tested. Although it is common to think of task specification as a front-end activity, it is possible to begin development guided by the force of narrative or of scenario attributes and then see what has been developed. At that point specification (or documentation) of learning and assessment relationships can be plotted. If there are obvious gaps, inappropriate redundancies, or errors, they can be caught and modified.

The value of the assessment architecture is that it represents the process of assessment design with different levels of specificity and complexity, enabling modifications to the game without having to start from scratch. For example, in a game designed to teach the importance of units when adding fractions with unlike denominators, varying the complexity of the tasks or levels in the game could be a function of various parameters such as the explicitness of the unit (e.g., an implicit unit of one interval with whole numbers versus real-world categories such as pizzas, tables, or groups of objects), the representations to be worked with (e.g., graphical versus symbolic), and the number of different fractions to be added and manipulated (e.g., $\frac{1}{2} + \frac{3}{4}$ versus $\frac{1}{2} + \frac{3}{4} + \frac{1}{4}$).

Thus, the assessment architecture allows for systematic modulations and appropriate sampling while maintaining alignment of learning goals and assessment purposes. In this way, it also supports the evaluation of our outcomes of interest. The assessment architecture makes transparent the rationale behind the design choices, from the specification of the range of the content to be covered to the appropriate supports that should be implemented (e.g., linguistic or instructional). Transparency is key in any review or adoption practice, as well as for developers seeking to revise or release improved versions of the game. In the light of explicit national standards in content, described above, a transparent mechanism is indispensable to display the relevance of game or other technologies to the goals for students. In the next section we present an example of one game we designed to support learning of fraction concepts of unit and fraction addition. While the game was intended for both learning and assessment, we focus mainly on the assessment dimension, particularly the linkage between (a) the knowledge and cognitive demands underlying the math content, and (b) how the game play operationalizes the cognitive demands.

The Assessment Design Process Applied to the Design of a Math Game

We illustrate the assessment design process with an example of a game designed to assess the concept of a unit in rational numbers. We first developed general specifications around two ideas in rational numbers. The first idea is that all rational numbers (integers and fractions) are defined relative to a single unit quantity (e.g., a unit of count, measure, area, volume). The second idea is that rational numbers can be summed only if the unit quantities are identical (e.g., ¼ + ¾ is permissible but ½ + ¾ is not because the unit or size of the fractions is unequal). These two ideas formed the basis of what we expected to measure from students' game play. Table 9.1 shows an example of the specifications for the idea of unit. Additional specifications included the meaning of addition, the meaning of the denominator in a fraction, the meaning of the numerator in a fraction, and the idea that any rational number can be written as a fraction.

The specifications in Table 9.1 guided the development of the game mechanics (the main game-play operations). A key property of the game, if it was to have assessment utility, is that game play required the cognitive demands outlined in Table 9.1 (i.e., the two central ideas of unit and addition of like-sized unit quantities). The game design reflected these key ideas in two ways. First, the basic task presented students with essentially a number line, where whole units were demarked with vertical bars and each whole unit could be further divided into fractional pieces (demarked

---

TABLE 9.1   Sample Excerpt of the Specification for the Idea of *Unit* in Rational Numbers

1.0.0 Does the student understand the meaning of one unit in the context of rational number? One unit can be descriptive (e.g., apple, car, rocket) or quantitative (interval on a number line, a kilometer, a square foot, etc.) and may be stated implicitly or explicitly.

    1.1.0 The size of a rational number is relative to how one Whole Unit is defined.

    1.2.0 In mathematics, one unit is understood to be one of some quantity (intervals, areas, volumes, etc.).

    1.3.0 In our number system, the unit can be represented as one whole interval on a number line.

        1.3.1 Positive integers are represented by successive whole intervals on the positive side of zero

        1.3.2 The interval between each integer is constant once it is established.

        1.3.3 Positive non-integers are represented by fractional parts of the interval between whole numbers.

        1.3.4 All rational numbers can be represented as additions of integers or fractions.

---

by green dots). The game scenario was to help the character, *Patch*, move from his initial position to the goal position (the *X* in screenshot in Table 9.2). *Patch* could only move by bouncing on trampolines, and the distance *Patch* bounced was determined by the value of the trampoline. Players moved trampolines onto the grid and energized them by adding coils to it. Coils were of whole or fraction unit values (right upper panel in screenshot in Table 9.2).

Successful game play required students to determine the size of the whole unit for a given grid and also the size of any fractional pieces. The second component, additive operations only allowed on like-sized units, was carried out via the game scenario of energizing the trampolines so *Patch* would bounce the appropriate distance. The distance of the bounce was a function of how many spring "coils" were added to a trampoline. The size of the coil corresponded to a whole unit (1/1) or a fractional unit (e.g., 1/2), and when adding coils to a trampoline, only same-sized coils were allowed. This adding operation corresponded to adding fractions with common denominators to a trampoline, and also in the solution to the level. A successful solution resulted in *Patch* bouncing from trampoline to trampoline to the goal position, which mathematically was the sum of all trampoline values.

TABLE 9.2   Sample Task Design Specification for the First Game Level

Design information   Description

Design information	Description
Math goal	Defining the whole unit
Knowledge specifications	1.3.0 In our number system, the unit can be represented as one whole interval on a number line.
	1.3.2 The interval between each integer is constant once it is established.
Stage and level	1, 1
Level design	Bounce = 1; Grid unit = 1; Distance = 3 units total
	Resources: 1 trampoline; 1 location to place trampoline; 4 1-unit coils
Level solution	Standard: 1 + 1 + 1 (right); Alternate solution: none
Screenshot	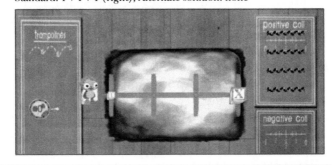

Table 9.2 presents the task specifications for the first game level. Note that the fundamental cognitive demands are encoded in the game mechanics itself; thus, the task specifications allowed variation in the complexity of the task (e.g., by making the grid have fractional units of 1/6 instead of whole units as shown in the screenshot; by providing fractional unit coils that do not correspond to the grid, thus requiring students to convert the coils to the appropriate size). The task specifications also allowed the game features to vary (e.g., by limiting resources; by allowing the grid to extend vertically; by making a complex path).

TOWARD THE FUTURE OF ASSESSMENT IN GAMES

What are the obvious modifications we can expect from present technology to improve the manner in which games will be evaluated and performance assessed in the future? We will consider statistical or behind the curtain options, social computing approaches to assessment, and new sources of validity evidence.

More Adaptive Games

Clearly we are able without much effort to imagine the improvement of current statistical models, such as Bayesian approaches that adjust performance against prior behavior and a myriad of individual features, including language status, prior performance in similar games, content knowledge, emotional states, and so on. These technical improvements may be developed by refining multiple models of expertise, various models of successful learning pathways, or periods of accelerated development, any or all of which are superimposed upon the performance of individuals at entry, during various points in progress, and at the conclusion of the intervention. This approach requires a higher level of planning than do methods that use probabilities based on results as their main adaptation strategy. Ideally, such manipulations will lead to game options that are just at or somewhat above the level of expertise demonstrated by the player. Like learning tennis with a professional who can hit the ball faster than one can typically return it and somewhat outside of the player's optimal movement radius, games can refine their adaptation in order to challenge but not frustrate the player. All options of course will enable the player to raise or lower challenge, in much the same way as in the present, but system constraints may retard an individual's desire to do easy work, or to take too many diversionary side trips. In addition, we can anticipate a wide range of changes in inputs from the player to the system, moving from experimental to wider use technologies supporting gaze detection, speed, hesitation, perspiration, breath control, and other sensors related to display, keystroke, mouse, or touch-screen behaviors.

Increased Use of Social Computing-Based Assessments

Social computing—the use of groups of people to evaluate content, recommend content, rate, and perform other forms of "computation"—is increasingly being used as a source of assessment. Today, users with mobile platforms can engage either the individual or a group of others, and depending upon one's reach and desire, the group can be constrained to an intimate size or run in the millions. Games and social computing occur in the context of the current explosion of social networks. Whether for good or evil, the principal form of assessment of such interactions is frequency of use and personal reflection.

How such games will aptly support individual learning goals is a question. If games were refereed and tagged as focusing on key cognitive demands, such as problem solving, pattern detection, and interpersonal communication, for instance, then the user and his circle of colleagues could pursue the attainments attached to such games and accumulate "points" or other indicators of accomplishment apart from any game's surface features, narrative, or scenario style.

However, the adoption of the collective rating system, how many stars, how many chef hats, how many thumbs down does an experience receive, has substituted normative values for some criterion expectations. In commercial games this has always been true, as market is inherently distributional. Yet normative values are slippery, to wit, the food ratings in restaurants in Hawaii versus the presumed same scale as rated in New York City. If the social definition of the group influences ratings, we are thrust, once again, into the Neverland of comparative performance—that is, "I'm better than you" rather than in documenting what I can do under certain constraints with particular help. So a corollary discussion is whether we are talking about learning as collectively defined, accessible and classified any way the learner wishes. A worrisome example is the number of citations of Wikipedia in research reports, clearly documenting that the teacher's role as gatekeeper to knowledge disappeared at least ten years ago.

If instead we focus on self-directed, informal learning, then one improvement that could be made in socially defined intellectual behaviors is to improve the quality of self-assessment. This topic reverts to earlier discussions of metacognitive skills, that is one's self-awareness of planning, feedback, effort, distractibility, efficacy, and affective mood, such as anxiety. If we are to teach people to be accurate estimators of their own intellectual,

244 ■ E. L. BAKER, G. K. W. K. CHUNG, and G. C. DELACRUZ

meta-cognitive, and emotional states, we could go a long way toward solving some of the looming problems. However, one's self-judged competency may still require corroborative evidence for tasks that are highly complex and mission-critical.

New Sources of Validity Evidence

Moving from the physiological inputs invoked by much of current game play, there are other indicators that may in fact provide strong evidence of persistence, engagement, and their relationship to learning. In mobile environments, for the most part, users connect physically with their phone or other small device to play either individual or socially connected games. Measures of dynamic connectivity, including types of colleagues or competitors, can provide real-time information about the type of challenge, supportive or antagonistic environment, and amount of interaction that the gamer prefers. Such information is most useful to the gamer himself or herself, in support of metacognitive goals relating to the development of efficacy, teamwork, deliberate planning, and other higher-level thinking goals.

In addition to measuring users' interaction with their environment, recent advances in neurophysiology make tenable the use of imaging of the brain and potentially the gut (the second brain) to determine impact of games on cognitive function, including activation of particular parts of the brain, speed of solving problems, and increased overall functioning (Dye, Green, & Bavelier, 2009; Green, Li, & Bavelier, 2009). Experts in neuroscience are busily creating magnetic and other imaging devices that can function outside of noisy machines, or inside with multiple fMRI environments, linked to permit the analyses of team brain function given certain problems and direction to solve in concert with one or more other individuals, similarly being imaged. Current constraints include human subjects approvals for experimentation, the potential invasiveness of approaches, and how silly (or how miniaturized) sensors can be. The embarrassment of walking around with electroencephalography (EEG) headgear to determine the sweet spot for learning certain skills and content might be mitigated if the apparatus were embedded inside a Boston Red Sox cap (Berka, Behneman, Kintz, Johnson, & Raphael, 2010).

In a world where thoughts drive computers, and electromagnetic waves may be used in nonconsensual ways, the discussion of privacy, revelations of test scores, and choice of what to learn seem almost primitive. Consider, however, the inception of games driven by brain waves (EEG), which according to analysts can determine, by analyzing theta waves, levels of concentration, and focus. Planned are games that use other well known physiological indicators through sensors such as electromyography (EMG) that measures muscle movement, galvanic skin response (GSR) that measures perspiration, and electrocardiograph (ECG) that measures heart rate (Stafford & Webb, 2004). If put together, we may at last have a rough cut measure of the whole person. Indicators need to be refined, but suppose we think of the set of neurophysiology indicators as an internal Wii to measure users' responses as they engage in a task designed around knowledge ontologies and particular cognitive problems or situations to stimulate participants. Because such sensors will decrease in size and be easily embedded in everyday things, read outs, intended for the participant or responsible adult related to game play, whether device driven or in the wild, will certainly be available. Criterion performance could be estimated by using expert-novice comparisons, so that boundaries or classifications can be devised.

If evidence of brain function is combined with a few typical samples of performance, the typical approaches to assessment may ultimately fade away. However, with a continuing focus on efficiency, global competitiveness, and selection for further education and careers, formal testing situations may still remain as the criteria for certification and admission. At minimum, they subdivide society into those who have access and those who do not. Less interest will be given to the amount of time served in schools or other educational institutions, and more concern to whether, if we teach through games, schools, books, and television, we have resources to handle all the students who could be successful.

REFERENCES

Airasian, P. W., & Jones, A. M. (1993). The teacher as applied measurer: Realities of classroom measurement and assessment. *Applied Measurement in Education, 6,* 241–254.

Arici, A. D. (2008). *Meeting kids at their own game: A comparison of learning and engagement in traditional and 3D MUVE educational-gaming contexts.* Doctoral dissertation. UMI Number: 3342204. Indiana University.

Baker, E. L. (1974). The role of the evaluator in instructional development. In G. D. Borich (Ed.), *Evaluating educational programs and products* (pp. 56–73). Englewood Cliffs, NJ: Educational Technology Publications.

Baker, E. L. (2009, June). *Assessment policy options: Three coins in the fountain: Beware the return of the bad penny.* Presentation in the session "Ensuring Technical Quality of Formative Assessments," at the Council of Chief State School Officers National Conference on Student Assessment "The Future of Student Assessment," Los Angeles.

Baker, E. L., Chung, G. K. W. K., & Delacruz, G. C. (2008). Design and validation of technology-based performance assessments. In J. M. Spector, M. D. Merrill, J. J. G. van Merriënboer, & M. P. Driscoll (Eds.), *Handbook of research on educational communications and technology* (3rd ed.) (pp. 595–604). Mahwah, NJ: Erlbaum.

Baker, E. L., & Delacruz, G. C. (2008a). A framework for the assessment of learning games. In H. F. O'Neil & R. S. Perez (Eds.), *Computer games and team and individual learning* (pp. 21–37). Oxford, UK: Elsevier.

Baker, E. L., & Delacruz, G. C. (2008b). *What do we know about assessment in games?* Paper presented at the annual meeting of the American Educational Research Association. In session 17.021 "Computer Games and Team and Individual Learning," New York.

Berka, C., Behneman A., Kintz, N., Johnson, R., & Raphael, G. (2010). Accelerated training using interactive neuro-educational technologies: Applications to archery, golf and rifle marksmanship. *International Journal of Sports and Society, 1*, 87–104.

Black, P., & Wiliam, D. (1998). Assessment and classroom learning. *Assessment in Education: Principles, Policy & Practice, 5*(1), 7–74.

Chung, G. K. W. K., & Baker, E. L. (2003). An exploratory study to examine the feasibility of measuring problem-solving processes using a click-through interface. *Journal of Technology, Learning, and Assessment, 2*(2). Available from http://escholarship.bc.edu/cgi/viewcontent.cgi?article=1006&context=jtla

Chung, G. K. W. K., & Delacruz, G. C. (in press). Cognitive readiness for solving equations. In H. F. O'Neil, R. S. Perez, & E. L. Baker (Eds.), *Teaching and measuring cognitive readiness*. Mahwah, NJ: Erlbaum.

Crooks, T. J. (1988). The impact of classroom evaluation practices on students. *Review of Educational Research, 58*, 438–481.

de Freitas, S. (2006, December). *Using games and simulations for supporting learning. Learning, Media and Technology* (Special Issue on Gaming), *31*(4), 343–358.

Delacruz, G. C. (2010). *Games as formative assessment environments: Examining the impact of incentives and amount of scoring scheme information on math learning, game performance, and help seeking*. Unpublished doctoral dissertation, University of California, Los Angeles.

Delacruz, G. C., Chung, G. K. W. K., & Baker, E. L. (2009). Finding a place: Developments of location-based mobile gaming in learning and assessment environments. In A. de Souza e Silva & D. M. Sutko (Eds.), *Digital cityscapes: Merging digital and urban playspaces* (pp. 251–268). New York: Peter Lang.

Dye, M. W. G., Green, C. S., & Bavelier, D. (2009). Increasing speed of processing with action video games. *Current Directions in Psychological Science, 18*(6), 321–326.

Green, C. S., Li, R., & Bavelier, D. (2009). Perceptual learning during action video game playing. *Topics in Cognitive Science, 2*, 202–216.

Holyoak, K. (1995). Problem solving. In E. E. Smith & D. N. Osherson (Eds.), *Thinking: An invitation to cognitive science* (pp. 267–296). Cambridge, MA: MIT Press.

Johnson, W. L., & Valente, A. (2009). Tactical language and culture training systems: Using AI to teach foreign languages and cultures. *AI Magazine, 30*(2), 72–83.

Kirriemuir, J. K., & McFarlane, A. (2003). *Use of computer and video games in the classroom.* Proceedings of the Level Up Digital Games Research Conference, Universiteit Utrecht, Netherlands. Available from: http://www.silversprite.com

Kluger, A. N., & DeNisi, A. (1996). The effects of feedback interventions on performance: Historical review, a meta-analysis and a preliminary feedback intervention theory. *Psychological Bulletin, 119*, 254–284.

Koenig, A., Lee, J. J., Iseli, M., & Wainess, R. (2009, November). *A conceptual framework for assessing performance in games and simulations.* Paper presented at the 2009 annual Inter-service/Industry Training, Simulation and Education Conference (I/ITSEC), Orlando, FL.

Markle, S. M. (1967). Empirical testing of programs. In P. C. Lange (Ed.), *Programmed instruction, sixty-sixth yearbook of the National Society for the Study of Education, Part II* (pp. 104–138). Chicago: University of Chicago Press.

Mayer, S. (in process). *CRESST problem solving ontology.* Los Angeles: University of California, National Center for Research on Evaluation, Standards, and Student Testing.

Mitchell, A., & Savill-Smith, C. (2004). *The use of computer and video games for learning: A review of literature.* London: Learning and Skills Development Agency.

Morrison, J. E., & Fletcher J. D. (2002). *Cognitive readiness.* Alexandria, VA: Institute for Defense Analyses, IDA Paper P–3735.

National Research Council. (2001). *Classroom assessment and the National Science Education Standards.* Washington, DC: National Academy Press.

National Research Council. (2003). *Assessment in support of learning.* Washington, DC: National Academies Press.

Natriello, G. (1987). The impact of evaluation processes on students. *Educational Psychologist, 22,* 155–175.

Nyquist, J. B. (2003). *The benefits of reconstructing feedback as a larger system of formative assessment: A meta-analysis.* Unpublished master's thesis. Vanderbilt University, Nashville, TN.

O'Neil, H. F., & Perez, R. S. (Eds.). (2008). *Computer games and team and individual learning.* Elsevier, Oxford, UK.

O'Neil, H. F., Wainess, R., & Baker, E. L. (2005). Classification of learning outcomes: Evidence from the computer games literature. *The Curriculum Journal, 16*(4), 455–474.

Organisation for Economic Co-operation and Development. (2009). *PISA 2009 Assessment Framework: Key competencies in reading, mathematics and science.* Paris: OECD. Available at http://www.oecd.org/dataoecd/11/40/44455820.pdf

Project Tomorrow. (2010). *Creating our future: Students speak up about their vision for 21st century learning. Speak Up 2009 national findings: K–12 students and parents.* Available at http://www.tomorrow.org/speakup/pdfs/SU09NationalFindings Students&Parents.pdf

Sandford, R., Ulicsak, M., Facer, K., & Rudd, T. (2006). *Teaching with games: Using commercial off-the-shelf computer games in formal education.* Available at http://archive.futurelab.org.uk/resources/documents/project_reports/teaching_with_games/TWG_report.pdf

Scriven, M. (1967). Aspects of curriculum evaluation. In R. Tyler (Ed.), *Perspectives of curriculum evaluation.* Chicago: Rand McNally.

Scriven, M. (1991). Beyond formative and summative evaluation. In M. W. McLaughlin & D. C. Phillips (Eds.), *Evaluation and education: At quarter century* (90th yearbook of the National Society for the Study of Education) (pp. 19–64). Chicago: University of Chicago Press.

Shilling, R., Zyda, M., & Wardynski, C. E. (2002, 30 November). *Introducing emotion into military simulation and videogame design: America's army: Operations and VIRTE.* Paper presented at the GameOn Conference, London.

Stafford, T., & Webb, M. (2004). *Mind hacks.* Cambridge, MA: O'Reilly Media.

Wiliam, D. (2006). Formative assessment: Getting the focus right. *Educational Assessment, 11*(3,4), 283–287.

Wiliam, D. (2010). An integrative summary of the research literature and implications for a new theory of formative assessment. In H. L. Andrade & G. J. Cizek (Eds.), *Handbook of formative assessment* (pp. 18–40). New York: Routledge.

Wiliam, D., Lee, C., Harrison, C., & Black, P. J. (2004). Teachers developing assessment for learning: Impact on student achievement. *Assessment in Education: Principles Policy and Practice, 11*(1), 49–65.

CHAPTER 10

INQUIRY AND ASSESSMENT

Future Developments from a Technological Perspective

Ton de Jong, Pascal Wilhelm, and Anjo Anjewierden
University of Twente, The Netherlands

ABSTRACT

In this chapter we present an overview of on-line assessment of inquiry learning. We take learners who are involved in a technology enhanced inquiry learning environment as our starting point. These learners leave traces in the form of activity logs, chats, and products designed (models, hypotheses etc.). The traces can be used to analyze different aspects of the inquiry process, such as, for example, the students' experimentation behavior or hypothesis quality. Results can also be used to inform students on their inquiry process or developing knowledge or to trigger instructional interventions. In this chapter we present a few examples of on-line assessment and its use, and we highlight techniques that are used for this.

Technology-Based Assessments for 21st Century Skills, pages 249–265
Copyright © 2012 by Information Age Publishing

INTRODUCTION

Currently, a shared vision on education is that learning for understanding and transfer can only take place when students process learning material actively and engage in deeper processes such as asking questions, searching for structures, and creating abstractions (Bransford, Brown, & Cocking, 1999; Jonassen, 1991; Mayer, 2002). One way to engage students in those active processes is to involve them in inquiry learning. This type of learning is a common pedagogy in science education. The core components of inquiry learning activities are 1) engaging in scientifically oriented questions, 2) focusing on evidence, 3) formulating explanations on the basis of evidence, 4) evaluating explanations and 5) communicating and justifying explanations (Minner, Levy, & Century, 2009; National Research Council, 2000). In this way, students learn science by actively engaging in the practices of science by conducting investigations and by modelling. This includes managing the process, making sense of data, and discussion and reflection on the results (National Research Council, 2007; National Science Foundation, 2000). Evidence is accumulating that inquiry learning has advantages over traditional, more expository, forms of instruction (see e.g., Eysink et al., 2009; Hickey, Kindfield, Horwitz, & Christie, 2003; Linn, Lee, Tinker, Husic, & Chiu, 2006; Minner et al., 2009). Inquiry learning results may be manifold. Students learn about the domain that they inquire, but they may also acquire specific inquiry skills or learn about scientific practices, form attitudes towards science, and acquire knowledge about the Nature of Science (NOS) (Norman, 1992). In this chapter, we will focus on assessment issues that relate to these various inquiry learning outcomes in the context of technology enhanced learning.

Nowadays, inquiry learning is often supported by means of technology enhanced learning (TEL), for example based on simulations (de Jong, 2006a). Technology, and more particularly simulation, is especially suited to afford inquiry learning (de Jong, 2010). For example, technology offers the opportunity to perform experiments that would otherwise require laboratory settings, presents students with unique instructional capabilities (cognitive tools for different inquiry learning activities, intelligent support), can link learners to information resources, and can help students to visualize problems and solutions (Zacharias & Anderson, 2003). Technology also can make the invisible visible—for example by offering dynamic representations of physical concepts like gravity, force, and electricity (van der Meij & de Jong, 2006). The current, more advanced technology based learning environments can even offer sensory augmentations through which students can "feel" phenomena that have no sensory counterpart in reality (e.g., forces that accompany transportation through a cell membrane, Minogue & Jones, 2009). In addition, technology allows for on-line synchronous collaborative inquiry including video and chat communication tools (van Joolingen, de Jong, Lazonder, Savelsbergh, & Manlove, 2005). Of course, these technological affordances do not automatically imply more proficient learning. To make them efficient, instructional innovations also produce serious challenges. See, for example, the work of Bell and colleagues (Bell, Urhahne, Schanze, & Ploetzner, 2010) who discuss challenges in the development of collaborative inquiry learning in TEL. Several papers discuss how inquiry learning can be scaffolded in the process of learning itself (e.g., de Jong, 2006b; Quintana et al., 2004; Zhang, Chen, Sun, & Reid, 2004).

These and other examples illustrate the opportunities that technology offers to scaffold or guide the learning process. At the same time, technology offers opportunities for assessment. The most simple and direct way is that technology replaces traditional assessment methods. For example, paper-and-pencil domain pre- and post-tests can be integrated as templates in a TEL environment. However, technology also allows us to follow learners in real time, on-line, and without impeding their activities. The latter use of technology will be the focus of this chapter. Before describing three examples of on-line assessment, we first present an overview of the goals of inquiry learning, several characteristics of assessment, the ways results of assessment can be applied, and the on-line sources that can be used for assessment.

INQUIRY RELATED ASSESSMENT

What Is Being Assessed?

Assessment in the context of inquiry learning is related to the learning goals in inquiry and these goals, as indicated above, refer to a) domain knowledge, b) inquiry skills c) attitudes towards science and d) nature of science.

Domain knowledge as acquired in simulation based inquiry has a multifaceted character. Students may acquire factual and/or procedural knowledge, but overall the focus is more directed towards conceptual knowledge and even conceptual knowledge with a more intuitive character (de Jong, 2006a; Swaak & de Jong, 1996). This implies that students develop a "feeling" for relations in the underlying model, but with the disadvantage that students may not be able to explicate their knowledge. One way to overcome this is to ask students to "explain" their knowledge, for example in the form of a runnable computer model. In this way, students acquire more explicit knowledge of the domain or even about models in general (van Borkulo, van Joolingen, Savelsbergh, & de Jong, 2009).

Inquiry skills refer to an overall idea of the inquiry cycle or to more specific inquiry heuristics. The inquiry cycle normally contains processes such as hypothesis generation, experimentation, and evidence evaluation. Also, a distinction can be made between learning processes that relate to knowledge construction and processes that relate to self-regulation or metacognition (Veenman, Prins, & Elshout, 2002). One of the best known inquiry heuristics is the Control-of-Variables (CVS) or VOTAT (Vary One Thing At a Time) heuristic that signifies the idea that only one variable at a time should be manipulated (Chen & Klahr, 1999; Wilhelm, Beishuizen, & Van Rijn, 2005), but a whole range of other heuristics exist, such as, for example, the heuristic to try extreme values to see if ideas still hold in different circumstances (Veermans, van Joolingen, & de Jong, 2006).

Attitudes towards science relate to personal ideas about the use of inquiry in general, for society, for one's career, and so on. Attitudes are a part of a larger concept called science motivation. Research on the relationships between science motivation and TEL learning is emerging (Mistler-Jackson & Butler Songer, 2000; Wang & Reeves, 2006).

Nature of Science (NOS) concerns the views an individual has on science. It includes, for example, if an individual sees scientific knowledge as an absolute truth or not (Lederman, 1992). Being involved in inquiry learning may affect some aspects of the nature of science. Students may, for example, experience the role of measurements errors, which makes them aware of how knowledge is dependent on correct observations. Inquiry context may serve the development of adequate NOS views (Akerson & Hanuscin, 2007; Schwartz, Lederman, & Crawford, 2004).

In this chapter we focus on the first two goals of inquiry learning: domain knowledge and inquiry skills.

Characteristics of Assessment

If assessment is carried out on one or a combination of the inquiry goals above it may still have different characteristics.

First, assessment may compare students' achievements to a specific criterion or be criterion free. For example, if we judge the quality of a model developed by a student, this requires a criterion model to which the model of the student is compared (Bravo, van Joolingen, & de Jong, 2006, 2009). Also, if we judge if a student is working orderly (for example, following CVS/VOTAT), we need an idea of the ideal way of performing inquiry. In their work on assessing students' inquiry behavior Veermans et al. (2006) judged whether conclusions that students draw could be based on the experiments they had been performing. This required a model of what experiments were related to a specific hypothesis. As an alternative, assessment may just describe knowledge or processes without taking any criterion into account. As an example, in the work of Kay, Maisonneuve, Yacef, and Reimann (2006), activity levels of students in a collaborative setting are calculated and shown to the participating students in a graphical way.

A second characteristic of assessment is whether it refers to individuals or groups. In individual assessment, the personal behavior or achievement of a student is analyzed and this could, for example, be presented in the form of feedback to a student. But also the behavior or achievements of groups can be assessed. An example is the work by Perera, Kay, Koprinska, Yacef, and Zaïane (2009) who characterized with educational data mining techniques the cooperation behavior of both individuals and groups of students.

A third feature of assessment concerns who is performing the assessment. In a classroom, ongoing assessment is performed by teachers. They constantly monitor performance of individuals or groups of individuals and make assessments of the process and/or the developing knowledge. Students themselves of course can also make assessments of their own learning process or knowledge. This is often called a process of reflection. Peer assessment is another often used way of assessment, sometimes supported by technology (Vold, Wasson, & de Jong, in press). Finally, and of specific interest for this chapter, in TEL environments also the software may assess the knowledge and behavior of learners.

A final characteristic is if the assessment is performed during the learning process or afterwards (immediate or delayed). If the assessment is performed afterwards, often traditional tests are used. For assessing knowledge a whole range of (standard) knowledge tests is available, with test for intuitive knowledge in simulation based learning as a special case (Swaak & de Jong, 2001). If deeper knowledge is to be assessed, tests that ask students to write explanations can be used (McNeill, Lizotte, Krajcik, & Marx, 2006). For assessing inquiry skills, a set of paper-and-pencil tests is available (for example, Tannenbaum, 1971; Tobin & Capie, 1982; van Borkulo et al., 2009), as are computerized tests such as the Peter task (Wilhelm, et al., 2005). Also for measuring students' view on the nature of science different tests exist (e.g., Lederman, Abd-El-Khalick, Bell, & Schwartz, 2002). On-line assessment is taking place concurrently with the learning process and is often performed unobtrusively using the "traces" that students leave behind in a TEL environment. As an example, we can take the work by Veermans, et al. (2006), who analyzed the experimentation behavior of students on the basis of logfiles in relation to the conclusion that these students drew about a hypothesis they were investigating and used this as a basis to provide students with feedback on the way the data collected supported the hypothesis.

In the examples we present in this chapter, we focus on on-line assessment performed by a computer program, of individuals, and for knowledge and inquiry skills with and without a criterion.

ON-LINE ASSESSMENT

Sources

On-line assessment may be based on obtrusive measures (such as on-line questionnaires) or unobtrusive measures (see, Schraw, 2010). In this chapter we will focus on the unobtrusive ones.

On-line assessment of learning processes often uses *logfiles* containing all interactions of the learners(s) with the TEL environment (Hulshof, 2004). For example, systematic experimentation indicated by the consistent use of the control-of-variables strategy (Chen & Klahr, 1999) can be extracted from logfiles (Wilhelm et al., 2005). To do this, data from the logfile need to be reformatted, filtered, and analyzed to allow for statistical analysis. The SCY environment (de Jong et al., 2010) also contains a tool to discover systematic learning behavior. A sophisticated example of logfile analysis can be found in Aleven, Roll, McLaren, and Koedinger (2010), who describe the on-line, unobtrusive assessment of student help seeking behavior in which this behavior is interpreted by the software in the context in which it appears.

A second source can be found in the products that students design on-line. The SCY project (de Jong et al., 2010) specifically focuses on these products. These can be hypotheses, models, concept maps, (experimentation) plans, reports, data sets (e.g., from simulations), free hand drawings and so on.

A third source, in the case of collaborative learning, comes from the chats of learners. Chats form an interesting source to get a view on the learning process of students since they may express, for example, which topic is in the focus of students or what conclusions are drawn on the basis of experiments. An example of on-line assessment of chats can be found in Anjewierden, Gijlers, Kolloffel, Saab, and de Hoog (2011). In their work they automatically analyzed the relative presence of domain related chat of students working in dyads on a simulation environment in the physics domain of collisions and found that if a dyad is using more domain related chat, this is related to progress in intuitive knowledge gained. A similar approach is reported by Azevedo, Moos, Johnson, and Chauncy (2010), who describe a system to assess students' self-regulative behavior on the basis of a quantitative and qualitative analysis of their logfiles.

A fourth (unobtrusive) source can come from devices specifically built to collect information from students, such as eye movements or mouse movements (Azevedo, 2010).

GOALS

The information that is gathered from on-line assessment can be used for different goals. First, researchers can use this information to test their hypotheses. If we can use logfile analysis to find specific characteristics of learner behavior, this is advantageous compared to, for example, thinking aloud techniques since it is less intrusive for the learner and less subjective in the scoring method. An example of a tool using on-line data for research purposes is ChatIc, a tool for the automatic analysis of learner chats. This tool, after being trained by a coder, can automatically categorize chat messages as domain, regulatory, technical, or off-line/social messages (Anjewierden & Gijlers, 2008). The analysis can be done after all chats are recorded, but also during the learning process.

On-line assessment may also be used to inform the learner. The system then generates a representation of the activities of the learner (e.g., in a graph), but does not give any directions as to what to do next. In this case, the learner can monitor the learning processes. The input is the learner's own activity in the TEL environment. An example of this can be found in a study by Janssen, Erkens, Kanselaar, and Jaspers (2007), who showed learners' patterns of their interaction behavior very similar to the study by Kay et al. (2006) cited above. Another example can be found in SimQuest learning environments (van Joolingen & de Jong, 2003), in which learners can see the experiments they have been doing in a simulation, re-order the experiments and redo them in a so-called monitoring tool.

When on-line assessment of learning processes is used as input for tailor-made prompt and hints, assessment for learning has taken place. For example, in the system Model-It (Jackson, Krajcik, & Soloway, 1998) this type of scaffolding is provided as messages which appear as relevant. A "Stop reminding me" button can be clicked by the learner to ignore the messages, but if learners neglect certain activity a message will appear saying: "I know you asked me not to remind you about this, but I noticed that you haven't been..." In this case, assessment of learner activity results in tailored instruction. In the remainder of this chapter we will present some state of the art examples of this type of assessment.

EXAMPLES OF ON-LINE ASSESSMENT OF INQUIRY LEARNING

Analyzing Models Created by Learners

Runnable models created by learners in a TEL environment can be compared in real time to expert models (criterion) and result in feedback on how learners are progressing towards a correct model. In two consecutive papers Bravo et al. (2006, 2009) describe a system that is able to automatically assess models created by students. The models were created with the Co-Lab system and based on system dynamics (van Joolingen et al., 2005).

In the Bravo et al. work the assessment of models was based on a comparison with an expert criterion model on an element by element and relation by relation basis. For example, if the learner requested advice to improve the model, Bravo's system might respond: "a constant is missing;" the second time the advice would be more detailed: "constant X is missing." In work by Anjewierden, Mulder, Bollen, and Lazonder (in preparation), also based on system dynamics modeling, a tool was developed in which the researcher can specify both a reference model and sets of rules to compare the model created by the learner with the reference model. A rule can be simple—"is constant X present"—or more complex. For instance, in the domain of electrical circuits it is possible to specify a rule that assesses whether Ohm's law is in the learner model. In a study by Mulder, Lazonder, and de Jong (in press) the learning environment provided a simulation facility for experimentation, a system dynamics modeling tool and a rule-based assessment agent. On the student's request the agent presents the number of correct and incorrect elements and relations in the learner's model in a bar chart (see Figure 10.1). In this study, assessment feedback was of a tacit nature: learners were only informed when something was wrong. With the appropriate sets of rules, automatic assessment can also be used for more specific feedback based on the quality of the model created by the learner.

To inform the researcher, overviews of group behavior can be generated (see Figure 10.2). The figure shows the "ideal" reference model from the Mulder et al. (in press) study for learners who obtained feedback from the agent (bottom) and learners who did not obtain agent feedback. The elements in the final model of the learners are represented using gradient

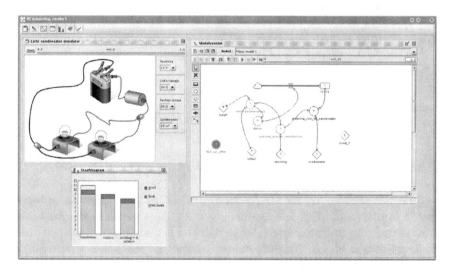

Figure 10.1 Feedback to the learner on model quality.

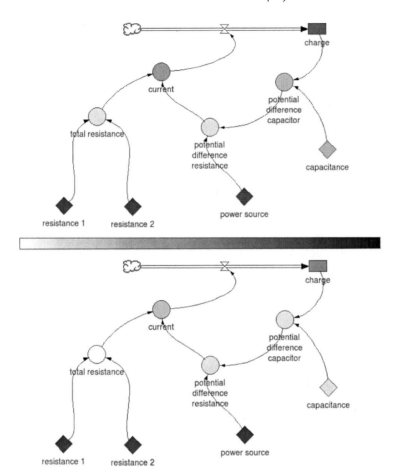

Figure 10.2 Students' model quality. *Note:* The two figures show the reference model of a system dynamics modelling task. Each element in the model is filled with a color gradient ranging from white (0% of the learners included the element in their model) to black (100%). The above figure corresponds to learners who obtained tacit feedback from an agent and the one below to learners who did not obtain feedback. As can be seen, receiving feedback resulted in a higher percentage of learners including the elements in their model.

colors, ranging from red (0% had this element in the final model) through dark blue (100%) (in the figure displayed in black, grey, and white).

In the SCY project (de Jong et al., 2010) the assessment of student generated concept maps is done in a similar way. Concepts maps that learners create are compared to a criterion map. Results are used to a) help students extend or change their maps or b) suggest collaboration with other students who have similar maps.

ANALYZING LOG-FILES TO FIND ERRATIC BEHAVIOR

The next examples focus on on-line assessment of activity logs of learners in a TEL environment with the purpose of intervening in an individual student's learning process. The assessment is criterion-based and the corresponding interventions are focused on providing awareness of non-systematic learning behavior and offer tailor-made advice on how learning can be made more systematic and efficient.

The examples come from the SCY project. In SCY, all students' actions are logged and pedagogical agents are used to analyze students' behavior. The overall goal of pedagogical agents is to adapt to the context and abilities of a particular learner in order to monitor his or her behavior and provide scaffolds just in time.

In SCY, three aspects of learner activity can be used to alert students on non-systematic experimentation behavior. The first pertains to so-called canonical behavior. A sensor agent detects whether the learner chooses simple, canonical manipulations or not. Specifically, the agent counts if the learner uses equal increments to change a particular input variable. For this, an underlying optimal criterion is specified. Another (decision) agent then offers advice on how to change variables while testing a certain hypothesis. A monitoring system mediates this process, allowing for other sensor data to be combined and integrated, so the advice will suit the learner in the best optimal way.

The second type of behavior that SCY can monitor is whether a learner applies the Control-of-Variables Strategy (CVS; Chen & Klahr, 1999) and describes an important heuristic related to hypothesis testing (Klahr & Dunbar, 1988). The heuristic suggests that a variable that is not relevant for the specific hypothesis should be held constant (e.g., hold the same value as in the previous experiment). The task of the CVS agent in SCY is to detect which and how many variables have been modified within a specific time frame and offer the learner hints and advice when his or her learning behavior becomes inefficient.

A third type pertains to user experience. A tool experience agent in SCY detects and offers information about how familiar the user is with a specific tool. Basically, this is solved by looking into the logs to determine how much time the user spent using that tool.

So, in all three examples log data are used to detect aspects of experimental behavior that are evaluated with built-in rules or criteria. Depending on the outcome of this evaluation, the system then offers specific feedback and hints on how to change learner behavior for learning to become more efficient. In this way a system might also detect non-productive behavior like "gaming the system" (Baker, Corbett, Roll, & Koedinger, 2008) and "floundering" (de Jong & van Joolingen, 1998).

ANALYZING CHATS TO FIND ORIENTATION OF STUDENTS

In inquiry learning environments a chat tool can be used to facilitate co-operative problem solving. The resulting chats can be seen as externalized "products" reflecting the focus of the learning process. They are descriptive and informative, especially for researchers. The chats tend to be short; for example in the simulation environment from Saab (2005), average chat length was 3.77 tokens (words, smileys, numbers, etc.) (SD = 3.51).

Chat analysis can contribute to assessment in several ways. Each chat can be categorized according to a coding scheme reflecting what the researcher is interested in. Grammatical and semantic analysis can be applied to obtain an understanding of the meaning of the chats, for example to determine whether a chat contains a hypothesis or some other content-oriented observation (Anjewierden et al., 2011). An example of the application of a coding scheme related to inquiry learning environments is given by Gijlers and de Jong (2005). They propose a coding scheme in which each chat is classified as one of *domain* (the domain of learning, "the speed increases"), *technical* (related to the learning environment, "could you click start"), *regulative* ("yes," "do you have an idea"), or *social* (off-task). Figure 10.3 shows a screendump

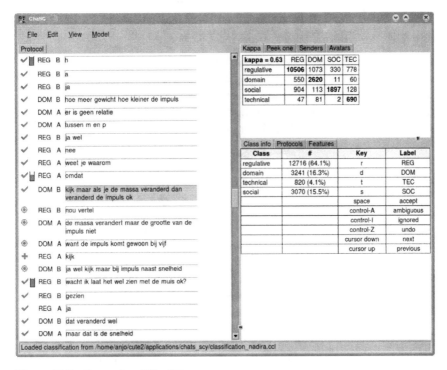

Figure 10.3 Example of ChatIC.

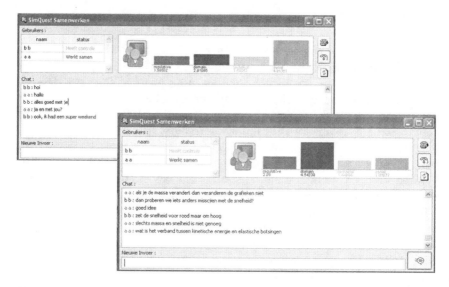

Figure 10.4 Examples of on-line coding of chats. *Note*: The heights of the bars indicate the relative amount of regulative, domain-specific, technical, and social talk between two learners as a means of feedback on their collaborative learning process. This feedback is generated automatically on the basis of the chats.

of ChatIC (Anjewierden & Gijlers, 2008), an interactive tool that supports chat coding by researchers. The tool also uses a machine learning algorithm to learn a *model* using the codes entered by the researcher as training data. In the screendump, the markers in the second column indicate chats in which human and automatic coding differ and at the top right is a confusion matrix summarizing agreement on coding.

The model resulting from the machine learning algorithm can be used to analyze messages on-line and thus provide feedback to learners. Based on the coding scheme mentioned above, feedback could be related to the ratio of domain versus non-domain oriented messages. Figure 10.4 combines a chat tool and feedback about the most recent messages as a bar chart (e.g., blue is domain).

DISCUSSION AND OUTLOOK

In this chapter we discussed several areas of assessment in the context of inquiry learning supported by TEL environments. We focused on the assessment of (domain) knowledge and skills and discussed important characteristics of these assessments. Assessments can be criterion-based or not; on an individual or group level; delivered by teachers, peers and systems; and may be immediate (e.g., log file assessment) or delayed (e.g., posttests). We then focused on assessments by a system incorporated in a TEL environment and defined three sources of data on the basis of which assessment can be made: logfiles, products (e.g., tables, graphs, concept maps) and communication data (e.g., data logs). The goals of these assessments might be to test certain research hypotheses, inform or alert learners, and to offer tailor-made prompts and hints for more productive learning.

The state of the art in inquiry learning assessment lies in this third goal, which relates to assessment for learning. In principle, computing power poses no constraints on on-line assessment and feedback algorithms; moreover data mining techniques are becoming more and more sophisticated. It is a question of time before a TEL environment is developed which fully adapts to learner behavior, integrating all kinds of data sources and offers specific tailor-made prompt and hints. However, the greatest challenge for assessment lies in the fact that inquiry learning is, to a great extent, open-ended. Processes have to be assessed more uniquely because there is no overall "good model" and what is good depends on the context, the learner and many other factors. In principle, learners can decide for themselves what they want to learn. Although this is an extreme case, it poses serious challenges. Educational goals in specific subject areas (e.g., physics, chemistry) are more or less fixed, and we want learners to become knowledgeable in particular subjects. The question is then: how can we achieve this without sacrificing the unique aspects of inquiry (e.g., self-regulative, flexibility)? On the one hand, the TEL environment can pose constraints on what can be learned while learners can still have the feeling they have ample opportunities to explore the TEL environment in their own ways. On the other hand, the road ahead involves a step-by-step integration of more and more adaptive scaffolding offered in an integrated way. Research in inquiry learning has to inform on the pedagogical interventions while technology assists in implementing these.

ACKNOWLEDGEMENTS

Part of this work was conducted in the context of Science Created by You (SCY), which is funded by the European Community under the Information and Communication Technologies (ICT) theme of the 7th Framework Programme for R&D (Grant agreement 212814). This document does not represent the opinion of the European Community, and the European Community is not responsible for any use that might be made of its content.

REFERENCES

Akerson, V. L., & Hanuscin, D. L. (2007). Teaching nature of science through inquiry: Results of a 3-year professional development program. *Journal of Research in Science Teaching, 44*, 653–680.

Aleven, V., Roll, I., McLaren, B. M., & Koedinger, K. R. (2010). Automated, unobtrusive, action-by-action assessment of self-regulation during learning with an intelligent tutoring system. *Educational Psychologist, 45*, 224–233.

Anjewierden, A., & Gijlers, H. (2008). An exploration of tool support for categorical coding. In G. Kanselaar, J. van Merriënboer, P. Kirschner & T. de Jong (Eds.), *International conference of the learning sciences (icls)* (pp. 35–44). Utrecht (The Netherlands): ICLS.

Anjewierden, A., Gijlers, H., Kolloffel, B., Saab, N., & de Hoog, R. (2011). Examining the relation between domain-related communication and collaborative inquiry learning. *Computers & Education, 57*, 1741–1748.

Anjewierden, A., Mulder, Y. G., Bollen, L., & Lazonder, A. (in preparation). Tacit pedagogical agent support for modelling activities in an inquiry learning environment.

Azevedo, R. (2010, August). *Using metatutor to scaffold and foster self-regulated learning and science understanding.* Paper presented at the TACONET conference: Self-regulated Learning in Technology Enhanced Learning Environments: Challenges and Promises, Barcelona.

Azevedo, R., Moos, D. C., Johnson, A. M., & Chauncy, A. D. (2010). Measuring cognitive and metacognitive regulatory processes during hypermedia learning: Issues and challenges. *Educational Psychologist, 45*, 210–223.

Baker, R., Corbett, A., Roll, I., & Koedinger, K. (2008). Developing a generalizable detector of when students game the system. *User Modeling and User-Adapted Interaction, 18*, 287–314.

Bell, T., Urhahne, D., Schanze, S., & Ploetzner, R. (2010). Collaborative inquiry learning: Models, tools and challenges. *International Journal of Science Education, 32*, 349–377.

Bransford, J. D., Brown, A. L., & Cocking, R. R. (Eds.). (1999). *How people learn: Brain, mind, experience, and school.* Washington, D.C: National Academy Press.

Bravo, C., van Joolingen, W. R., & de Jong, T. (2006). Modeling and simulation in inquiry learning: Checking solutions and giving intelligent advice. *Simulation: Transactions of the Society for Modeling and Simulation International 82*, 769–784.

Bravo, C., van Joolingen, W. R., & de Jong, T. (2009). Using co-lab to build system dynamics models: Students' actions and on-line tutorial advice. *Computers & Education, 53*, 243–251.

Chen, Z., & Klahr, D. (1999). All other things being equal: Acquisition and transfer of the control of variables strategy. *Child Development, 70*, 1098–1120.

de Jong, T. (2006a). Computer simulations—technological advances in inquiry learning. *Science, 312*, 532–533.

de Jong, T. (2006b). Scaffolds for computer simulation based scientific discovery learning. In J. Elen & R. E. Clark (Eds.), *Dealing with complexity in learning environments* (pp. 107–128). London: Elsevier Science Publishers.

de Jong, T. (2010). Instruction based on computer simulations. In R. E. Mayer & P. A. Alexander (Eds.), *Handbook of research on learning and instruction* (pp. 446–466): Routledge Press.

de Jong, T., & van Joolingen, W. R. (1998). Scientific discovery learning with computer simulations of conceptual domains. *Review of Educational Research, 68,* 179–202.

de Jong, T., van Joolingen, W. R., Giemza, A., Girault, I., Hoppe, U., Kindermann, J.,... Van Der Zanden, M. (2010). Learning by creating and exchanging objects: The SCY experience. *British Journal of Educational Technology, 41,* 909–921.

Eysink, T. H. S., de Jong, T., Berthold, K., Kollöffel, B., Opfermann, M., & Wouters, P. (2009). Learner performance in multimedia learning arrangements: An analysis across instructional approaches. *American Educational Research Journal, 46,* 1107–1149.

Gijlers, H., & de Jong, T. (2005). The relation between prior knowledge and students' collaborative discovery learning processes. *Journal of Research in Science Teaching, 42,* 264–282.

Hickey, D. T., Kindfield, A. C. H., Horwitz, P., & Christie, M. A. (2003). Integrating curriculum, instruction, assessment, and evaluation in a technology-supported genetics environment. *American Educational Research Journal, 40,* 495–538.

Hulshof, C. D. (2004). Log file analysis. In K. Kempf-Leonard (Ed.), *Encyclopedia of social measurement,* Vol. 2 (pp. 577–583). San Diego, CA: Academic Press.

Jackson, S. L., Krajcik, J., & Soloway, E. (1998). *The design of guided learner-adaptable scaffolding in interactive learning environments.* Paper presented at the Conference on Human Factors in Computing Systems, Los Angeles, California.

Janssen, J., Erkens, G., Kanselaar, G., & Jaspers, J. (2007). Visualization of participation: Does it contribute to successful computer-supported collaborative learning? *Computers & Education, 49,* 1037–1065.

Jonassen, D. H. (1991). Objectivism versus constructivism: Do we need a new philosophical paradigm? *Educational Technology: Research & Development, 39,* 5–14.

Kay, J., Maisonneuve, N., Yacef, K., & Reimann, P. (2006). The big five and visualisations of team work activity. In M. Ikeda, K. D. Ashley & T. Chan (Eds.), *Intelligent tutoring systems* (pp. 197–206). New York: Springer.

Klahr, D., & Dunbar, K. (1988). Dual space search during scientific reasoning. *Cognitive Science, 12,* 1–48.

Lederman, N. G. (1992). Students' and teachers' conceptions of the nature of science: A review of the research. *Journal of Research in Science Teaching, 29,* 331–359.

Lederman, N. G., Abd-El-Khalick, F., Bell, R. L., & Schwartz, R. S. (2002). Views of nature of science questionnaire: Toward valid and meaningful assessment of learners' conceptions of nature of science. *Journal of Research in Science Teaching, 39,* 497–521.

Linn, M. C., Lee, H. -S., Tinker, R., Husic, F., & Chiu, J. L. (2006). Teaching and assessing knowledge integration in science. *Science, 313,* 1049–1050.

Mayer, R. E. (2002). Rote versus meaningful learning. *Theory into Practice, 41,* 226–232.

McNeill, K. L., Lizotte, D. J., Krajcik, J., & Marx, R. W. (2006). Supporting students' construction of scientific explanations by fading scaffolds in instructional materials. *Journal of the Learning Sciences, 15,* 153–191.

Minner, D. D., Levy, A. J., & Century, J. (2009). Inquiry-based science instruction—what is it and does it matter? Results from a research synthesis years 1984 to 2002. *Journal of Research in Science Teaching, 47,* 474–496.

Minogue, J., & Jones, G. (2009). Measuring the impact of haptic feedback using the solo taxonomy. *International Journal of Science Education, 31,* 1359–1378.

Mistler-Jackson, M., & Butler Songer, N. (2000). Student motivation and internet technology: Are students empowered to learn science? *Journal of Research in Science Teaching, 37,* 459–479.

Mulder, Y.G., Lazonder, A.W., de Jong, T. (2011). Comparing two types of model progression in an inquiry learning environment with modelling facilities. *Learning & Instruction, 21,* 614–624.

National Research Council. (2000). *Inquiry and the national science education standards. A guide for teaching and learning.* Washington DC: National Academy Press.

National Research Council. (2007). *Taking science to school: Learning and teaching science in grade k–8.* Washington, DC: Author.

National Science Foundation. (2000). An introduction to inquiry. In *Foundations. Inquiry: Thoughts, views and strategies for the k–5 classroom.* (Vol. 2, pp. 1–5). Arlington, VA: Author.

Norman, G. L. (1992). Students' and teachers' conceptions of the nature of science: A review of the research. *Journal of Research in Science Teaching, 29,* 331–359.

Perera, P., Kay, J., Koprinska, I., Yacef, K., & Zaïane, O. R. (2009). Clustering and sequential pattern mining of online collaborative learning data. *IEEE Transaction on Knowledge and Data Engineering, 21,* 759–772.

Quintana, C., Reiser, B. J., Davis, E. A., Krajcik, J., Fretz, E., Duncan, R. G.,... Soloway, E. (2004). A scaffolding design framework for software to support science inquiry. *The Journal of the Learning Sciences, 13,* 337–387.

Saab, N. (2005). *Chat and explore: The role of support and motivation in collaborative inquiry learning.* Amsterdam: University of Amsterdam.

Schraw, G. (2010). Measuring self-regulation in computer-based learning environments. *Educational Psychologist, 45,* 258–266.

Schwartz, R. S., Lederman, N. G., & Crawford, B. A. (2004). Developing views of nature of science in an authentic context: An explicit approach to bridging the gap between nature of science and scientific inquiry. *Science Education, 88,* 610–645.

Swaak, J., & de Jong, T. (1996). Measuring intuitive knowledge in science: The development of the what-if test. *Studies in Educational Evaluation, 22,* 341–362.

Swaak, J., & de Jong, T. (2001). Discovery simulations and the assessment of intuitive knowledge. *Journal of Computer Assisted Learning, 17,* 284–294.

Tannenbaum, R. S. (1971). The development of the test of science processes. *Journal of Research in Science Teaching, 8,* 123–136.

Tobin, K. G., & Capie, W. (1982). Development and validation of a group test of integrated science processes. *Journal of Research in Science Teaching, 19,* 133–141.

van Borkulo, S., van Joolingen, W. R., Savelsbergh, E. R., & de Jong, T. (2009). A framework for the assessment of learning by modelling. In P. Blumschein, W. Hung & D. Jonassen (Eds.), *Learning by modeling systems* (pp. 179-199). Rotterdam: Sense Publishers.

van der Meij, J., & de Jong, T. (2006). Supporting students' learning with multiple representations in a dynamic simulation-based learning environment. *Learning and Instruction, 16*, 199–212.

van Joolingen, W. R., & de Jong, T. (2003). Simquest: Authoring educational simulations. In T. Murray, S. Blessing & S. Ainsworth (Eds.), *Authoring tools for advanced technology educational software: Toward cost-effective production of adaptive, interactive, and intelligent educational software* (pp. 1–31). Dordrecht: Kluwer Academic Publishers.

van Joolingen, W. R., de Jong, T., Lazonder, A. W., Savelsbergh, E., & Manlove, S. (2005). Co-lab: Research and development of an on-line learning environment for collaborative scientific discovery learning. *Computers in Human Behavior, 21*, 671–688.

Veenman, M. V. J., Prins, F. J., & Elshout, J. J. (2002). Initial inductive learning in a complex computer simulated environment: The role of metacognitive skills and intellectual ability. *Computers in Human Behavior, 18*, 327–341.

Veermans, K. H., van Joolingen, W. R., & de Jong, T. (2006). Using heuristics to facilitate scientific discovery learning in a simulation learning environment in a physics domain. *International Journal of Science Education, 28*, 341–361.

Vold, V., Wasson, B., & de Jong, T. (in press). Assessing emerging learning objects: Eportfolios and peer assessment. In K. Littleton, E. Scanlon & M. Sharples (Eds.), *Orchestrating inquiry learning: Contemporary perspectives on supporting scientific inquiry learning.* New York: Routledge.

Wang, S.-K., & Reeves, T. (2006). The effects of a web-based learning environment on student motivation in a high school earth science course. *Educational Technology Research and Development, 54*, 597–621.

Wilhelm, P., Beishuizen, J. J., & Van Rijn, H. (2005). Studying inquiry learning with file. *Computers in Human Behavior, 21*, 933–943.

Zacharias, Z., & Anderson, O. R. (2003). The effects of an interactive computer-based simulation prior to performing a laboratory inquiry-based experiment on students' conceptual understanding of physics. *American Journal of Physics, 71*, 618–629.

Zhang, J., Chen, Q., Sun, Y., & Reid, D. J. (2004). Triple scheme of learning support design for scientific discovery learning based on computer simulation: Experimental research. *Journal of Computer Assisted Learning, 20*, 269–282.

CHAPTER 11

ASSESSING ESSENTIAL SCIENCE OF NASCENT INQUIRERS

Nancy Butler Songer
University of Michigan

ABSTRACT

What is essential science that all American students will need to know for the 21st century? At what age should educators begin to guide learners towards the development of this essential science knowledge? In this chapter, I define essential science as knowledge that is a fusion of science content knowledge and science practices, that develops slowly over time, and that is often dynamic and therefore best represented through representations such as simulations. The chapter also presents the argument that if we value essential science for all learners, we need environments that will foster and assess learning of this knowledge at all stages of the learning trajectory, including nascent learners who are embracing types of essential science such as prediction-making and explanation-building about focal science topics for the first time. Building on existing work to foster and evaluate elementary and middle school students' development of explanation-building about biodiversity and ecology, this chapter presents and illustrates three features available with existing and emerging technologies for the assessment of essential science throughout a

Technology-Based Assessments for 21st Century Skills, pages 267–284

learning trajectory, with special emphasis on formative assessment for nascent inquirers as they are embarking on their first efforts to develop essential science knowledge.

INTRODUCTION

As America shifts from an industrial-based economy to an information-based economy, there is much talk and some disagreement (e.g., Toppo, 2009) about the knowledge, pedagogy, and learning environments that are needed to prepare individuals for the twenty-first century. Hirsch and his Core Knowledge Foundation (Hirsch, 1996) suggest that at least 50% of instructional time should be dedicated to grade-by-grade specific lists of declarative content in grades K–8, called Core Knowledge. Hirsch prioritizes traditional pedagogy as the means to acquire knowledge and skills essential for the twenty first century because, "no matter how much musical ability a person has, he or she will not learn to play the piano well without a lot of drill and practice" (Hirsch, 1996, p. 87).

In contrast, the Partnership for 21st Century Skills (2003), a conglomerate representing both large American computer industries and the U.S. Department of Education, places an emphasis on twenty-first century schooling to help students to "know more than core subjects. They need to know how to use their knowledge and skills—by thinking critically, applying knowledge to new situations, analyzing information, comprehending new ideas, communicating, collaborating, solving problems, making decisions." These skills are emphasized because "... they are increasingly important in workplaces and community life" (P21, 2003, p. 9).

Focusing exclusively on the science knowledge that is needed for the future, this chapter discusses a third perspective that might not fit comfortably within either of these other two perspectives. This third perspective suggests that the important knowledge of science that is needed is knowledge that is a fusion of the information emphasized in the other perspectives—a fusion of science content knowledge with skills such as analyzing data and information. This third perspective draws from what we know about how children learn science (e.g., National Research Council, 2007) towards an emphasis on what we call *essential science*. In this chapter, I define essential science as knowledge that is necessary for twenty-first century decision-making and employment, knowledge that is a fusion of science content knowledge and science practices, knowledge that develops slowly over time, and knowledge that is often dynamic and therefore best represented through dynamic representations such as simulations.

Across educational specialties, there is a growing recognition that a new generation of technologies present brand new possibilities to develop assessment systems for classroom-based and large scale testing of essential science and other knowledge we believe is important for twenty-first century learners (e.g., Laser et al., 2010; Quellmalz & Pellegrino, 2009). In particular, we propose that new advances with emerging online technologies are already presenting opportunities for the systematic and ongoing assessment of the development of essential science, including early, guided attempts at the development of essential science by elementary-age school individuals. Building on existing work to foster elementary and middle school students' development of scientific explanations about biodiversity and ecology, this chapter discusses three aspects of essential science knowledge followed by a discussion of existing and emerging online technologies that can be harnessed to assess essential science.

What Is Science Knowledge, and What Do Existing Tests Measure?

Historically, science knowledge has been defined as consisting of three types of knowledge: (1) content knowledge in, for example, the life, physical, and earth sciences; (2) science practices such as making predictions or building evidence-based explanations (National Research Council, 2007; Songer, Kelcey and Gotwals, 2009; College Board, 2009); and (3) and the nature of science knowledge (National Research Council, 1996). In recent history, a common organizational format for science knowledge in policy documents or standards is to list content, science practices and, at times, the nature of science knowledge as separate lists (e.g., AAAS, 1993; National Research Council, 1996) even when the narrative sections of these same documents explicitly place a great deal of emphasis on the fusion of content and science practices.

The division of these types of knowledge into separate lists has predictably led to difficulties by textbook writers, educators and students in successfully understanding what fused content and practices knowledge might look like and how this fusion might occur. A recent analysis of middle school life science textbooks points to weaknesses in popular and new textbooks in linking science practices with content, for example in connecting relevant evidence (a central dimension of a complete scientific explanation) with the related scientific content (e.g., Stern & Roseman, 2004). In addition, assessment and measurement experts admit that existing standardized tests are often not well suited to the evaluation of fused content and practices knowledge. Koretz (2009) refers indirectly to this issue when he states that "test scores usually do not provide a direct and complete measure of educational achievement... these tests can measure only a subset of the goals of education" (p. 9). Test developers support these ideas when they state that the subsets of knowledge most test developers believe current high stakes tests measure reasonably well is stand alone content knowledge such as facts or stand alone procedures. For example, the National Research Council reported, "The most common kinds of educational tests do a reasonable job with certain functions of testing, such as measuring knowledge of basic facts and procedures and producing overall estimates of proficiency for an area of the curriculum. But both their strengths and limitations are a product of their adherence to theories of learning and measurement that fail to capture the breadth and richness of knowledge and cognition" (National Research Council, 2001, p. 26). In addition, when assessments are designed to evaluate higher order thinking in science, American students underperform relative to their peers internationally. American students' performance on PISA (OECD, 2008), a test designed to evaluate complex and applied thinking in science and other topics, demonstrated an overall low average, with a comparatively large proportion of American students demonstrating poor performance—24.4% of US 15-year olds did not reach Level Two, the baseline level of achievement on the PISA scale that represents "competencies that will enable them to participate actively in life situations related to science and technology" (OCED, 2008, p. 3).

What Does Essential Science Knowledge Look Like?

Recently, The Center for Essential Science (CES, www.essentialscience. umich.edu) was established to develop online curricular and assessment programs focused on fostering and evaluating the development of essential science with populations of students in American fourth through the tenth grades. Our team consists of professional scientists, educational researchers and teachers who work together to develop educational materials to support the development of complex inquiry reasoning about ecology, biodiversity and the impacts of climate change. Our work has adopted a learning progression approach to the development of our research studies and products (see Songer, Kelsey, Gotwals, 2009). Learning progressions are one approach that arise from studies of how people learn (NRC, 2007) that are focused on prioritizing and sequencing focal concepts and fostering systematic development of higher-order thinking in science across years and grade bands (e.g., NRC, 2007; Songer, Kelcey and Gotwals, 2009). In our work, we see learning progressions as having both content and practice components that are fused into learning goals associated with each curricular activity.

The synthesis of content and practices that occurs in the form of learning goals makes the fusion concrete, as it also supports a systematic building of content and practices throughout each unit and across the units comprising

> **Science content knowledge**: *There are observable features of living things (grow, breathe, move, reproduce, need energy, have cells), once living things, and non-living things.*
>
> **Science practice knowledge**: *Students build and justify predictions matched to the scientific question.*
>
> **Learning goal**: Students <u>build and justify predictions</u> to address the question, What is alive in my schoolyard?

Figure 11.1 Fourth grade content and practice knowledge fused into learning goal.

the seven-year span. Figure 11.1 presents an example of a content knowledge idea, a science practice, and their fusion to create the first learning goal that launches the first (fourth grade) unit. Each unit contains approximately three learning goals a week for each of the eight week time periods.

HOW CAN NEW TECHNOLOGIES BE HARNESSED TOWARDS ASSESSMENT OF ESSENTIAL SCIENCE?

Concurrent with the development of curricular units, we are challenged with the development of assessment systems that are well suited to the assessment of essential science. As mentioned earlier, the research literature suggests that many existing assessments, both large scale and classroom-based, are not well suited towards the assessment of fused knowledge such as essential science. Drawing on evidence for the design of assessment systems that can capitalize on emerging technologies, we are optimistic about emerging assessment systems focused on gathering evidence of the development of knowledge we believe is important for twenty-first century learners like essential science. The following sections present three features of essential science knowledge that might make it particularly difficult to assess well, coupled with illustrations of existing designs for a potentially more fruitful online assessment environment for essential science.

Feature One: Essential Science Is Knowledge that Takes Time, Repeated Exposures, and Guidance

Our work, and that of others, suggests that while children as young as eight are capable of developing knowledge that fuses content and practices, this knowledge development takes time, repeated exposures, and guidance (Songer, Kelcey & Gotwals, 2009; Metz, 2000). Over the past several years, the Center for Essential Science has built three consecutive, eight-week curricular units to foster essential science in ecology and biodiversity for fourth, fifth and sixth grade students in urban Detroit Public Schools (Songer, Kelcey & Gotwals, 2009; Songer, 2006). In each curricular unit, students work with seven (fourth grade) or nine (fifth and sixth grades) different activity sheets within each unit, each of which scaffolds students to develop claims + evidence or full explanations[1] to address a different scientific question. We provide these extensive, repetitive scaffolds and fades in fourth, fifth and sixth grade in order to provide a systematic and guided approach for the development of fused content and practices associated with different scientific questions focused around the same larger content area (biodiversity). Figure 11.2 presents a sample student activity sheet that illustrates the scaffolds used to guide the development of essential science within a sixth grade unit on biodiversity and ecology. In this example, the scaffolding guides the student in the development of a scientific explanation to address the question focused on a local ecosystem: *If the Rouge River bottom becomes mostly gravel, what will happen to the canvasback ducks in the Rouge River?* To address this question and to construct the components of their scientific explanation, students draw on two types of scaffolding: content hints (gray boxes) and explanation guides (squares and prompts) to guide them in the fusion of content knowledge and practices (e.g., the development of a claim, reasoning and two pieces of evidence that support the scientific question).

Our results demonstrate that our urban Detroit students that experience these multiple exposures to the guided development of essential science outperform their peers on two types of summative assessments: traditional standardized tests and tests designed to measure fused content and inquiry knowledge about ecology and biodiversity (Songer, Kelcey, & Gotwals, 2009). In addition, earlier work in summative assessment design in which we implemented a full information factor analysis (Thissen & Wainer, 2006) indicated that our essential science test items were a strong match to the curricular activities. In addition, a comparison of the fit of one-dimensional and two-dimensional Item Response Theory (IRT) models demonstrated that our assessment items were best represented by a uni-dimensional construct (Gotwals 2006). We believe these research results collectively support our theory about the fused nature of content and practices knowledge that makes it challenging to uncouple the deep conceptual understanding of the content knowledge from the practices aspects of that knowledge.

5. Canvasback ducks live around the Rouge River and eat wild celery. Wild celery grows well in areas of the Rouge River that have soft, sandy bottoms. Wild celery does not grow very well in areas that have gravel bottoms.

Write a scientific explanation to the following question.

<u>Scientific Question</u>: **If the Rouge River bottom becomes mostly gravel, what will happen to the canvasback ducks in the Rouge River?**

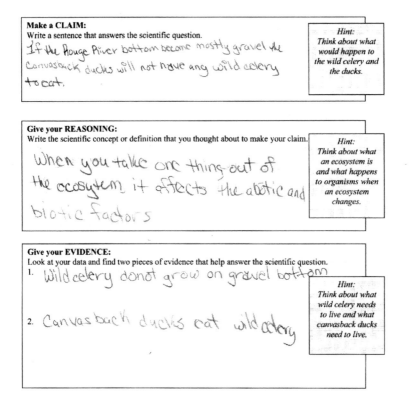

Make a CLAIM:
Write a sentence that answers the scientific question.

If the Rouge River bottom become mostly gravel the Canvasback ducks will not have any wild celery to eat.

> *Hint:*
> *Think about what would happen to the wild celery and the ducks.*

Give your REASONING:
Write the scientific concept or definition that you thought about to make your claim.

When you take one thing out of the ecosystem it affects the abotic and biotic factors

> *Hint:*
> *Think about what an ecosystem is and what happens to organisms when an ecosystem changes.*

Give your EVIDENCE:
Look at your data and find two pieces of evidence that help answer the scientific question.

1. *Wild celery donot grow on gravel bottom*

2. *Canvasback ducks eat wild celery*

> *Hint:*
> *Think about what wild celery needs to live and what canvasback ducks need to live.*

Figure 11.2 Example of sixth grade format for explanation-building associated with the scientific question, "If the Rouge River bottom becomes mostly gravel, what will happen to the canvasback ducks in the Rouge River?"

How Can an Online Assessment System Provide Important Information About the Guided Development of Essential Knowledge Over Time?

Existing work coupling online technologies with assessments present tremendous potential for the gathering and delivery of information about students' knowledge development associated along a learning trajectory. Research by Paul Black and others has established the educative benefits of formative assessments in the classroom (e.g., Black & Wiliam, 1998), although more work is needed into how this research translates into the design of online formative assessments. While most large-scale summative assessments are still primarily delivered by paper and pencil, new versions of the National Assessment for Educational Progress (NAEP), some state tests and other tests internationally present a range of computer adaptive and ongoing data collection-based features. For classroom and formative assessment, systems exist and are under development for customizable prompts and coaching, immediate feedback, gathering data over multiple years and topics, and interactivity through voice recognition as well as click and type entry.

In the Center for Essential Science, we are developing an online system that builds from these exemplars and that utilizes the knowledge information in our learning progressions towards ongoing, customized coaching and feedback for learners at a range of age and ability levels. In our system, as all the learning activities are anchored to the same learning progressions, the online resource can gather students' information from the first online activity in fourth grade and continue addition to that information throughout the several unit sequence.

This work will be more productive than our earlier offline assessments for several important reasons. While our earlier assessments drew from our understanding of the knowledge in the learning progressions towards a series of summative offline assessment instruments designed specifically for either a fourth, fifth or sixth grade audience, our test information analysis revealed that our fourth grade test had too few cognitive supports for many students' first attempts at essential science development and was therefore not an optimal assessment instrument to gather a wealthy of information from several fourth graders (Songer & Gotwals, submitted). Building from these efforts, our new online system will include a wider range of interactive and customizable scaffolds, both for curricular activities and formative assessment, that would support and gather information on young students' performances under a range of supported contexts and conditions.

Figure 11.3 presents a prototype of our CES (Center for Essential Science) online curricular and formative assessment environment associated with an eighth grade unit focused on assessing the effects of climate change on organisms. In our system, windows are available representing interactive mapping information (shown), prompted data collection information (shown), online dialogue with others, and note taking. All windows are adjustable both in size and location. The prototype in Figure 11.3 is focused on material associated with the first of three sequential learning goals that build systematically on each other. This part of the activity is focused on the learning goal, *Students will collect data to determine which abiotic factors are present in the habitat of selected local species.* Students build on this activity with two

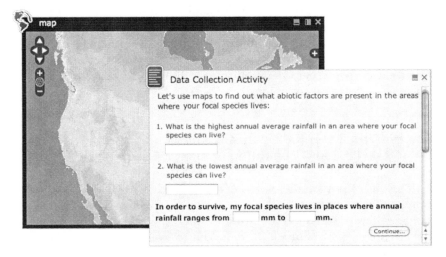

Figure 11.3 Prototype of task to assess students' ability to collect data associated with the learning goal "*Students will collect data to determine which abiotic factors are present in the habitat of selected local species.*"

additional online activities focused around focal species, abiotic features and the practices of analyzing data and building explanations. These learning goals are: *Students will analyze data from maps to identify patterns in abiotic conditions that influence where a focal species live,* and *Students build explanations about how abiotic factors influence species distributions.* The final learning goal is also a target concept for a formative assessment activity.

This example illustrates a sequence of learning goals that represent essential science knowledge as it develops somewhat slowly under guided conditions, and the relationship between online learning goals and the online formative assessment we have planned for feedback to students and teachers on essential capstone ideas. As illustrated in this example, the formative assessment system mirrors curricular designs that include scaffolds and fades for the ongoing development of essential science throughout the three-learning goals material (and the series of coordinated curricular units). At any point, we envision customizable support or fade of content material (like the material in grey boxes in Figure 11.2), science practice material (e.g., prompts associated with data collection, analysis or explanation-building), or the fusion of these two into, for example, a comprehensive explanation. As we envision it, this customizable support or fade could be set by the teacher or responsive to request. In addition, the material in particular windows, such as the zoom or overlay information in the mapping window, could be either set or adjusted for particular curricular or assessment outcomes, time or task. In these ways, we anticipate the combination of the advances of online technologies, research on formative assessment, research on learning progressions, and our previous design of assessments can lead towards more powerful formative assessment resources for a more systematic understanding of not only how essential science develops over time and topic, but what challenges and successes are realized under a range of scaffold and conditions.

Feature Two: Essential Science Is Knowledge that Should be Fostered Beginning in Elementary School

A second important dimension of essential science is that it is attainable by relatively young students through careful scaffolds embedded within the online system. In addition, we postulate that to best prepare our students for the twenty-first century, it is important to foster and evaluate essential science with elementary-age students. In our work, we draw from the work by Kathy Metz (2000) and others in our belief that younger students such as fourth graders are capable of developing sophisticated explanations to address scientific questions if they are provided a system of guides and prompts focused on known areas of difficulty, such as the components of a complete scientific explanation (Songer, 2006). In our most recent work, we designed interview protocols for fourth and sixth graders that were specifically focused on known errors by these different grade level students. In both grade level interviews, we presented students with other students' hypothetical worksheets that were designed to illustrate a common error of either fourth or sixth grader's knowledge development. Figure 11.4 presents one of these worksheets used in the student interviews representing the work of a hypothetical student, Kenisha, that illustrates one piece of incorrect evidence (#2) that does not match the scientific question or claim. The interview questions probed students' abstract understandings of claim, evidence, and reasoning outside of a given situation as well as their ability to detect and correct errors in essential science within problem contexts. The following interview excerpt illustrates the range of detailed information we are able to gather from one student, Dean, in response to a general prompt about the definition of evidence and what he thought of the evidence Kenisha presented:

> **I:** How would you know if you had good evidence?
> **D:** the evidence would show ... would give examples of what goes where.
> **I:** What do you think of Kenisha's response?
> **D:** Well Kenisha she has a good claim, she has good reasoning. The reasoning is good because it tells what ... how ... the definition of

competition between the ring billed gulls and the walleye. And then the second evidence doesn't go with the question. It says "the mayflies eat algae."

I: Okay. So if I asked you if this was a correct explanation, what would you say?

D: It is a correct explanation up to the second piece of evidence.

Our interview with Dean revealed that, like many young students, Dean was not able to provide an abstract definition of what makes some evidence good evidence. On balance, when provided with Kenisha's responses con-

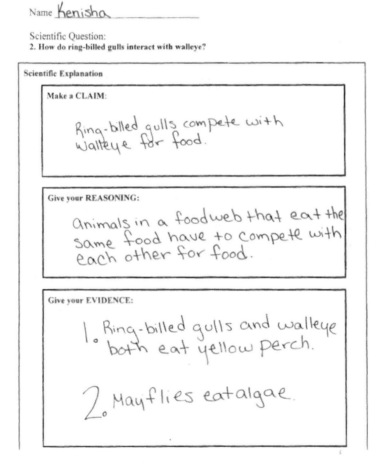

Name Kenisha

Scientific Question:
2. How do ring-billed gulls interact with walleye?

Scientific Explanation

Make a CLAIM:

Ring-billed gulls compete with walleye for food.

Give your REASONING:

Animals in a foodweb that eat the same food have to compete with each other for food.

Give your EVIDENCE:

1. Ring-billed gulls and walleye both eat yellow perch.

2. Mayflies eat algae.

Figure 11.4   Interview item representing a hypothetical student response with a known EVIDENCE error (only the first piece of evidence addresses the scientific question).

taining fused content and practice within a contextual situation, Dean was able to recognize that Kenisha's claim, reasoning, and the first part of the evidence she provided were correct. He was also able to correctly state that her response actually already had two pieces of evidence present, evidence associated with both the walleye and the ring billed perch eating the same food, and therefore it was likely they were competing for food. We characterize students' ability to correctly diagnose and correct errors in context through verbal interviews while not being able to provide abstract definitions of key terms as a common pattern among students encountering fused content and practices knowledge for some of the first times. We also see this type of response as support for the situated nature of knowledge, in other words the view that all knowledge is situated in activity that is bound to social, contextual and physical contexts (e.g., Brown, Collins & Dugid, 1989).

How Can an Online Assessment System Provide Important Information that Capitalizes on Learning Progressions and Known Types of Errors?

This work to explore the types of errors young students make when first attempting to construct essential science suggests a need for formative assessments that are sensitive to growth along learning trajectories and over time and topic. Assessment experts suggest performance assessments can be well suited as measurements of growth in the development of higher order knowledge if they are based on analyses of problem solving tasks conducted by the target audience (Mislevy, 1993). Existing efforts to develop assessment systems that are based on the characterization of common errors along a progression continue to suggest a strong direction to capture a sophisticated range of correctly and incorrectly fused essential knowledge on the path towards successful knowledge development (e.g., Minstrell, 2001), although more work is needed to develop these systems that are focused on learning progressions associated with complex higher-order thinking such as essential science (Darling-Hammond & Adamson, 2010). Nevertheless, these online assessment systems seem well poised to deliver a new set of formative assessments that are better matched to not only a range of learners' abilities but young students' first attempts at the knowledge development appropriate to their complexity level. An online assessment system that can be developed in conjunction with the knowledge along a learning progression can also help emphasize the growth criteria in formative assessment, as they help us obtain a wealth of information about our correct, or incorrect, guesses about learning progressions and curricular sequences to best foster the development of essential science at all ages.

Another dimension we are considering adding to our online formative assessment resource is verbal information gathering and feedback. We view verbal interactivity as a potentially valuable addition to support and illuminate younger students' struggles with the development of essential science knowledge. Most especially with younger learners, we know we need a greater range of data gathering approaches that serve as complements to traditional written or typed data entry. We can envision online coaches that interact verbally with the learner as an engaging means for homework or game-like practice sessions to guide young learners in the development of, for example, scientific explanations. In the same way in which existing language development resources provide learners with real-time evaluation of pronunciation (Rosetta Stone, 2010), we can visualize an avatar for Kenisha who can interact with Dean to provide game-like individualistic prompts, suggestions, or guidance as another means to provide to formative or diagnostic information in assessing the nuances and complexity of Dean's knowledge development.

Feature Three: Essential Science is Dynamic Science Knowledge

As we come to understand the nature of science knowledge in many disciplines, we are recognizing that much science knowledge is represented within systems that have complex and dynamic properties. Whether we are tracking a weather system across our continent or making predictions about the impact of climate changes on humans or organisms (e.g., Guisan & Zimmermann, 2000), much of the science we see as essential for twenty-first century learners includes dynamic information.

In our latest work, scientists, teachers and educators are collaborating to create middle and high school units focused on students' understanding of the ecological impacts of climate change. In our online system, students investigate scientific questions focused on, for example, the relationships between temperature changes in the ocean and Staghorn corals, the name for approximately 160 species of corals that comprise essential roles in reef-building (IUCN, 2009). In these activities, the Center for Essential Science research team struggled to characterize the science knowledge essential for building and justifying predictions associated with the impact on different temperature changes on animal distributions. So far, we recognize that students will need to understand some basic science concepts in atmospheric science, ecology, geography and map reading combined with science practices associated with prediction making, explanation-building and modeling. As an example, two of the essential science learning goals towards the end of our unit are as follows:

A. Students will <u>analyze data</u> to identify patterns in global temperature increases associated with different Intergovernmental Panel on Climate Change (IPCC) prediction scenarios.
B. Students will <u>build and justify predictions</u> of the effects of IPCC scenarios on focal species distribution.

As illustrated in these learning goals, students need to draw on and fuse science practices with content knowledge, including science content from at least two different science disciplines (atmospheric science and ecology), in their efforts to analyze dynamic simulations and make predictions. The data are represented in spatially represented maps that illustrate patterns through the running of simulation scenarios. Like scientists, learners of the future need to be not only comfortable with dynamic presentations of information, they will need to learn how to read and interpret information from these representations successfully. Therefore, the knowledge necessary not only includes the fusion of content, practices, and the ability to work with dynamic simulations, but it requires content knowledge from two or more different areas of science.

In a traditional middle school or high school science classroom, atmospheric science and life science topics are not taught together or even very often by the same teacher. This illustration is just one example of a growing trend: science knowledge is also becoming more multi-disciplinary and fused across science disciplines. A related issue is that our current teacher education programs most often focus on training in either earth science or life science but not both or a fusion of the two. As the nature of scientific information is becoming more multidisciplinary and requiring fluency with dynamic and digital content, learners of the twenty first century are going to need educational and assessment systems that can guide, and evaluate, this dynamic, multi-disciplinary and essential science knowledge.

How Can an Online Assessment System Provide Important Information on Students' Development of Dynamic Essential Science?

Experts in test design already recognize that technology can be used to design assessment resources representing complex, interactive tasks and students' understanding of relationships between a set of changing variables (Quellmalz & Pellegrino, 2009). Our online assessment system includes visualizations and models of authentic, dynamic scenarios for students' input and feedback. In particular, we are designing our system to gather students' ongoing creation and justification of predictions and explanations associated with essential science in a range of dynamic scenarios.

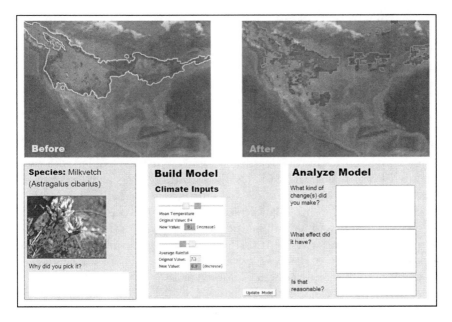

Figure 11.5 Prototype interface. Students select species, choose climate inputs. After changing inputs, student updates model to see a distribution map on the right. Reflection (lower right panel) guides generating and comparing explanations.

Figure 11.5 presents a prototype of another window of our online assessment resource, a modeling tool that would probe middle school students' essential science related to the question: "How does a two degree change in temperature effect the distribution of a particular species (in this case a milkvetch plant) in North America?" In this system, student inputs can be gathered and analyzed associated with a range of simulated scenarios available from adjustment of the slider bars for temperature and precipitation. Much like the interdisciplinary nature of experts' knowledge, our students participating in our online formative assessment could draw on their previously developed material already stored in our system to provide assistance with either biology, weather and climate, geography (map reading skills) or prediction-making in order to navigate this task. On balance, while the simulation supports students' fusion of these different domains of knowledge, the system can also be used to select for particular types of questions or knowledge that are less complicated if desired. Student feedback can be not only rapid, in the form of distribution maps and temperature information, but also varied in form (e.g., also include feedback on the strength of their reflections or predictions). Students can perform these tasks as individuals or pairs, and the work of more than one individual can be captured at one time. In addition, prompts or features can be faded to shift the assessment environment into a less structured task. In this way, we envision simulation resources that can capture students' developing problem solving and decision-making associated with dynamic, multidisciplinary essential science under more or less structured scenarios.

CONCLUSIONS

This chapter identified three features of a new type of knowledge we see as foundational for twenty-first learners, essential science. Coupled with each feature of essential science, we described features of existing or planned online assessment systems that are well suited to the formative evaluation of essential science. In particular, we see promise in the combined potential of existing and emerging online assessment systems, learning progression research, formative assessment research and dynamic simulations for the delivery of a wealth of data and a greater understanding of the challenges in developing this kind of science knowledge.

As much of the ideas in this essay are already available, we hold strong and optimistic views about the near future of the assessment of essential science. On balance, we recognize the need to gather information longitudinally and systematically over many time points, age bands, and time durations to achieve strong research-based products and outcomes. We value continued dialogue coupled with sound research outcomes towards an understanding of how to foster, and evaluate, essential science for all learners.

NOTE

1. In our work, we define a scientific explanation as consisting of a claim, two pieces of evidence (empirical information or observations) and reasoning that links the claim to the evidence. For more information see Songer, 2006.

REFERENCES

American Association for the Advancement of Science. (1993). *Benchmarks for science literacy*. New York, NY: Oxford University Press.

Black, P. & Wiliam, D. (1998). Inside the black box: raising standards through classroom assessment. *Phi Delta Kappan, 80*(2), 139–148.

Brown, J. S., Collins, A., & Dugid, P. (1989). Situated cognition and the culture of learning. *Educational Researcher, 18*(1), 32–41.

Darling-Hammond, L., & Adamson, F. (2010). *Beyond basic skills: The role of performance assessment in achieving 21st century standards of learning*. Palo Alto, CA: Stanford Center for Opportunity Policy in Education.

College Board. (2009). *Science College Board standards for college success.* New York: Author.

Gotwals, A. (2006) *The nature of students' science knowledge bases: Using assessment to paint a picture.* Unpublished doctoral dissertation. Ann Arbor, MI: The University of Michigan.

Guisan, A., & Zimmermann, N. E. (2000). Predictive habitat distribution models in ecology. *Ecological Modeling, 135,* 147–186.

Hirsch, E. D. (1996). *The schools we need and why we don't have them.* New York: Doubleday.

IUCN. (2009). Species and climate change: More than just the polar bear. Downloaded on June 24, 2010 from www.iucnredlist.org

Koretz, D. (2009). Measuring up: What educational testing really tells us. Cambridge, MA: Harvard University Press.

Laser, S., Mazzeo, J., Twing, J., Way, W., Carnara, W., & Sweeney, K. (2010). *Thoughts on an Assessment of Common Core Standards.* Educational Testing Service, Pearson and the College Board white paper. Princeton, NJ: Educational Testing Service.

Metz, K. (2000). Young children's inquiry in biology: Building the knowledge bases to empower independent inquiry. In J. Minstrell & E. van Zee (Eds.), *Inquiring into inquiry learning and teaching in science* (pp. 371–404). Washington, DC: AAAS.

Minstrell, J. (2001). Facets of students' thinking: Designing to cross the gap from research to standards-based practice. In K. Crowley, C.D. Schunn, & T. Okada (Eds.), *Designing for science: Implications from everyday, classroom, and professional settings* (pp. 415–443). Mahwah, NJ: Lawrence Erlbaum Associates.

Mislevy, R. (1993). Foundations of a new test theory. In N. Fredricksen, R. Mislevy & I. Bejar (Eds.), *Test theory for a new generation of tests* (pp. 19–40). Hillsdale, NJ: Erlbaum.

National Research Council. (1996). *National Science Education Standards.* Washington, DC: Author.

National Research Council. (2001). *Knowing what students know: The science and design of educational assessment.* Washington, DC: Author.

National Research Council. (2007). *Taking science to school: Learning and teaching science in grades K–8.* Washington, DC: Author.

OECD. (2008). *PISA 2006: Science competencies for tomorrow's world,* OECD briefing note for the United States. Downloaded on May 26, 2010 from www.oecd.org/document/2/0,3343,en_32252351_32236191_39718850_1_1_1_1,00.html

Partnership for 21st Century Skills. (2003). *Learning for the 21st Century: A report and mile guide for 21st century skills.* Downloaded June 1, 2010 from www.21stcenturyskils.org

Quellmalz, E .S. & Pellegrino, J. W. (2009). Technology and testing. *Science, (323),* 75–79.

Rosetta Stone. (2010) Introduction video retrieved on June 21, 2010 from http://www.rosettastone.com/personal/demo on June 21

Songer, N. B. & Gotwals, A. (submitted). Late elementary students' guided development of scientific explanations. *Journal of Research in Science Teaching.*

Songer, N. B. (2006). BioKIDS: An animated conversation on the development of curricular activity structures for inquiry science. In R. K. Sawyer (Ed.), *Cam-*

bridge handbook of the learning sciences (pp. 355–369). New York: Cambridge University Press.

Songer, N. B., Kelcey, B., & Gotwals, A. (2009). How and when does complex reasoning occur? Empirically driven development of a learning progression focused on complex reasoning about biodiversity. *Journal of Research in Science Teaching, 46*(6), 610–631.

Stern, L., & Roseman, J. E. (2004). Can middle-school science textbooks help students learn important ideas? Findings from Project 2061's curriculum evaluation study: Life science. *Journal of Research in Science Teaching, 41*(6), 538–568.

Thissen D., & Wainer, H. (Eds.). (2001). *Test scoring.* Mahwah, NJ: Lawrence Erlbaum.

Toppo, G. (2009, March 5). What to learn: Core knowledge or 21st century skills? *USA Today.* Downloaded from www.usatoday.com/news/education/2009-03-04-core-knowledge_N.htm

CHAPTER 12

DIGITAL ASSESSMENT OF THE ACQUISITION AND UTILITY OF BIOLOGICALLY SECONDARY KNOWLEDGE

Perspectives Based on Human Cognitive Architecture

Renae Low, Putai Jin, and John Sweller
The University of New South Wales, Australia

ABSTRACT

Acknowledging the rapid development and proliferation of digital assessment in schools, universities, and other organizational contexts, we attempt to a) evaluate the congruence between modern technology-based assessment and human cognitive architecture, and b) offer some suggestions that are derived from accumulated research findings of effective learning based on cognitive load approaches. We argue that, since the knowledge to be learned in modern educational and training settings is by and large biologically secondary (which can only be acquired through an effortful process), the associated assessment

Technology-Based Assessments for 21st Century Skills, pages 285–303
Copyright © 2012 by Information Age Publishing

should reflect corresponding cognitive principles of human information processing that deal with such knowledge. Furthermore, the format and operation of technology-based assessment should be carefully chosen and implemented to ensure that the demands of cognitive load during the assessment are appropriate. Suggestions to avoid some pitfalls in the design of assessment and to maximize the advantages of adopting digital technology are provided.

INTRODUCTION

Assessment, including ability, knowledge and skill testing, whether in a formal or informal context, has been embedded in human history, culture, and civilization. The dialogues between Socrates and his students or Confucius and his followers are examples of assessment in informal settings in ancient time. With respect to formal assessment, the high-stake, large-scale, organized examinations for the selection of civil officials can be traced as early as the seventh century in China (Bai, 1982). In that important, statewide assessment in ancient China, candidates, regardless of where they resided, had to travel to the Capital to sit for an examination that could last several days. Candidates were required to write essays on topics decided by an examination board, often about policy making, analysis of state affairs, and strategies for effective administration. The examinees' essays were cross-marked by an ad hoc committee formed by well-established scholars and experts, whose rankings of the papers were further verified by a higher governing body that usually comprised the emperor (the figurehead) and delegates. Such assessments required huge resources and were often very time-consuming. Nevertheless, to a large extent, modern assessment has adopted this format along with its inherent problems like high logistic costs, vague validity of task content, questionable reliability of test items, and examiners' bias (Clauser, Kane, & Swanson, 2002; Mislevy, Steinberg, Breyer, Almond, & Johnson, 2002; Yang, Buckendahl, Juszkiewicz, & Bhola, 2002).

In recent decades, the rapid development of information technology has provided an alternative means to either high-stake or regular assessment. Three decades ago, researchers and educational practitioners were excited about the promise of computer-assisted assessments; nowadays, various formats as well as procedures of computerized assessments are truly on the agenda. In addition to relatively simple machine scoring of multiple-choice tests, computer-based and increasingly web-facilitated complex tests have been developed for streamlining purposes or professional licensure, such as the architect registration test, patient-management skills assessment, dental interactive simulation test, and essay grading (e.g., Abedi, 2009; Mislevy et al., 2002; Yang et al, 2002). The 21st century is characterized by the proliferation of digital tools with a number of researchers arguing that digital assessments, in comparison to conventional assessments, can be not only more cost-effective but also more reliable (e.g., Clauser et al., 2002; de Jong, 2006; Haladyna, Downing, & Rodriguez, 2002; Parsons-Pollard, Lacks, & Grant, 2008).

At the commencement of this digital age, what is the role of assessment in education, training, and selection? What are the theoretical bases from a cognitive perspective? In this chapter, acknowledging the rapid development and proliferation of digital assessments in schools, universities, and other organizational contexts, we attempt to a) evaluate the congruence between modern technology-based assessment and human cognitive architecture, and b) offer some suggestions that are derived from accumulated findings in the research of effective information processing. Furthermore, we highlight the feasibility of applying cognitive principles to the format and operation of technology-based assessment in order to avoid some pitfalls in the design of assessment and to maximize the advantages of adopting digital technology.

THE NATURE OF ACADEMIC KNOWLEDGE LEARNED IN MODERN EDUCATION

Despite technological advances, there still are two essential issues related to assessment: validity and reliability. Validity refers to "the degree to which evidence and theory support the interpretation of test scores entailed by proposed uses" (AERA/APA/NCME, 1999, p. 9). Reliability refers to the extent that results from an assessment procedure can be generalized to other occasions (Salvia & Ysseldyke, 1995). Both validity and reliability are major considerations in the evaluation of assessment procedures. Reliability is a necessary but not a sufficient condition for valid assessment. Thus, all valid tests are reliable, unreliable tests are not valid, and reliable tests may or may not be valid. Clauser and colleagues (2002) provided a discussion of potential threats to validity in the context of computer-automated scoring. These include expert-articulated rules and rules inferred from expert ratings, models based on expert behavior, and rules based on psychological models. Although the use of an automated system may eliminate the random errors associated with the direct scoring by experts and thus to some extent improve reliability, it may also introduce systematic error. How should we develop a valid and reliable digital assessment design? According to Mislevy et al. (2002), in a construct-centered approach to assessment, the type of knowledge, skills or other attributes should be assessed in the contexts that are relevant to the goals of education and are valuable for participants' career development or potential contribution to society. Therefore it is important to decide a) the appropriate test content, b) the criteria of essential and desired responses, and c) the task and the conditions in which the task is executed. All these issues are related to the nature of academic knowledge that is supposed to be learned in modern education.

In line with theorists holding a Darwinian evolutionary perspective, Geary (2002, 2005, 2007, 2008) suggests that knowledge can be classified into two categories: biologically primary knowledge and biologically secondary knowledge. Biologically primary knowledge is knowledge we have evolved to acquire over countless generations and is essential for humans to survive as a species. The learning of a mother tongue, including listening, speaking, and understanding basic facial expressions as well as body language, is an example; counting by fingers is another example. This category of knowledge can be acquired simply by one being immersed in a social environment. In contrast, biologically secondary knowledge is what we have developed in a very recent stage of civilization. Therefore we have not explicitly evolved to acquire this type of knowledge, such as written language (whether in the form of alphabets or hieroglyphs), mathematics, physical sciences rather than folk physics, biological sciences rather than folk biology, and psychological sciences rather than folk psychology. Acquiring secondary knowledge is far more difficult than the process of acquiring primary knowledge, because in the evolutionary process biologically secondary knowledge is not critical for human survival and thus its acquisition is not as effortless as the mastery of biologically primary knowledge. In fact, such knowledge has been developed for societal advancement only during the last few thousand years. According to Geary (2002, 2008), children cannot be assumed to be always intrinsically motivated to acquire academic knowledge (i.e., biologically secondary knowledge) simply because a) this knowledge is not indispensable for their natural growth, and b) it requires great conscious effort and additional assistance from others. However, modern societies demand that children as well as adults acquire a certain amount of biologically secondary knowledge so that they can become functioning citizens in those societies.

COGNITIVE ARCHITECTURE NEEDED TO ACQUIRE BIOLOGICALLY SECONDARY KNOWLEDGE AND ITS IMPLICATIONS FOR ASSESSMENT

Since the knowledge to be acquired in modern educational and training settings is by and large, biologically secondary, the associated assessment should reflect corresponding cognitive principles of human information processing that deal with such knowledge. It is this category of biologically secondary knowledge for which schools and other educational institutions were proposed and established. The cognitive architecture required to allow the acquisition of biologically secondary knowledge mirrors the processes and structures of evolution by natural selection. Both the acquisition of biologically secondary knowledge and the processes of evolution by natural selection are examples of natural information processing systems. Sweller and Sweller (2006) proposed five principles that depict the information processes involved in acquiring biologically secondary knowledge.

Information store principle. In order to function in a natural environment, natural information processing systems must include a large information store to deal with the various contingencies with which individuals will be faced. Long-term memory provides this cognitive function and serves as the foundation in human learning, thinking and problem solving. The main aim of assessment is to test the extent to which organized information associated with particular domains has been learned and stored in long-term memory.

Borrowing and reorganizing principle. This mechanism enables us to rapidly build up a large information store. Natural information processing systems construct their stores primarily by borrowing information from other stores. The massive amount of biologically secondary information held in our long-term memory is mainly borrowed from others and then reorganized. We imitate other people, follow their spoken or written instructions, comprehend what they show us, and interpret the underlying meanings. Assessment, by and large, is to test to what extent the examinees have understood and mastered knowledge taught in a particular domain.

The randomness as genesis principle. Whereas most information contained in our long-term memory is borrowed from others, elements of that information need to be generated in the first instance. The random generate-and-test mechanism used during problem solving is the source of human creativity. When solving unfamiliar problems, we use prior knowledge to generate moves whenever possible and random generate-and-test when familiar moves are unavailable. If critical information for possible solution moves is not available in our long-term memory, we have no alternative but to randomly generate moves and then test the effectiveness of those moves. Since this random generate-and-test cognitive process contributes to creativity and new knowledge, the design of assessment should include items that allow examinees to demonstrate such creative ideas or moves. It should be noted that increases in knowledge can increase the sophistication of novel, creative moves generated by a random generate-and-test procedure.

The narrow limits of change principle. The type of cognitive processes associated with randomness can influence our mental structures and functions. When random moves result in the creation of novel structures and functions, such changes have to be small and incremental. A large, randomly generated change is likely to destroy the functionality of mental structures and functions. In other words, if there is no control of randomness as genesis, the cognitive system could be in danger of malfunctioning. The human cognitive system avoids this problem via a limited working memory that prevents large, rapid changes to long-term memory. Working memory has well-known temporal (Peterson & Peterson, 1959) and capacity (Miller, 1956) limits when dealing with novel information. These limits should be considered in any assessment design in order to ensure that examinees are not cognitively overloaded.

The environmental organizing and linking principle. The limitations of working memory only apply to novel information. Familiar, organized information stored in long-term memory has neither temporal nor capacity limitations when transferred to working memory. Working memory links long-term memory and the environment. During problem solving, large amounts of relevant, organized information from long-term memory can be retrieved and transmitted to working memory in order to produce a solution. For instance, to solve an equation $1-1/\cot^2\theta = 0$ in an on-line test, examinees with appropriate mathematical knowledge/skills may retrieve their organized information about trigonometry and algebra stored in long-term memory, such as $\tan\theta = 1/\cot\theta$ and $a^2 - b^2 = (a + b)(a - b)$, upload such helpful information to working memory, and then work out a series of appropriate moves, choosing either a path of $1-\tan^2\theta = 1$ or another path of $(1+\tan\theta)(1-\tan\theta) = 0$ to meet environmental demands—in this case, trigonometric equation solving. To differentiate this mechanism from the short-duration, limited-capacity work memory described in *the narrow limits of change principle*, this function has been referred to as long-term working memory (Ericsson & Kintsch, 1995). In particular, *the environmental organizing and linking princip*le highlights that the prior knowledge stored in long-term memory can be activated as a high-level organized structure depending on environmental conditions and then be uploaded to working memory for cognitive processing. This process should be reflected in any form of valid assessment. In other words, the test should be designed to reveal the quality and quantity of organized information that examinees are able to bring to their working memory for task activities.

Several consequences flow from this cognitive architecture:

- There are fundamental limits to the human cognitive system: a) human working memory can hold no more than about five to nine chunks or elements of information and process even less; and b) without rehearsal, individuals are likely to lose most of the contents of working memory within about 20 seconds. These psychological constraints can exert a considerable impact on thinking and problem solving (Cowan, 2005; Miller, 1956; Peterson & Peterson, 1959; Simon, 1990). In the design or execution of assessment, it is reasonable to take those features and limitations of information processing into account.

- Compared to novices, experienced individuals with expertise can effectively retrieve and employ their extensive knowledge stored in long-term memory for designated tasks (Chase & Simon, 1973; Chi, Glaser, & Farr, 1988; de Groot, 1946/1965). For those individuals with sufficient expertise in a particular domain, the capacity of working memory "can grow to a vast size as individual acts of recognition access larger and richer stores of information in long-term memory" (Simon, 1990, p. 16). This powerful characteristic of human cognitive architecture enriches the potential of working memory by allowing highly structured and automated information from long-term memory to be transferred to working memory. This architecture suggests that the primary cause of differential test performance is knowledge and its organized structures held in long-term memory. If so, the function of testing is to assess knowledge as well as the structures held in long-term memory.

The recent advances in computer technology have provided innovative ways to present, conduct, score, and report tests. For example, the task presentation can request examinees to type text-based response, use a keyboard to enter a numerical answer, click on-screen icons, and use a mouse to select and place objects. In addition to these commonly used means, electronic ink using a special pen with a tablet PC, touch screens, microphones equipped with speech recognition software, pressure-feedback (haptic) devices, PDAs, joysticks, and clickers are available for assessment activities. As summarized by Zenisky and Sireci (2002), these devices have been used in large-scale assessment using a series of item formats that are either uncommon or not feasible in conventional tests. Examples of novel item formats are drag-and-drop, graphical modeling, concept mapping, sorting tasks, ordering information, passage editing, highlighting text, and animation-embedded questioning. Empirical data regarding the effects of such novel test formats on examinees' working memory capacity and elicited performance are not commonly collected. However, it is possible to discuss the cognitive effects of digital assessments from perspectives based on human cognitive architecture, which have generated useful information for instruction design.

In the development of computer-based assessment designs, there is a tendency to integrate two general strategies: one based on empirically derived statistical relationships and the other based on subjective, cognitive rules, mental models, principles or policies (Yang et al., 2002). The following discussion will attempt to highlight the utility of long-term memory in both examinees and examiners based on research on various cognitive characteristics.

SOME THOUGHTS ON TECHNOLOGY-BASED ASSESSMENT FROM THE PERSPECTIVE OF HUMAN COGNITIVE ARCHITECTURE

Reducing Extraneous Load Imposed on Working Memory in Digital Assessment

Extraneous load in assessment occurs when a) part of the task content contains non-essential/irrelevant information that jeopardizes construct validity, and b) the manner in which the assessment task is presented forces examinees to exert extra effort to integrate disparate sources of the information. Because of the limits of working memory, an excessive extraneous load may divert examinees' cognitive process to irrelevant issues. Extraneous load is related to testing knowledge or skills that may not be the ultimate objective of the assessment. For instance, a well documented phenomenon in educational psychology is the split-attention effect, which occurs when learners are required to integrate multiple sources of critical information that are physically or temporally separate from each other (Low, Jin, & Sweller, 2009; Mayer, 2005; Mayer & Anderson, 1991, 1992; Mayer & Sims, 1994; Moreno & Mayer, 1999; Sweller, Chandler, Tierney, & Cooper, 1990; Tarmizi & Sweller, 1988; Yeung, Jin, & Sweller, 1998). If separation of resources in a test task is unnecessary and requires individuals to hold some elements of the information in their working memory, search for other elements contained in the question, and then mentally combine all of them in order to comprehend the question, examinees may find that the given conditions in the question are provided in such a difficult to understand manner that it hampers their essential problem solving process. For example, to request examinees to solve a geometry problem such as calculating the area of an irregular triangle, it is preferable to use a physically integrated presentation in which the given conditions (angle sizes, line lengths) are marked on the figure of the triangle rather than in a list next to the triangle. Separating the figure from the characteristics of the figure by listing them may result in split-attention, since examinees must split their attention between the figure and the list in order to understand the question. The need to mentally integrate the split source question is likely to impose an extraneous cognitive load. A physically integrated format is likely to have a higher validity than a split source version, unless one of the objectives of the task is to construct an appropriate triangle.

An extraneous working memory load in digital assessment may also occur when examinees are not familiar with computerized testing procedures. In this case, the assessment may require examinees to possess a) sufficient domain knowledge on a targeted topic (e.g., infection control in dental surgery), and b) a certain level of computer skills (e.g., typing symbols, using menus and tool bars, and navigating). However, the latter may not be an objective of the syllabus and so is redundant. The redundancy effect (Chandler & Sweller, 1991), like the split-attention effect, has working memory consequences. The negative consequences of processing redundant information that is not relevant to the information being tested can be overcome by ensuring that learners are fully familiar with the computer system being used for testing (Clarke, Ayres, & Sweller, 2005). A practice section (Schnotz & Rasch, 2005) before the assessment may be introduced to let examinees become familiar with the operation of the computerized test. In some circumstances, a pre-test training session is needed to make sure that all examinees reach a minimal level of computer competence before the exam (Palaigeorgiou, Siozos, & Konstantakis, 2006).

Optimizing Intrinsic Load Conveyed in Digital Assessment

Intrinsic load refers to a type of mental load that reflects the degree of perceived complexity associated with the material (Low & Sweller, 2009; Sweller, 1994, 1999). It is determined by the degree to which elements that learners must process interact. Some elements can be processed one element at a time without loss of intelligibility, while other elements must be processed simultaneously in order for them to be understood. In assessment design, we may consider testing and adopting those techniques used in instructional design, such as introducing isolated elements before indicating how they should be integrated (Pollock, Chandler, & Sweller, 2002), simple-to-complex sequencing (van Merriënboer, Kirschner, & Kester, 2003), and modular-like presentations (Gerjets, Scheiter, & Catrambone, 2004).

The following example from a test of a statistics course illustrates that intrinsic load can be adjusted in correspondence to the stages of examinees' progress. The objective of this assessment is to check whether the students are able to select and run an appropriate t-test or analysis of variance (ANOVA) to compare means produced from a particular design (between-subjects or within-subjects) by using statistical software. In the early stages of the course, although the students were supposed to be able to conduct a designated hypothesis test, it was too demanding to request them to conduct this complex task consisting of a descriptive analysis, hypothesis development, choosing a proper statistics test, and forming a correct statistical procedure, in a single attempt. They were likely to be cognitively overloaded by considering all the newly-learned concepts simultaneously, even though they had been exposed to all of them. Learners were capable of handling those elements one by one. In other words, experiencing too much intrinsic load in a test may prevent the examinees from demonstrating their knowledge, thus defeating the purpose of the assessment. One way to design a valid test is to present the early-stage examinees a series of sub-tasks within a general question or in a coherent context as shown below:

> Q. Noise is an ever-present phenomenon in modern society and we are interested in finding if it has any physiological effects. Suppose we randomly assigned 22 individuals to either a control or an experimental group (ncontrol = nexperimental). Subjects in the control group relaxed in a comfortable chair for 30 minutes. At the end of the 30-minute period, we measured their systolic blood pressure (i.e., the blood pressure during the contraction of the heart). Subjects in the experimental group also sat in the same chair for 30 minutes. During the 30-minute wait, however, they listened to a recording of traffic noise from a large city during rush hour. After listening to the noise for 30 minutes, the systolic blood pressure of these individuals also was recorded. Suppose we obtained the following blood pressure measures (in millimeters of mercury, i.e., mmHg).
>
> Under the quiet condition: 127 136 128 115 106 117 129 124 115 131 121
>
> Under the noise condition: 140 134 128 115 147 119 136 141 124 139 121
>
> Q (1) Find the mean and standard deviation for each group.
>
> Q (2) State the null hypothesis.
>
> Q (3) State a reasonable alternative (working) hypothesis.
>
> Q (4) Run an appropriate test to answer the question: Does noise affect systolic blood pressure? Use a two-tailed test and a .05 significance level.

This type of built-in guidance in assessment may be helpful to ascertain the extent of individual mastery of particular knowledge and associated skills. If only the last question is asked, that knowledge and skill may not become apparent because the high element interactivity associated with the question may prevent many students from providing any valid answer. However, at a later stage when students have consolidated all recently obtained schemata and are able to deal with a research question independently in order to generate a comprehensive research report, the guidance in the assessment question can be gradually faded out. For instance, in a quiz of hypothesis testing given at this stage, the presentation can be simply as follows:

> Q. As part of an anti-cancer program to reduce smoking, the Institute of Health Education ran a media campaign, using all TV channels for advertising the benefits of non-smoking behavior, to convince people to quit or reduce their smoking. The investigator asked 15 subjects to record the average number of cigarettes smoked per day in the week before and the week after exposure to the advertisement. The data follow:

Subject:	1	2	3	4	5	6	7	8	9	10	11	12	13	14	15
Before:	45	16	20	33	30	19	33	25	32	32	26	15	36	28	40
After:	43	20	17	30	25	19	34	28	23	34	23	16	40	26	41

Run an appropriate test to evaluate the effectiveness of this advertising campaign.

In a digital environment, assessment designers can conduct timely analyses of students' responses at different mastery stages, adjust the structure and sequence of test items to control intrinsic load, and map their concrete cognitive gains. In this way, examinees' true learning outcomes can be effectively appraised. It should be noted that low demands on working memory and low levels of difficulty may lead to decreased task motivation and thus minimum effort. Accordingly, assessment designers should optimize the intrinsic load imposed on examinees so that the assessment task is sufficiently challenging and motivating.

Enhancing Working Memory Capacity in Digital Assessment

As discussed earlier, one of the critical factors of learning and problem solving processes is working memory, which is characterized by its limited capacity (Miller, 1956) and short duration (Peterson & Peterson, 1959) when the problem solvers are dealing with novel information. If the capacity of working memory is exceeded, then comprehension, understanding, and thus learning and problem solving cannot effectively occur. According to a review by Yuan, Steedle, Shavelson, Alonzo, and Oppezo (2006), individual working memory indicators are positively correlated with cognitive functioning and academic achievement. Since working memory appears to be the bottle-neck of human cognitive performance, it is of interest whether assessment can be designed so that examinees' effective working memory capacity may be enhanced. If so, a further step is to examine the feasibility of such enhancement in digital environments. An inspection of previous research in cognitive psychology and instructional design provides relevant information.

Researchers (e.g., Baddeley, 1986, 1992, 2003; Paivio, 1986) have proposed that working memory can be divided into two relatively independent paths: 1) a visual-spatial sketchpad that temporally holds and processes information from diagrams, pictures, and other visually based forms; and 2) a phonological loop to deal with auditory information. The relative independence of the two paths was demonstrated in Murdock's (1971) study, in which providing a visual probe had noticeable impact on the recall of visual targets but did not have significant effect on the recall of auditory target words. Similarly, the auditory probe interfered with only the recall of auditory targets but not with visual ones. It is evident that working memory can be expanded by using both visual and auditory processors instead of a single-mode processor (Penney, 1989; Brünken, Plass, & Leutner, 2004; Brünken, Steinbacher, Plass, & Leutner, 2002; Low & Sweller, 2005).

This modality effect has been demonstrated in experiments conducted in both conventional classroom settings (e.g., Mousavi, Low, & Sweller, 1995; Tindall-Ford, Chandler, & Sweller, 1997) and computer-aided multimedia environments (e.g., Mayer & Moreno, 1998; Moreno & Mayer, 1999; Moreno, Mayer, Spires, & Lester, 2001). The data obtained from these experiments demonstrated that a) students in the audio-visual presentation group performed much better than did those in the visual-visual presentation group, and b) students performed better at problem solving when scientific explanations were given as pictures plus narration (or spoken text) than under the condition of pictures together with on-screen text. According to Mayer's (2001) interpretation, when students are dealing with pictures and related on-screen text, their visual channel may become overloaded while their auditory channel is unused. When words are narrated or the spoken text is provided, students can use their auditory channel to process such information, and the visual channel will deal with the pictures only. The redistribution of information flow can lead to enhanced cognitive processing capacity. Education research also shows that when the information contained in a picture is too complex, simultaneous presentation of corresponding auditory information may still be beyond the capacity of working memory. In this case, the sequencing method can be used to reduce cognitive load (Kulhavy, Stock, & Caterino, 1994; Schnotz, 2005).

In computer-based assessment, test information can be prepared, organized, and presented in various multimedia ways, such as dual-mode, picture and text, picture before text, and animation. These test presentation techniques can make use of knowledge gained from instructional experiments on the modality effect. Students being presented a test question consisting of a diagram and spoken text may respond in a manner very different to the same diagram and written text presented in split-attention format. They may be better able to demonstrate their knowledge when cognitive load is reduced by the use of a dual presentation technique.

Using Long-Term Working Memory Capacity in Digital Assessment

As pointed out by Simon (1990), long-term memory provides "a major way to relax the limits" (p. 7) of working memory. Long-term memory is not merely a "warehouse" for storage, nor a tangential component to information processing. Research has clearly demonstrated that a) long-term memory is the core of human cognition, essential to thinking, recognizing, and self-identity; b) long-term memory participates actively in information processes; and c) the ultimate gains from learning should be indicated by changes in long-term memory. The evidence comes from research of chess playing pioneered by de Groot (1946/1965), Chase and Simon (1973), and Chi, Glaser, and Farr (1988). In comparison with novices, expert chess players are able to recognize and reproduce more meaningful board configurations drawn from real games but do not respond better than novices if random, nonsense board configurations were presented. Based on these results we can conclude that individuals with prior knowledge can effectively activate and use their extensive experience and massive knowledge stored in long-term memory for domain-specific tasks. This mechanism should be included in the equation of assessment design. The example below illustrates how a test item can be designed in accordance with examinees' prior knowledge. In a university-entry preparation course of physics, a question appears as follows:

> Q. The Vanguard rocket is equipped with a pulsed jet engine. If the rocket of mass 5200 kg ejects a 400 kg mass of gas every 1.5 seconds with a velocity of 600 $m \cdot s^{-1}$, what is the velocity of the Vanguard rocket after one pulse?

In this question, the actual amount of time per pulse (here, $t = 1.5$ s) is unnecessary. The answer will be the same irrespective of the value of t. However, if this assessment item is for students who have just learned Newton's Laws of Motion, the given amount of time per pulse may act as a necessary factor in their reasoning. They may use the given amount of time per pulse (t), the mass of gas per pulse (m_1), and the velocity of immediately ejected gas (v_1) to find those parameter relations with acceleration (a) in the formula $v_t = v_{0} + \frac{1}{2} at^2$ (Newton's First Law retrieved from their long-term memory and then transferred to their working memory). They can continue to use the formula $F = ma$ (Newton's Second Law) to find the ejecting force. Next, they may be able to apply the formula $F = -F'$ (Newton's Third Law) to logically determine the force that pushes the rocket. Then those examinees may employ a reversed order to find the acceleration for the rocket and finally the velocity of the Vanguard rocket after one pulse (by using the schemata of Newton's Second Law and Newton's First Law activated as elements of long-term working memory, respectively). Thus, in this assessment, for newly enrolled, inexperienced examinees of preliminary physics, the parameter of amount of time per pulse, though unnecessary, may be used as sort of a "walking aid" to fetch information from long-term memory and then build up long-term working memory for problem solving.

On the other hand, for students who have gained more relevant schemata, such as linear momentum (P) and collisions (Serway & Jewett, 2010), the assessment may be adjusted to a higher, more abstract level. Examinees having stored those extra schemata in their long-term memory are expected to use simultaneous equations (P_{total} = Constant = 0, in this case, and $P_{total} = m_1 v_1 + m_2 v_2$) to solve the problem without specific information of the amount of time per pulse. Hence, the question should be modified as follows to eliminate t as a "catalyst" in problem solving:

> Q. The Vanguard rocket is equipped with a pulsed jet engine. If the rocket of mass 5200 kg ejects a 400 kg mass of gas every pulse with a velocity of 600 m·s⁻¹, what is the velocity of the Vanguard rocket after one pulse?

In digital environments, assessment designers have more means than in traditional classroom contexts to check potential examinees' prior knowledge together with associated schemata stored in long-term memory, and consequently to be able to provide appropriate test items that match the required long-term working memory patterns for the completion of designated assessment tasks. Assessment designers can a) use computerized pre-test modules to classify appropriate cohorts for specific tests, b) employ an on-line system to allow potential examinees to choose their entry level in computer-based adaptive assessment, c) analyze on-going assessment logs (time spent on each step, critical moves, random trials, common mistakes, etc.) so that a streamlined test can be based on an accurate diagnostic report, and d) provide examinees with immediate feedback to consolidate their gains to be stored in long-term memory in a progressive, assessment featured, learning program.

Accommodating Needs of Certain Sub-Population or Special Groups

As indicated earlier, digital assessment is currently focused on the mastery of biologically secondary knowledge in schools, universities and other training institutions. Digital technologies can be useful for assessing and identifying various developmental stages of the mastery of biologically primary knowledge as well. The assessment of verbal native language, elementary numeracy and spatial concepts for children in the kindergarten, preschool, clinics, and even at home can be embedded in interactive computer games (Jin, 2010; Low, 2010; Low, Jin, & Sweller, 2010). To ascertain the knowledge that is possessed by some children who have yet to develop their psychomotor skills to effectively use a mouse and keyboard, the technology of touch screens can be an alternative assessment means.

We should pay attention to conducting assessment research on subpopulations having special needs. For instance, we should be mindful of the educational, training, diagnostic, and other issues associated with the phenomenon of an increasing aging sub-population. The corresponding assessment issues are not merely constrained to the areas of pathological or normal testing of their cognitive functioning (e.g., diagnosing dementia or renewing a driving licence), but also relate to professional development for those postponing their retirement, new job requirements for those seeking a second career, and new subjects for those pursuing their academic or recreational study as leisure activities. A general trend for this sub-population is declining cognitive efficiency, weakening working memory capacity, reducing cognitive speed, weakening inhibition, and down-graded integration (Paas, van Gerven, & Tabbers, 2005; van Gerven, Paas, van Merriënboer, Hendriks, & Schmidt, 2003). Digital assessment must be tailored for the changed cognitive capacity of the elderly, and perhaps special sessions of "digital literacy" training/assessment should be organized before a formal assessment. Likewise, similar assessment strategies should be developed for cognitively impaired groups. For instance, during assessment, individuals with attentional deficits may need more direct, explicit instructions and game-like testing formats to raise their motivation of task fulfillment and enhance their adherence to testing procedures (Ford, Poe, & Cox, 1993; Low, 2010; Low, Jin, & Sweller, in press; Ota & DuPaul, 2002).

CONCLUSIONS

Despite the proliferation of digital assessment practices, research that focuses on the link between computer-based assessment and human cognitive structure is still in its infancy. Since the knowledge that needs to be acquired in modern educational or training settings is by and large biologically secondary, the associated assessment correspondingly should reflect the cognitive principles of human information processing that deal with such knowledge. The format and operation of technology-based assessment should be carefully chosen and implemented to reduce extraneous load imposed on working memory, optimize intrinsic load conveyed in the test items, enhance working memory capacity in testing, use long-term working memory capacity in assessment tasks, and accommodate the needs of certain sub-population or special groups. A consideration of human cognitive architecture has the potential to substantially improve testing procedures in education.

REFERENCES

Abedi, J. (2009). Computer testing as a form of accommodation for English language learners. *Educational Assessment, 14*(3), 195–211.

American Educational Research Association, American Psychological Association, and National Council on Measurement in Education. (1999). *Standards for educational and psychological testing.* Washington, DC: Author.

Baddeley, A. D. (1986). *Working memory.* Oxford, England: Oxford University Press.

Baddeley, A. D. (1992). Working memory. *Science, 255,* 556–559.

Baddeley, A. D. (2003). Working memory: Looking back and looking forward. *Nature Reviews Neuroscience, 4,* 829–839.

Bai, S. (1982). *An outline history of China.* Beijing: Foreign Languages Press.

Brünken, R., Plass, J. L., & Leutner, D. (2004). Assessment of cognitive load in multimedia learning with dual task methodology: Auditory load and modality effects. *Instructional Science, 32,* 115–132.

Brünken, R., Steinbacher, S., Plass, J. L., & Leutner, D. (2002). Assessment of cognitive load in multimedia learning using dual-task methodology. *Experimental Psychology, 49,* 109–119.

Chandler, P., & Sweller, J. (1991). Cognitive load theory and the format of instruction. *Cognition and Instruction, 8,* 293–332.

Chase, W. G., & Simon, H. A. (1973). Perception in chess. *Cognitive Psychology, 4,* 55–81.

Chi, M. T. H., Glaser, R., & Farr, M. (Eds.). (1988). *The nature of expertise.* Hillsdale, NJ: Erlbaum.

Clarke, T., Ayres, P., & Sweller, J. (2005). The impact of sequencing and prior knowledge on learning mathematics through spreadsheet applications. *Educational Technology Research and Development, 53,* 15–24.

Clauser, B. E., Kane, M. T., & Swanson, D. B. (2002). Validity issues for performance-based tests scored with computer-automated scoring systems. *Applied Measurement in Education, 15*(4), 413–432.

Cowan, N. (2005). *Working memory capacity.* New York: Psychology Press.

de Groot, A. (1965). *Thought and choice in chess.* The Hague, Netherlands: Mouton. (Original work published 1946)

de Jong, T. (2006). Computer simulations: Technological advances in inquiry learning. *Science, 312,* 532–533.

Ericsson, K. A., & Kintsch, W. (1995). Long-term working memory. *Psychological Review, 102,* 211–245.

Ford, M. J., Poe, V., & Cox, J. (1993). Attending behaviour of children with ADHD in math and reading using various types of software. *Journal of Childhood Education, 4,* 183–196.

Geary, D. (2002). Principles of evolutionary educational psychology. *Learning and Individual Differences, 12,* 317–345.

Geary, D. (2005). *The origin of mind: Evolution of brain, cognition, and general intelligence.* Washington, DC: American Psychological Association.

Geary, D. (2007). Educating the evolved mind: Conceptual foundations for an evolutionary educational psychology. In J. S. Carlson & J. R. Levin (Eds.), *Psychological perspectives on contemporary educational issues* (pp. 1–99). Greenwich, CT: Information Age Publishing.

Geary, D. (2008). An evolutionarily informed education science. *Educational Psychologist, 43,* 179–195.

Gerjets, P., Scheiter, K., & Catrambone, R. (2004). Designing instructional examples to reduce intrinsic cognitive load: Molar versus modular presentation of solution procedures. *Instructional Science, 32*, 33–58.

Haladyna, T. M., Downing, S. M., & Rodriguez, M. C. (2002). A review of multiple-choice item-writing guidelines for classroom assessment. *Applied Measurement in Education, 15*(3), 309–333.

Jin, P. (2010). Methodological considerations in educational research using serious games. In R. Van Eck (Ed.), *Interdisciplinary models and tools for serious games: Emerging concepts and future directions* (pp. 147–176). Hershey, PA: IG1 Global.

Kulhavy, R. W., Stock, W. A., & Caterino, L. C. (1994). Reference maps as a framework for remembering text. In W. Schnotz & R. W. Kulhavy (Eds.), *Comprehension of graphics* (pp. 153–162). Amsterdam: Elsevier Science B. V.

Low, R. (2010). Examining motivational factors in serious educational games. In R. Van Eck (Ed.), *Interdisciplinary models and tools for serious games: Emerging concepts and future directions* (pp. 103–124). Hershey, PA: IG1 Global.

Low, R., Jin, P., & Sweller, J. (2009). Cognitive architecture and instructional design in a multimedia context. In R. Zheng (Ed.), *Cognitive effects of multimedia learning* (pp. 1–16). Hershey, PA: IG1 Global.

Low, R., Jin, P., & Sweller, J. (2010). Learner's cognitive load when using educational technology. In R. Van Eck (Ed.), *Gaming and cognition: Theories and practice from learning* (pp. 169–188). Hershey, PA: IG1 Global.

Low, R., Jin, P., & Sweller, J. (in press). Cognitive load theory, attentional processes and optimized learning outcomes in a digital environment. In C. Roda (Ed.), *Human attention in digital environments.* New York: Cambridge University Press.

Low, R., & Sweller, J. (2005). The modality principle in multimedia learning. In R. E. Mayer (Ed.), *Cambridge handbook of multimedia learning* (pp. 147–158). Cambridge, UK: Cambridge University Press.

Mayer, R. E. (2001). *Multimedia learning.* New York: Cambridge University Press.

Mayer, R. E. (2005). Introduction to multimedia learning. In R. E. Mayer (Ed.), *The Cambridge handbook of multimedia learning* (pp. 1–16). New York: Cambridge University Press.

Mayer, R. E., & Anderson, R. (1991). Animations need narrations: An experimental test of a dual-coding hypothesis. *Journal of Educational Psychology, 83,* 484–490.

Mayer, R. E. & Anderson, R. (1992). The instructive animation: Helping students build connections between words and pictures in multimedia learning. *Journal of Educational Psychology, 84,* 444–452.

Mayer, R. E. & Moreno, R. (1998). A split-attention effect in multi-media learning: Evidence for dual processing systems in working memory. *Journal of Educational Psychology, 90,* 312–320.

Mayer, R. E. & Sims, V. K. (1994). For whom is a picture worth a thousand words? Extensions of a dual-coding theory of multimedia learning. *Journal of Educational Psychology, 86,* 389–401.

Miller, G. A. (1956). The magical number seven, plus or minus two: Some limits on our capacity for processing information. *Psychological Review, 63,* 81–97.

Mislevy, R. J., Steinberg, L. S., Breyer, F. J., Almond, R. G., & Johnson, L. (2002). Making sense of data from complex assessments. *Applied Measurement in Education, 15*(4), 363–389.

Moreno, R., & Mayer, R. E. (1999). Cognitive principles of multimedia learning: The role of modality and contiguity. *Journal of Educational psychology, 91*, 358–368.

Moreno, R., Mayer, R. E., Spires, H. A., & Lester, J. C. (2001). The case for social agency in computer-based multimedia learning: Do students learn more deeply when they interact with animated pedagogical agents? *Cognition and Instruction, 19,* 177–214.

Mousavi, S., Low, R., & Sweller, J. (1995). Reducing cognitive load by mixing auditory and visual presentation modes. *Journal of Educational Psychology, 87,* 319–334.

Murdock, B. B., Jr. (1971). Four-channel effects in short-term memory. *Psychonomic Science, 24,* 197–198.

Ota, K. R., & DuPaul, G. (2002). Task engagement and mathematics performance in children with attention-deficit hyperactivity disorder: Effects of supplemental computer instruction. *School Psychology Quarterly, 17,* 242–257.

Palaigeorgiou, G. E., Siozos, P. D., & Konstantakis, N. I. (2006). CEAF: A measure for deconstructing students' prior computer experience. *Journal of Information Systems Education, 17*(4), 459–468.

Parsons-Pollard, N., Lacks, R. D., & Grant, P. H. (2008). A comparative assessment of student learning outcomes in large online and traditional campus-based introduction to criminal justice courses. *Criminal Justice Studies, 21*(3), 239–251.

Paivio, A. (1986). *Mental representing: A dual coding approach.* Oxford, England: Oxford University Press.

Paas, F., van Gerven, P., & Tabbers, H. K. (2005). The cognitive aging principle in multimedia learning. In R. E. Mayer (Ed.), *The Cambridge handbook of multimedia learning* (pp. 339–351). New York: Cambridge University Press.

Penney, C. G. (1989). Modality effects and the structure of short-term verbal memory. *Memory & Cognition, 17,* 398–422.

Peterson, L., & Peterson, M. J. (1959). Short-term retention of individual verbal items. *Journal of Experimental Psychology, 58,* 193–198.

Pollock, E., Chandler, P., & Sweller, J. (2002). Assimilating complex information. *Learning and Instruction, 12,* 61–86.

Salvia, J., & Ysseldyke, J. E. (1995). *Assessment* (6 ed.). Boston: Houghton Mifflin Company.

Schnotz, W. (2005). An integrated model of text and picture comprehension. In R. E. Mayer (Ed.), *The Cambridge handbook of multimedia learning* (pp. 49–69). New York: Cambridge University Press.

Schnotz, W., & Rasch, T. (2005). Enabling, facilitating, and inhibiting effects of animations in multimedia learning: Why reduction of cognitive load can have negative results on learning. *Educational Technology Research & Development, 53,* 47–58.

Serway, R. A., & Jewett, J. W., Jr. (2010). *Physics for scientists and engineers with modern physics* (8th ed.). Belmont, CA : Brooks/Cole.

Simon, H. A. (1990). Invariants of human behavior. *Annual Review of Psychology, 41,* 1–19.

Sweller, J. (1994). Cognitive load theory, learning difficulty, and instructional design. *Learning and Instruction, 4,* 295–312.

Sweller, J. (1999). *Instructional design in technical areas.* Melbourne: ACER Press.

Sweller, J., Chandler, P., Tierney, P., & Cooper, M. (1990). Cognitive load as a factor in the structuring of technical material. *Journal of Experimental Psychology: General, 119,* 176–192.

Sweller, J., & Sweller, S. (2006). Natural information processing systems. *Evolutionary Psychology, 4,* 434–458.

Tarmizi, R., & Sweller, J. (1988). Guidance during mathematical problem solving. *Journal of Educational Psychology, 80,* 424–436.

Tindall-Ford, S., Chandler, P., & Sweller, J. (1997). When two sensory modes are better than one. *Journal of Experimental Psychology: Applied, 3,* 257–287.

van Gerven, P. W. M., Paas F., van Merriënboer, J. J. G., Hendriks M., & Schmidt, H. G. (2003). The efficiency of multimedia learning into old age. *British Journal of Educational Psychology, 73,* 489–505.

van Merriënboer, J. J. G., Kirschner, P. A., & Kester, L. (2003). Taking the load off a learner's mind: Instructional design for complex learning. *Educational Psychologist, 38,* 5–14.

Yang, Y., Buckendahl, C. W., Juszkiewicz, P. J., & Bhola, D. S. (2002). A review of strategies for validating computer-automated scoring. *Applied Measurement in Education, 15*(4), 391–412.

Yeung, A. S., Jin, P., & Sweller, J. (1998). Cognitive load and learner expertise: Split-attention and redundancy effects in reading with explanatory notes. *Contemporary Educational Psychology, 23,* 1–21.

Yuan, K., Steedle, J., Shavelson, R., Alonzo, A., & Oppezo, M. (2006). Working memory, fluid intelligence, and science learning. *Educational Research Review, 1,* 83–98.

Zenisky, A. L., & Sireci, S. G. (2002). Technological innovations in large-scale assessment. *Applied Measurement in Education, 15*(4), 337–362.

CHAPTER 13

ENHANCING DIAGNOSTIC ASSESSMENT OF EXPERTISE IN ADAPTIVE LEARNING ENVIRONMENTS

Slava Kalyuga
University of New South Wales, Sydney, Australia

ABSTRACT

Optimizing cognitive load factors in learning requires that instructional methods and procedures be dynamically tailored to changing levels of knowledge and skills of individual learners as they proceed through instructional sessions. This chapter focuses on the role of diagnostic assessment procedures in adaptive learning environments such as adaptive online tutors. Special attention is devoted to some recently suggested rapid diagnostic assessment instruments and their potential use in adaptive learning.

INTRODUCTION

Cognitive diagnostic assessment is becoming a major trend in the field of educational assessment. It aims at determining levels of acquisition of spe-

Technology-Based Assessments for 21st Century Skills, pages 305–323

305

cific cognitive processes and operations, and providing fine-grained information about learner strengths and weaknesses. The need for cognitively-based assessment has been advocated by many educational assessment theorists for some time (Embretson, 1993; Mislevy, 1996; Pellegrino, Baxter, & Glaser, 1999; Snow & Lohman, 1989). Cognitive assessment theories rely on models of cognition developed in cognitive science as the foundation for the assessment design process (Pellegrino, Chudowsky, & Glaser, 2001) and apply modern psychometric models appropriate to the assessment of cognitive constructs involved in complex tasks (Embretson, 1991, 1993; Martin & van Lehn, 1995; Mislevy, 1994; Tatsuoka, 1990; Wilson, 1989).

Traditional evaluation of students' performance (e.g., based on responding to a set of multiple-choice items) may not provide sufficient levels of precision for guiding instructional decisions, even though appropriately designed multiple-choice items with response options that mirror persistent students' errors may provide valuable diagnostic information. In contrast, cognitive diagnostic assessment evaluates specific cognitive processes required for successful performance in targeted tasks and provides information about students' mastery of these processes that could be used to adjust instruction responsively to students' needs. Cognitive diagnostic assessment combines specific cognitive models (theories of cognition in a domain) and statistical models of student response patterns. Cognitive models are based on task analyses and empirical research including expert interviews, verbal protocols of thinking processes, and identify cognitive attributes involved in successful learning of specific tasks.

Cognitive diagnostic assessment may provide invaluable information required for the design of advanced individualized instructional interventions for students at different levels of expertise. However, a limitation of the available cognitive diagnostic models is that they are still mostly used for post-learning assessment with the intention of guiding the follow-up remediation procedures (e.g., for students who are at risk of failure in specific topics as determined by the diagnostic assessment procedure) rather than for dynamic assessment during learning with the aim of using adaptively appropriate interventions on the fly.

Another limitation of many current cognitive assessment theories is that they are focused primarily on developing sophisticated statistical measurement models rather than on obtaining valid evidence about the relevant cognitive attributes to which those models are applied. No matter how sophisticated a measurement model, it is unlikely to result in a precise diagnostic decision if applied to vague empirical data. It is necessary to have appropriate complementing means for obtaining empirical evidence about students' cognitive structures that would match the level of precision of new measurement models.

Cognitive diagnostic assessment has been proven to maximize learning outcomes. For example, Russell, O'Dwyer, and Miranda (2009) demonstrated that students participating in a diagnostic assessment and instructional intervention in algebra performed significantly better on a measure of algebra proficiency than did students participating in typical classroom instruction without guidance from diagnostic information. However, with most currently used diagnostic assessment techniques, developing and administering the tests, obtaining assessment data, and interpreting results of diagnostic assessments, as well as incorporating appropriate instructional interventions based on these results may require a considerable amount of time. Therefore many practitioners may not be particularly inclined to use cognitive diagnostic assessment to guide their instructional decisions. More dynamic and rapid assessment techniques are required to accelerate the process. Another possible solution to this problem is in developing adaptive computer-based tutors with embedded diagnostic assessment tools.

This chapter focuses on the role of diagnostic assessment procedures in adaptive learning environments. It approaches the issue from a perspective of optimizing cognitive load factors in learning that require instructional methods and procedures to be dynamically tailored to changing levels of knowledge and skills of individual learners as they proceed through instructional sessions. Special attention is devoted to some recently suggested rapid diagnostic assessment instruments and their potential role in adaptive learning.

EXPERTISE REVERSAL EFFECT AND ADAPTIVE LEARNING

Individualized learner-tailored instruction has been on educators' minds for a long time; however, practically, on any significant scale, it still remains an unaccomplished objective. Even though access to sufficient computing power is not an issue anymore, some other issues essential for the development of learner-tailored environments still need to be resolved. One of them is the availability of cognitive diagnostic assessment techniques that can be used dynamically in real time for guiding the selection of appropriate instructional methods.

Typical student attributes used in the field of adaptive e-learning for the tailored selection of instructional content include learner preferences, interests, history of previous on-line choices, and performance on simple quizzes. Student attributes can also be used for adapting training procedures for relatively simple learning materials. For example, in learning foreign vocabulary items, adaptive training could be successfully implemented by using an analogy of stacks of learning cards or equivalent computer software. Correctly answered cards are placed on piles that are subsequently re-tested less often while incorrectly answered ones are re-tested more often until they finally also belong to the former category (Meltzer-Baddeley & Baddeley, 2009). However, most of such attributes are surface-level rather than deep-level cognitive characteristics of learners that may not be critical for learning complex cognitive tasks. What are the critical cognitive characteristics that should be used for building adaptive learning environments in complex task domains?

Studies of expert-novice differences have clearly demonstrated that a learner's knowledge base is the single most important cognitive characteristic that influences learning and performance (e.g., Chi, Feltovich, & Glaser 1981; Larkin, McDermott, Simon, & Simon, 1980; see Pellegrino et al., 2001for a review). In accordance with this general conclusion, studies within the cognitive load theory framework have demonstrated that instructional methods that are effective for low-knowledge learners can lose their effectiveness and even have negative consequences for more proficient learners (an expertise reversal effect; see Kalyuga, 2007 for a recent overview). The need to tailor instructional methods and procedures to levels of learner knowledge as they acquire more expertise in a specific domain is the main instructional implication of these studies. The characteristics of human cognitive architecture that underlie the expertise reversal effect are described in Chapter 12 (Low, Jin, & Sweller) of this volume. This chapter is focused on the main empirical findings associated with the expertise reversal effect and some means for implementing this effect in the design of adaptive learning environments.

According to the expertise reversal effect, the effectiveness of learning materials depends on matching levels of instructional guidance to levels of learner expertise. When learners are novices in a domain, effective instruction usually provides detailed and comprehensive guidance. The lack of such guidance may force novices to use random search processes that impose a heavy cognitive load to handle a task or situation. On the other hand, when learners have significant and relevant domain-specific knowledge in long-term memory, the simultaneous use, cross-referencing and integration of similar knowledge-based and instruction-based guidance may require additional cognitive sources. Wasting these resources on essentially redundant activities may decrease resources available for meaningful learning. The process of *optimization of cognitive load* in learning involves providing essential instructional guidance at the appropriate time and removing its redundant components as the level of learner expertise gradually increases.

For example, it has been demonstrated that worked examples may constitute optimal instructional formats for novice learners, while at higher levels of expertise, problem-solving or exploratory learning environments with limited guidance may represent optimal instructional methods (Kalyuga, Chandler, & Sweller, 2000, 2001; Kalyuga, Chandler, Tuovinen, &

Sweller, 2001). At intermediate levels of expertise, worked-out steps may be gradually faded out as learners acquire more knowledge to be eventually replaced by problem solving tasks (Atkinson & Renkl, 2007; Renkl, Atkinson, Maier, & Staley, 2002). Renkl et al. (2002), Renkl and Atkinson (2003), and Renkl, Atkinson, and Große (2004) demonstrated the advantage of gradually reducing guidance with increases in expertise in comparison with an abrupt switch from worked examples to problems. The timing of fading should be linked to the learner's understanding and proficiency in executing the corresponding steps. Therefore, optimizing cognitive load in instruction should be based on continuously monitoring changes in the learner knowledge base and accordingly tailoring dynamically appropriate instructional methods that are optimal for individual learners. In turn, this requires cognitive diagnostic methods for determining learners' levels of expertise suitable for dynamic real-time applications.

Thus, because the acquisition of expertise is a gradual process, the switch from fully guided instructional procedures to unguided problem-solving practice or exploration needs to be designed as a continuing process. Faded worked examples and completion assignments represent suitable approaches for instructional implementation of such a gradual change in guidance. A completion strategy is based on a sequence of instructional procedures from fully worked-out examples with complete task solutions to conventional problems. Accordingly, completion assignments include a problem description, an incomplete worked-out solution, and steps that need to be completed (van Merriënboer, 1990; van Merriënboer, Kirschner, & Kester, 2003).

Similar considerations may be applicable to other instructional environments. For example, the effectiveness of web-based hypermedia and hypertext learning environments also depends on levels of learner prior knowledge that allows the separation of essential and non-essential information (Alexander & Jetton, 2003; Chen, Fan, & Macredie, 2006; Gall & Hannafin, 1994). Therefore, adequate instructional support needs to be provided to novices, while relatively more experienced learners may benefit from exploring less supported hypermedia environments guided by their available knowledge base (Gerjets & Scheiter, 2007).

Spiro and Jehng (1990) suggested designing interactive exploratory environments in complex, ill-structured domains based on learners traversing the information space along several intersecting dimensions so they study the same content from different perspectives. From a cognitive load point of view, even though the provided dimensions for exploration represent a limited form of instructional guidance that may partially prevent random search with its accompanying heavy cognitive load, such guided traversing should be used only with relatively more advanced learners. Even for knowledgeable learners, multidimensional traversing in ill-structured domains may require some external instructional scaffolding (Jacobson & Spiro, 1995)

Simons and Klein (2007) compared three instructional conditions in an exploratory problem-based hypermedia environment (an inquiry project on designing and planning a balloon trip around the world for grade seven students): (1) an environment without scaffolding; (2) an optional scaffolding condition; and (3) a compulsory scaffolding condition. Results indicated that high prior knowledge students benefited more from the problem-based environment than low knowledge students; the no-scaffolding condition was worse than both scaffolding conditions; and students in the compulsory scaffolding condition made more relevant entries. Designing this learning environment as one that is adaptive to learner prior knowledge levels could have possibly further improved its learning effect for all students.

The available empirical studies indicate that higher-level structure and instructional guidance should be provided for novices, but reduced levels of guidance could be used with more experienced learners. In contrast to novices, more knowledgeable learners may not be overloaded in hypermedia learning environments because their knowledge base may flexibly support their navigation through the environments, processing unordered segments of information, and handling interruptions by connecting these segments to existing knowledge structures (DeStefano & LeFevre, 2007). Therefore, while high prior knowledge learners are capable of handling different types of interactive environments, for low prior knowledge learners, more structured and guided versions should result in greater learning benefits (Amadieu, Tricot, & Marine, 2009; Amadieu, van Gog, Paas, Tricot, & Marine, 2009; Balcytiene, 1999; Calisir & Gurel, 2003; Shapiro, 1999; Shin, Schallert, and Savenye, 1994).

The main implication of the expertise reversal effect is that instructional techniques and procedures need to be continuously tailored to levels of learner expertise in specific learning areas. Adaptive computer-based learning environments represent the best possible way of implementing this effect in practice. In this regard, from the currently available adaptive learning environments, intelligent cognitive tutoring systems may offer a possible design approach. Such systems have been developed for teaching problem-solving skills in well-defined areas (Anderson, Corbett, Koedinger, & Pelletier, 1995). Cognitive tutors select learning tasks based on a continuously updated model of the student that traces current levels of knowledge state. Accordingly, the system provides feedback and hints, and evaluates learning progress.

Cognitive tutors have embedded knowledge assessment tools for evaluating individual learners' progress in real time, and these tools can be used for implementing adaptively adjusted guidance procedures. Also, procedures for providing varied degrees of instructional guidance such as faded worked examples could potentially complement these tutors if they do not duplicate already available forms of learner support. Since most cognitive tutors provide extended feedback and hints that effectively represent a form of annotated worked examples, additional embedded worked examples may be redundant and impose more rather than less cognitive load (Koedinger & Aleven, 2007). Whether with feedback and hints, or with worked examples, the issue of determining the optimal timing for fading levels of instructional support remains critical in cognitive tutors. This issue has been associated with a broader "assistance dilemma" in making a decision on when the assistance or guidance should be provided to learners, and when it should be fully or partially withdrawn (Koedinger & Aleven, 2007).

HOW GOOD IS OUR EVIDENCE OF EXPERTISE?

If instructional methods and techniques in different learning environments need to be adapted to levels of learner prior knowledge (or expertise) in a domain, then the quality of adaptive procedures may depend significantly on the accuracy of information about current levels of learner expertise. Unfortunately, as indicated previously, widespread and easy to implement multiple-choice tests based on the solution of a series of problems may not be very effective measurement tools for this purpose because they are neither precise in cognitive diagnosis nor sufficiently rapid. With such traditional assessment methods, it may not be possible to make reliable inferences about learners' actual knowledge structures because their results are not always directly related to cognitive processes and structures targeted by the assessment. Such inferences could also be rather misleading for cognitive diagnosis resulting in inadequate instructional decisions.

For example, based on student correct answers to a series of multiple-choice test items in solving algebra equations, it is not possible to conclude how those problems were actually solved and what cognitive processes were involved. Some students could have solved them by applying appropriate knowledge about solution procedures, but others could achieve the same outcomes by using a novice-like random search or simple trial-and-error methods. We usually use such weak problem-solving techniques in the absence of a relevant knowledge base. Such methods may often succeed in reaching a solution, but they are not indicative of an appropriate knowledge base, and the obtained evidence would be useless for cognitive diagnosis.

Furthermore, even those students who used appropriate knowledge structures could have used them differently. Some students could slowly apply low-level, fine-grained, step-by-step procedures learned "by the book," while others could use expert-like or higher-level automated procedures with final answers obtained quickly by skipping many intermediate steps.

Expert performance is characterized by rapid retrieval and application of previously acquired solution procedures stored in long-term memory. The above two types of knowledge-based performance would obviously be characterized by different levels of expertise (e.g., intermediate and experts) in this domain. However, traditional tests would place all of them (as well as novices who reached correct solutions using weak problem-solving methods) in the same category of successful learners. These assessment results would not be suitable for cognitive diagnosis.

In many existing adaptive online environments, knowledge evaluation methods are often based on a learner history of interactions with the environment and use only a few, discrete, global, coarse-grained levels of learner experience (e.g., high or low levels). Such methods are unlikely to be sufficiently precise instruments for effective adaptive procedures. In intelligent cognitive tutors, sophisticated production rule-based learner models significantly increased the precision of ongoing information about the learner knowledge state by assessing acquisition of specific production rules (Anderson et al., 1995; Corbett & Anderson, 1992; Draney, Pirolli, & Wilson, 1995). However, such tutors have been limited to domains that are relatively easy to model computationally, such as programming or mathematics.

The levels of learner expertise in a specific domain are determined by the levels of acquisition of organized knowledge structures (schemas) in long-term memory that should be the major target of assessment. Higher degrees of diagnostic precision can be achieved by methods used in cognitive science laboratory studies designed to uncover knowledge structures held by individuals. Such methods are usually based on interviews, observations, and "think aloud" protocols collected during problem solving (Chi, Bassok, Lewis, Reimann, & Glaser, 1989; Ericsson & Simon, 1993a, 1993b; Magliano & Millis, 2003). However, these methods are very time consuming, slow, and not suitable for real-time assessment in realistic educational settings. Thus, there seems to be a trade-off between the precision and the rapidity of diagnostic assessment. Even though cognitive assessment instruments that combine high levels of diagnostic power with rapidity of assessment and simplicity of implementation appear counterintuitive, such tools would obviously be advantageous to adaptive learning environments. The next section describes an attempt to develop such diagnostic instruments.

RAPID DIAGNOSTIC ASSESSMENT METHODS

If an organized knowledge base in long-term memory is the main factor determining differences between experts and novices, then indicators of levels of expertise in a specific task area may be obtained by observing how learners approach briefly presented tasks. Learners who are more knowledgeable in the domain should be better able to recognize presented problem states and retrieve appropriate solution steps than less knowledgeable learners. Experts may immediately recognize a problem state within their higher-level knowledge structures and activate appropriate solution schemas. Novices may only locate random, lower-level components.

This idea was realized as the first-step diagnostic method: learners were presented with a series of selected tasks (some of which were incomplete intermediate solution stages for other higher-level tasks) for a limited time and asked to rapidly indicate their first step towards solution of each task. In this situation, more knowledgeable learners will use their higher-level (in some cases, automated) solution procedures to rapidly generate steps of the solution and skip some intermediate steps (Blessing & Anderson, 1996; Sweller, Mawer, & Ward, 1983). Thus, different first steps generated by learners for the same task could be used to indicate different levels of expertise. The method was validated in a series of studies using tasks in algebra, coordinate geometry, and arithmetic word problems. Results indicated high levels of correlations between performance on the rapid tasks and detailed traditional measures of knowledge (Kalyuga, 2006c, 2008a; Kalyuga & Sweller, 2004), with test time reductions up to about five times.

In an alternative rapid assessment method, learners were presented with a series of possible steps (some of which were incorrect) at various stages of the solution procedure, and asked to rapidly verify the validity of these steps. Again, the assumption was that the knowledge structures of more expert learners would allow them to accomplish such rapid verifications more successfully than less knowledgeable learners. This method was validated using sentence comprehension tasks based on a series of sentences with different levels of complexity (e.g., simple, composite, and multiple-embedded sentences). Each sentence was displayed on the computer screen for a limited but sufficient reading time followed by a sequence of four simple statements related to the content of the sentence (both correct and incorrect) for rapid verification. A significant correlation was found between performance on the rapid verification tasks and traditional measures of reading comprehension, with test time reduced by factor of 3.7 (Kalyuga, 2006b).

The results of rapid verification tests in which learners were required to verify the validity of alternative steps were also compared with the results of observations (using video-recordings and concurrent verbal reports) of the same students' problem solving steps in kinematics and mathematics. Again, a sufficiently high degree of concurrent validity for the rapid method was obtained, with reductions in testing times by around three to four times (Kalyuga, 2008b). This alternative to a first step rapid assessment method was designed for use in online and computer-based learning environments. For many types of tasks (e.g., those involving drawing graphs), especially in science and technical areas, it may be technically challenging to collect and evaluate students' first-step responses in an electronic form. Verifying the validity of alternative steps might also be used with relatively poorly defined tasks that accept different possible solution paths. For such tasks, only a limited number of steps (both acceptable and unacceptable) representing different levels of problem solutions can be presented for rapid verification.

Our cognitive architecture consists of two major interrelated components: working memory as a conscious information processor with limited capacity and duration, and long-term memory as a knowledge base effectively unlimited in capacity and duration. Long-term memory knowledge structures allow us to encapsulate or chunk many elements of information within one schema that can be treated as a single element in working memory, thus effectively increasing its capacity (e.g., see Ericsson & Kintsch, 1995 for a possible mechanism). Therefore, experts' extensive domain-specific knowledge base can make working memory capacity limitations irrelevant.

From this theoretical perspective, rapid assessment methods essentially evaluate the degree to which the learners' working memory capacity is augmented by the availability of a knowledge base in long-term memory, thus providing an indicator of levels of expertise. If an expert learner faces a task in a familiar domain, the relevant available knowledge structures in long-term memory are rapidly activated and brought into the learner's working memory, allowing the encapsulation of many elements of information (e.g., fine-grained intermediate solution steps) into a single element (e.g., a single advance-level solution step). Different first-step responses reflect different levels of acquisition of corresponding knowledge structures in the learner's long-term memory. Therefore, the diagnostic power of the rapid assessment methods exceeds the power of equivalent traditional tests that ask for final answers to the same tasks. The rapid assessment evaluates not only the availability of knowledge of solution procedures, but also the level at which they have been acquired.

The design of rapid diagnostic tests follows a general conceptual framework for the design of cognitively based assessment (Mislevy, Steinberg, Breyer, Almond, & Johnson, 2002) that contains the student model, the task model, and the evidence model. For a rapid diagnostic test in a specific area, the student model includes characteristics of organized knowledge structures that underpin the evaluated cognitive processes. The task model describes patterns of tasks or situations necessary to elicit evidence about these knowledge structures. Finally, the evidence model defines observable variables, the scoring procedure, and a specific measurement model that should be applied to the collected evidence. Thus, according to this framework, a set of relevant knowledge structures should be described and a pattern of corresponding tasks outlined. An appropriate scoring procedure for evaluating performance on these tasks should be defined (with specific scores allocated to responses corresponding to different levels of expertise), and a suitable multidimensional measurement model applied to the data to make statistical inferences about levels of acquisition of each cognitive construct.

APPLYING RAPID ASSESSMENT METHODS IN ADAPTIVE LEARNING ENVIRONMENTS

The described rapid assessment methods were used in adaptive computer-based tutorials in solving linear algebra equations (Kalyuga & Sweller, 2004; 2005) and vector addition motion problems in kinematics (Kalyuga, 2006a) for high school students. It was suggested that the gradual fading of worked examples could be more effective if the rate of fading was tailored to individual learner progress. Early exposure to cognitive demands of problem solving could overload learners' working memory capacity and inhibit learning.

The adaptive tutorials selected the levels of fading or levels of instructional guidance based on rapid measures of individual learners' current knowledge. At the beginning of each session, the initial rapid pretest was administered in order to select an appropriate level of instructional guidance. During the session, ongoing rapid tests were used to select an appropriate learning pathway. The learner was either allowed to proceed to the next phase of learning with a lower level of guidance (more worked-out steps were omitted), or was required to repeat the same stage and then take the rapid test again. The adaptive tutorials were compared with similar non-adaptive tutorials in which learners either studied all tasks that were included in the corresponding stages of the training session of their yoked participants, or were required to study the whole set of tasks available in the tutorial.

In Kalyuga and Sweller (2004), the selection of appropriate levels of instructional guidance was based on the rapid first-step tests, while Kalyuga and Sweller (2005) combined the rapid first-step scores with measures of cognitive load based on subjective ratings of task difficulty into a composite indicator of instructional efficiency. Expertise is usually associated with both higher-level performance and lower-level cognitive load. Therefore, instructional efficiency was defined by Kalyuga and Sweller (2005) as a ratio of the current level of performance to the current level of cognitive load according to the common understanding of efficiency as performance relative to cost. Results of both studies indicated that the learner-adapted tutorial resulted in significantly better knowledge gains (differences between post-instruction and pre-instruction test scores) than the non-adapted tutorial. Kalyuga (2006a) compared two adaptive instructional tutorials, one based on rapid verification tests and another based on the efficiency indicator, and a non-adaptive tutorial as a control group. Both adaptive conditions outperformed the control group; however no significant differences were found between the adaptive conditions.

The above adaptive fading procedures could be further improved by incorporating (at least partially, at higher levels of expertise) learner control over the fading rate into the adaptation algorithm to enhance the development of self-regulation skills. Shared control models of task selection (Van Merriënboer et al., 2006; Corbalan, Kester, & van Merriënboer, 2006) or advisory models based on adaptive guidance (Bell & Kozlowski, 2002) could supplement system-controlled adaptive procedures with possible benefits for learners. However, a cautious evidence-based approach should be taken in allowing higher levels of learner control as relying on learners' own decisions in selecting external guidance on-demand may not necessarily be more effective that using a system-controlled provision of guidance, especially for novice learners (Koedinger & Aleven, 2007). Salden, Paas, van der Pal, and van Merriënboer (2006) demonstrated that selecting the next learning task and the level of instructional guidance based on self-assessment of performance and mental effort produced similar learning results on transfer tasks to those obtained when the selection was based on the assessment by the system. Both these approaches were superior to the no-assessment approach that used a fixed sequence of learning tasks. Thus, according to the available data, while dynamic adaptive task selection leads to more efficient learning than non-adaptive task selection, no significant differences have been demonstrated between different types of adaptation methods.

The quality of any adaptive tutor depends on the accuracy of information about levels of learner knowledge incorporated into the student model. Existing sophisticated intelligent cognitive tutors (Anderson et al., 1995) select problems based on a continuously updated model of the learner. Appropriate forms of instructional guidance (e.g., faded worked examples) can effectively complement such tutors if (according to the expertise reversal effect) the fading of worked examples is dynamically tailored to growing levels of expertise of individual learners. Since cognitive tutors already have a mechanism for evaluating individual student's progress over time, this knowledge assessment tool could be used for potentially implementing adaptive fading procedures within the tutors.

For example, Salden, Aleven, Schwonke, and Renkl (in press) investigated whether adaptively faded worked examples in a tutored problem solving environment dealing with the geometric properties of angles could lead to higher learning gains by comparing two example-enhanced versions of a cognitive tutor with the standard problem-solving tutor. In one version, the fading of worked examples occurred in a fixed manner, while in another, fading occurred adaptively according to individual learners' levels of understanding. The results demonstrated improved learning from the adaptive fading condition compared to the fixed fading and problem solving conditions.

In these intelligent cognitive tutors, the transition between different levels of guidance was based on student ability to explain example steps in terms of the principles targeted in the instruction. The level of understanding of each principle was tracked by the software, and steps that involved corresponding principles were faded when a certain threshold was reached. Salden et al. (in press) suggested that the advantage of using self-explanations rather than rapid assessment for adaptive fading of worked examples in cognitive tutors is that no separate assessment instrument is needed, as students' self-explanations are already a part of the tutors' usual procedure, and they are sufficiently rapid, frequent, and non-intrusive. However, the self-explanations that students select from the suggested fixed options in a multiple choice computer-based format may be limited in their diagnostic precision.

Thus, computational knowledge-tracing methods or rapid diagnostic assessment techniques could be used for real-time evaluation of levels of learner expertise and tailoring levels of instructional guidance in adaptive learning environments. Available evidence indicates that adaptive learning environments using either of these diagnostic methods produce better learning outcomes than equivalent non-adaptive learning environments (Kalyuga, 2006a; Kalyuga & Sweller, 2005; Koedinger & Aleven, 2007). Faded worked examples based on either self-explanations or rapid assessment methods resulted in better learning outcomes than non-adaptive fading. It is possible that they could also be used in complementary ways to better optimize the fading procedures according to changing levels of learner knowledge. For example, since most intelligent cognitive tutors do not take into account learners' actual initial knowledge levels, their self-explanations-based adaptive procedures could possibly be further improved by using levels of learner prior knowledge measured by rapid assessment methods to determine the initial level of fading.

THEORETICAL AND PRACTICAL IMPLICATIONS FOR FUTURE TECHNOLOGY-BASED ASSESSMENTS

The level of learner expertise is the most significant factor influencing learning. Adaptive interactive learning environments may allow efficient dynamic tailoring of the nature and levels of interactivity to changing knowledge levels of individual learners. Some general practical implications of the role of learner expertise for the design of interactive adaptive learning environments include: (1) direct guidance needs to be provided to low-prior knowledge learners at the appropriate time or on-demand using various forms of worked-out procedures, feedback, and hints; (2) unnecessary or redundant scaffolding should be removed in a timely manner as learners progress through the task domain; (3) content presentation formats (e.g., using on-screen and/or narrated versions of explanations) also need to be tailored to changing levels of knowledge of individual learners.

The procedures for adapting instruction to individual learners have been described above in conjunction with the empirically established expertise reversal effect that relates to interactions between levels of learner knowledge and instructional methods. The major instructional implication of the expertise reversal effect is the need to tailor dynamically external instructional guidance to current levels of learner expertise as they gradually change during learning. Completion tasks and faded worked examples can be effectively used for managing levels of instructional guidance in adaptive learning environments based on detailed diagnosis of learner knowledge and skills. The ability to diagnose levels of learner expertise rapidly in real time is an important prerequisite to building dynamically-tailored learning environments.

Real-time monitoring of levels of learner expertise using rapid cognitive diagnostic methods may be instrumental in selecting appropriate levels of instructional guidance at different stages of acquisition of complex cognitive skills. As learner knowledge in a domain increases, processing redundant worked examples and integrating them with previously learned knowledge structures may generate high levels of unnecessary cognitive load. Therefore, external instructional guidance should be gradually faded and a relative share of the students' own problem-solving or exploratory activities increased.

As the research in cognitively-optimized adaptive procedures implementing technology-based diagnostic assessments of deep cognitive characteristics (such as knowledge base and levels of learner expertise) is still very limited, it needs to be further extended. In addition to domain-specific knowledge structures, other cognitive characteristics of learners such as self-regulation skills and levels of motivation (Azevedo & Cromley, 2004) or epistemological beliefs (Jacobson & Spiro, 1995) may also influence the instructional effectiveness of interactive learning environments. Interactive metacognitive tutors have been developed to help students in acquiring advanced metacognitive skills by providing effective means for understanding learning processes, representing and tracing metacognitive knowledge, and assessing metacognitive skills (Azevedo, Cromley, Winters, Moos, & Greene, 2005; Azevedo & Hadwin, 2005). Metacognitive prompts can be integrated into learning environments; however, they may also increase cognitive load by demanding additional cognitive resources. More powerful research tools using, for example, eye-tracking techniques and think-aloud protocols could be used to establish the instructional efficiency of these methods. Dynamic visualizations techniques may allow students to represent their knowledge in cognitively efficient graphical forms such as dynamic concept maps and diagrams.

The accuracy of diagnostic information concerning levels of learner knowledge is an essential factor that influences the quality of adaptive environments. In most cases, especially when the diagnostic information is based on tracing user interactions with the system, the levels of granularity in representing available knowledge are still rather coarse (e.g., just "yes" or "no" categories). As new technologies for tracking student interactions in real time are developed, more appropriate adaptive procedures may be implemented, and more support could be integrated into interactive learning environments to provide higher levels of customized guidance, optimal content and learner activities.

REFERENCES

Alexander, P. A., & Jetton, T. L. (2003). Learning from traditional and alternative texts: New conceptualization for an information age. In A. Graesser, M. Gernsbacher, & S. Goldman (Eds.), *Handbook of discourse processes* (pp. 199–241). Mahwah, NJ: Erlbaum.

Amadieu, F., Tricot, A., & Marine, C. (2009). Prior knowledge in learning from a non-linear electronic document: Disorientation and coherence of the reading sequences. *Computers in Human Behavior, 25*, 381–388.

Amadieu, F., van Gog, T., Paas, F., Tricot, A., & Marine, C. (2009). Effects of prior knowledge and concept-map structure on disorientation, cognitive load, and learning. *Learning and Instruction, 19*, 376–386.

Anderson, J. R., Corbett, A. T., Koedinger, K. R., & Pelletier, R. (1995). Cognitive tutors: Lessons learned. *The Journal of the Learning Sciences, 4*, 167–207.

Atkinson, R. K., & Renkl, A., (2007). Interactive example-based learning environments: Using interactive elements to encourage effective processing of worked examples. *Educational Psychology Review, 19*, 375–386.

Azevedo, R. & Cromley, J. G. (2004). Does training on self-regulated learning facilitate students' learning with hypermedia? *Journal of Educational Psychology, 96*, 523–535.

Azevedo, R, Cromley, J. G., Winters, F. I., Moos, D.C., & Greene, J.A. (2005). Adaptive human scaffolding facilitates adolescents' self-regulated learning with hypermedia. *Instructional Science, 33*, 381–412.

Azevedo, R. & Hadwin, A. (2005). Scaffolding self-regulated learning and metacognition—Implications for the design of computer-based scaffolds. *Instructional Science, 33*, 367–379.

Balcytiene, A. (1999). Exploring individual processes of knowledge construction with hypertext. *Instructional Science, 27*, 303–328.

Bell, B. S. & Kozlowski, S. W. J. (2002). Adaptive guidance: Enhancing self-regulation, knowledge, and performance in technology-based training. *Personnel Psychology, 55*, 267–306.

Blessing, S. B., & Anderson, J. R. (1996). How people learn to skip steps. *Journal of Experimental Psychology: Learning, Memory, and Cognition, 22,* 576–598.

Calisir, F. & Gurel, Z. (2003). Influence of text structure and prior knowledge of the learner on reading comprehension, browsing and perceived control. *Computers in Human Behavior, 19,* 135–145.

Chen, S. Y., Fan, J. -P., & Macredie, R. D. (2006). Navigation in hypermedia learning systems: Experts vs. novices. *Computers in Human Behavior, 22,* 251–266.

Chi, M. T. H., Bassok, M., Lewis, M. W., Reimann, P., & Glaser, R. (1989). Self-explanation: How students study and use examples in learning to solve problems. *Cognitive Science, 13,* 145–182

Chi, M. T. H., Feltovich, P., & Glaser, R. (1981). Categorization and representation of physics problems by experts and novices. *Cognitive science, 5,* 121–152.

Corbalan, G., Kester, L., & van Merriënboer, J. J. G. (2006). Towards a personalized task selection model with shared instructional control. *Instructional Science, 34,* 399–422.

Corbett, A. T., & Anderson, J. R. (1992). LISP intelligent tutoring systems: research in skill acquisition. In J. H. Larkin & R. W. Chabay (Eds.), *Computer-assisted instruction and intelligent tutoring systems: Shared goals and complimentary approaches* (pp. 73–110). Hillsdale, NJ: Lawrence Erlbaum.

DeStefano, D., & LeFevre, J. -A. (2007). Cognitive load in hypertext reading: A review. *Computers in Human Behavior, 23,* 1616–1641.

Draney, K. L., Pirolli, P., & Wilson, M. (1995). A measurement model for a complex cognitive skill. In P. D. Nichols, S. F. Chipman, & R. L. Brennan (Eds.), *Cognitively diagnostic assessment* (pp. 103–125). Hillsdale, NJ: Lawrence Erlbaum Associates.

Embretson, S. E. (1991). A multidimensional latent trait model for measuring learning and change. *Psychometrika, 56,* 495–516.

Embretson, S. (1993). Psychometric models for learning and cognitive processes. In N. Frederiksen, R. J. Mislevy, & I. I. Bejar (Eds.), *Test theory for a new generation of tests* (pp. 125–150). Mahwah, NJ: Erlbaum.

Ericsson, K. A., & Kintsch, W. (1995). Long-term working memory. *Psychological Review, 102,* 211–245.

Ericsson, K. A., & Simon, H. A. (1993a). Verbal reports as data. *Psychological Review, 87,* 215–251.

Ericsson, K. A., & Simon, H. A. (1993b). *Protocol analysis: Verbal reports as data.* Cambridge, MA: MIT Press.

Gall, J. E., & Hannafin, M. J. (1994). A framework for the study of hypertext. *Instructional Science, 22,* 207–232.

Gerjets, P., & Scheiter, K. (2007). Learner control in hypermedia environments. *Educational Psychology Review, 19,* 285–307.

Jacobson, M. J., & Spiro, R. J. (1995). Hypertext learning environments, cognitive flexibility, and the transfer of complex knowledge: An empirical investigation. *Journal of Educational Computing Research, 12,* 301–333.

Kalyuga, S. (2006a). Assessment of learners' organized knowledge structures in adaptive learning environments. *Applied Cognitive Psychology, 20,* 333–342.

Kalyuga, S. (2006b). Rapid assessment of learners' proficiency: A cognitive load approach. *Educational Psychology, 26,* 613–627.

Kalyuga, S. (2006c). Rapid cognitive assessment of learners' knowledge structures. *Learning and Instruction, 16,* 1–11.

Kalyuga, S. (2007). Expertise reversal effect and its implications for learner-tailored instruction. *Educational Psychology Review, 19,* 509–539.

Kalyuga, S. (2008a). Rapid computer-based diagnostic tests of learners' knowledge. In D. H. Robinson & G. Schraw (Eds.), *Current Perspectives on cognition, learning, and instruction: Recent innovations in educational technology that facilitate student learning* (pp. 195–219). Charlotte, NC: Information Age Publishing.

Kalyuga, S. (2008b). When less is more in cognitive diagnosis: A rapid online method for diagnostic learner task-specific expertise. *Journal of Educational Psychology, 100,* 603–612.

Kalyuga, S., Chandler, P., & Sweller, J. (2000). Incorporating learner experience into the design of multimedia instruction. *Journal of Educational Psychology, 92,* 126–136.

Kalyuga, S., Chandler, P., & Sweller, J. (2001). Learner experience and efficiency of instructional guidance. *Educational Psychology, 21,* 5–23.

Kalyuga, S., Chandler, P., Tuovinen, J., & Sweller, J. (2001). When problem solving is superior to studying worked examples. *Journal of Educational Psychology, 93,* 579–588.

Kalyuga, S., & Sweller, J. (2004). Measuring knowledge to optimize cognitive load factors during instruction. *Journal of Educational Psychology, 96,* 558–568.

Kalyuga, S., & Sweller, J. (2005). Rapid dynamic assessment of expertise to improve the efficiency of adaptive e-learning. *Educational Technology, Research and Development, 53,* 83–93.

Koedinger, K., & Aleven, V. (2007). Exploring the assistance dilemma in experiments with cognitive tutors. *Educational Psychology Review, 19,* 239–264.

Larkin, J., McDermott, J., Simon, D., & Simon, H. (1980). Models of competence in solving physics problems. *Cognitive Science, 4,* 317–348.

Magliano, J. P., & Millis, K. K. (2003). Assessing reading skill with a think-aloud procedure and latent semantic analysis. *Cognition and Instruction, 13,* 251–283.

Martin, J., & van Lehn, K. (1995). A Bayesian approach to cognitive assessment. In P. D. Nichols, S. F. Chipman, & R. L. Brennan (Eds.), *Cognitively diagnostic assessment* (pp. 141–165). Hillsdale, NJ: Erlbaum.

Metzler-Baddeley, C., & Baddeley, R. (2009). Does adaptive training work? Applied *Cognitive Psychology, 23,* 254–266.

Mislevy, R. J. (1994). Evidence and inference in educational assessment. *Psychometrika, 59,* 439–483.

Mislevy, R. J. (1996). Test theory reconceived. *Journal of Educational Measurement, 33,* 379–416.

Mislevy, R. J., Steinberg, L. S., Breyer, F. J., Almond, R. G., & Johnson, L. (2002). Making sense of data from complex assessments. *Applied Measurement in Education, 15,* 363–389.

Pellegrino, J. W., Baxter, G. P., & Glaser, R. (1999). Addressing the "two disciplines" problem: Linking theories of cognition and learning with assessment and instructional practice. In A. Iran-Nejad & P. D. Pearson (Eds.), *Review of research in education. Vol. 24* (pp. 307–353). Washington, DC: AERA.

Pellegrino, J., Chudowsky, N., & Glaser, R., (Eds.). (2001). *Knowing what students know: The science and design of educational assessment*. National Research Council's Committee on the Foundations of Assessment. Washington, DC: National Academy Press.

Renkl, A., & Atkinson, R. K. (2003). Structuring the transition from example study to problem solving in cognitive skills acquisition: A cognitive load perspective. *Educational Psychologist, 38*, 15–22.

Renkl, A., Atkinson, R. K., & Große, C. S. (2004). How fading worked solution steps works—A cognitive load perspective. *Instructional Science, 32*, 59–82.

Renkl, A., Atkinson, R. K., Maier, U. H., & Staley, R. (2002). From example study to problem solving: Smooth transitions help learning. *Journal of Experimental Education, 70*, 293–315.

Russell, M., O'Dwyer, L, & Miranda, H. (2009). Diagnosing students' misconceptions in algebra: Results from an experimental pilot study. *Behavior Research Methods, 41*(2), 414–424.

Salden, R. , Aleven, V., Schwonke, R., & Renkl, A. (in press). The expertise reversal effect and worked examples in tutored problem solving. *Instructional Science*.

Salden, R. J. C. M., Paas, F., van der Pal, J., & van Merriënboer, J. J. G. (2006). Dynamic task selection in a flight management system training. *The International Journal of Aviation Psychology, 16*, 157–174.

Shapiro, A. M. (1999). The relationship between prior knowledge and interactive overviews during hypermedia-aided learning. *Journal of Educational Computing Research, 20*, 143–167.

Shin, E. C., Schallert, D. L., & Savenye, W. C. (1994). Effects of learner control, advisement, and prior knowledge on young students' learning in a hypertext environment. *Educational Technology Research and Development, 42*, 33–46.

Simons, K. D., & Klein, J. D. (2007). The impact of scaffolding and student achievement levels in a problem-based learning environment. *Instructional Science, 35*, 41–72.

Snow, R. E., & Lohman, D. F. (1989). Implications of cognitive psychology for educational measurement. In R. Linn (Ed.), *Educational measurement* (pp. 263–331). New York: Macmillan.

Spiro, R. J., & Jehng, J. (1990). Cognitive flexibility and hypertext: Theory and technology for the nonlinear and multidimensional traversal of complex subject matter. In D. Nix & R. Spiro (Eds.), *Cognition, education, and multimedia: Exploring ideas in high technology*. Hillsdale, NJ: Lawrence Erlbaum Associates.

Sweller, J., Mawer, R., & Ward, M. (1983). Development of expertise in mathematical problem solving. *Journal of Experimental Psychology: General, 12*, 639–661.

Tatsuoka, K. (1990). Toward an integration of Item-Response Theory and cognitive error diagnosis. In N. Frederiksen, R. Glaser, A. Lesgold, & M. G. Shafto (Eds.), *Diagnostic monitoring of skill and knowledge acquisition* (pp. 453–487). Hillsdale, NJ: Lawrence Erlbaum Associates.

Van Merriënboer, J. J. G. (1990). Strategies for programming instruction in high school: Program completion vs. program generation. *Journal of Educational Computing Research, 6*, 265–287.

Van Merriënboer, J. J. G., Kirschner, P. A., & Kester, L. (2003). Taking the load off a learner's mind: Instructional design principles for complex learning. *Educational Psychologist, 38*, 5–13.

Van Merriënboer, J. J. G., Sluijsmans, D., Corbalan, G., Kalyuga, S., Paas, F., & Tattersall, C. (2006). Performance assessment and learning task selection in environments for complex learning. In D. Clark, & J. Elen (Eds.). *Advances in learning and instruction* (pp. 201–220). Maryland Heights, MO: Elsevier Science.

Wilson, M. (1989). Saltus: A psychometric model of discontinuity in cognitive development. *Psychological Bulletin, 105,* 276–289.

CHAPTER 14

COLLABORATIVE VERSUS INDIVIDUAL DIGITAL ASSESSMENTS

Priya K. Nihalani and Daniel H. Robinson
University of Texas at Austin

ABSTRACT

Changes in the economic context within which today's students will function as adults have increased the value of perennial skills such as collaborative and communication skills (Binkley et al., 2009; Dede, 2010; Levy & Murnane, 2004). Today, proficiency in collaborative problem solving is requisite for success in both school and work (O'Neil & Chuang, 2008). At the same time, structuring assessments that evaluate attainment of these skills in 21st century education, specifically collaboration or teamwork, is challenging. When using collaborative assessments, important issues to consider are how to assign credit to each group member and how to account for differences across groups that may bias a given student's performance. This chapter addresses these challenges as well as discusses inappropriate, yet common, implementation of collaborative techniques and preliminary research on applications of cognitive load theory (CLT) to task selection procedures for individual versus collaborative assessments (Hansen & Zapata-Rivera, 2010; Kirschner, Paas, & Kirschner, 2008). We conclude by proposing a framework for structuring both collaborative and individual digital assessments to facilitate collaborative skill in line with 21st century educational objectives.

Technology-Based Assessments for 21st Century Skills, pages 325–344

Proficiency in collaboration and teamwork is requisite for success in today's world of work and school (O'Neil & Chuang, 2008). Research conducted and synthesized over the last decade confirms that information and communication technology (ICT) adoption has transformed an individual's probability for success to be heavily dependent on higher level skill sets related to information use (Buckingham & Willett, 2006; Gera & Gu, 2004; Zohgi, Mohr, & Meyer, 2007). Of the key skills that have been re-conceptualized for 21st century learners, only collaboration and communication—which supports the very nature of collaboration—have been identified as skills that support the observed shifts in the way people work (Binkley et al., 2009; Keen, 1992).

The recent emphasis on developing these skills results from an economy transformed into one that is globalized and characterized by decentralized decision-making, widely shared information, and project teams (Binkley et al., 2009). Work world progress is now often contingent on teams that, as opposed to individuals, often collaborate and communicate through digital technologies (Buckingham & Willett, 2006; O'Neil & Chuang, 2008). It is hardly surprising, then, that organizations experiencing the greatest productivity gains have also reported the enabling communicative affordances provided by ICT (Pilat, 2004) and are conveying the need for educational institutions to produce students capable of teamwork. Furthermore, although employers still base recruitment decisions on formal school-based qualifications, they are increasingly making decisions to fire people on the basis of their poor collaborative styles and team-working skills (Scardamalia, Bransford, Kozma, & Quellmalz, 2010). Such shifts provide the rationale for aligning students' formal qualifications with 21st century skills.

Because education plays a role in priming society's awareness of valued skills via whatever is formally evaluated, a challenge is how assessments should be structured to evaluate 21st century skills. Focusing specifically on collaborative skills, the present chapter addresses this challenge by providing educators with a framework for structuring and implementing assessments that support development of collaborative skill. The framework is built on a synthesis of (1) preliminary applications of cognitive load theory (CLT) to group functioning and assessment task selection procedures (i.e., Hansen & Zapata-Rivera, 2010; Kirschner et al., 2008), (2) robust human memory processes that occur during social interaction, and (3) recent findings of studies further evaluating the nature of group-level assessments (Nihalani, Mayrath, & Robinson, 2010; Nihalani, Schallert, & Sweet, 2009; Nihalani, Wilson, Thomas, & Robinson, 2010). Finally, we conclude by designing a digital collaborative assessment guided by the presented framework.

ASSESSING COLLABORATIVE SKILL

Two key points lay the foundation for designing collaborative assessments. First, ICT support for learning and teaching is further advanced than the more patchy use of ICT to support digital assessment (Gipps, 2005) and thus some trial-and-error or iteration is to be expected. Second, collaboration within education has traditionally been described as a technique for *learning* and thus the term "collaborative learning" has been arbitrarily applied in instances when collaboration techniques are used for summative assessment tasks. However, *collaboration* is a dual concept in that *collaboration for learning* can be distinguished from *collaboration for assessment*—acknowledging that there are overlapping features. These terms will be elaborated on shortly.

DIGITAL ASSESSMENT

ICT plays a well-established role for learning and teaching in higher education compared to the role played to the use of digital assessment (Gipps, 2005). For example, the number of web-based curricula and instructional activities that can be integrated in the classroom continues to grow at exponential rates (Duffy & Cunningham, 1996). Increased capabilities of learning management systems, such as Blackboard and Moodle, provide further evidence for this point (Rubin, Fernandes, Avgerinou, & Moore, 2009). In contrast, the use of digital assessments is only now beginning to extend beyond its infancy. A thorough review is beyond the scope of this chapter (see Mayrath, Clarke-Midura, & Robinson, Chapter 1 in this volume); however, it is important to distinguish between uses of digital assessment to replicate traditional assessments versus those that test new competences.

The most common digital assessment is computer-based assessment (CBA), which is simply the use of computers to deliver, mark, and analyze assignments or exams. CBAs are normally comprised of multiple-choice and short-answer questions, both of which can be automatically scored and are generally used in subject areas with high amounts of factual information (e.g., geography). Use of CBAs to assess relatively recent skills such as ICT literary, or iSkills, is beginning increasing in prevalence as well (Katz, 2007).

The real power of digital assessments is in their potential to expand far beyond simply replicating traditional assessments. For example, online collaborative tasks offer new proficiency estimates that synthesize information from individuals *and* teams along cognitive dimensions (Laurillard, 2009). Design features that can support online measurement are the user interface, predefined messages, and Bayesian networks (O'Neil, Chuang, & Chung, 2003). For example, for online discussion alone, we can now automatically generate data on students' use of domain-specific vocabulary, visually display social relationships based on discourse patterns (Zhang, Scardamalia, Reeve, & Messina, 2007), and enable instructors to generate learner-tailored feedback (Wittwer & Renkle, 2008). However, we will be equipped to create digital assessments that appropriately leverage affordances like these only once we better understand how to develop the 21st century skills we want to evaluate.

COLLABORATION FOR LEARNING

Collaborative learning refers to a small group of students who cognitively and cooperatively engage in a common task to achieve a shared learning goal (Kuhn, Hoppe, Lingnau, & Wichmann, 2006; Slavin, 1996; Soller, 2004; Teasley & Roschelle, 1993). Shared efforts to learn, to understand, and to solve a range of problems are central for constructing collective flexible knowledge structures that can be efficiently applied to successfully complete novel tasks (Murphy & Alexander, 2005). Collaboration fosters such structures by requiring group members to integrate their varying cognitive strengths, monitor their conceptual understanding, and articulate their tacit knowledge during group discussions (Hagman & Hayes, 1986; Johnson, Johnson, & Stanne, 2000; Ormrod, 2008).

Computer-supported collaboration. Due to the surge of distance learning, computer-mediated collaboration for spatially distributed people has rapidly increased in prominence (Leskovac, 1998; Nardi, Kuchinsky, Whittaker, Leichner & Schwarz, 1997). Computer-supported collaboration (CSC) involves use of technology to enable a group of spatially distributed individuals to work together on a common problem or project. The software and online environments run the gamut from simple asynchronous discussion lists to groupware for asynchronous work to synchronous multimedia environments that allow workspace or document sharing (Duffy & Cunningham, 1996; Jonassen, Peck, & Wilson, 1999; Koschmann, 1996). CSC software can generally support many different functions, such as the knowledge-building process, by providing students with a forum for collaboratively presenting arguments to achieve consensus on new and difficult-to-understand information (Kolodner & Guzdial, 1996).

Collaboration for "ineffective" learning. With regards to real world practice, students frequently express disappointment when instructors inform them that a component of their grade will be based on collaborative assignments. Why might this be?

As an observable skill, adeptness at collaboration is best demonstrated while students are engaged in group-level tasks, and understandably so (Salomon & Perkins, 1998). For a given task, collaboration has been deemed effective when the group-level score is greater than that of a nominal group, the sum of individual level performance scores of a fictitious set of individuals with ability levels comparable to the group (e.g., Weldon & Bellinger, 1997; Wright, 2007). Consequently, this benchmark of collaborative assessment provides little insight into within-group interactions or between-group task performance, and is representative of the majority of available collaborative learning research.

The few studies that focus on individual contributions, as opposed to group performance, often report extreme discrepancies between performance scores reported at the group level versus those reported at the individual member level (e.g., Hatano & Inagaki, 1991; Johnson & Johnson, 1991; Salomon, Perkins, & Globerson, 1992; Straus & McGrath, 1994; Webb, 1992). Such discrepancies imply that collaborative tasks disadvantage certain members and have been shown as resulting a number of different ways. The most common pattern is *social loafing*, which describes the tendency of certain members to reduce the amount of effort they exert when working in a group, compared to when working alone (Latane, Williams, & Harkins, 1979). Social loafing manifests as: (1) the free rider effect (Kerr & Brunn, 1983), where some members do not put in their share of work under the assumption that others' efforts will cover their shortfall, and thus causes (2) the sucker effect (Kerr, 1983), where the fully performing members decrease the effort expended in response to the free riders. Yet, even with the prevalence of these dysfunctional processes, collaborative techniques have widespread use and continued support at every tier of education from preschool to graduate school (Johnson & Johnson, 2000). So much so, in fact, that it is almost considered heretical to not include some form of small-group work in one's teaching repertoire. Nevertheless, the "elephant in the room" is that many students loathe group work, so it comes as no surprise that simply placing individuals in groups and assigning tasks may lead to dysfunctional processes and disappointing performance scores (Johnson & Johnson, 1989).

COLLABORATION FOR ASSESSMENT

Efforts to increase the effectiveness of collaboration (group performance versus nominal group performance) have mostly concentrated on variables that are external to the collaborative process itself, such as "optimal" group size or communication mode (e.g., Dillenbourg, 2002; Johnson et al., 2000; Slavin, 1996; Straus & McGrath, 1994; Webb, 1992). Factors that are more fundamental to interpreting the effects of a collaborative environment are typically absent. For example, conclusions on the effects of collaboration should be drawn through a multifaceted technique, combining overall group performance *and* the contribution made by each group member. Another more pressing factor not accounted for has been assessing students' ability to collaborate by considering this skill as a construct on a continuum ranging from novice to mastery. This notion is discussed next.

Collaborative skill. In current frameworks where 21st century learning is described, collaboration has been taught indirectly, through the curricula of various subjects, and, having said that, it is unclear whether collaboration actually has features in common with those subjects through which it is prescriptively taught (Pellegrino, Chudowsky, & Glaser, 2004). Existing collaborative assessment tasks fail to directly measure the knowledge, skills, and abilities (KSAs) reflecting collaborative proficiency (Kester & Paas, 2005). Often, because of the indirect evaluation, the measures used simply determine the quality of the overall group product and do not measure individual members' abilities or contributions. Numerous studies have found that directly instructing students on how to work jointly on activity problems may counter dysfunctional group processes (e.g., the Matthew effect; Cooke, Gorman, Duran, & Taylor, 2007). Before the validity of collaborative assessments can be considered, support for students to develop some degree of collaborative skill must be in place.

To develop and evaluate *collaborative skill*, an operational definition, described in terms that are measurable and aligned with 21st century learners, must be provided (Hargreaves, 2007). Table 14.1 provides these operational definitions as described by the first white paper from the Assessment and Teaching of 21st Century Skills project (Binkley et al., 2009, p. 23). Thus, we define a *collaborative assessment* as one that includes three interrelated components: (1) peer evaluations, (2) group-level tasks that evaluate overall group accountability, and (3) individual tasks that evaluate individual accountability. Using this definition, the following challenging questions emerge:

- What are the task-related features to consider when selecting tasks for the individual versus a collaborative group?
- How can credit be assigned to each member of the group?
- Can between-group differences that may bias a given student's performance be accounted for?
- How can we integrate assessment information from these three components?
- What constitutes "good collaborative assessments"?

The remainder of this chapter focuses on identifying factors that predict when collaboration facilitates greater outcomes compared to working alone, as well as addresses the questions listed above to structure digital assessments so that collaborative skill manifests as one that is consistent with 21st century educational objectives.

TABLE 14.1

Knowledge	Skills	Attitudes/Values/Ethics
Interact effectively with others • Know when it is appropriate to listen and when to speak Work effectively in diverse teams • Know and recognize the individual roles of a successful team and know own strengths and weaknesses recognizing and accepting them in others Manage projects • Know how to plan, set and meet goals and to monitor and re-plan in the light of unforeseen developments	Interact effectively with others • Speak with clarity and awareness of audience and purpose. Listen with care, patience, and honesty • Conduct themselves in a respectable, professional manner Work effectively in diverse teams • Leverage social and cultural differences to create new ideas, increase innovation and quality of work Manage projects • Prioritize and plan work towards the intended result Guide and lead others • Use interpersonal and problem-solving skills to guide others toward a goal • Leverage strengths of others to accomplish a common goal • Demonstrate integrity and ethical behavior in guiding others	Interact effectively with others • Know when it is appropriate to listen and when to speak • Conduct themselves in a respectable, professional manner Work effectively in diverse teams • Show respect for cultural differences • Respond open-mindedly to different ideas and values Manage projects • Persevere to achieve goals, even in the face of competing pressures Be responsible to others • Act responsibly with interests of the larger community in mind

INDIVIDUAL VERSUS COLLABORATIVE INFORMATION PROCESSING

A collaborative assessment, we maintain, includes both individual and group-level tasks. However, differentiating between tasks that are appropriate for an individual learner versus a collaborative group of learners is not necessarily intuitive. Activities assigned to a student are designed based on how an individual processes information. This information-processing approach states that human working memory has a limited processing capacity and can only operate on a few pieces of information at one time

(Baddeley, 1986; Miller, 1956). Thus, as an information processing system, the individual will complete a problem-solving task by organizing and processing task-related information elements in working memory; unrelated information is ignored. The notion that groups may process complex task-related information similarly to individuals has been observed over the previous three decades (Hinsz, Tindale, & Vollrath, 1997; Levine, Resnick, & Higgins, 1993; Stasser, Taylor, & Hanna, 1989) so it makes sense that we explore this approach for comparison. The following section describes how we can differentiate between tasks appropriate for the individual versus the collaborative group by considering both as information processing systems.

GROUP-LEVEL INFORMATION PROCESSING.

As an information processing system, groups experience a distribution advantage where task-associated information elements are divided across multiple working memories (Kirschner, Paas, & Kirshner, 2009). The expanded processing capacity of members' collaborative working memories also creates a collective working space (Laughlin, Vander-Stoep, & Hollingshead, 1991; Stewart & Stasser, 1995) conducive to managing highly complex tasks. However, assigning individuals to groups and assigning tasks to groups does not guarantee effective collaborative completion of those tasks. What does?

Small group research over the past two decades has shown that although basic a priori task-related knowledge is necessary for groups to operate, a high degree of task-related knowledge is not the primary predictor of group effectiveness (Dillenbourg, 2002). Instead, collaborative group success is primarily contingent on the collective knowledge structures that form when members communicate to each other (Barron, 2000; Murphy & Alexander, 2005). Sharing information allows members to reach an agreement regarding each other's reasoning processes, which reduces the potential for within-group variability (Beers, Boshuizen, Kirschner, & Gijselaers, 2005). Group effectiveness then varies as a function of *group-level information processing*, defined as the degree of communication and coordination within a group (Kreijns, Kirschner, & Jochems, 2003). Communication refers to information held by each group member being actively shared and exchanged (Teasley & Roschelle, 1993). Coordination is the extent to which activities being completed by each member are known and is contingent on individual members' ability to engage in communication (Hinsz et al., 1997). The greater the degree to which groups function as information processing systems, the greater their processing capacity, and the more effectively they complete complex tasks that have high volumes of interactive task elements or induce a high processing load due. Recent application of cognitive load considers groups processing capacity to predict when collaboration facilitates greater outcomes compared to working alone (Paas, Touvinen, Tabbers, & van Gerven, 2003).

A cognitive load perspective of group-level information processing. Based on information processing approaches, cognitive load theory (CLT) has traditionally been concerned with how individuals learn from complex cognitive activities and associated element interactivity (Sweller, van Merriënboer, & Paas, 1998). CLT distinguishes between three types of load a given task can impose on the learner: *intrinsic* load describes the inherent element interactivity associated with the to-be-learned material; *germane* load results from use of relevant cognitive resources for meaningful investment in schema construction; and *extraneous* load is the irrelevant cognitive load caused by instruction that does not contribute to learning (Sweller & Chandler, 1994; van Merriënboer & Sweller, 2005). Both germane and extraneous load can be directly manipulated and, because the three loads are additive, the total cognitive load associated with an instructional design should stay within working memory limits (Paas et al., 2003; Paas, Renkl, & Sweller, 2004).

From a CLT perspective, collaboration allows for task-related load to be distributed among group members' working memories, through the distribution advantage discussed previously, so that more complex problems can be addressed within the group's collective working space. When performing complex tasks, collaboration will reduce the high intrinsic load *if* the group is performing as an information processing system. However, the very nature of collaboration induces its own extraneous cognitive load because there are also cognitive costs to establish and maintain these group processes (Baker, Hansen, Joiner, & Traum, 1999). A recent study by Kirschner and colleagues (2009) applied CLT to individual and group-level complex cognitive tasks. They speculated that in collaborative environments, the inherent communication and coordination required for task completion determines the associated intrinsic load. Germane load then results when the extraneous cognitive costs for collaboration pay off because they foster use of requisite skill sets. Extraneous load is imposed when the cognitive costs are ineffective for task completion because it fosters errors, dysfunctional processes, or unnecessary duplication. Thus, if cognitive costs are too high, the advantages to sharing complex task-related load (i.e., distribution of task-associated information elements among collaborative working memories) may be inhibited (Kirschner et al., 2009).

REDUCING COLLABORATIVE-RELATED COGNITIVE COSTS.

Enough small group research has speculated that the high cognitive costs paid during collaboration are significant enough inhibitors of positive outcomes that methods for reducing these costs are warranted (i.e., Johnson

& Johnson, 1994; Paas et al., 2003; Webb & Palincsar, 1996; Whyte, 1991). As it happens, these same options will also support collaborative skill development aligned with 21st century educational objectives. From a CLT perspective, this can be accomplished through (1) reducing intrinsic load associated with collaborative skill by explicitly facilitating related schemata and (2) structuring collaborative assessments as a function of task complexity so that available working memory capacity is allocated to the task itself rather than unnecessary group processes.

Facilitating collaborative skill. According to CLT, the total load is comprised of interacting information elements related to collaboration *and* the tasks that are, in this case, digitally-based; however, the intrinsic load can be reduced by explicitly facilitating collaborative schemata, so that parts of the group process require less mental effort. As a consequence, the overall cognitive load will decrease and working memory capacity that can be allocated towards complex tasks will increase (Baker et al., 1999; Sweller et al., 1998). Recall that collaborative effectiveness varies as a function of group-level information processing (Beers et al., 2005; Salas, Sims, & Burke, 2005), two observables of which are managing subtasks and knowing when to listen versus speak (see KSAs listed in Table 14.1). Experimental studies have demonstrated fruitful interactions and high performance when scripted rules enforcing communication were embedded in collaborative environments (e.g., Dillenbourg, 2002; O'Donnell & Dansereau, 1992; Reiserer, Ertl, & Mandl, 2002). But, rarely were there long-term effects (i.e., collaborative skill development; Deci & Ryan, 1985). A possible reason may be that scripts do not offer feedback or encourage reflection and students' failure to understand specific script elements prevents authentic skill development (Rummel & Spada, 2005). As a consequence, potential group outcomes are inhibited (Johnson & Johnson, 1994; Whyte, 1991). There is a need for practical techniques to ensure positive collaboration—for instance, providing all members opportunities to impart their perspective or encourage members with less task-related knowledge to request explanatory help.

In a recent study conducted by Meade, Nokes, and Morrow (2009), aviation students' verbal protocol analyses demonstrated that direct teamwork training was positively related to group dynamics. Students who received training were significantly more likely to discuss other group members' perspectives if different from their own and engage in collective reasoning. In contrast, students who did not receive training were more likely to simply ignore conflicting perspectives or perceive their group members' contributions as disruptive. Additional research on direct instruction has demonstrated that students experience greater success at managing joint task attention and perceive collaborative tasks as more engaging than their counterparts who did not receive the same instruction (Clark, 1996; Cooke et al., 2007; Retnowati, Ayres, & Sweller, 2010).

In particular, formative digital assessments can be used to reinforce collaborative skill because they guide and encourage social and cognitive processes and help steer teachers' attention to students needing additional support (Beers et al., 2005; Sweller, 2010). Students become more cognizant and reduce off-task behavior.

Competencies reflective of collaborative skill, such as developing positive attitudes towards group members and group cohesion, can also be assessed formatively to support students' development (Johnson & Johnson, 1999; Kirschner, van Vilsteren, Hummel, & Wigman, 1997). Evaluating collaborative skill development through formative assessments is challenging, but technological advances have allowed us to move past relying on time-intensive observational methods such as recording, transcribing, and coding discourse (e.g., Nihalani, Wilson, et al., 2010). Online tools provide new measurement opportunities such as analyzing group discourse, during or after activities, to investigate an individual student's cognizant increase in providing their group members with explanations with elaboration (Laurillard, 2009). Ownership over such skill development can also be given to students themselves. External representations or visualization features can also support fading where the extent of detail provided gradually reduces as collaborative skill develops or expertise increases (Kester & Paas, 2005). *Meta-perspectives*, for instance, is a brainstorming tool that allows students to read through their discourse and tag artifacts such as explanations given but not with elaboration, and, once tagged, a discourse-visualization feature can make thinking visible and indicate areas needing extra work (Nunes, Nunes, & Davis, 2003). As students develop the necessary skill, reduced scaffolds is a vital component (Nihalani, Mayrath, et al., 2010). Studies using *Belvedere*, a program to facilitate collaborative inquiry, have shown that continuing guidance after skill development imposes extraneous cognitive load and may lead to off-task behavior (Buckingham-Shum, & Hammond, 1993; Suthers & Weiner, 1995).

Collaborative skill can also be developed through peer assessment where students (anonymously) evaluate each other after several opportunities for interaction. Knowing that their peers will hold them accountable for their actions is a good way of preventing students from loafing, domination, and other behaviors that are detrimental to group functioning. Peer assessment forces learners to recognize weaknesses and strengths of their peers and to provide justifications that, in turn, makes them more aware of their own behavior (Sluijsmans, Brand-Gruwel, van Merriënboer, & Martens, 2004).

Recently, Nihalani and colleagues (Nihalani, Wilson, et al., 2010) conducted recursive qualitative analyses to identify patterns of discourse that took place within low-performing and high-performing peer teams. Within low-performing teams, certain facilitating interactions that were already present within high-performing teams emerged soon after administering peer assessments. For example, during multiple-choice collaborative assessments, "tabling," momentarily skipping a question when group members were unable to come to consensus, was identified as a collaborative facilitator because tabling allowed students to gather more information about who among their teammates had better mastery of the course material. They could then return to the tabled question with different knowledge about each other as well as about their mastery as a team of the content. Requests to table were common in all teams; however, they were granted more often among high-performing teams reflecting team members' respect for one another. Although peer assessments were unavailable, there was a significant increase in low-performing teams' productive use of tabling moves, leading the researchers to consider the potential impact of students' feedback on their teammates' displayed behavior.

Task selection. According to CLT, cognitive costs associated with the task-related interacting elements may also inhibit positive outcomes (Paas et al., 2003). If a collaborative task has too few associated interacting elements or if a student has sufficient expertise to carry out a task alone, group-level information processing may interfere because it imposes extraneous load (Janssen, Kirschner, Erkens, Kirschner, & Paas, 2010).

Research in the area of memory has provided additional support regarding the consequences of assigning groups with tasks containing too few interacting elements. Investigations comparing individual and group performance have shown that collaborative environments tend to disrupt members' knowledge retrieval for these tasks. Further, this finding has been labeled as one of the most robust within this field of inquiry (e.g., Andersson & Rönnberg, 1995; Finlay, Hitch, & Meudell, 2000; Lorge & Solomon, 1955; Steiner, 1972). For a collaborative assessment task, the demands involved in completing the task alone must exceed an individual's working memory capacity in addition to the cognitive costs needed to deal with ineffective group functioning (Janssen et al., 2010). Although similar cognitive costs do not exist for individuals completing the same task, they have less working memory capacity to work with the interrelated information elements and, consequently, are likely to experience cognitive overload.

PRACTICAL GUIDANCE AND CONCLUSIONS

Operational Constraints

In investigating CSC environments, some researchers have suggested that collaborative tasks will impose a greater load due to additional task elements resulting from coordinating each member's syntax and semantics to establish some form of common ground as compared to face-to-face groups

(Boshuizen & Schijf, 1998). In contrast, several studies have compared collaborative productivity differences for CSC tasks and face-to-face tasks as a function of CSC training. These studies found that the number of words typed by CSC groups were less than those spoken by face-to-face, groups; however, no differences in the *quality* of discourse or group performance scores were evident (Brennan & Lockridge, 2006; Brennan & Ohaeri, 1999; Ekeocha & Brennan, 2008; Whittaker, 2002). Thus, when implementing digital assessments, expertise regarding the assessment tool mediates performance on both the individual and group level. Without sufficient training on the tools in question, student performance will likely be disappointing and misrepresentative of their proficiency level (Meade et al., 2009; Nihalani, Mayrath et al., 2010). Also, students need to have sufficient access to technology such as laptops, smart phones, and so on for such collaborative assessments to be even possible.

With regards to forming groups, there is little definitive research concerning ideal group sizes and interactions. Most research recommends a group size of four or five in an educational setting (Johnson & Johnson, 1994; Mevarech, 1985; Webb, 1992). It is widely accepted that the smaller the group size, the higher the chance for each member to actively participate. Conversely, large groups result in less individual accountability. Regardless of group size, enough time must be allocated for individuals working on their own to ensure that members can bring individual domain knowledge to group for individual accountability (Schmidt, Loyens, van Gog, & Paas, 2007; van Boxtel, van der Linden, & Kanselaar, 2000). Further, just as it is important to include all three components in any collaborative environment, it is just as important to strike the right balance in terms of the relative weight each assessment is assigned. If too much weight is assigned to the peer evaluation, for example, students may become overly concerned with their peers' perceptions of them. After having used these three assessment components in undergraduate courses for several years, we have found a balance that seems to work.

COLLABORATIVE ASSESSMENT: A REAL EXAMPLE

We have used a weighting system where the clear majority of a student's grade consists of individual performance. We have found that individual accountability is absolutely essential before any meaningful group work can occur. Thus, in our undergraduate courses in statistics and learning, students typically take several quizzes and/or exams first as individuals and then with their teams. Bonus points are available to students whose teams outperform other teams. For example, on a 30-item quiz, students may earn up to three bonus points if their team scores the highest among all the teams. They can earn two points if their team gets second place, and one point if their team gets third place. Individuals are *never* penalized for poor team performance. However, enough incentive exists so that teams exert considerable effort into the team testing procedure.

With regard to peer evaluations, we have students complete evaluations of their teammates twice per semester and distribute the anonymous results to each individual. We tell students that the results of the evaluations will only be used at the end of the course for those individuals who find themselves a few points short of a desired grade. Such students must contact the instructor and request an examination of the peer evaluation results. If a student's teammates have said nothing but positive things both times, or if the first was a bit rough but clearly improved by the second time, then the student will be "bumped up" to receive the desired grade. However, for students who have raised the ire of their teammates both times, they do not receive the bump. The advantage of this system is that students will not know if they will be on the cusp of a desired grade until the very end of the course. Thus, it is hoped that they will strive to "play nice in the sandbox" until then and exhibit behaviors that benefit their team.

To increase the validity and practical implementation of collaborative assessments, future research should explore protocol measures as unique indices of domain knowledge or collaborative skill processes. Because we are aiming to develop 21st century skills, it may also be important to investigate collaboration in more realistic task environments and to develop measures of collaborative processes in those contexts.

REFERENCES

Andersson, J., & Rönnberg, J. (1995). Recall suffers from collaboration: Joint recall effects of friendship and task complexity. *Applied Cognitive Psychology, 9,* 199–211.

Baddeley, A. D. (1986). *Working memory.* New York, NY: Oxford University Press.

Baker, M., Hansen, T., Joiner, R., & Traum, D. (1999). The role of grounding in collaborative learning tasks. In P. Dillenbourg (Ed.), *Collaborative learning: cognitive and computational approaches* (pp. 31–63). Amsterdam: Pergamon Press.

Barron, B. (2000). Achieving coordination in collaborative problem-solving groups. *The Journal of the Learning Sciences, 9,* 403–436.

Beers, P. J., Boshuizen, H. P. A., Kirschner, P. A., & Gijselaers, W. H. (2005). Computer support for knowledge construction in collaborative learning environments. *Computers in Human Behavior, 21,* 623–643.

Binkley, M., Erstad, O., Herman, J., Raizen, S., Ripley, M., & Rumble, M. (2009). *Developing 21st century skills and assessments.* White paper from the assessment and learning of 21st Century Skills Project.

Boshuizen, H. P. A., & Schijf, H. J. M. (1998). Problem solving with multiple representations by multiple and single agents: an analysis of the issues involved.

In M. W. van Someren, P. Reimann, H. P. A. Boshuizen, & T. de Jong (Eds.), *Learning with multiple representations* (pp. 137–151). Amsterdam: Pergamon Press.

Brennan, S. E., & Lockridge, C. B. (2006). Computer-mediated communication: A cognitive science approach. In K. Brown (Ed.), *Encyclopedia of language and linguistics* (pp. 775–780). Oxford, UK: Elsevier Ltd.

Brennan, S. E., & Ohaeri, J. O. (1999). Why do electronic conversations seem less polite? The costs and benefits of hedging. *Proceedings, International Joint Conference on Work Activities, Coordination, and Collaboration* (WACC) (pp. 227–235). San Francisco, CA: ACM.

Buckingham, D., & Willett, R. (2006). *Digital generations: Children, young people, and new media.* Mahwah, NJ: Lawrence Erlbaum Associates.

Buckingham-Shum, S., & Hammond, N. (1993). Argumentation-based design rationale: What use at what cost? *International Journal of Man-Machine Studies, 40,* 603–652.

Clark, H. H. (1996). *Using language.* Cambridge, UK: Cambridge University Press.

Cooke, N. J., Gorman, J. C., Duran, J. L., & Taylor, A. R. (2007). Team cognition in experienced command-and-control teams. *Journal of Experimental Psychology: Applied, 13,* 146–157.

Deci, E. L., & Ryan, R. M. (1985). *Intrinsic motivation and self-determination in human behavior.* New York: Plenum.

Dillenbourg, P. (2002). Over-scripting CSCL: The risks of blending collaborative learning with instructional design. In P. A. Kirschner (Ed.), *Three worlds of CSCL: Can we support CSCL?* (pp. 61–91). Heerlen, The Netherlands: Open University of The Netherlands.

Duffy, T. M., & Cunningham, D. J. (1996). Constructivism: implications for the design and delivery of instruction. In D. H. Jonassen (Ed.), *Handbook of research for educational communications and technology* (pp. 170–198). New York: Macmillan Library Reference USA.

Ekeocha, J. O., & Brennan, S. E. (2008). Collaborative recall in face-to-face and electronic groups. *Memory, 16*(3), 245–261.

Finlay, F., Hitch, G. J., & Meudell, P. R. (2000). Mutual inhibition in collaborative recall: Evidence for a retrieval-based account. *Journal of Experimental Psychology: Learning, Memory, & Cognition, 26,* 1556–1567.

Gera, S., & Gu, W. (2004). The effect of organizational innovation and information technology on firm performance. *International Performance Monitor, 9,* 37–51.

Gipps, C. V. (2005). What is the role for ICT-based assessment in universities? *Studies in Higher Education, 30*(2), 171–180.

Hagman, J., & Hayes, J. (1986). *Cooperative learning: Effects of task, reward, and group size on individual achievement.* Alexandria, VA: Army Research Institute for the Behavioral and Social Sciences.

Hansen, E. G., & Zapata-Rivera, D. (2010, May). *ECD and cognitive load theory for improving the accessibility and effectiveness of learning-centered assessments.* Paper presented at the annual meeting of the American Educational Research Association (AERA), Denver, Colorado.

Hargreaves, E. (2007). The validity of collaborative assessment for learning. *Assessment in Education, 14*(2), 185–199.

Hatano, G., & Inagaki, K. (1991). Sharing cognition through collective comprehension activity. In L. B. Resnick, J. M. Levine, & S. D. Teasley (Eds.), *Perspectives on socially shared cognition* (pp. 331–348). Washington, DC: American Psychological Association.

Hinsz, V. B., Tindale, R. S., & Vollrath, D. A. (1997). The emerging conceptualization of groups as information processors. *Psychological Bulletin, 121*(1), 43–64.

Janssen, J., Kirschner, F., Erkens, G., Kirschner, P. A., & Paas, F. (2010). Making the black box of collaborative learning transparent: Combining process-oriented and cognitive load approaches. *Educational Psychology Review, 22*, 139–154.

Johnson, D. W., & Johnson, R. T. (1989). *Cooperation and competition: Theory and research.* Edina, MI: Interaction Book Co.

Johnson, D. W., & Johnson, R. T. (1991). Social interdependence theory and university instruction: Theory into practice. *Swiss Journal of Psychology, 61*, 119–129.

Johnson, D. W., & Johnson, R. T. (1994). *Learning together and alone: Cooperative, competitive and individualistic learning.* Columbus, OH: Allyn & Bacon.

Johnson, D. W., & Johnson, R. T. (1999). *Human relations: Valuing diversity.* Edina, MN: Interaction Book Co.

Johnson, D. W., & Johnson, R. T. (2000). *Joining together: Group theory and group skills* (7th ed.). Boston, MA: Allyn & Bacon.

Johnson, D., Johnson, R. & Stanne, M. (2000). *Cooperative learning methods: A meta-analysis.* Retrieved May 25, 2010 from http://www.co-operation.org/pages/cl-methods.html

Jonassen, D. H., Peck, K. L., & Wilson, B. G. (1999). *Learning with technology: a constructivist perspective.* Upper Saddle River, NJ: Prentice Hall.

Katz, I. (2007). Testing information literacy in digital environments: ETS's iSkills assessment. *Information Technology and Libraries, September,* 1⊠12.

Keen, K. (1992). Competence: what is it and how can it be developed? In J. Lowyck, P. de Potter, & J. Elen (Eds.), *Instructional design: implementation issues* (pp. 111–122). Brussels, Belgium: IBM Education Center.

Kerr, N. L. (1983). Motivation losses in small groups: A social dilemma analysis. *Journal of Personality and Social Psychology, 45*, 819–828.

Kerr, N. L., & Brunn, S. E. (1983). Dispensability of member effort and group motivation losses: Free-rider effects. *Journal of Personality and Social Psychology, 44*, 78–94.

Kester, L., & Paas, F. (2005). Instructional interventions to enhance collaboration in powerful learning environments. *Computers in Human Behavior, 21*, 689–696.

Kirschner, F., Paas, F., & Kirschner, P. A. (2009). A cognitive load approach to collaborative learning: United brains for complex tasks. *Educational Psychology Review, 21*, 31–42.

Kirschner, F., Paas, F., & Kirschner, P. A. (2008). Individual versus group learning as a function of task complexity: An exploration into the measurement of group cognitive load. In J. Zumbach, N. Schwartz, T. Seufert, & L. Kester (Eds.), *Beyond knowledge: The legacy of competence* (pp. 21–28). New York: Springer.

Kirschner, P. A., van Vilsteren, P., Hummel, H., & Wigman, M. (1997). A study environment for acquiring academic and professional competence. *Studies of Higher Education, 22*(2), 151–171.

Kolodner, J. L., & Guzdial, M. (2000). Theory and practice of case-based learning aids. In D. H. Jonassen, & S. M. Land (Eds.), *Theoretical foundations of learning environments* (pp. 215–242). Mahwah, NJ: L. Erlbaum Associates.

Koschmann, T. (Ed.). (1996). *CSCL: Theory and practice of an emerging paradigm.* Mahwah, NJ: Lawrence Erlbaum Associates, Inc.

Kreijns, K., Kirschner, P. A., & Jochems, W. (2003). Identifying the pitfalls for social interaction in computer-supported collaborative learning environments: A review of the research. *Computers in Human Behavior, 19,* 335–353.

Kuhn, M., Hoppe, U., Lingnau, A., & Wichmann, A. (2006). Computational modeling and simulation fostering new approaches in learning probability. *Innovations in Education & Teaching International, 43,* 183–194.

Laurillard, D. (2009). The pedagogical challenges to collaborative technologies. *International Journal of Computer-Supported Collaborative Learning, 4*(1), 5–20.

Latane, B., Williams, K., & Harkins, S. (1979). Many hands make light the work: The causes and consequences of social loafing. *Journal of Personality and Social Psychology, 37*(6), 822–832.

Laughlin, P. R., Vander-Stoep, S. W., & Hollingshead, A. B. (1991). Collective versus individual induction: Recognition of truth, rejection of error, and collective information processing. *Journal of Personality and Social Psychology, 61,* 50–67.

Laurillard, D. (2009). The pedagogical challenges to collaborative technologies. *International Journal of Computer-Supported Collaborative Learning, 4,* 5–20.

Leskovac, H. (1998). Distance learning in legal education: Implications of frame relay videoconferencing. *Albany Law Journal of Science & Technology, 8,* 305–335.

Levin, J. M., Resnick, L. B., & Higgins, E. T. (1993). Social foundations of cognition. *Annual Review of Psychology, 44,* 585–612.

Lorge, J., & Solomon, H. (1955). Two models of group behavior in the solution of eureka-type problems. *Psychometrika, 20,* 139–148.

Meade, M. L., Nokes, T. J., & Morrow, D. G. (2009). Expertise promotes facilitation on a collaborative memory task. *Memory, 17*(1), 39–48.

Mevarech, Z. R. (1985). The effects of cooperative mastery learning strategies on mathematics achievement. *Journal of Educational Research, 78*(6), 372–377.

Miller, R. (1956). The magic number of seven plus or minus two: Some limits on our capacity for processing information. *Psychological Review, 63,* 81–97.

Murphy, P. K., & Alexander, P. A. (2005). *Understanding how students learn: A guide for instructional leaders.* Thousand Oaks, CA: Corwin Press.

Nardi, B. A., Kuchinsky, A., Whittaker, S., Leichner, R., & Schwarz, H. (1997). Video-as-data: Technical and social aspects of a collaborative multimedia application. In K. E. Finn, A. J. Sellen, & S. B. Wilbur (Eds.), *Video-mediated communication* (pp. 487–517). Mahwah, NJ: Lawrence Erlbaum Associates, Inc.

Nihalani, P. K., Mayrath, M. C., & Robinson, D. H. (2010). *Does level of expertise affect transfer when using a complex simulation in a collaborative learning environment?* Manuscript currently under review.

Nihalani, P. K., Wilson, B., Thomas, G., & Robinson, D. H. (2010). What determines high- and low-performing groups? The superstar effect. *Journal of Advanced Academics, 21*(30), 520–529.

Nunes, C. A. A., Nunes, M. M. R., & Davis, C. (2003). Assessing the inaccessible: Metacognition and attitudes. *Assessment in Education: Principles, Policy & Practice, 10,* 375–388.

O'Donnell, A. M., &, Dansereau, D. F. (1992). Scripted cooperation in student dyads: A method for analyzing and enhancing academic learning and performance. In R. Hertz-Lazarowitz & N. Miller (Eds.), *Interaction in cooperative groups. The theoretical anatomy of group learning* (pp. 120–141). New York: Cambridge University Press.

O'Neil, H. F., Chuang, S. H., & Chung, G. K. W. K. (2003). Issues in the computer-based assessment of collaborative problem solving. *Assessment in Education, 10*(3), 361–373.

Ormrod, J. E. (2008). *Human learning* (5th ed,). Alexandria, VA: Prentice Hall.

Paas, F., Renkl, A., & Sweller, J. (2004). Cognitive load theory: instructional implications of the interaction between information structures and cognitive architecture. *Instructional Science, 32,* 1–8.

Paas, F., Tuovinen, J. E., Tabbers, H., & Van Gerven, P. W. M. (2003). Cognitive load measurement as a means to advance cognitive load theory. *Educational Psychologist, 38,* 63–71.

Pellegrino, J. W., Chudowsky, N. & Glaser, R. (2004). *Knowing what students know: The science and design of educational assessment.* Washington, DC: National Academy Press.

Pilat, D. (2004). *The economic impact of ICT: A European perspective.* Paper presented at a conference on IT Innovation, Tokyo.

Reiserer, M., Ertl, B., & Mandl, H. (2002). Fostering collaborative knowledge construction in desktop videoconferencing. Effects of content schemes and cooperation scripts in peer-teaching settings. In G. Stahl (Ed.), *Proceedings of the Computer Support for Collaborative Learning (CSCL) 2002 Conference* (pp. 379–388). Mahwah, NJ: Lawrence Erlbaum Associates, Inc.

Retnowati, E., Ayres, P., & Sweller, J. (2010). Worked example effects in individual and group work settings. *Educational Psychology, 30,* 349–367.

Rummel, N., & Spada, H. (2005). Learning to collaborate: An instructional approach to promoting collaborative problem solving in computer-mediated settings. *The Journal of the   Learning Sciences, 14*(2), 201–241.

Salas, E., Sims, D., & Burke, C. (2005). Is there a 'Big Five' in teamwork? *Small Group Research, 36,* 555–599.

Salomon, G., & Perkins, D. N. (1998). Individual and social aspects of learning. *Review of Research in Education, 23,* 1–24.

Salomon, G., Perkins, D. N., & Globerson, T. (1992). Partners in cognition: Extending human intelligence with intelligent technologies. *Educational Researcher, 20*(3), 2–9.

Scardamalia, M., Bransford, J., Kozma, B., & Quellmalz, E. (2010). *New assessments and environments for knowledge building.* White paper from the Assessment and Learning of 21st Century Skills Project.

Schmidt, H. G., Loyens, S. M. M., Van Gog, T., & Paas, F. (2007). Problem-based learning is compatible with human cognitive architecture: Commentary on Kirschner, Sweller, and Clark (2006). *Educational Psychologist, 42*(2), 91–97.

Slavin, R. E. (1996). Research on cooperative learning and achievement: What we know, what we need to know. *Contemporary Educational Psychology, 21*, 43–69.

Sluijsmans, D. M. A., Brand-Gruwel, S., van Merriënboer, J. J. G., & Martens, R. (2004). Training teachers in peer-assessment skills: Effects on performance and perceptions. *Innovations in Education and Training International, 41*, 59–78.

Soller, A. (2004). Understanding knowledge-sharing breakdowns: A meeting of the quantitative and qualitative minds. *Journal of Computer Assisted Learning, 20*, 212–233.

Stasser, G., Taylor, L. A., & Hanna, C. (1989). Information sampling in structured and unstructured discussions of three- and six-person groups. *Journal of Personality and Social Psychology, 57*, 67–78.

Steiner, I. D. (1972). *Group process and productivity.* New York: Academic.

Stewart, D. D., & Stasser, G. (1995). Expert role assignment and information sampling during collective recall and decision-making. *Journal of Personality and Social Psychology, 69*, 619–628.

Straus, S. G., & McGrath, J. E. (1994). Does the medium matter? The interaction of task type and technology on group performance and member reactions. *Journal of Applied Psychology, 79*(1), 87–97.

Suthers, D., & Weiner, A. (1995) *Groupware for developing critical discussion skills.* Retrieved May 26, 2010 from http://www.cscl95.indiana.edu/cscl95/suthers.html

Sweller, J. (2010). Element interactivity and intrinsic, extraneous, and germane cognitive load. *Educational Psychology Review, 22*, 123–138.

Sweller, J., & Chandler, P. (1994). Why some material is difficult to learn. *Cognition and Instruction, 12*(3), 185–233.

Sweller, J., van Merriënboer, J., & Paas, F. (1998). Cognitive architecture and instructional design. *Educational Psychology Review, 10*, 251–296.

Teasley, S. D., & Roschelle, J. (1993). Constructing a joint problem space: The computer as a tool for sharing knowledge. In S. P. Lajoie, & S. J. Derry (Eds.), *Computers as cognitive tools* (pp. 229–261). Hillsdale, NJ: Erlbaum.

van Boxtel, C., van der Linden, J., & Kanselaar, G. (2000). Collaborative learning tasks and the elaboration of conceptual knowledge. *Learning and Instruction, 10*, 311–330.

van Merriënboer, J., & Sweller, J. (2005). Cognitive load theory and complex learning: Recent developments and future directions. *Educational Psychology Review, 17*, 147–177.

Webb, G. (1992). On pretexts for higher education development activities. *Higher Education, 24*, 351–361.

Webb, N. M., & Palincsar, A. S. (1996). Group processes in the classroom. In D. C. Berliner (Ed.), *Handbook of educational psychology* (pp. 841–873). New York, NY: Simon & Schuster Macmillan.

Weldon, M. S., & Bellinger, K. D. (1997). Collective memory: Collaborative and individual processes in remembering. *Journal of Experimental Psychology. Learning, Memory, and Cognition, 23*, 1160–1175.

Whyte, G. (1991). Decision failures: Why they occur and how to prevent them. *Academy of Management Executive, 5*(3), 23–31.

Whittaker, S. (2002). Theories and methods in mediated communication. In A. Graesser, M. Gernsbacher, & S. Goldman (Eds.), *The handbook of discourse processes* (pp. 243–286). Hillsdale, NJ: Lawrence Erlbaum Associates Inc.

Wittwer, J., & Renkl, A. (2008). Why instructional explanations often do not work: A framework for understanding the effectiveness of instructional explanations. *Educational Psychologist, 43,* 49–64.

Wright, D. B. (2007). Calculating nominal group statistics in collaborative studies. *Behavior Research Methods, 39,* 460–470.

Zhang, J., Scardamalia, M., Reeve, R., & Messina, R. (2007). Socio-cognitive dynamics of knowledge building in the work of nine- and ten-year-olds. *Educational Technology Research and Development, 55*(2), 117–145.

Zohgi, C., Mohr, R., & Meyer, P. (2007). *Workplace organization and innovation.* Washington, DC: Bureau of Labor Statistics.

CHAPTER 15

TECHNOLOGY-BASED ASSESSMENT IN THE INTEGRATED CURRICULUM

**Jeroen J. G. van Merriënboer and
Cees P. M. van der Vleuten**
Maastricht University, the Netherlands

ABSTRACT

This chapter describes guidelines for technology-based assessment in an integrated, competence-based curriculum. Such a curriculum may be developed on the basis of van Merriënboer's four-component instructional design model (4C/ID-model). The curriculum then consists of (a) learning tasks, which are based on real-life tasks and range from relatively simple tasks with ample learner support and guidance to more complex professional tasks without support and guidance; (b) supportive information, which aims to develop the mental models and cognitive strategies necessary to perform non-routine aspects (i.e., problem solving, reasoning) of tasks; (c) procedural information, which aims to develop the cognitive rules necessary to perform routine aspects of tasks; and (4) part-task practice, which aims to develop selected routine aspects to a high level of automaticity. For the highest levels of Miller's pyramid, guidelines for assessment in the integrated curriculum are presented and illustrated for the medical domain. For the educational setting, the

Technology-Based Assessments for 21st Century Skills, pages 345–369

assessment of part tasks and whole tasks is described at the "shows how" level; for the professional setting, the assessment of whole tasks is described at the "does" level. Together, discussed technologies provide the theoretical building blocks to underpin future assessment technologies.

INTRODUCTION

In many Western countries, there is a strong development in the direction of competence-based education (Weigel, Mulder, & Collins, 2007). In the field of curriculum design and development, the curriculum is no longer seen as a set of courses or subjects but as an integrated whole aiming at the long-term development of competencies: the integrated curriculum. In such an integrated curriculum, rich learning tasks called problems, projects or cases are typically used to drive student learning. In the field of assessment and educational measurement, assessments are no longer seen as a random indication of the student's knowledge, but as instruments that monitor progress and facilitate learning. In competence-based assessment, aggregation instruments such as logbooks and portfolios are often used to gather information from different assessors and to monitor and steer the learning process.

The problem that will be tackled in this chapter is that the fields of curriculum design and assessment are largely unrelated, with their own research communities and their own journals. As a result, most models of curriculum design provide little information, if any information at all, on the development of a matching assessment program. And the other way round, most models on new types of assessment provide little guidance, if any guidance at all, on how to include these assessments in a competence-based curriculum. Yet a perfect match between curriculum and assessment is necessary to effectively promote student learning (Carr & Harris, 2001). Therefore, this chapter aims to illuminate what good assessment looks like in an integrated, competence-based curriculum. Guidelines are presented and illustrated with examples from the medical domain.

The structure of this chapter is as follows. First, the integrated curriculum is described using van Merriënboer 's four-component instructional design model (4C/ID; van Merriënboer & Kirschner, 2007). Such a curriculum is built from four interrelated components: Learning tasks, which are based on real-life tasks and provide the backbone of the curriculum; supportive information; procedural information; and part-task practice, which are carefully connected to this backbone. Second, the highest levels of Miller's pyramid (1990) are used to describe ten guidelines for good assessment in the integrated curriculum. For the educational setting, the assessment of part tasks and whole tasks is described at Miller's "shows how" level; for the professional setting, the assessment of whole tasks is described at the "does" level. Third, main conclusions and future research directions for assessment in the integrated curriculum are presented.

THE INTEGRATED CURRICULUM

The basic message of the four-component instructional design model (van Merriënboer, 1997; van Merriënboer, Clark, & de Croock, 2002; van Merriënboer & Kirschner, 2007) is that an integrated curriculum aimed at the development of professional competencies can always be described in terms of four interrelated components.

1. Learning Tasks: concrete, authentic "whole-task" experiences provided to learners in order to promote the simultaneous development of both non-routine (reasoning, problem solving) and routine behaviors.
2. Supportive Information: information that helps to learn and perform non-routine aspects of learning tasks. It provides the bridge between learners' prior knowledge and the learning tasks.
3. Procedural Information: information that is prerequisite to the learning and performance of routine aspects of learning tasks. Procedural information is not only relevant to learning tasks but also to:
4. Part-task Practice: additional practice in order to promote automation of selected routine aspects of learning tasks.

Learning Tasks

A sequence of learning tasks is the backbone of an integrated curriculum aimed at the development of professional competencies (see Figure 15.1, which represents the learning tasks as large circles). The learning tasks are typically performed in a simulated or real task environment and provide whole-task practice. They confront the learners with a sizeable set of constituent skills from the whole complex skill or professional competency taught. It is important to stress that learning tasks should engage learners in activities that require them to work with the constituent skills, as opposed to activities in which they have to study general information about or related to the skills. For the non-routine aspects, learning tasks promote the construction of cognitive schemas by inductive processing (e.g., Halford, Bain, Maybery, & Andrews, 1998). That is, the learning tasks stimulate learners to construct cognitive schemas by mindfully abstracting away from the concrete experiences that the learning tasks provide.

Variability. A high level of variability of learning tasks is of utmost importance. That is, learning tasks should differ from each other on all dimensions on which tasks in the real world also differ from each other—for example, in terms of the saliency of defining characteristics, the context in which the task has to be performed, the familiarity of the task, and so forth. This high variability is necessary to promote the development of rich cognitive schemas, which allow for transfer from the educational program to the real world (Bowden & Marton, 2004; Norman, 2009).

Task classes. It is clearly impossible to provide highly complex learning tasks right from the start of the training program because this would yield excessive cognitive load for the learners, which impairs learning and performance (Van Merriënboer & Sweller, 2005, 2010). Thus, learners will typically start their work on relatively easy learning tasks and progress towards more difficult tasks. Task classes are used to define easy-to-difficult categories of learning tasks and to steer the process of selection and development of suitable learning tasks (see the dotted boxes around the circles in Figure 15.1). Learning tasks within a particular task class are equivalent in the sense that the tasks can be performed on the basis of the same body of knowledge. A more difficult task class requires more knowledge or more

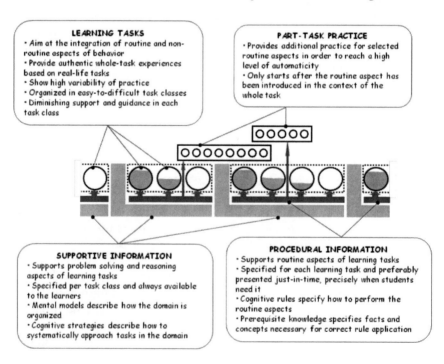

LEARNING TASKS
• Aim at the integration of routine and non-routine aspects of behavior
• Provide authentic whole-task experiences based on real-life tasks
• Show high variability of practice
• Organized in easy-to-difficult task classes
• Diminishing support and guidance in each task class

PART-TASK PRACTICE
• Provides additional practice for selected routine aspects in order to reach a high level of automaticity
• Only starts after the routine aspect has been introduced in the context of the whole task

SUPPORTIVE INFORMATION
• Supports problem solving and reasoning aspects of learning tasks
• Specified per task class and always available to the learners
• Mental models describe how the domain is organized
• Cognitive strategies describe how to systematically approach tasks in the domain

PROCEDURAL INFORMATION
• Supports routine aspects of learning tasks
• Specified for each learning task and preferably presented just-in-time, precisely when students need it
• Cognitive rules specify how to perform the routine aspects
• Prerequisite knowledge specifies facts and concepts necessary for correct rule application

Figure 15.1 An integrated curriculum consisting of four components.

elaboration of knowledge for effective performance. The basic idea is to use a whole-task approach where the first task class refers to the easiest version of whole tasks experts may encounter in the workplace. For increasingly more difficult task classes, the assumptions that simplify task performance are relaxed. The final task class represents all tasks, including the most complex ones that professionals encounter in the workplace.

Support and guidance. While there is no increasing difficulty for the learning tasks within the same task class, they do differ with regard to the amount of support and guidance provided to learners. Much support is given for learning tasks early in a task class, and no support is given for the final learning tasks in a task class. This process of diminishing support as learners acquire more expertise is called "scaffolding." It is repeated for each subsequent task class, yielding a saw-tooth pattern of support throughout the whole training program (see the filling of the circles in Figure 15.1). In effect, each learning task is in the "zone of proximal development" of the learner (Vygotsky, 1978). The basic idea is that learners learn most when they are confronted with a task that is actually too difficult for them, but that they can nevertheless perform thanks to the support and guidance given to them.

The difference between supported and unsupported learning tasks is particularly relevant to the assessment of learners' performance. Usually, assessment of supported learning tasks (i.e., "filled" learning tasks in Figure 15.1) will be formative and improvement oriented. It is used to monitor learners' progress and to remediate when necessary. The assessment of unsupported learning tasks may also be summative. Ideally, unsupported learning tasks are performed in the real professional setting so that assessments indicate if learners are able to perform authentic tasks *at a particular level of difficulty* up to the standards. If learners reach the standards, they can proceed to a next task class, that is, continue their learning based on more difficult tasks for which they receive support and guidance again. If they do not reach the standards, they need to continue practicing tasks at the same level of difficulty.

Supportive Information

Obviously, learners need information in order to work fruitfully on (non-routine aspects of) learning tasks and to genuinely learn from those tasks. This supportive information provides the bridge between what learners already know and what they need to know to work on the learning tasks. It is the information that teachers typically call "the theory" and which is often presented in study books and lectures. Because the same body of general knowledge underlies all learning tasks in the same task class, and because it is not known beforehand which knowledge is precisely needed to success-fully perform a particular learning task, supportive information is not cou-pled to individual learning tasks but to task classes (see the grey L-shapes in Figure 15.1). The supportive information for each subsequent task class is an addition to or an elaboration of the previous information, allowing the learners to do things that could not be done before. Instructional methods for the presentation of supportive information primarily promote schema construction through elaboration, by helping students to establish rela-tionships between newly presented information elements and their prior knowledge. The cognitive schemas that may help learners to perform non-routine aspects of complex tasks come in two forms. Mental models allow them to reason within the learning domain, and cognitive strategies allow them to systematically approach problems in this domain.

Mental models. Mental models are declarative representations of how the world is organized and may contain both general, abstract knowledge and concrete cases that exemplify this knowledge. So, strong models allow for both abstract and case-based reasoning. Mental models may be viewed from different perspectives and can be analyzed as conceptual models, structural models, or causal models. Conceptual models (what is this?) allow for the classification or description of objects, events or activities. For example, knowledge about the names of the many parts in the human body helps medical doctors to communicate with each other about injuries, diseases, and so forth. Structural models (how is this organized?) describe how things are built or constructed. For example, knowledge about the relative loca-tions of the organs in the human body helps a surgeon to make decisions on where to make an incision. Causal models (how does this work?) focus on how principles affect each other and help to interpret processes, give ex-planations for events and make predictions. For example, knowledge about the working of the human respiratory system, and how each element of it affects other elements, helps medical doctors to make diagnoses.

Cognitive Strategies. Like mental models, cognitive strategies contain both general, abstract knowledge and concrete cases that exemplify this knowl-edge. They may be analyzed as systematic approaches to problem solving (SAPs), describing the successive phases in a problem solving process and the rules-of-thumb or heuristics that may be helpful to successfully com-plete each of the phases. For example, the main phases for conducting a surgical intervention are initialization, the main interventional cycle, termi-nation, aftercare, and follow-up. For each phase, there may be sub phases and rules-of-thumb of what might be effective actions under particular cir-cumstances. The rules-of-thumb will typically specify which actions may be taken given factors such as type of lesions or injuries, risk-benefit relations, available instruments, and so forth.

Procedural Information

Whereas supportive information pertains to the non-routine aspects of a complex skill, procedural information pertains to the routine aspects—that is, constituent skills that should be performed after the educational program in a highly similar way over different problem situations. Procedural information provides learners with the step-by-step knowledge they need to know in order to perform the routine aspects of learning tasks. They can be in the form of, for example, directions teachers or tutors typically give to their learners during practice, acting as an "assistant looking over your shoulder." Because the procedural information is identical for many learning tasks, which all share the same routine aspects, it is typically provided during the first learning task for which the routine is relevant (see the dark grey beam with upward-pointing arrows in Figure 15.1). For subsequent learning tasks, procedural information is quickly faded away as the learners gain more expertise (a principle called "fading"). Instructional methods for the presentation of procedural information primarily promote the construction of cognitive rules through a process called knowledge compilation (Anderson, 1987). The procedural information is specified at the entry level of the learners, that is, at a level that is suitable to present to the lowest-level ability learner. It is not critical that the information is embedded in existing schemas in declarative memory. Because of this, during presentation no particular reference has to be made to related knowledge structures in long-term memory. Cognitive rules help learners to perform routine aspects of learning tasks, and prerequisite knowledge is conditional to the development of such rules.

Cognitive rules. The process of knowledge compilation, which leads to the construction of cognitive rules, is facilitated when the information necessary for forming the rules is available in working memory when learners need it during task performance. It concerns information that describes the rules themselves (how-to instructions) or procedures that combine those rules. For instance, when a doctor in training is conducting a particular surgical operation for the first time, the supervisor will preferably give *just-in-time* instructions on how to hold the instruments, how to position the patient, and how to make an incision, that is, during task performance and not in a theory lesson beforehand. Organization in small units is considered to be essential because only the presentation of relatively small amounts of new information at the same time can prevent processing overload during practice.

Prerequisite knowledge. Another part of the procedural information is the knowledge that is prerequisite to a correct performance of the rules discussed above. Often, the description of the rule that must be applied and the description of the knowledge that is prerequisite for correctly applying this rule are combined with each other. For example, a rule may state that "in order to start this piece of equipment, you must first switch it on" and also indicate that the on/off-switch is located on the back of the machine (i.e., a fact that is prerequisite to a correct application of the rule). These examples make clear that procedural information may best be characterized as "how-to instruction" or "rule-based instruction" (Fisk & Gallini, 1989).

Part-Task Practice

Learning tasks make an appeal to both non-routine and routine behaviors. Often, learning tasks provide enough opportunity to practice both the non-routine and the routine aspects of the complex skill up to the standards. However, if a high level of automaticity of particular routine aspects is required, the learning tasks may provide insufficient repetition to reach this. Then, it is necessary to include additional part-task practice for those selected routine aspects in the educational program (see the series of small circles in Figure 15.1). Part-task practice promotes the strengthening of cognitive rules, which is a very slow process that requires extensive amounts of practice. Well-known examples of part-task practice are letting children drill on multiplication tables or playing scales on musical instruments. It is critical to start part-task practice within an appropriate "cognitive context" because it has been found to be most effective after exposure to a simple version of the whole complex skill (Carlson, Khoo, & Elliot, 1990). This allows learners to identify the activities that are required to integrate the routine aspect in the whole learning tasks.

Summarizing, we described an integrated curriculum as a skeleton built from four components. The backbone of the skeleton consists of learning tasks, which serve as the vertebrae. It is critical that the other three components (supportive information, procedural information, part-task practice) are connected to this backbone at the right places; if not, this will jeopardize the sturdiness of the whole skeleton. Thus, supportive information should be linked to classes of equally difficult learning tasks, procedural information should be linked to the first learning tasks for which it is relevant, and part-task practice should only be introduced after the routine aspect it is dealing with has been introduced in a whole learning task. A lack of integration will always have negative effects on learning and transfer (van Merriënboer, 1997).

ASSESSMENT IN THE INTEGRATED CURRICULUM

How should learners be assessed in an integrated curriculum? First, the 4C/ID-model makes clear that it is useful to make a distinction between assessments for the four different components. Assessment technologies for meaningful learning tasks that involve problem solving are different from assessment technologies for part tasks that focus on routine behaviors, assessment technologies for part-task performance are different from assessment technologies for knowledge of supportive information, and so forth. Second, the 4C/ID-model indicates that it is useful to make a distinction between the assessment of *supported* learning tasks, which provide guidance and support to learners in an educational setting, and *unsupported* learning tasks, which are typically performed in a professional setting. The next sections will first relate the 4C/ID-model to Miller's pyramid, which makes a distinction between different levels of assessment (Miller, 1990). The lowest level (Knows) refers to factual knowledge. If one is able work with the factual knowledge, apply it to problems or authentic tasks, this is called Knowing How and represents the second level. At the third level (Showing How), a learner is able to perform complex tasks in a simulated or laboratory environment. Typically this is what happens in assessment centers. The tasks are complex and behavioral, but the situation is not completely authentic. When these tasks are conducted in the real life setting, we speak of the final and fourth level of Miller's pyramid. We will describe assessment technologies for the two highest levels in Miller's pyramid, the "shows-how" level for, in order, assessment of part tasks and assessment of supported whole tasks in an educational setting, and the "does" level for assessment of unsupported whole tasks in a professional setting.

Miller's Pyramid

Figure 15.2 relates the four components in an integrated curriculum to Miller's pyramid of competence assessment (1990). We have linked this pyramid to the 4C/ID framework. First, on the lower levels, an additional distinction has been made by us between routine and non-routine aspects; at the higher levels, this distinction does not make sense because whole learning tasks always make on appeal to both routine and non-routine behaviors. Second, the four components are placed in the pyramid to indicate at which level they need to be assessed.

Procedural information is placed in the lower left area of the pyramid: It relates to the "knows-how" level (e.g., tell me how to start up this equipment) and "knows" level (e.g., where is the on/off button located on this piece of equipment?) for the routine aspects of behavior. Supportive information is placed in the lower right area of the pyramid: It also relates to the "knows-how" (e.g., tell me how you would approach this problem) and "knows" level (e.g., explain how the human heart works), but now for the non-routine aspects of behavior that involve reasoning and problem solv-

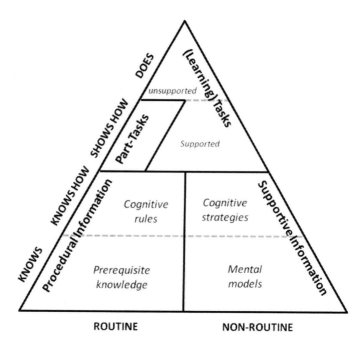

Figure 15.2 The four components in Miller's pyramid.

ing. Part-task practice is placed on the left side of the "shows-how" level. Learners demonstrate their ability to perform particular skills, but the focus is on routine behaviors. Finally, learning tasks are placed on the highest levels, in such a way that they always make on appeal on both routine and non-routine behaviors. On the "shows-how" level, assessments are based on predesigned, supported tasks that will typically be performed in an educational setting. Finally, on the "does" level, assessments are based on professional, unsupported tasks that will typically be performed in clerkships or internships in the workplace, that is, in a professional setting.

The pyramid clearly indicates that single-point assessments have their limitations and any form of assessment will be confined to one part of the pyramid. An integrated curriculum should thus always be combined with a comprehensive program of assessment (Baartman, Bastiaens, Kirschner, & van der Vleuten, 2006; van der Vleuten & Schuwirth, 2005). Such a program acknowledges that each single assessment is a biopsy and a broad collection of biopsies, from different parts of the pyramid, is needed to provide a complete picture.

Although a comprehensive program of assessment should always deal with the whole pyramid, we will focus the remainder of this chapter on the two highest levels of the pyramid. This is in line with historical developments, because the literature shows a steady movement from assessment on the "knows" level to assessment on the "does" level. Assessment at the two bottom layers, aimed at the testing of (factual) knowledge and the application of knowledge, has a long history and could almost be labeled "established" assessment technology. The following sections, therefore, will focus on assessment technologies at the "shows how" level, where a further distinction is made between showing how to perform part tasks and showing how to perform whole tasks in an educational setting, and the "does" level, where assessments focus on the performance of whole tasks in a professional work setting.

The "Shows How" Level: Assessment of Part Tasks

In many curricula, assessments on the "shows-how" level are limited to part tasks. In medical curricula, for example, the Objective Structured Clinical Examination (OSCE) (Harden, Stevenson, Downie, & Wilson, 1975) is a popular approach based on objective testing and direct observation of student performance during planned clinical encounters. The OSCE includes several "test stations" in which examinees are expected to perform specific clinical tasks within a specified time period. To complete the examination, students rotate through a series of stations that each measure one particular aspect of whole-task performance (as few as two or as many as 20). OSCE stations are most often planned clinical encounters in which a student interacts with a standardized simulated patient. A trained observer scores the student's performance for part tasks such as taking a patient history, performing a physical examination or diagnostic procedure, or advising a patient. A standardized rating form or checklist specifies the evaluation criteria and the scoring system to be used for each station. The more items are marked as "done" on the checklist, the higher the score.

Research has identified a number of serious shortcomings of OSCEs and led to an increased interest in the use of whole tasks for assessment. The shortcomings mainly relate to authenticity and variability. With regard to authenticity, OSCEs tend to focus more on the response format (i.e., what the learner has to do) than on the stimulus format (i.e., the nature of the task given to the learner). What one is measuring or the validity of assessment, however, is more determined by the stimulus format than by the response format (Schuwirth & van der Vleuten, 2004). Actually, written forms of assessment can predict OSCE performance to a large extent (van der Vleuten, van Luijk, & Beckers, 1989). An implication is that we need to worry more about constructing appropriate stimulus formats than response formats. Just like good learning tasks, good assessment tasks should be authentic and be based on real-life tasks. The classic OSCE in medical curricula consists of short stations assessing clinical skills in fragmentation (e.g., station 1: examination of the abdomen, station 2: communication). This is not authentic to the real situation the OSCE intends to emulate. The use of whole tasks and integrated skills assessment, more closely reflecting the real clinical encounter, seems thus more important as a stimulus format.

With regard to variability, a disconcerting finding is that a learner's performance on one assessment task is a poor predictor of his or her performance on another assessment task. This is called the "content specificity" problem. Research on OSCEs showed that content specificity is the dominant source of unreliability (Petrusa, 2002). All other sources of error (i.e., assessors, patients, checklists) are either small or can be controlled for (van der Vleuten & Swanson, 1990). The original motivation of OSCEs to increase reliability by objectifying and standardization (the "O" and "S" in the acronym) did thus not come true. The OSCE is as reliable as any method, all depending on the sampling of stations (i.e., assessment tasks) and assessors (Petrusa, 2002). The conclusion is that we cannot rely on small samples of assessment tasks across content. Large samples are required to make reliable inferences about the competence of a learner. Like variability in a set of learning tasks is needed to develop competence, variability in a set of assessment tasks is needed to measure this competence. In more simplistic terms, one measure is no measure and we should always be extremely careful with single-point assessments—not only because they are unreliable, but also because learners will quickly learn about the assessments and start to memorize checklists, making them trivial (van Luijk, van der Vleuten, & van Schelven, 1990).

To conclude, part-task practice may be an important component of the integrated curriculum to automate routine aspects of behavior. As such, part tasks may also be used for assessment, but *only* if they are limited to routines. Then, assessments should not focus on accuracy (is the learner able to show how the task is performed?), but on speed and the ability to perform the task under high workload, for instance, combined with other tasks. Assessments using part tasks not limited to routines, such as OSCEs, have all sorts of undesirable effects such as lack of authenticity and content specificity. For the assessment of meaningful behaviors, combining routine and non-routine aspects, whole tasks seem to be more suitable for assessment purposes.

The "Shows-How" Level: Assessment of Whole Tasks

This section describes assessments that require the learners to show whole, meaningful task performance in an educational setting. Like learning tasks, the assessment tasks are pre-designed tasks at a level of difficulty and with a level of support and guidance that is attuned to the learners. We discuss ten research-based guidelines for the assessment of whole tasks. The guidelines are summarized in Table 15.1.

Scoring rubrics. The specification of performance objectives is part of the 4C/ID model; these objectives specify the standards for acceptable performance including relevant criteria, values, and attitudes (van Merriënboer & Kirschner, 2007). Criteria refer to minimum requirements that must be met in terms of accuracy, speed, productivity, percentage of errors, tolerances and wastes, time requirements, and so forth. Values typically do not specify a quantifiable minimum requirement, but indicate that particular aspects of tasks should be performed according to appropriate rules, regulations, or conventions. Finally, particular aspects of performance may also require the exhibition of particular attitudes, such a client-centeredness ("with a smile on your face"), punctuality ("performing regular checks"), or persuasiveness ("frequently giving relevant arguments").

TABLE 15.1   Ten Guidelines for the Assessment of Whole Learning Tasks

1. Scoring rubrics	Develop for all relevant aspects of performance scoring rubrics, which provide rating scales indicating to which degree standards (criteria, values, attitudes) have been met by the learner.
2. Constant set of standards	Use the same set of standards throughout the whole curriculum or educational program.
3. Mix of assessment methods	Use a rich mix of assessment methods so that the disadvantages of particular methods are counterbalanced by the strengths of other methods.
4. Multitude of assessors	Use a multitude of assessors to provide multisource feedback, taking different perspectives on the learner's performance.
5. Self assessments	Use self-assessments to include the learner's point of view, to help develop lifelong learning skills, and to make the assessment process more efficient.
6. Broad sampling of tasks	Use a broad sample of tasks for assessment purposes, with different assessment methods and different assessors.
7. Vertical and horizontal assessments	Provide both vertical assessments, which indicate the degree to which standards are met for one particular aspect of performance, and a horizontal assessment, which indicates the degree to which standards for overall performance are met.
8. Narrative information	Always complement quantitative assessment information with narrative, descriptive, linguistic information.
9. Feedback sessions	Schedule feedback sessions with the learner to discuss assessment results, evaluate progress, and plan future learning.
10. Development portfolios	Use an electronic development portfolio to implement guidelines 1–9 and to provide overviews and summaries of assessment results.

Performance assessments based on clear standards provide important information on the quality of a learner's performance as well as opportunities for improvement of this performance. The standards are best included in *scoring rubrics*, which contain an indication of each aspect of behavior that will be assessed, the standards for acceptable performance of this particular aspect, and a scale of values on which to rate each standard. For non-routine aspects of performance, standards will not only take the form of criteria but also of attitudes and values. While criteria relate to minimum requirements, which are either met or not met (yes/no), values and attitudes typically require narrative reports or, at least, more scale values with qualitative labels (e.g., insufficient, almost sufficient, just sufficient, good, excellent). Each point on the scale should be clearly labeled and defined; the rule-of-thumb is to best avoid scales with more than six or seven points. For the routine aspects of performance, standards are typically relatively firm. In contrast to non-routine aspects, the accuracy of routine aspects can thus be judged more often with a simple correct or incorrect (i.e., either according to the specified criteria or not). Judgments on only one or a few aspects of performance provide the learner with little detail about how to improve performance. Therefore, a well-designed scoring rubric will pay attention to most or all relevant aspects of performance, and typically contain more than one standard for each of those aspects (Baartman et al., 2006).

Constant set of standards. The standards for acceptable behavior are part of the performance objectives, which correspond with all constituent skills that make up the complex skill or professional competency the educational program is aiming at. These standards should remain constant throughout the whole program. Thus, in the beginning of the first task class, the learner already tries to reach the relevant standards but only for performing the simplest versions of the task and with ample support and guidance; at the end of the first task class, the learner should be able to perform the simplest versions of the unsupported tasks up to the relevant standards. This continues until in the beginning of the final task class, the learner tries to reach the same standards for the most difficult versions of the task with ample support and guidance, and at the end of the final task class, the learner should be able to perform the most difficult versions of unsupported tasks up to those standards. Thus, in this approach, it is not the level of the standards that changes throughout the educational program but, in contrast, the difficulty of the learning tasks and the available support and guidance.

Whereas there is a constant set of standards for the whole educational program, this does *not* imply that each separate learning task is assessed with exactly the same set of standards. First, not all standards are relevant for all tasks because more difficult tasks typically make an appeal on more constituent skills and thus on more standards. In general, more and more standards will become relevant if learners progress through the curriculum.

Second, standards may be hierarchically ordered, making it possible to vary the level of detail of assessments. For example, tasks in the field of nursing may be assessed at the global level of starting the care, preparing the patient, preparing the environment and so on. At the more detailed level of starting the care this may include introducing yourself, explaining the goals of the care and so on, or at the even more detailed level, introducing yourself, shaking hands, calling your name, mentioning the organization you are representing, and so on. The use of standards higher in the hierarchy will assess performance at a global level, and the use of standards lower in the hierarchy will assess performance at increasingly more detailed levels. In general, highly detailed assessments will be limited to aspects of performance that are not yet mastered by the learners or for which they still have to improve their performance.

Mix of assessment methods. There are many methods to assess task performance. For example, situational judgment tests describe work-related situations and require the learner to choose a course of action by responding to questions (e.g., what would you do first or what is the most important action to take?); work sample tests require the learner to perform tasks that are similar to those that are performed on the job; and performance-on-the-job assessments observe a learner's task performance under regular working conditions. The point is that all assessment methods have their own advantages and disadvantages. In general, assessment methods with a high reliability have a relatively low external validity and, vice versa, assessment methods with a high external validity have a relatively low reliability. Therefore, it is recommended to use a rich mix of assessment methods. Then, the disadvantages of particular assessment methods are counterbalanced by the strengths of other assessment methods.

Multitude of assessors. Next to a mix of assessment methods, a mix of assessors should be used. Important assessors include teachers, instructors and other experts in the task domain: clients, customers and other people served by the learners, as well as employers and other responsible managers. In addition, peer assessments may be used to gather input from fellow learners or colleagues (Sluijsmans, Moerkerke, van Merriënboer, & Dochy, 2001; Sluijsmans, Brand-Gruwel, & van Merriënboer, 2002). The whole group of assessors is able to provide 360-degree assessments or multi-source feedback, taking different perspectives on the learner's performance.

It should be noted that the selection of assessors may introduce worrying biases (Bullock, Hassell, Markham, Wall, & Whitehouse, 2009). Assessors might be inclined to use only the positive part of the scale in order not to compromise their relationship with the learner or to avoid more work (and trouble) for the assessor often contingent on giving more negative evaluations. Yet, a good relationship between the assessor and the learner is instrumental for learning (Boor et al., 2008) and persons who know the learner best potentially provide the most valuable information for assessment. Three approaches might help to reduce biases. First, assessors should be trained in the use of assessment instruments and also become aware of the most important sources of bias in performance assessment. Second, multiple roles of the assessors should be separated by removing the summative assessment decisions from the formative ones and the coaching role. And third, inconsistencies in assessment data should be discussed between assessors for benchmarking of the process and the results.

Self assessments. Self-assessments may be an important part of multi-source assessments. The literature, however, is very clear with regard to the quality of self-assessments: We are poor self-assessors (Davis et al., 2006; Eva & Regehr, 2005, 2007; Gordon, 1991). Nevertheless, there are three arguments to include self-assessment in the assessment process. First, it is important to incorporate the learner's point of view in the assessment process. This helps the learner to feel responsible for his or her own learning process and it has positive effects on motivation (Boud, 1995). Second, the development of self-assessment skills is a condition for self-directed and lifelong learning (van Merriënboer & Sluijsmans, 2009). Confronting learners with conflicts between self-assessments and assessments of others helps them to reflect on and further develop their self-assessment skills. Third, the efficiency of the assessment process may be increased because self-assessments can replace part of the assessments made by teachers or others, provided that the balance does not tip in the direction of self assessment. The implication is that self-assessment can never stand on its own and should always be triangulated with other information. But the continuous exercise of relating self-assessments with information from others is hopefully an effort that pays off in the long run because it stimulates lifelong learning skills.

Broad sampling of tasks. One measure of performance is *no* measure of performance. There have been several studies looking at how many assessments are needed for adequate reliability (Atwater, Waldman, & Brett, 2002; Kogan, Holmboe, & Hauer, 2009; Wood, Hassell, Whitehouse, Bolluck, & Wall, 2006). Although the studies vary, we conclude that reliable inferences can be made with feasible samples. The magical number seems to be somewhere between eight and ten, irrespective of the type of assessment instrument and what is being measured. This confirms that reliability is primarily a matter of sampling, not a matter of standardization or structuring the assessment. In order to reach reliable assessments, assessments should thus be repeated for a series of different tasks (i.e., tasks that differ from each other on the dimensions on which real-life tasks also differ from each other), using different methods and different assessors.

Vertical and horizontal assessment. A complication with sampling of tasks already indicated in the section on the constant set of standards is that usually not all tasks are assessed with the same set of standards. For example, if learners work on Tasks 1, 2 and 3, it is well conceivable that Task 1 can only be assessed on aspects *a* and *c*, Task 2 on aspects *b* and *c*, and Task 3 on aspects *a* and *d*—yielding two assessments for *a*, one assessment for *b*, two assessments for *c*, and one assessment for *d*. Consequently, a multitude of eight to ten tasks may be necessary to reach reliable assessments for all relevant aspects of performance. In this respect, Sluijsmans, Straetmans and van Merriënboer (2008) make a distinction between vertical and horizontal assessment. Vertical assessments indicate the degree to which the standards are met for one particular aspect of performance, as assessed with various assessment methods and by a multitude of assessors over a range of learning tasks. It reflects the learner's mastery of distinct aspects of performance and yields important information for the identification of points of improvement. Horizontal assessments, in contrast, indicate to which degree the standards for overall performance are met. It reflects the student's mastery of the whole professional competency and is thus more appropriate to base progress decisions on.

Narrative information. If feedback is a central issue in assessment, numerical and quantitative information has clear limitations while narrative, qualitative information has benefits. Qualitative, narrative information carries a lot of weight. This is also reported in empirical studies: Narrative, descriptive, linguistic information is often much richer and appreciated more by learners (Govaerts, van der Vleuten, Schuwirth, & Muijtjens, 2005; Sargeant et al., 2010). Narrative and qualitative information clearly is an issue that the assessment field needs to get used to. The assessment literature is strongly associated with quantification, scoring and averaging—called the "psychometric discourse" by Hodges (2006). It is quite clear that having obtained a rating of two out of five for counseling skills in a patient encounter should probably raise some concern with the learner, but it does not disclose what the learner actually did and what are points of improvement for future performance. In order to provide more richness to the assessment we have an excellent tool: language. We argue that for effective assessment qualitatively rich information is required. We should encourage instrument developers to provide facilities for that in the instrument (like for example open space to write down narrative comments), and we should stimulate and train assessors to provide and document such information routinely.

Feedback sessions. In an integrated curriculum, performing learning tasks and assessing learning tasks are the two basic elements of a cyclical process. In this cyclical process, regular feedback sessions between assessor(s) and the learner should be scheduled. The first function of these sessions is to look back in a systematic fashion. If decisions are made on the basis of assessments, these sessions give the learner the possibility to appeal to these decisions. If there is conflicting assessment information it may be necessary to gather additional information before a definite decision is made.

In a formative framework, feedback sessions also give the opportunity to elaborate on the assessments and to identify individual learning needs. The second, related function of feedback sessions is to look forward. It should be discussed what are, given the assessment results, important points of improvement for the learner. The identification of learning activities and learning tasks that may help the learner to work on these points of improvement is critical to fulfill the formative assessment function.

Development portfolios. Electronic development portfolios provide good opportunities to implement the nine guidelines discussed above (Kicken, Brand-Gruwel, van Merriënboer, & Slot, 2009; van Merriënboer & Kirschner, 2007). In addition, they take over administrative duties and computational tasks to detect conflicts between different assessors, to provide overviews and summaries, to give vertical and horizontal assessments, and so forth. A development portfolio includes scoring rubrics (guideline one) that allow an assessor to assess the learner's performance on one or more learning tasks. The assessor can select the relevant aspects of performance—for example, from a hierarchical list with global objectives at the top and more detailed objectives lower in the hierarchy. For each objective, the portfolio shows the standards (criteria, values, attitudes) for acceptable performance and the associated scoring rubric, allowing the assessor to rate the aspect of performance under consideration. This process is repeated for all aspects relevant for the learning task assessed, and if more than one task is assessed, it is repeated for all tasks. The same development portfolio with the same scoring rubrics and thus the same standards (guideline two) should be used throughout the whole curriculum. An advantage of this approach is that the learner is confronted with all relevant standards right from the start of the educational program. Although he or she will not be assessed on all these standards immediately, the final attainments levels of the program are communicated right from the beginning and help the learner to work towards them. A mix of assessment methods should be used to collect the data that are entered in the portfolio (guideline three) and a multitude of assessors (guideline four) should be responsible for updating the portfolio; performed tasks can be assessed by the teacher, clients or (simulated) patients, and other stakeholders. Obviously, the learner can also use the portfolio to conduct self-assessments (guideline five). Possible conflicts between assessments made by different assessment methods or by different assessors (including self assessments) can be automatically detected by the portfolio and used as input for discussion in feedback sessions.

A development portfolio allows for broad sampling of tasks (guideline six), because in principle *all* learning tasks might be used as a basis for assessment and, according to the 4C/ID-model, variability is ensured for the whole set of learning tasks. In order to keep the workload manageable, a representative subset of tasks can be used for assessment purposes. The portfolio can also use automatic functions for the computation of vertical and horizontal assessments (guideline seven). For vertical assessments, an overview can be given for each relevant aspect of performance, including an overview of all learning tasks for which this particular aspect has been assessed, development over time, identified individual learning needs, points for improvement, and so forth. For horizontal assessments, an overview can be given of overall progress over learning tasks and/or over time. To improve the informative value of the portfolio, scoring rubrics need not be limited to quantitative ratings of particular aspects of performance, but may also include narrative information (guideline eight), which might be given by the assessor in a separate textbox, or multimedia information, including spoken messages, photographs and video fragments that are uploaded in the portfolio. With regard to feedback sessions (guideline nine), the overviews and summaries generated by the portfolio provide helpful information for regular meetings with an assessor, coach, or supervisor. The main aim of such regular meetings may be to reflect on the work on previous learning tasks (including the use of assessments to make formal decisions), to identify future opportunities for performance improvement, or a combination of both. Although portfolios run the risk of a positive bias of evidence, they can be robust if done well. That is with prolonged engagement of a mentor with the learner (Driessen, van Tartwijk, van der Vleuten, & Wass 2007) and pass/fail decision guidelines based on qualitative research methodology (van der Vleuten et al., 2010).

To conclude, we discussed a number of guidelines to assess learners' performance on whole learning tasks in an integrated curriculum. These guidelines can, in our opinion, best be applied and implemented in an electronic development portfolio. Such a portfolio should not be limited to the function of assessment, but should also help to monitor, reflect, plan and coach (van Tartwijk & Driessen, 2009). We assume that development portfolios will work best in an integrated curriculum if these functions are fully combined, and if the portfolio has a very central function for guiding the learning, monitoring, and coaching of longitudinal development of professional competencies as well a central function or weight in the assessment program.

The "Does" Level: Assessing Unsupported Tasks

On the "shows how" level, learners perform tasks in an educational setting and the learning tasks or test tasks are typically designed or selected beforehand. On the "does" level, in contrast, learners perform tasks in a professional setting (e.g., internships or clerkships) and the tasks are professional tasks not designed beforehand. Thus, the stimulus format is the authentic context and is essentially non-standardized and relatively unstructured. The response format is usually more or less generic and not tailored to the specific context. Essentially all assessments in the professional setting rely on knowledgeable others or on "expert judgment." Whereas the guidelines discussed in the previous section can also be applied here, the professional setting has some important additional implications for the assessment process, including the nature of assessed competencies, the function of assessment, and the decisions based on the assessment.

With regard to the nature of assessed competencies, in comparison with assessments on the "show how" level the focus typically shifts from domain-specific competencies to more generic competencies. In the medical domain, two well-known integral competency structures are the general competencies from the U.S. Accreditation Council of Graduate Medical Education (ACGME, 2009) and the Canadian CanMeds competencies (Frank & Danoff, 2007). They both emphasize competencies that are not only specific to the medical domain but may also hold to any other professional domain. For example, the CanMeds competencies "collaborator" and "communicator" are generically applicable, although we acknowledge immediately that they are still equally context specific as any other skill or competency. There are good reasons to emphasize these more generic competencies: When things go wrong in medical practice, these kinds of competencies are often at stake and research has shown that success on the labor market is more determined by these generic skills than by specific domain-specific skills (Meng, 2006). But whereas the importance of generic competencies is widely acknowledged, they are particularly difficult to grasp. Attempts to define, for example, "professionalism" in detail and to measure it with checklists easily risks trivialization (Norman, van der Vleuten, & de Graaff, 1991). Yet, we all have an intuitive notion of what is meant by professionalism, especially when we see it in actual performance. In our view, expert judgment is one of the key factors making assessment of generic competencies work at the "does" level.

With regard to the function of assessment, it should be clear that in an educational setting assessment is typically seen as an integral part of the learning process, but in a professional setting this is—unfortunately—not the case. If assessments on the "does" level do not fulfill a strong formative function and do not have a recognized learning value to the learners, they become trivialized and will not work. For example, if the reflection in a portfolio is written to please the assessment committee it will have no significance to the learner, and the members of the committee will provide judgment without much information and quickly return to their routine. Whenever the assessment becomes a goal in itself, the assessment will become "infected" and will ultimately "swear" until it is removed. Especially in a professional setting, assessments will only work if they succeed in driving the learning process, become part of the daily routine, and ultimately appear indispensable for the learning practice.

With regard to the decisions based on the assessment process, supervisors in a postgraduate teaching role traditionally judge the maturity of learners by their ability to bear responsibility and to safely perform their professional tasks without strict supervision. In the medical domain, for example, the assessment program at the "does" level has been promoted to result in Statements of Awarded Responsibility or STARs (Ten Cate & Scheele, 2007). In Figure 15.2 these STARs, representing the competence of safe and independent practice, would be placed on top of Miller's pyramid, but below the highest level of competency to be assessed: The track record of the results of professional practice. This is where the ultimate goal of competence, being able to perform your job independently and with good results, comes into scope.

CONCLUSIONS

In this chapter, we tried to answer the question of what good assessment looks like in an integrated, competence-based curriculum. We first described how such a curriculum can be developed on the basis of the 4C/ID-model. The four components learning tasks, supportive information, procedural information, and part-task practice were placed in Miller's pyramid to gain an impression of the main elements of a competence-based assessment program. The remainder of the chapter focused on the highest levels of the pyramid: The assessment of part tasks and the assessment of whole tasks on the "shows how" level, that is, in an educational setting, and the assessment of whole tasks at the "does" level, that is, in a professional setting. Considerations and guidelines for assessment were presented for each of the three categories.

Three main conclusions emerged for assessment in the integrated curriculum. First, assessments of part tasks on the "shows how" level should be limited to the assessment of *routine* behaviors; the assessment of part tasks that also include non-routine aspects (e.g., OSCEs) shows serious problems due to a lack of authenticity and the content specificity problem. Second, assessments of whole tasks on the "shows how" level turned out to be very well possible in an integrated curriculum. We presented ten guidelines for such assessments and argued that an electronic development portfolio is probably the best instrument to implement the guidelines. Third, assessment of whole tasks on the "does" level poses some additional requirements. Because generic, difficult-to-define competencies are particularly important in a professional setting and because assessments are only accepted in such a setting if they patently obvious contribute to learning and performance, expert judgment is of utmost importance in the workplace.

Future research should first focus on the design of comprehensive assessment programs, which do not only include the "shows how" and "does" level but also the lower levels of Miller's pyramid. So far, almost all literature on competence-based assessment is related to individual assessment methods. Very little is yet known about how to combine these individual methods in one assessment program. A second and related issue for future research goes even one step further and aims to bridge the gap between the construction of assessment instruments and curriculum design, in both undergraduate education and the complicated world of postgraduate training programs. Unfortunately, the research fields of curriculum design and assessment are separate worlds, though, in our opinion, a marriage between both is necessary to effectively support innovation in the direction of competence-based education. Third, more research on expert judgment is needed because especially in professional settings there seems to be no real alternative. Such research might, for example, study how expert judgments can best be optimized by the provision of probabilistic and empirical information, how expertise in judgment skills develops, which biases and novice-expert differences exist, and so forth.

To conclude, this chapter combined research-based guidelines for the development of a competence-based curriculum, derived from the 4C/ID-model, with current ideas about competence-based assessment. Overall, this exercise has been successful and yielded ten guidelines for the assessment of whole tasks in an integrated curriculum. Yet, we are still far away from a complete integration of the integrated curriculum with a competence-based assessment program. At least, this should include the lower levels of Miller's pyramid and better guidelines for the assessment of routine behaviors. Next steps should be taken to reach a full integration of curriculum design and "assessment design" because a perfect match between curriculum and assessment is a condition sine qua non for effectively promoting student learning.

REFERENCES

ACGME. (2009). *Common program requirements: General competencies.* Chicago, IL: Accreditation Council for Graduate Medical Education. Available from http://www.acgme.org/outcome/comp/GeneralCompetenciesStandards21307.pdf

Anderson, J. R. (1987). Skill acquisition: Compilation of weak-method problem solutions. *Psychological Review, 94,* 192–210.

Atwater, L. E., Waldman, D. A., & Brett, J. F. (2002). Understanding multi-source feedback. *Human Resource Management, 41*(2), 193–208.

Baartman, L. K. J., Bastiaens, T. J., Kirschner, P. A., & van der Vleuten, C. P. M. (2006). The wheel of competency assessment. *Studies in Educational Evaluations, 32*(2), 153–170.

Boor, K., Teunissen, P. W., Scherpbier, A. J., van der Vleuten, C. P., van de Lande, J., & Scheele, F. (2008). Residents' perceptions of the ideal clinical teacher: A qualitative study. *European Journal of Obstetrics & Gynecology and Reproductive Biology, 140(2)*, 152–157.

Boud, D. (1995). *Enhancing learning through self assessment.* New York: Routledge-Falmer.

Bowden, J., & Marton, F. (2004). *The university of learning.* London: RoutledgeFalmer.

Bullock, A. D., Hassell, A., Markham, W. A., Wall, D. W., & Whitehouse, A. B. (2009). How ratings vary by staff group in multisource feedback assessment of junior doctors. *Medical Education, 43*(6), 516–520.

Carlson, R. A., Khoo, H., & Elliot, R. G. (1990). Component practice and exposure to a problem solving context. *Human Factors, 32*, 267–286.

Carr, J. F., & Harris, D. E. (2001). *Succeeding with standards: Linking curriculum, assessment, and action planning.* Alexandria, VA: Association for Supervision & Curriculum Development.

Davis, D. A., Mazmanian, P. E., Fordis, M., van Harrison, R., Thorpe, K. E., & Perrier, L. (2006). Accuracy of physician self-assessment compared with observed measures of competence: A systematic review. *JAMA, 296*(9), 1094–1102.

Driessen, E., van Tartwijk, J., van der Vleuten, C., & Wass, V. (2007). Portfolios in medical education: Why do they meet with mixed success? A systematic review. *Medical Education, 41*(12), 1224–1233.

Eva, K. W., & Regehr, G. (2005). Self-assessment in the health professions: A reformulation and research agenda. *Academic Medicine, 80*(10), S46-S54.

Eva, K. W., & Regehr, G. (2007). Knowing when to look it up: A new conception of self-assessment ability. *Academic Medicine, 82*(10), S81-S84.

Fisk, A. D., & Gallini, J. K. (1989). Training consistent components of tasks: Developing an instructional system based on automatic-controlled processing principles. *Human Factors*, 31, 453–463.

Frank, J. R., & Danoff, D. (2007). The CanMEDS initiative: Implementing an outcomes-based framework of physician competencies. *Medical Teacher, 29*(7), 642–647.

Gordon, M. J. (1991). A review of the validity and accuracy of self-assessments in health professions training. *Academic Medicine, 66*(12), 762–769.

Govaerts, M. J., van der Vleuten, C. P., Schuwirth, L. W., & Muijtjens, A. M. (2005). The use of observational diaries in in-training evaluation: Student perceptions. *Advances in Health Sciences Education, 10*(3), 171–188.

Halford, G. S., Bain, J. D., Maybery, M. T., & Andrews, G. (1998). Induction of relational schemas: Common processes in reasoning and complex learning. *Cognitive Psychology, 35*(3), 201–245.

Harden, R. M., Stevenson, W., Downie, W. W., & Wilson, G. M. (1975). Assessment of clinical competence using objective structured examination. *British Medical Journal, 1*, 447–451.

Hodges, B. (2006). Medical education and the maintenance of incompetence. *Medical Teacher, 28*(8), 690–696.

Kicken, W., Brand-Gruwel, S., van Merriënboer, J. J. G., & Slot, W. (2009). Design and evaluation of a development portfolio: How to improve students' self-directed learning skills. *Instructional Science, 37*, 453–473.

Kogan, J. R., Holmboe, E. S., & Hauer, K. E. (2009). Tools for direct observation and assessment of clinical skills of medical trainees: A systematic review. *JAMA, 302*(12), 1316–1326.

Meng, C. (2006). *Discipline-specific or academic? Acquisition, role and value of higher education competencies.* Unpublished PhD thesis. Maastricht, the Netherlands: Maastricht University.

Miller, G. E. (1990). The assessment of clinical skills / competence / performance. *Academic Medicine, 65*(9), S63-S67.

Norman, G. R., van der Vleuten, C. P. M., & de Graaff, E. (1991). Pitfalls in the pursuit of objectivity: Issues of validity, efficiency and acceptability. *Medical Education, 25*, 119–126.

Norman, G. (2009). Teaching basic science to optimize transfer. *Medical Teacher, 31*(9), 807–811.

Petrusa, E. R. (2002). Clinical performance assessments. In G. R. Norman, C. P. M. van der Vleuten, & D. I. Newble (Eds.), *International handbook for research in medical education* (pp. 673–709). Dordrecht, the Netherlands: Kluwer Academic Publishers.

Sargeant, J., Armson, H., Chesluk, B., Dornan, T., Eva, K., Holmboe, E., . . . van der Vleuten, C. (2010). The processes and dimensions of informed self-assessment: A conceptual model. *Academic Medicine, 85*(7), 1212–1220.

Schuwirth, L. W., & van der Vleuten, C. P. (2004). Different written assessment methods: What can be said about their strengths and weaknesses? *Medical Education, 38*(9), 974–979.

Sluijsmans, D. M. A., Brand-Gruwel, S., & van Merriënboer, J. J. G. (2002). Peer assessment training in teacher education: Effects on performance and perceptions. *Assessment & Evaluation in Higher Education, 27*, 443–454.

Sluijsmans, D. M. A., Moerkerke, G., van Merriënboer, J. J. G., & Dochy, F. J. R. C. (2001). Peer assessment in problem-based learning. *Studies in Educational Evaluation, 27*, 153–173.

Sluijsmans, D. M. A., Straetmans, G., & van Merriënboer, J. (2008). Integrating authentic assessment with competency based learning: the Protocol Portfolio Scoring. *Journal of Vocational Education and Training, 60*, 157–172.

Ten Cate, O., & Scheele, F. (2007). Competency-based postgraduate training: Can we bridge the gap between theory and clinical practice? *Academic Medicine, 82*(6), 542–547.

Van der Vleuten, C. P. M., & Swanson, D. (1990). Assessment of clinical skills with standardized patients: State of the art. *Teaching and Learning in Medicine, 2*(2), 58–76.

Van der Vleuten, C. P. M., & Schuwirth, L. W. T. (2005). Assessment of professional competence: From methods to programmes. *Medical Education, 39*, 309–317.

Van der Vleuten, C. P. M., Schuwirth, L. W., Scheele, F., Driessen, E. W., & Hodges, B. (2010). The assessment of professional competence: Building blocks for theory development. *Best Practice & Research Clinical Obstetrics & Gynaecology, 24*, 703–719.

Van der Vleuten, C. P. M., van Luijk, S. J., & Beckers, H. J. M. (1989). A written test as an alternative to performance testing. *Medical Education, 23*, 97–107.

Van Luijk, S. J., van der Vleuten, C. P. M., & van Schelven, R. M. (1990). Observer and Student opinions about performance-based tests. In W. Bender, R. J. Hiemstra, A. J. Scherpbier, & R. P. Zwierstra (Eds.), *Teaching and assessing clinical competence* (pp. 199–203). Groningen, The Netherlands: Boekwerk Publications.

Van Merriënboer, J. J. G. (1997). *Training complex cognitive skills: A four-component instructional design model for technical training.* Englewood Cliffs, NJ: Educational Technology Publications.

Van Merriënboer, J. J. G., Clark, R. E., & de Croock, M. B. M. (2002). Blueprints for complex learning: The 4C/ID-model. *Educational Technology, Research and Development, 50*(2), 39–64.

Van Merriënboer, J. J. G., & Kirschner, P. A. (2007). *Ten steps to complex learning.* Mahwah, NJ: Erlbaum.

Van Merriënboer, J. J. G., & Sluijsmans, D. A. (2009). Toward a synthesis of cognitive load theory, four-component instructional design, and self-directed learning. *Educational Psychology Review, 21*, 55–66.

Van Merriënboer, J. J. G., & Sweller, J. (2005). Cognitive load theory and complex learning: Recent developments and future directions. *Educational Psychology Review, 17*, 147–177.

Van Merriënboer, J. J. G., & Sweller, J. (2010). Cognitive load theory in health professional education: Design principles and strategies. *Medical Education, 44*(1), 85–93.

Van Tartwijk, J., & Driessen, E. W. (2009). Portfolios for assessment and learning: AMEE Guide no. 45. *Medical Teacher, 31*(9), 790–801.

Vygotsky, L. S. (1978). *Mind in society: The development of higher psychological processes.* Cambridge, MA: Harvard University Press.

Weigel, T., Mulder, M., & Collins, K. (2007). The concept of competence in the development of vocational education and training in selected EU member states. *Journal of Vocational Education & Training, 59*(1), 53–66.

Wood, L., Hassell, A., Whitehouse, A., Bullock, A., &Wall, D. (2006). A literature review of multisource feedback systems within and without health services, leading to 10 tips for their successful design. *Medical Teacher, 28*(7), e185–e191.

CHAPTER 16

ACCESSIBLE NEXT GENERATION ASSESSMENTS

Michael Russell
Boston College

Over the past two decades, the infusion of computer-based technologies into schools has presented an important opportunity to enhance the technology of assessment. During this time period, assessment experts have presented visions of next generation assessments that capitalize on various capabilities of computer-based technologies. This chapter focuses narrowly on one innovation enabled by digital assessment delivery, namely tailoring the presentation of, interactions with, and response modes to assessment items to improve accessibility (Russell, Hoffmann, & Higgins, 2009).

Over the past thirty years, considerable controversy has brewed about accessibility and assessment. Initially, concerns about accessibility focused on students with physical and visual disabilities. Over time, the population of students for whom concerns were identified expanded to students with learning disabilities, language processing needs, attention and stimulus needs, auditory needs, and most recently students who are English language learners. In each case, advocacy has focused on a sub-population of students with common characteristics (e.g., students who are blind or have low vision, students with dyslexia, students who communicate in sign, etc.).

Technology-Based Assessments for 21st Century Skills, pages 371–386
Copyright © 2012 by Information Age Publishing

In response, assessment programs created provisions that allowed assessment instruments to be modified, through what has become known as a test accommodation, so that their content was more accessible for a specific sup-population of students. But test accommodations have proven to be expensive and, in many cases, controversial.

The expense arises primarily from the need to change or retrofit an existing instrument, and in the process revisit the intent of each item to assure that any changes do not violate the knowledge or skill measured by the item. In some cases, this process identifies some items that could not be appropriately modified, which complicates the scoring and reporting process. For an initial period of time, the provision of test accommodations resulted in scores for students who received accommodations being flagged, reported separately, or not included in school or classroom averages. In some cases, students who required accommodations were excluded entirely from participating in assessment programs. More recently, however, federal policies have reduced these practices (NCLB and IDEA). Nonetheless, the provision of test accommodations remains an expensive component of an assessment program.

Over the past five years, efforts to apply principles of universal design to the development and delivery of educational assessments have helped improve the quality with which access is provided to students with a variety of access needs. This work has led to the development of the Accessible Test Design model. When applied throughout the development and delivery on an assessment instrument, accessible test design enables an assessment program to capitalize on the flexibility that digital technologies offer to tailor the presentation of content, interactions with that content, and methods of recording the outcome of those interactions based on the specific needs of each individual student.

UNIVERSAL DESIGN AND ASSESSMENT

The concept of Universal Design focuses on "the design of products and environments to be usable by all people, to the greatest extent possible, without the need for adaptation or specialized design" (Center for Universal Design, 1997, p. 1). Rather than creating a single solution, Universal Design has come to embrace the concept of allowing users to select from among multiple alternatives. As Rose and Meyer (2000) emphasize, "Universal Design does not imply 'one sizes fits all' but rather acknowledges the need for alternatives to suit many different people's need . . . the essence of [Universal Design] is flexibility and the inclusion of alternatives to adapt to the myriad variations in learner needs, styles, and preferences" (p. 4).

In the field of education, Universal Design for Learning applies these same design principles by considering the variety of accessibility and learning needs of students when developing instructional materials. The three key principles of UDL (Rose & Meyer, 2000) focus on the provision of:

- Alternative formats for presenting information.
- Alternative means for action and expression.
- Alternative means for engagement.

When applied to student assessment, these three aspects of universal design for learning have important implications for the development of item content, the interface used to deliver items, and the interaction among the examinee, the item content, and the delivery interface. Accessible Test Design provides a model that addresses these three elements to maximize the ability of an assessment item to measure a targeted construct.

ACCESSIBLE TEST DESIGN

Accessible test design provides a model that allows assessment programs to specify methods for flexibly tailoring the presentation of, interaction with, and response methods for an assessment item such that the influence of non-targeted constructs is minimized for each individual student. As depicted in Figure 16.1, the accessible test design model begins by defining the access needs of each individual student. These needs are then used to present specific representational forms of the item content specified in the item itself (e.g., text, Braille, sign, audio, alternate language, etc.) and to activate specific access tools embedded in a test delivery interface that align

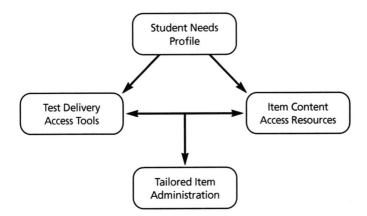

Figure 16.1 Accessible test implementation model.

with the student's access needs. Through this interaction with item content and the delivery system, the administration of an assessment item is tailored to maximize the measurement of the intended construct and minimize the influence of unintended constructs.

Flexible tailoring of a student's experience with an assessment item depends on the access needs of each student and may require adaptations to the presentation of item content, the interaction with that content, the response mode, or the representational form in which content is communicated. The forms of adaption are explored and separated in the sections that follow. Before doing so, however, it is useful to review how assessment items are designed to function and consider how accessibility can be hindered during each step of a student's interaction with an item.

ASSESSMENT ITEMS AND ACCESSIBILITY

At its core, an educational test is a sample of behaviors that are intended to be the product of the application of a cognitive construct. The sample of behaviors is provided through an examinee's interactions with a set of items or tasks. Items are designed to present a context in which the examinee must apply the targeted construct in order to produce a response. Since cognitive constructs cannot be directly observed, items and tasks are constructed to stimulate or activate the construct of interest. In addition, to provide an observable record of the construct, an item or task requires a student to produce an observable product. While the focus of a student's interaction with an item or task is often on the answer or product produced, that product is only useful if it accurately reflects the activation of the construct of interest.

When thinking about a test item as both a stimulant of the construct and a subsequent observable product of the construct, there are three important factors about a test item to consider. First, in order for an item to activate a construct, the content of the item must transfer from the medium in which it is presented (e.g., paper, computer, orally, etc.) to the student. Without a successful and fully accurate transfer, the item is unlikely to activate the construct of interest.

Second, the contents of the task must be carefully designed to stimulate or activate the construct of interest. A task placed on a test intended to measure a mathematical construct, but which does not contain any mathematical content, is unlikely to activate the construct of interest. Similarly, a task that contains mathematical content but uses confusing language, poorly constructed images, or is formatted in an unfamiliar manner may also be unsuccessful in stimulating the construct of interest because other unrelated constructs (e.g., reading ability, visual acuity) are activated as the student attempts to understand what is being presented or asked.

Third, to produce an observable product, the task must allow a student to produce a response that accurately reflects the outcome of the activation of the construct. Accurate reflection requires that the response results from the construct of interest and not some other construct, and that the method used to render a response allows the student to accurately transfer his/her thinking to the medium used to record the response (e.g., a bubble sheet, a text box on a computer screen, a video file that provides a recording of a student performing an experiment, etc.).

Collectively, the accuracy with which a task is able to sample a specific behavior depends on the extent to which a task is able to allow content to be transferred accurately from the medium of presentation to the student, stimulate the construct of interest, and support accurate recording of a response that is the product of the construct of interest. Subsequently, the extent to which a test provides information that allows a user to make accurate inferences about a given construct depends on the quality of each of the tasks used to form the sample of observable behaviors.

In the context of assessment, accessibility focuses on the accuracy with which each of these three steps occurs during the measurement process. The extent to which an item is able to accomplish these three tasks is influenced by a variety of factors. These factors can be sorted into three broad categories, each of which relates to a step in the measurement process, namely: a) presentation, b) interaction, and c) response. A fourth category, representational form, is also relevant in some cases.

Accessible test design considers these four categories throughout the test development and delivery of a test. At its core, accessible test design focuses on three important aspects of a test: item content, representational forms used to communicate that content, and the delivery interface through which an examinee is presented, interacts with, and responds to item content. As we will see, unless all three of these aspects are addressed, the accessibility of a test will be limited.

REPRESENTATIONAL FORMS

As Mislevy and colleagues (2010) explain, several different representational forms can be used to present instructional or test content to a student. To enable a student to recognize and process content, the form used to present that content may need to be tailored based on the student's representational form need. As an example, a student who is blind cannot access content presented in print-based form. However, when that same content is presented in Braille, the content becomes accessible for the student if the student is a Braille reader. Reading aloud content, presenting text-based content in sign language, Braille, tactile representations of graphical images, symbolic representations of text-based information, narrative representations of chemical compounds (e.g., "sodium chloride" instead of "NaCl") or mathematical formulas, and translating to a different language are all forms of alternate representations.

For paper-based instructional and test materials, alternate representations often require the development of different versions or forms of the materials, or the use of translators or interpreters who present alternate representations to the student. In a digital environment, alternate representations of content can be built into item information and a digital test delivery system can then tailor the representational form presented to examinees based on their individual needs. The Accessible Portable Item Profile (APIP) Standard item model (Mattson & Russell, 2010) provides item writers with the tools to specify the exact manner in which tailored representations are to be provided by a test delivery engine for examinees with a given access need.

Default, Alternate, and Supplemental Item Content

An important concept that intersects with alternate representations is the distinction between default content and alternate content. Default content is item information that is intended to be presented to an examinee who does not have any defined access needs. Traditionally, this default content defines the original form of the item developed for the general population of examinees. Typically, default content includes text, graphics, and/or tables that form the item that would be presented to a student who does not have any defined access needs. However, default content might also include other media elements such as sound files or movies that are intended to be presented as part of the item for the general population of examinees.

Alternate content presents a different version of the item to students with specific access needs. In essence, some or all of the original default content is replaced by alternate content. When this occurs, the alternate content that replaces default content is intended to be presented to an examinee with a specific access need in replace of the default content. Examples of replacements that result in alternate content include a translated version of an item, replacing text or formulas with symbolic representations, or simplifying the language contained in an item.

In contrast, for many access needs, improved access does not require content to be replaced, but instead requires the presentation of information that supplements default content. As an example, text displayed as part of default content might be presented in audio, Braille, or signed form. When doing so, the default content will remain displayed to the examinee and the additional content (audio, Braille or sign) will be presented as supplementary information. Similarly, changes intended to assist the examinee in identifying important aspects of default content present the default content along with supplementary information (e.g., highlighting key words, translation or definitions for key words, flags that point the student to key information, etc.).

The Accessible Portable Item Profile (APIP) item model allows supplemental information provided to meet a specific access need to be placed in a digital item file (Mattson & Russell, 2010). Similarly, pointers to alternate versions of an item can also be placed in a digital item file. To make the alternate versions accessible for some students, supplementary information can be provided for specific content contained in the alternate item (e.g., audio presentation of a translated item). This concept is foundational, for the Accessible Portable Item Profile standard and digital technologies are essential for tailored presentation of default, supplemental, and alternate content.

ACCESSIBLE TEST DELIVERY INTERFACE

Capitalizing on the flexibility of computer-based technologies, computer-based test delivery interfaces can tailor the delivery of assessment items and tasks based on each individual's access needs. To do so, principles of universal design play an important role in designing systems that can personalize the testing experience based on each individual student's needs.

As an example, NimbleTools® is a universally designed test delivery system that embeds several different accessibility and accommodation tools within a single system. A few examples of accessible tools include read aloud of text-based content, oral descriptions of graphics and tables, magnification of content, altered contrast and color of content, masking of content, auditory calming to support sustained concentration, signed presentation of text-based content, and presentation of text-based content in Braille (Russell, Hoffmann, & Higgins, 2009).

For students who have not been identified with one or more access needs, an accessible test delivery interface delivers content using a standard computer-based delivery interface. For students who need a given accommodation or set of accommodations, a proctor/teacher settings tool is used to customize the tools available for each student. As the student performs an assessment, he/she is able to use available tools as needed. This flexibility allows assessment programs to customize the delivery interface to meet the specific needs of each student and for the student to then use specific tools as needed for each item on the assessment task.

STUDENT ACCESS PROFILE

In addition to a flexible test delivery interface with embedded access tools and items that contain accessibility specifications, the final element required to make a task accessible for a given user is a Student Access Profile. An access profile defines access needs for a given student and indicates which tools and/or representational forms should be made available for each individual student. The profile might also specify specific settings, such as magnification levels, color contrasts, or default representational forms preferred by the student. Once defined, an access profile interacts with both the delivery interface and the item content. The interaction with the delivery interface focuses on specific tools or features embedded in the interface, activates those tools and features that are defined in the profile, and, in some cases, controls the exact settings for those tools and features. The interaction with the item content focuses on which of the specific representational forms embedded in the item should be presented and/or activated for a given student in order to meet his/her specific need. The access profile effectively controls the behavior of the interface and the components of an item that are presented to the student. The result is test delivery that is tailored to meet the specific access needs of each individual student.

LOOKING TO THE FUTURE

Accessible test design requires careful thought when developing test items, designing test delivery interfaces and test systems, and when developing an access profile for a given student. Specifically, to make item content accessible, item developers must specify supplementary and alternate information associated with each item and assure that these alternate representations do not alter the measure of the intended construct. When a test delivery interface is designed, an assessment program must specify the variety of accessibility tools and features that may be required for specific students. When developing an access profile, educators must be sure that the needs of each student are accurately defined and the methods for meeting those needs are specified appropriately. Finally, the test delivery system must be able to integrate examinee access information, item accessibility information, and interface accessibility tools and features to tailor item delivery to meet access needs for each individual examinee.

Accessible test design depends heavily on digital technologies to flexibly tailor the delivery of tasks. To date, accessible test design has been applied primarily to traditional multiple-choice and short-response test items. As digital technologies are applied to develop new types of items and tasks, it will important to extend accessible test design to these new methods in order to avoid access issues that challenged valid measure of students with access needs prior to the development of test accommodations. Moreover, to avoid the challenges that have occurred when traditional item types were retrofitted with accommodations, it will be important to apply the concept of accessible test design throughout the process of developing next generation item and task-types. As part of the development process, it will also be essential to clearly define the construct(s) that are intended to be measured by a task, to determine which constructs are not intended to be measured, and to acknowledge when an intended construct overlaps with an access need. Below, these two issues—building accessibility into new tasks and clearly defining constructs—are explored in the context of three task types that hold promise to comprise next generation assessments.

Manipulating Objects to Demonstrate Understanding

Traditional item types require students to either select a response or produce a text-based response. Several efforts, however, have explored other methods for responding to items to demonstrate knowledge and understanding. In many cases, these alternate methods require students to manipulate or maneuver objects displayed on a screen in order to produce a response. In some cases, these items may be referred to as "drag-and-drop." A common drag-and-drop task may require students to categorize objects by dragging them into a pre-defined category (e.g., categorizing a list of words as nouns or verbs by moving them into one of two columns). In other cases, an item may ask students to move or re-orient an object, such as a line on a graph. In still other cases, multiple objects may need to be manipulated to demonstrate understanding of a given concept. As a concrete example, Figure 16.2 displays an item that requires students to manipulate line segments to create objects (in this case rectangles). Similar items may ask students to manipulate a set of words or images to create a food web or a water cycle.

While these types of manipulations may provide greater insight into student understanding compared to a multiple-choice item, they also introduce potential accessibility barriers. As one example, requiring students to manipulate objects, sometimes with precision, may be challenging for students with fine and gross motor skill needs. Similarly, without knowing the level of precision required to demonstrate understanding of a concept,

The line segments shown below can be translated (they can slide) around on the screen, but you cannot rotate (turn) them. Create as many rectangles as you can with the segments (each line segment can only be used once). Then drag the extra segments into the shaded area.

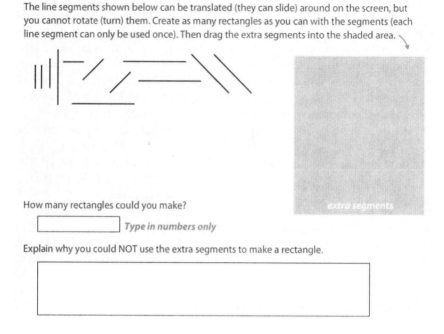

How many rectangles could you make?

☐ *Type in numbers only*

Explain why you could NOT use the extra segments to make a rectangle.

Figure 16.2   Item requiring the manipulation of line segments.

some students may become focused on aligning objects exactly and, as a result invest considerable time making very minor and fine-grained manipulations that are not requisite for making an inference about their understanding. For students with vision needs, items that require manipulations may also present challenges when the manipulations require students to visually align or orient objects in an open workspace.

To minimize the influence of these potential construct irrelevant factors, it is important to build tools and methods into the item model that allow students with a variety of needs to interact with the item. As an example, for students who have fine or gross motor needs, methods can be incorporated that allow objects (e.g., line segments in Figure 16.2) to be selected and maneuvered without the use of a mouse. One method for doing so would allow Tab-Enter manipulation at two levels. At the first, or higher level, students would be able to Tab between line segments to select any segment for manipulations. Once selected, students could work at a lower level to perform actual manipulations. Depending on the task, manipulations may include moving the object right, left, up or down, each of which could be accomplished by tabbing to the desired direction, pressing Enter, and pressing Tab to move the object by a pre-defined amount in the selected direction. For items that require additional types of manipulations, Tab options could allow an object to be rotated in multiple directions, resized, and/or to have its properties altered (e.g., solid versus dotted, arrow head or no arrow head, color, etc.). While performing these manipulations using Tab-Entering is not as efficient as using a mouse, the inclusion of Tab-Enter options ensures that a broader spectrum of students can interact with the item type. It should be pointed out that we do not have any idea of whether such tab manipulations introduce other kinds of complexity factors that interfere with measuring the construct of interest.

As a further support, interactive items can include "snap" or pre-defined increment rules. As an example, a snap rule may automatically align the end-point of two line segments when they are brought into close proximity (e.g., 5 pixels) of each other. Similarly, pre-defined increments may move line segments a specific number of pixels with each movement (e.g., 10 pixels) or may rotate the object by a pre-defined number of degrees (e.g., 10 degrees) whether manipulated with a mouse or by Tab-Entering. Pre-defined rules for manipulating objects can simplify manipulations and support the student's effort to demonstrate knowledge and understanding, rather than the process of performing a digital manipulation.

Locating Objects in Virtual 3-Dimensional Space

Digital assessment environments provide opportunities to measure student understanding by requiring them to explore an environment to locate and identify specific objects. As an example, Figure 16.3 displays an item that requires students to use a virtual microscope to locate a paramecium on a virtual slide. In addition to one or more paramecium, the slide also contains amoebas and specks of dirt. To change the level of magnification, change the focal point, and move the slide beneath the microscope, the item allows the student to use a mouse or use a control panel that allows those same manipulations to be performed via Tab-Entering. In this way, the item is accessible for students with fine and gross motor skill needs.

For students with vision needs, however, this type of item presents additional challenges. Without being able to clearly see what is displayed in the virtual microscope field, it would be challenging to interact with this item. More importantly, the construct measured by this item implicitly requires vision. By definition, one uses a microscope to magnify objects so that the objects are more visible. For the item displayed in Figure 16.3, the skills intended to be measured by the item include: a) the ability to use controls found on a typical microscope to adjust the field of vision; b) the ability to observe features of organisms; and c) the ability to distinguish a paramecium from other microscopic organisms and/or small objects (e.g., speck of sand). To make the contents displayed within the microscope field of

Use the microscope below to find a paramecium. Leave the
paramecium focused in the microscope as your answer.

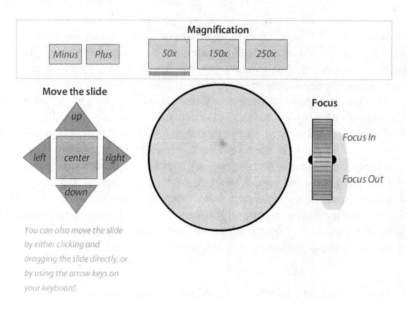

Figure 16.3   Virtual microscope item.

vision accessible for students with vision needs, one might provide audio
descriptions of the contents. However, such descriptions would need to be
carefully crafted so that they focus on physical descriptions of objects that
were currently displayed. Moreover, the descriptions would need to be updated with each change in magnification level, position of the slide, and
adjustment to the focus. But, by providing such descriptions, the constructs
measured by the item shift such that the student no longer must observe
features of a microscopic organism, but instead is only distinguishing between features identified by a third party (i.e., the item writer who produced the script accompanying each screen display). In such cases when
it is not possible to provide supplemental information to meet a need or
when the need overlaps with what is measured, it is important to recognize
this and perhaps accept that the targeted construct cannot be validly measured for students with that need.

When new item types are developed to measure skills that may overlap
with access needs, it will be important to clearly define the skills and knowledge that are intended to be measured by a given item. It is also vital to
recognize that in some cases, those skills will overlap with access needs.
When such overlap occurs, that overlap will need to be included in the

item's metadata and the assessment program must decide whether it is appropriate to present that item to students whose access needs overlap with the measured construct.

Exploring Virtual Worlds to Demonstrate Knowledge and Skills

Chapter Five describes efforts by researchers at Harvard University and Simon Fraser University to develop performance assessments designed to measure scientific inquiry that require students to explore and solve problems within a virtual world. This approach allows a student to apply a variety of data gathering and analytic skills to develop and explore hypotheses. Tasks can also establish complex challenges that simulate problems encountered in the real world, yet can embed supports to minimize the influence of construct irrelevant variance. For example, to reduce the influence that content knowledge or familiarity with specific vocabulary has on the measure of scientific inquiry, definitions and examples of vocabulary terms encountered within the virtual environment can be provided to students upon request. Similarly, when students encounter roadblocks or experience difficulty determining how to proceed with an investigation, hints or scaffolded instructions can be built into the system. These supports help maximize the measure of the intended construct and minimize the influence of unintended constructs.

For students with access needs, however, assessment in virtual environments provide additional challenges. For students with vision needs, the visual display of the environment and need to visually identify zones within the environment that can be explored present challenges. For students with reading-support needs, the presentation of dialogues between characters in a text-based format introduce construct irrelevant variance. When sound is used to portray character dialogues, challenges are introduced for students who communicate in sign language. And the abstract nature of a virtual world presents challenges for students who are developing spatial-relations skills or who require concrete representations.

In reality, the challenges presented by assessments conducted in virtual environments are similar to those encountered when more traditional item types are employed to measure a given construct. However, the complexity of the environments, tasks, interactions, and actions that may occur while the student is engaged with the assessment require careful planning and decisions to provide access for the full spectrum of students who are expected to demonstrate the knowledge and skills measured by the assessment task.

To meet the needs of students who have vision, auditory, or text-processing needs, the assessment systems can be designed to present alternate representations of content encountered during interactions between characters or through information presented during data collection activities. In fact, the methods incorporated in the APIP standards can be applied to assign Braille, signed (ASL or signed English), and auditory representations to the text-based information presented on-screen to students. Alternate representations can then be presented to students based on needs defined in the student's access need profile.

For students whose vision needs present challenges to navigating through a virtual environment and for students who encountered challenges with abstract tasks, the manner in which students navigate through an environment can also be altered. While such an alteration requires careful design, one option is to present the task as a series of options, with each option representing an action a student can take. As an example, when first entering an environment, the task may be designed to allow students to scan the environment to view various features and to then move to a given feature for further investigation. In the current version of the Virtual Performance Scientific Inquiry Assessment task, the initial environment allows students to make contact with a person walking on a beach, access a helicopter to transport to a new location, go scuba diving to explore a kelp bed, interact with a scientist, or visit various landmarks such as a dock, a water plant, and a golf course. As the student rotates his/her avatar within the virtual environment, these options become visible and the student can select them by moving his/her avatar to his/her location within the virtual environment. These options, however, could be presented in a menu format, allowing the student to select a given activity. Each activity could then be presented as a set of additional options. As an example, if the student opted to explore the kelp forest, options might include moving to a specific location to make an observation or to collect data. If data collection is selected, the student might then be presented with a list of data collection instruments that are available, and so on. For students with vision needs, actions that may require them to observe features presented in the virtual environment can be substituted with reports from an independent observer. By restructuring the task as a series of options, students with visual support needs and students who may have difficulty working within a virtual environment can still gain access to the optional activities associated with the task and to the content provided through those activities. This branching approach to presenting the task may also be preferred by students with motor skill needs who might have difficulty manipulating an avatar in a virtual environment.

Without question, providing these supports requires considerable investment by task developers. However, tools like APIP make the provision of alternate representations feasible once content has been finalized. Similarly, allowing students to work through tasks using a branching schema does not require additional planning time since this branching structure would be defined while developing the storyboard for the task.

FINAL REFLECTION

The history of test access documents a difficult path paved by advocates for sub-groups with specific access needs. Forty years ago, little thought was given to the variety of access needs that may interfere with the valid measure of student knowledge and skill. Through lawsuits and regulations, traditional assessments have retrofitted a variety of accommodations designed to reduce the influence of construct irrelevant access needs. More recently, the concept of accessible test design has resulted in building in alternative methods for accessing and interacting with test content during the development of test items. APIP takes a priori inclusion of access methods to a higher level by providing a systematic method and set of tools for specifying how item content is to be presented in order to reduce the influence of a construct irrelevant access need.

To avoid a similar cycle of advocacy and retrofits, current efforts to develop new approaches to student assessment provide an opportunity to consider access during the prototyping and piloting phases. While it may not be affordable to embed the full body of accessible elements into prototypes and to then adequately sample sub-populations with specific access needs during initial pilot studies, the design specifications should consider these needs and provide placeholders for the integration of methods for providing access. As a concrete example, it may not be practical to develop signed versions of the text-based content contained in the initial prototype of the Science Inquiry Virtual Performance Assessment being developed at Harvard University. However, a tagging structure that allows assignment of signed content to text-based content could be included in the xml schema employed by that system. Once the initial prototypes have been piloted and shown to be promising, this predefined schema can be employed to add signed content to future inquiry tasks.

As tools like NimbleTools® demonstrate, computer-based technologies provide powerful opportunities to more fully include all students in assessment programs. By flexibly tailoring the presentation of and interaction with content, assessment tasks can also yield measures that enable more valid inferences about student learning. As we apply computer-based technologies to develop new methods of assessing student knowledge and skill, we have a unique opportunity to avoid the mistakes of the past by embedding flexible access to content included in these new assessments. Capitalizing on this opportunity may incur additional short term expense and additional thought. This investment, however, will help avoid the expensive retrofits experienced by more traditional assessment methods.

REFERENCES

Center for Universal Design (1997). *What is universal design?* Center for Universal Design, North Carolina State University. Retrieved December, 2002, from http://www.design.ncsu.edu:8120/cud/univ_design/princ_overview.htm

Mattson, D., & Russell, M. (2010). Meeting interoperability and accessibility requirements by adopting the accessible portable item profile (APIP) standards (White Paper). St. Paul, MN: Minnesota Department of Education.

Mislevy, R. J., Behrens, J. T., Bennett, R. E., Demark, S. F., Frezzo, D. C., Levy, R., . . . Winters, F. (2010). On the roles of external knowledge representations in assessment design. *Assessment, 8*(2), 1–58.

Rose, D., & Meyer, A. (2000). Universal design for individual differences. *Educational Leadership, 58,* 39–43.

Russell, M., Hoffmann, T., & Higgins, J. (2009). NimbleTools: A universally designed test delivery system. *Teaching Exceptional Children, 42*(2), 6–12.

CPSIA information can be obtained at www.ICGtesting.com
Printed in the USA
LVOW070123240312

274530LV00002B/9/P